In the Beginning

*A concise biblical look at creation from its
inception through the early patriarchs*

Andrew Myers

WESTBOW°
PRESS
A DIVISION OF THOMAS NELSON
& ZONDERVAN

WestBow Press books may be ordered through booksellers or by contacting:

WestBow Press
A Division of Thomas Nelson & Zondervan
1663 Liberty Drive
Bloomington, IN 47403
www.westbowpress.com
1 (866) 928-1240

ISBN: 978-1-4908-6511-9 (sc)
ISBN: 978-1-4908-6512-6 (hc)
ISBN: 978-1-4908-6510-2 (e)

Library of Congress Control Number: 2015900358

Printed in the United States of America.

WestBow Press rev. date: 01/15/2015

Epigraph – "Every good gift and every perfect gift is from above, and cometh down from the Father of lights, with whom is no variableness, neither shadow of turning."
(James 1:17)

Contents

Preface

You can't turn on a TV or a computer without being inundated with opinions and theories about how the earth and all of its organisms came into existence. Upon getting off the couch and heading to church you hear a whole different set of ideas about the earth's existence advocated from the pulpit. The problem is that while advocates for each position present convincing arguments, usually the two viewpoints are so diametrically opposed that the endgame is really just confusion and shame. You want to stay true to your scriptural base, but the traditional interpretation just doesn't make sense in light of undisputed scientific evidence.

Enclosed is a journey to understand what the Bible actually has to say about the creation of the earth and man's place on it. Because God is not the author of confusion, there has to be continuity between verifiable biblical truths (backed up with other Scriptures) and genuine scientific discoveries. Sometimes the conclusions found within the Bible will match modern scientific ideas, other times they do not. In the end, the goal is to obtain a deeper understanding of what the Bible has to say about creation.

For me, this is a personal journey, because I was that person on the couch and in the pew who was bewildered by biblical truths in light of scientific findings. Believing the Bible to be true, I sought to understand if the two could find some common ground. As I looked further into the timing and events of the creation, I realized how big this topic is. The timeline of the creation and man's place in it does not stop at "God said," but continues throughout the lives of the earliest saints.

Introduction

For by him were all things created, that are in heaven, and that
are in earth, visible and invisible... (Colossians 1:16)

In the beginning God created. By His right hand He initiated everything that is seen and known. This earth and the rest of the universe is not an accident, it is all His. (Psalm 24:1.) It did not just haphazardly appear from the cosmic soup of unknowing, but was delicately guided and carefully called forth into existence by His power. Everything in the entire universe can be attributed to Him and He encourages mankind to discover what He has to say about it and its beginnings.

Certainly His creative power resonates throughout the earth today and we can see His presence manifested through events such as the mere diversity of the creation itself. And it is through this creation that He has provided a window to witness a piece of who He is. Paul says that, "the invisible things of him from the creation of the world are clearly seen" (Romans 1:20). He clearly states that if one were to only look around at the majesty of the creation itself an individual would be able to discover the truth about the Creator. The evidence for creation is seen in the creation itself.

Yet, He has given this earthly creation to the sons of men (Psalm 115:16), handing over the reins of power to humanity with a commandment to subdue and dominate the earth, whom He set here with purpose, function, and meaningful intent. Man was created not as a result of some flippant causeless accident as some would reason, but to be His ambassadors and stewards in order to control and administer His creation.

Unfortunately, modern ideology and conventional wisdom has entered in and distracted people from the truth; replacing the simply majesty of the creation with enlightened thought and scientific theory, causing mankind to miss some of the great wonders that God has bestowed upon the earth. In turn, this has caused humans to take their very existence for granted and caused their foolish hearts to be darkened. By ignoring the Creator and professing themselves to be wise they changed the glory of the incorruptible God into an image. (Romans 1:21–23.)

As humanity has increased its scientific knowledge about the earth many have lost sight of the Creator in their journey to understand the creation. Quickly forgetting who the Creator is, they change the glory of God into an image of man's imagination and ultimately dispute the need for God at all. Once God is removed from the equation an individual leaves their future only in the hands of man's opinion. Hereby the Bible declares that they have deceived themselves. (Galatians 6:3) "Cynics look high and low for wisdom - and never find it; but the open-minded find it right on their doorstep!" (Proverbs 14:6 Message).

If one is truly willing and able to keep an open mind about the things of God they will discover there is no dichotomy between the biblical and the scientific. To wit, even though the creation itself is enough to declare His existence, He provided several other methods of communication to keep people in tune with His purpose. First, He passed out a handbook to lead all people to the truth: the Bible. Given to mankind it takes on various roles: it is a guidebook, a novel, a storybook, an historical text, a songbook, a prophecy, a journal, a biography, an autobiography, a chronicle, an adventure, a worship book, a book of poetry, a memoir, a prayer book, and much more. It cautions, heralds, praises, prophecies, cries, and directs mankind.

Through its pages, it recalls all of the mighty deeds that He has done and will do during man's time on earth and into eternity. He reminds His people who He is and what He is capable of doing. Mostly it is a compilation of truths written by men and women of God to provide a guide and instruction manual to help His children navigate this life and beyond. It is an infallible collection of writings by hundreds of different scribes and prophets who provide innumerable keys to Him and His creation. Transcending all time, it tells of the past, present, and future. "For therein is the righteousness of God revealed from faith to faith..." (Romans 1:17).

The word gospel means good news and the good news is that Jesus is the Creator. God graciously gave us both creation and the Bible to prove his existence to humanity. After giving us these dual revelations He was still not finished, but continued to reinforce the information they provided by sending the very incarnation of His Word to walk the earth. That physical incarnation of the word, of course, is Jesus who walked the earth and confirmed the purposes and intentions of His Father.

As if this wasn't enough, once Jesus had left the earth, He said that He would not leave us Fatherless, and He sent His Spirit to testify with our individual spirits that indeed He is the Creator. So, although the Bible makes it clear that the creation speaks for itself regarding its Creator, God has given several other avenues to prove and provide infallible verification of His divine creation. Each one, in and of itself, is sufficient to convince people of the truth of His existence, but by utilizing all three He gave undeniable verification to all men that He is God; so that every person is without excuse.

Within the following pages is an exploration into what the Bible says about the creation of God. Undoubtedly there has been much confusion about His creation, but hopefully the following journey will bring insight into His creation beginning with the earliest history of the earth until the introduction of humanity before finally concluding at the Tower of Babel. It is a history of the earth from the perspective of the Bible; the original historical textbook.

CHAPTER 1

Why Creation?

Creation

*I know that everything God does will last forever. You can't add
anything to it or take anything away from it. And one thing God does
is to make us stand in awe of him. (Ecclesiastes 3:14 GNB)*

Throughout time, mankind has spawned hundreds of different philosophies
and beliefs about the origins of mankind on the planet earth; conjuring up
ideas of mythological gods, alien beings, and infinite existence. Today the
pre-eminent school of thought among the scientific community is evolution,
which is an intriguing theory with compelling evidence to support its premise.
However, the Bible promotes a unique idea outside the realm of this new
doctrine. This, of course, is that God created everything that is seen and
known; the one true origin of the species.

Unfortunately, even adherents of creation have differing theories and
each of these ideological thoughts have caused division amongst its own
ranks. Some have attempted to add in a scientific model, while others
completely forgo the scientific facts, choosing to hold on to a more dogmatic
approach, resulting in various ideas splintering into their own iconoclasms
of creationism.

There are literally dozens of differing ideas about the biblical creation
currently being promoted by various individuals who are truly genuine in
their quest for the truth. Such ideologies include: young-earth creation,

old-earth creation, day-age creation, progressive creation, gap creation, and theistic evolution, to name just a few. Each brand of creation doctrine has a different slant and interpretation on the facts as to how God created. One purports that the earth is 6,000 years old, yet another alleges that creation days are actually eons of time, while a third states that creation time is segmented into distinct time lines in which God intervened.

Most branches of creationism have incorporated some of the gathered scientific knowledge and incorporated it into their particular biblical creation account. One will use science and blatantly humanize the story of creation while another will take a scientific theory and try to spiritualize it, combining the latest flash-in-the-pan scientific theory and show how "perfectly" it fits into God's thoughts on creation. A final group is the antithesis of both and will totally forgo scientific discovery and dogmatically hold to a literal six day creation.

Most of them do a good job of taking the science and revealing how God did it by essentially proving that all that is in the earth came into being solely by the hand of God. While this is a noble and important quest to bring people back to the truth of creation, is this the proper method of understanding the real events of creation?

Often the Christian community gets so tangled up in the latest move of science that they forgo basic tenets of Scripture. Not to mention, that several of these creation premises require in-depth knowledge of dozens of different fields of study to fully understand their extrapolations. The science and mathematics used to draw conclusions in these various fields can be difficult to decipher and even harder to truly determine whether their science is actually correct or not. Interestingly, each premise uses the Bible to support its claims, proving that each one of these ideologies has been nobly undertaken to uphold the gospel and is rooted in the right spirit.

Nevertheless, each subsequent ideology is seemingly more steeped in tradition than the next, making it difficult to determine what is truth and what is not. This book is not meant to condemn or condone any one belief system, but it does purport one biblical view of creation and the early earth. Its intent is to first determine what the Bible says and then allow the physical evidence to fall into place. This approach means that in some instances what is presented here will not match with the current scientific hypothesis.

That being said, just as scientific knowledge is incomplete, in the same respect the biblical picture of all things that happened during the events of creation is incomplete. Of a truth, people from all walks of life and religious backgrounds stumble over misconceptions and vagueness about God's masterpiece. This fact is simply a *quid pro quo* in today's society. The Bible doesn't seem to give enough information and science continues to inundate us with massive quantities of conflicting reports.

Many say that the creation story is unreasonable in light of today's knowledge base and it appears to have no relevance when laid alongside the sheer amount of information that the scientific community is producing. Undoubtedly, one reason why the scientific model has been largely adopted is because the Bible seemingly does not delve into many of the questions arising in today's vast knowledge pool.

The truth is that the Bible does not spend vast amounts of time detailing prior events on the earth, nor does it give an exhaustive account of everything that transpired in the earth's history. The Bible even admits this fact when it says that if it were to include all the information about Jesus the Creator, "I suppose that the whole world could not hold the books that would be written" (John 21:25). This verse asserts that the reason why the Bible does not disclose all the unknown facts of the creation is because it is not primarily designed to provide a basis for scientific discussion, but is intended to be used to discuss God and the relationship He has with His people.

Since much of the Bible's existence occurred thousands of years prior to the vast trove of scientific information we have today, it would have been unnecessary to include large amounts of information about creation events that would have been confusing for most of the biblical audience. Furthermore, it is clear that an exhaustive account of everything that the Lord has done in the earth would result in information overload.

The Bible says that the information contained within its pages is more than enough to provide a lifetime of studying. (Ephesians 3:8.) Indeed, it is not a far stretch to state that most people have not even read through its pages once and are still living on the most basic diet of milk. (Hebrews 5:13.) However, there are others who have continued on their biblical quest and found an unending source of reference and revelatory material, pursuant to all facets of their daily lives. Therefore, it is unnecessary for the Bible to address all the scientific issues that may seem relevant in light of today's scientific discoveries, because it is not meant to be an in depth study into God's science, but rather as an instruction manual for His followers.

As such, it does not answer all of the questions that science is proposing today. That is, although it does not provide answers to all the how's and wherefores of the physical universe, there is still more than enough information in its pages to provide an in-depth study concerning the chronological events of the creation. By looking closely and delving into its truths there is much to be learned about the earth and its history. And just as there are unknowns in the physical universe there are still unknowns hidden within the pages of the Bible. There are untold multitudes of mysteries waiting to be discovered within its pages that will reveal more about the physical creation. Some of those biblical mysteries are what this book hopes to uncover and settle as tenets of truth.

The Tightrope

The line between science and Scriptures has always been a fine line to tread. Be not dismayed, as always the answer lies within the word of God wherein there is no hypocrisy. It does not contradict itself, or factual events in the earth's history. Since God cannot lie, the events chronicled in the Bible must match the geological and physical events in the earth's history that definitively happened. If it does not, then it is man's interpretation of the facts that were wrong. "For God is not the author of confusion, but of peace..." (1 Corinthians 14:33). His words are clear and simple, not ambiguous and perplexing, and there are enough clues in the Scriptures to paint a realistic portrait of creation and the world before, during, and shortly after man's time here on earth.

So where should one walk in the never-ending battle between the creation and the scientific community? Certainly, scientific knowledge in the face of religion is nothing to shy away from, but rather true science is something to embrace as it continues to uncover more about the history of the earth. As new and better technology is used, we are able to delve deeper into His original creation and uncover more about God and His personality. With each technological advance, mankind is able to gaze into the vastness of space and gasp at its breathtaking beauty and majesty, all the while gathering a greater understanding of its origins. As this information is amassed, it is increasingly apparent how very little is still known about God's limitless creation.

Even in the face of the enormity of creation, science has done a good job finding answers to some of the basic questions of human existence. Only a few hundred years ago, a Christian astronomer called Galileo stood against the church and boldly proclaimed why the earth was revolving around the sun and not the other way around. Since that time, science has uncovered prodigious ideas of time, space, and the earth, and yet there still remains much more to be discovered.

For instance, one would believe that mankind is close to cataloging all of the creatures on the face of the planet. But in reality, creation is so large that it is believed only about one third of the species currently on the earth have been cataloged; meaning that there are untold thousands of creatures that humans have never documented or possibly even seen. Mankind's inadequacy is further enhanced when considering the vast, untold mysteries of space, the inner workings of the earth, the depths of the oceans, and the intricacies of the human body to name just a few.

Certainly there are many unknowns about the creation, but the scientific community continues to look for answers by hypothesizing and testing in their various fields. In recent years there has been exponential growth in fields of study that most people have never heard of, but in some cases affect us every day. The only thing for certain in this ever-changing scientific environment is that God's extravagant creation is so vast that mankind will never be able to reach the end of it.

Nevertheless, the search continues and much of the scientific knowledge that has been accumulated has come about in the last 200 years or so. In fact, it is believed that in the current technological environment, human knowledge on average doubles in a matter of years rather than centuries as it did in generations past. These scientists in their respective fields have done an excellent job gaining some understanding into the how, what, where, and even the when. But it is the why that alludes them in their quest for understanding. It is the why that always requires the spiritual. It requires faith. Questions such as: why are we here, what's our purpose, and where are we going? These and other questions need a spiritual interpretation to draw a proper conclusion.

So the analytical and quantitative scientific questions are sufficient to help us understand more about the Creator and His Creation, but it is nice to have both; the Bible to set a foundation and science to understand more about its intricacies. Therefore, it is not necessary for all of creation to be harmonized with the latest scientific theory. As different ideas are confirmed with fact, the landscape of human understanding changes, but it does not change the basic premise of the Scriptures. God is the Creator and the early history of the earth is laid out in the pages of the Bible. Once a scientific fact is established, it must always conform to biblical truth. If the scientific model does not jive with the creation model, then the "facts" were misinterpreted.

This in turn leads back to the premise that there are still several seemingly endless questions surrounding the events of creation. For instance, what are the exact proceedings that transpired during creation? Was it created in a matter of days or was it created in billions of years? Why was it only six days, why not two weeks, ten years, or for that matter why any amount of time at all? If it did only take six days, wouldn't it take a longer time to create all the stars and the heavens than it would to create the fish and birds on the fifth day? Are biblical days really restricted to a single rotation of the earth?

If He created the heaven and earth in verse one, then why is He creating the sun, moon and stars again on other days? How much growth could there have been from the day He created the plants (day three) until three days later when He creates man and it already needs to be kept up? Is there a discrepancy between Genesis chapter one and Genesis chapter two? The first chapter says that God created the plants, followed by the animals, and finally humans. But in the second chapter it appears as if He created man, followed by the plants, and finally the animals. And the list goes on-and-on.

Faith

If the Bible is the infallible word of God then there has to be parts of the creation sequence that are missing or that are not adequately being described in the Christian nomenclature of today. Hence, one of the goals of this book is to help piece together the events of creation that seemingly have gone astray. This will be primarily accomplished by examining the Scriptures. Other detailed scientific questions about geological strata, fossils, climatology, etc., can be answered by legitimate research and science; resulting in scientific conclusions that will be congruent with the biblical timeline. Some of that scientific information will be used to reveal a more concise biblical overview and time line.

That being said, it is unfortunate that people tend to put all their eggs into one basket when it comes to believing in either God or science. Either they believe in God and aren't sure how the science fits in or they believe in the scientific model and don't understand why one would want to insert God into the equation. The key word here is believe, for no matter which one a person chooses, it takes faith.

Undeniably, from a Christian standpoint, there is an element of faith if most of the Bible is to be believed. It takes faith to believe that Jesus died and was resurrected and sits at the right hand of God. The single most important doctrine in the Christian community and by faith, people around the world embrace this as the key to life in God. It is by faith that Christians believe in the virgin birth. That Joshua called on God to stop the earth for a day. That Moses parted the Red Sea. That Jesus performed healings and miracles. And it is by faith that one believes that God created the universe and all that it therein.

The Bible says a relationship established on faith will supply more than enough evidence of a Creator. (Hebrews 11:1.) Everything that God did in creation was by faith and by faith humanity is called upon to accept some things that are beyond the realm of human understanding and perception. (Hebrews 11:3.) Most definitely, the Bible purports things that mankind does not understand, but that does not make them false. It simply means we may not be able to see them, but instead we accept them as truth. "For we walk by faith, not by sight" (2 Corinthians 5:7).

The same thing is true from a scientific perspective. No human was present during the majority of the earth's growth stages, so without visual empirical evidence it takes faith to believe that evolution is science. Mankind's time on earth is a mere fraction of the ages of the earth, so no one can scientifically say that they definitively know how the earth and life evolved. It takes faith to believe in evolution. Though accepted as truth, visual empirical evidence will never be gathered. The end game is that both science and religion require faith to believe their respective premise.

In this same fashion, from a biblical standpoint it is presumptuous to think we can know all there is to know about His creation. "For we know in part, and we prophesy in part. But when that which is perfect is come, then that which is in part shall be done away" (1 Corinthians 13:9–10). We will never be able to know all there is to know about creation from either a scientific or biblical perspective in this lifetime. "He hath made every thing beautiful in his time: also he hath set the world in their heart, so that no man can find out the work that God makes from the beginning to the end" (Ecclesiastes 3:11).

As humans, we will never understand all the vast inner workings of creation. God challenged Job by asking him, "Where wast thou when I laid the foundations of the earth?" (Job 38:4). To be sure, some of it is not for us to know, but in spite of this God gave mankind the tools and intellect to discover a greater and greater measure of His creation. He wants us to use the resources He has bestowed to us to come to a further understanding of who He is, both from a physical scientific standpoint and a spiritual biblical standpoint. Furthermore, even if God had supplied all the information about creation within the pages of the bible, most people still wouldn't believe it. The Bible states that even though people had seen the impossible, they still would have turned the other cheek; even though the proof was undeniable. (Luke 16:31.)

Deduction

As a society, we may not know how or why the universe is organized the way it is, but it is plain to see that God is the one controlling it all; and He calls upon His people to come and see the goodness of His works. (Psalm 46:8.) There is no condemnation of a person yearning to delve into and desire to understand the inner working of His creation.

Many of the Old Testament patriarchs questioned the functionality of the earth and stars. Job and other Bible authors were intrigued with how the earth is seated on its foundation; they were puzzled by the hydrological cycle, and yearned to understand why the wind blows. In modern society, God has allowed us to understand these things and much more, but there is still an infinite amount of things we do not grasp. All the knowledge accumulated in recent years has only led to more and more questions: Do black holes really exist? Is there life on other planets? How does the brain function?

It seems like the more knowledge the human race collects, the more there is to discover. This is why God continually reveals His design to us through science. As these various fields of study uncover more details of His creation, a deeper understanding of the Creator Himself emerges. It is now up to each individual to grab hold of the creation revelation and act upon it. Unfortunately, even with God continually revealing Himself through His creation, people's hearts still frequently remain closed to the intuition of the word of God due to years of tradition and denominational dogma.

That is why God gave us deductive reasoning and requests us to delve into His word to further understand His creation. In fact, He tells us to, "come now, and let us reason together..." (Isaiah 1:18). It is all right to delve into and question His creation. He is a God that gives wisdom to all who ask. (James 1:5.) "But the wisdom that is from above is first pure, then peaceable, gentle, and easy to be entreated, full of mercy and good fruits, without partiality, and without hypocrisy" (James 3:17 Webster).

It is for this reason that God wants us to reason together. If God did not want us to look for answers to difficult questions, He would not have allowed them to be proposed or He would not have created us with such inquisitive minds that long for answers. The questions are out there and we have the cognitive reasoning to try and decipher them. It is our duty to get the answer to the larger picture of creation; keeping in mind that the resolution to the various questions will always point to the Creator and His glory.

Paul is a prime example of someone who loved to delve into the word and discover the truth. Before he began his ministry, it is apparent that he spent three full years studying and preaching the word of God in Damascus. (Galatians 1:17–18.) Although he was previously a Pharisee and incredibly well-versed regarding the things of God, he wanted to become further settled with the proof of Christ in the Scriptures before beginning his public ministry. He used his knowledge to debate and cajole his case on three known missionary journeys throughout the Middle East.

When Paul entered Berea, he found a people whose hearts were open to the gospel, but questioned its truth in light of their understanding. (Acts 17:11.) Once they studied out the issue, many of the men and women of the region came to believe. (Acts 17:12.) Similarly, a couple of chapters later, he was seen "disputing daily in the school of one Tyrannus" (Acts 19:9). Although the outcome of their conversation is unknown, it shows that Paul was not ashamed to argue and debate the truth of the Scriptures.

Time and again, he was willing to stand before the magistrates and refute the local theological premises of the township. So, it is alright to question and prove the Scriptures; the people of Berea did and found that the preaching of Paul and Silas was correct. If the sheer beauty of His creation is not enough to convince, then it is necessary to allow the word to prove out the rest, being confirmed by the very Spirit of God.

Certainty

Only one thing is certain; God does not change, therefore He cannot lie. There is only one way that the earth was created and made, and the Bible tells how it was done. While it may not provide the minutia of details the scientific community is searching for, it does paint a wonderful picture of broad brush strokes, with a few surprises intermixed.

For a more detailed picture, science can be used to allow insight into the more precise handiwork of God's creation. It is not an omission of non-creation to gather a greater understanding of the creation by looking to science. God gave mankind intelligence and deductive reasoning to discover the intricacies of the beauty all around us. Indeed, His awesome workmanship has astonished the greatest philosophers and made even the most hardened atheist question their beliefs. Certainly, answers to the questions of God's creation deserve to be resolved as much as they deserve to be asked. It is through the asking that a better understanding about Him and His creation can be ascertained.

So although scientific and creation theories abound, don't be confused. "Beware lest any man spoil you through philosophy and vain deceit, after the tradition of men, after the rudiments of the world, and not after Christ" (Colossians 2:8). "The first person to speak in court always seems right until his opponent begins to question him" (Proverbs 18:17 GNB).

Question the Scriptures and allow the word of God to prove itself. That is how Paul did it when he debated the Scriptures by using Old Testaments passages to prove that Jesus Christ was the fulfillment of what the prophets were proclaiming. He convinced the local villagers of the errors of their ways, including one case where they were worshipping an unknown god when they could have been worshipping the one true God of all creation. Boldly proclaiming to the Athenians, "Whom therefore ye ignorantly worship, him declare I unto you" (Acts 17:23). The same can and should be done with all Scripture.

God has given mankind many aspects of His being to reveal Himself: His Spirit, His word, and His creation. Each one of these in and of itself is adequate in relaying the who, the what, and the why of God. To ignore all three is ludicrous. Only the fool in his heart has said that there is no God. (Psalm 14:1.)

Every person is going to give account of himself to God after physical death. Even if they have never heard of Jesus, there will be no excuse for not believing because God has revealed Himself to them through His Spirit and by His creation. (Romans 1:19–21.) Of course, those who have had the opportunity to know Jesus the Creator through a personal relationship have been given the greatest gift, life. All in all, it is imperative to gather a deeper understanding of His word because it leads to a greater understanding of the Creator. "Come and see the works of God; He is awesome in His deeds toward the sons of men" (Psalm 66:5 MKJV).

CHAPTER 2

In the Beginning

The Beginning

Thou art worthy, O Lord, to receive glory and honour and power: for thou hast created all things, and for thy pleasure they are and were created. (Revelation 4:11)

The one burning question in the creation story that has caused so much confusion in recent years is the question of timing. When did the earth begin? If this question alone could be answered, it seems that all of the other mysteries of the universe could be solved. From a Christian standpoint there are numerous ideologies in this area, the most prominent being that the earth was created in six actual rotations of its axis. This premise claims that the entirety of creation came into being during six literal days mentioned in Genesis; including all the plants, animals, and humanity.

There is another premise that asserts creation transpired over an undetermined period of time ranging from several thousand years to several million or even billions years. These ideas have come about by those who find it difficult to ignore the systematic evidence that continues to pour out of the scientific community.

Essentially, these are the two main schools of thought in Christianity: the earth was created recently, or the earth was created during an undated past age that usually corresponds to scientific conjecture. These two persuasions are constantly at odds with each other and have become a major point of

13

contention amongst Christians, causing many to stumble and unnecessarily question their beliefs.

For others, this dilemma is even more serious; they find themselves unable to reconcile the seemingly obvious science with their unwavering dogmatic biblical approach. Being more than they can logically wrap their heads around, it has actually caused them to reject their faith. Fortunately, there is a happy medium between the two that commingles them in perfect harmony and this is exactly what the Bible espouses.

The one point of union that both the Christian and scientific community have come to agreement on in recent years is that the earth had a beginning. Scientists today believe that the universe did not begin in time, but rather that time started when the universe began. This perfectly matches what Saint Augustine proposed more than 1,500 years ago. Augustine was a theologian in the early church and he agreed that the universe was not a product of time, but that rather time began following the creation of the universe. Of course, the church was slow to adopt his ideas and science was no help because it was antiquated at that point in history, adopting many of the church's stances.

It took science and theology nearly thirteen hundred years to catch up to each other and agree that the universe had a point of origin; a point in history where both matter and time began. This is the moment in time that God called all things into existence by faith; a point that the Bible has always called creation.

Additionally, since before the days of Augustine and even up into the 20th century much of the world believed that the earth and universe had always existed. God is an eternal God, so the rationale was that His creation must also be eternal. It had no beginning and no end, it just always existed. In the same vein, the scientific community abounded with theories of its existence, but they too largely conjectured along with the church community that the universe was eternal. They deduced that there never was a beginning, and that the universe's end cannot be confirmed (because it certainly appeared that the earth was designed to extend into the infinite future ages). Although logically this seemed to make sense, it contradicted all of Genesis one as well as the rest of the Bible. Ultimately, the Christian community forsook this argument, matching it to biblical principles and the scientific community subsequently followed suit.

The Bible phrases it, "In the beginning." Not an eternity past, but a predetermined moment in time when God called it all into existence. Therefore it is logical to state that everything created had a beginning or starting point. It has not always been, but the Lord says, it will always be. Over the past hundred years or so, the scientific community has come to agree that the universe did indeed have a starting point; corresponding to the biblical account. An event that both groups have agreed upon in the past several decades and it has brought some congruence between the often divided Christian and scientific communities.

Scientists today have dubbed this point of origin the "big bang." It is the point in time when all matter and energy in the universe were encased in a small area and erupted into the universe that we see today. Now, the idea of an explosion at some point in the dateless past consisting of unimaginable power that erupted and began to throw galaxies across the broadening universe is nearly universally accepted. Of course, since scientific conjecture often causes questions to abound, the idea is not without its critics, but this thought process does help unveil some of the earliest mysteries of the universe.

In Christian circles the big bang is joked about by saying, "Sure, I believe in the big bang ... God spoke and bang it happened." Without a doubt, according to the previous verse, this is the truth. In the beginning (a specific period in time) God spoke and the universe was created. A magnanimous Creator who was thoughtful enough to bring it to pass, and continues to love and care for it. Hereby, answering in one stroke both the physical and metaphysical questions that arise when looking at the origins of the creation.

So now that it has been determined that there was a starting point of the universe from both a Christian and scientific perspective, the conversation can continue, and this is only the preface to the whole of the argument. The next questions that are asked are the how's and why's of its existence and it is these questions that begin to divide the landscape.

The quest for understanding the surrounding universe is certainly admirable and needed in today's nonstop, ever-expanding-knowledge-based society. Regardless though, humans in their present state will never totally understand what can only be described as God. And the only explanation for the existence of the earth is found in the word of God, "Through faith we understand that the worlds were framed by the word of God, so that things which are seen were not made of things which do appear" (Hebrews 11:3). The only way the existence of the cosmos can be understood is by faith, knowing that this universe was made of things which we do not see.

Nevertheless, human inquisitiveness continues to press for answers concerning the big bang and other mysteries in the universe. Knowing that ultimately there are questions that science will never be able to answer does not stop the quest. Human inquisition continues to want to know the answers to all the questions. For instance, how did an entire universe with billions of planets, moons, and suns, come forth from only a handful of elements? Not to mention all the detailed intricacies of the earth at large down to the tiniest molecule. How could this all be possible from one softball size cosmic goo? What caused the initial explosion that forced the elements apart? And why do the current laws of physics not always agree with the big bang?

Certainly, there are attempts to answer each one of them, but there are no proven conclusions. New theories continually arise in an attempt to combat any holes in the original theory and to help with some of the unknown physical questions. But as more discoveries continue to push the bounds of known science they confound the simplest of answers, so that many of the "known" tenets in the universe seem even further out of reach.

Of a truth, the Bible shows that many of the questions will never be answered, instead declaring that the overall premise of creation should be accepted by faith. The only answer to these seemingly insurmountable questions is that a higher power was involved in its development. In short, the only answer is God; a spiritual being outside of space and time, who created the very physical universe that mankind grasps to understand.

Certainly, the ever-expanding universe that the big bang promotes only proves that He is God; for the Bible shows that He is the Creator who stretches out the heaven like a fisherman casting a net. "It is he that sitteth upon the circle of the earth, and the inhabitants thereof are as grasshoppers; that stretcheth out the heavens as a curtain, and spreadeth them out as a tent to dwell in" (Isaiah 40:22). This ever-expanding universe is part of His unending plan of creation to bring about life on this planet and beyond.

In recent years the consensus between science and the Christian community is that the earth was not eternal, but had a starting point: A big bang. Of course, this is the very premise the Bible promulgated from the beginning. Therefore, the big bang proves the existence of God. Better yet, the big bang screams for a Creator. For without a Creator then there was no bang at all.

Notwithstanding all of the scientific questions any theory conjures, there is one other side to the story that science will never be able to answer and that is the metaphysical. Questions arise, such as; how can something come from nothing? Why did the universe and life come into existence? Was their some innate indwelling trait that caused life to spring forth? And the ultimate question, "Why are we here?" Of course, these questions have never and will never be understood using the scientific model, because there is no way to empirically measure desire, predilection, or predisposition for life. Thus, science is unable give answers to even basic questions regarding the causation of the universe.

That is why it is imperative to look to the one true answer: He is the purpose behind all that is seen and known. He is a loving God who created an ever-increasing universe and placed mankind on the earth to enjoy, increase, and bring forth life. And it was God that gave man a spirit and the desire to know more about Him and His creation in our hearts. (Ecclesiastes 12:7.)

So, the answer as to why there is life on this planet is so the Creator could fellowship with mankind though their spirit that He placed within them. This is why we are called to be friends of God, so that we can learn more about His ways and His creation. (John 15:15.) We are not an accident; but rather humanity and this creation were designed by a loving Creator who seeks the best for His creation. No matter how many billions of people there are, He is able to accommodate them all. "God made everything with a place and purpose" and "Everything that happens in this world happens at the time God chooses" (Proverbs 16:4 MSG, Ecclesiastes 3:1 GNB.)

In the Beginning

In the beginning God created the heaven and the earth. (Genesis 1:1)

The fact that the universe had a beginning is an accepted standard in this dialogue. But this leads to the point of contention that has caused a rift in the Christian community. Since there was a beginning, when was it and how did God bring it about? Was it a matter of days or was it a matter of eons? Science puts the big bang as occurring approximately 15 billion years ago, but is this what the Bible promotes? Was it instantaneous or was it an intermittent creative process?

The obvious place to start unraveling this conundrum is in the very beginning itself: Genesis 1:1. Without question, this one verse has caused seemingly unlimited amounts of confusion in religious circles as to its part in the creation story. Essentially there are two schools of thought about the first verse of the Bible.

First, many believe that it is an introduction to the chapter. All the verses that follow go on to describe the events revealed in this initial summary verse in greater detail. In other words, God is generally proclaiming that He created everything and the rest of the chapter explains how He did it. This idea has been promoted and generally accepted by the Christian community for centuries. Thus, by backtracking through biblical events, the first mention of creation would be in the range of 6,000 to 12,000 years ago. The premise is that from nothing God created everything and mankind has essentially occupied a position in His creation from the beginning.

Others believe that verse one is a summary of creation events that happened in the distant past. In other words, Genesis 1:1 declares the event of creation itself, and the actions that follow in chronological order in subsequent verses record events that happened sometime after the original creation. Thus, these verses are referring to more recent events that transpired in close proximity to the arrival of mankind on the earth. This premise supposes that at a point sometime in the dateless past, God created the heaven and the earth. Then the story is picked up at a point in history that is considerably more recent.

This premise takes the stance that the how and why of the original creation are not described in Genesis one, but are instead scattered throughout other passages in the Bible. So, in the second verse God moves to a more recent time; a time more relevant to the creation of mankind. Since the Bible was written to and for man, it stands to reason that it would spend considerably more time discussing the presence of man on the earth and how the creation relates to him, even though the original physical creation occurred much earlier than most of the Genesis creation account.

These two varying viewpoints have several differing offshoots, but in the end they basically boil down to these two different schools of thought. Regardless of what category of creation one subscribes to, it is undeniable that this one verse sets a precedent for the rest of the Scriptures. In one sentence it outlines everything that God is and will be. He is the Creator, the beginning and the end, the benevolent and caring one. He loves so much that He created: the sun, the moon, the stars, the earth, and mankind. He is the Creator of all physical things, both the heaven and the earth. He is a loving God who does all this for His creation with blessing upon blessing, and it's all illuminated within the first verse of Genesis. Praise the Lord.

Paralleling this initial creative verse is a second equally telling verse on creation found at the beginning of the New Testament in the book of John. Though chronologically it is not the first book of the New Testament; its first verse predates the other gospels. It says that, "In the beginning was the Word, and the Word was with God, and the Word was God" (John 1:1).

Here John unveils that Jesus is called the beginning. He is God's word in the flesh and by Him were all things created. This is possibly one of the most profound verses in the Bible, because it shows that God is truly multidimensional. He is both physical and spiritual, yet He is both the Father and Jesus. He is the Word and by His word all things were brought forth. The earth was framed by words of faith that He spoke at a point in time called the beginning.

John proceeds to say that without Jesus nothing was made that was made. (John 1:3.) Jesus was there in the beginning of creation and He is the Maker and Creator of all things that are seen. The Hebrew term for "word" in the original text is logos or spoken word. Therefore, the spoken word of God is

Jesus, He is one with God, and He is God. That same word that was spoken in the beginning, who is Jesus, became a man and lived on the earth. (John 1:14.) So, the Bible shows that two things happened in the beginning, God spoke and God created. Both events happened simultaneously, and it was at this moment in time that the spiritual became the physical.

In other words, the Bible is revealing the fact that the first act of creation was God the Father pulling the physical (Jesus), out of Himself and that Word became flesh in an eruption of creation. He was already there in the heart of God, but He came forth when God spoke Him forth at this initial moment of creation. "In the beginning was the Word, and the Word was with God, and the Word was God" (John 1:1).

When God spoke at that moment, the physical manifestation hatched in the heart of God was created. Hence, Jesus came forth and the physical creation was born. This is why God and Jesus are one. Jesus is the physical manifestation of God and was pulled from the very being of God Himself when He spoke Him into existence. Imagine the power that God poured forth as the spoken Word became a reality and the whole of the universe began to unfold before Him.

So, the first act was God speaking, and when the Lord by faith started to talk, it birthed the physical into existence from the unseen realm (Hebrews 11:3). It is the ultimate answer to both the physical and metaphysical, and it was these spoken words that stretched out of the heavens and spread forth the earth. "And, Thou, Lord, in the beginning hast laid the foundation of the earth; and the heavens are the works of thine hands" (Hebrews 1:10).

Hebrews confirms with Genesis that in the beginning God created both the heavens and the earth. For in the beginning was the Word, and in the beginning God created; and part of that creation in the beginning was the creation of the universe and the laying of the foundation of the earth. Not necessarily one instance, but the beginning is likely referencing to the first part of the timeline. Definitively, there were several actions the Lord performed during the initial creation of the earth. He laid it, measured it, and fastened it. (Job 38:4–6.) He established it. (Psalm 24:2.) He hung it in its place (Job 26:7), and He weighed the winds and the waters. (Job 28:25.)

These are multiple actions the Lord completed, but they all transpired during an unknown span of time designated as the beginning.

So although it is an undetermined amount of time, it is quantifiable. In other words, the beginning is not an ongoing perpetuity of time. These events happened during a period of time when the earth was created. This is not an argument that we are currently still in the beginning, rather the Bible is quite clear that this age is drawing to an end. "Better is the end of a thing than the beginning thereof" (Ecclesiastes 7:8).

A tale of two creations

If the timing of events in Genesis one is a summary of the events to follow, then it is difficult to correlate many of the events that transpired with the events in the Genesis account. Certainly, it is easy to perceive that on the first day of the Genesis creation, the very first thing the Bible says is that the Lord called forth the light. (Genesis 1:3.) Undoubtedly, an explosion of light might describe the events in spreading out the heavens and laying the foundation, but many of the following day's events do not parallel other passages of Scripture.

The discrepancy begins to become apparent on the third day when the Lord called forth the dry land. He instructed the earth to let the waters be gathered into one place and let the dry land appear. (Genesis 1:9.) Yet Hebrews says that His first act of creation was to lay the foundation of the earth. (Hebrews 1:10.) It was not an activity He performed on the third day or at a point after the beginning, but rather it was His first activity.

Additionally, there is a definite contrast in how the Bible describes these two events that appears to be the same activity. In one instance He spreads it forth, but in the other it is allowed to appear. The laying of the earth's foundation is an act of creation, but calling forth the earth out of the water on the third day is an act of permission. These two events are mutually exclusive. The only way these verses can be reconciled is if they were referring to two separate events. Isaiah says that He created all things both good and evil, but all of the creation in Genesis one is labeled as good. (Isaiah 45:7.)

These are a few of many contradictory verses in the Bible concerning the entirety of creation from the viewpoint of a literal six day creation. Many more of these discrepancies will come to light in the following pages, but as a necessary starting point it will be established from henceforth that the earth was originally created at a point in the distant past and the daily events of Genesis then took place at a later point in time.

Too many apparent contradictions among different verses in the Scriptures make the idea that the earth was created at essentially the same time as humanity suspect. Coupling this with the undeniable scientific findings being unearthed today makes it difficult to present a valid premise for a literal six day creation. Thus it is logical to conclude that Genesis 1:1 is more than an introduction to the rest of the text. It is a separate creative event by itself. In other words, the creation of the earth happened at some point in the undated past and the rest of Genesis chapter one is a separate event happening sometime after that original creation.

Obviously, for many this is already a stumbling block, but hold on because subsequent portions of this book are dedicated to exploring Scriptures to proving an elongated timeframe for creation. Just like Paul's admonition to the Thessalonians when he said to, "Prove all things; hold fast that which is good" (1 Thessalonians 5:21), the ultimate goal is to fully understand the events of the early earth, and whether or not they correspond to other interpretations of Scripture or scientific theories is not important. Once the Scriptures are examined and established, scientific fact can be mixed in to further salt the meat.

This book is in no way meant to judge or belittle any interpretation of the events of creation. It is difficult enough to draw people to the truth of the Scriptures without fraction and division amongst its own ranks. Undoubtedly there are several interpretations as to how the events of creation came forth. None of them has taken greater heat in recent years than those who purport that a day in the Bible refers to one complete rotation of the earth spinning on its axis, a period slightly under 24 hours.

Without question, the increased geological, archaeological, and other scientific knowledge that has come to the forefront in recent years, has put undeniable pressure on the belief that man was brought forth in six earth days. To hold on to this belief is certainly admirable, but in light of the biblical contradictions above, is it deserving? Certainly, God is still God, and whether He created the earth in one day or one hundred billion days, He is the Creator. Therefore, this is not an attempt to uproot ones faith, nor is it a concession to the scientific model. Rather it is an in-depth examination of the truths revealed in the Bible to obtain a more complete picture of the timelines involved and in turn uncover a greater insight into the whole of creation.

It takes faith to believe that He is the Creator. For it is by faith that God called all of creation forth and it is by faith that we believe that He is the Creator. So, could God have created the earth in six revolutions of the earth on its axis? Absolutely, He could have. In the same regard, if one has faith to believe that he created the earth in six days, could He have created it in six minutes or six seconds? Certainly He could have, He is God.

This belief system is where many people get hung up. Did God really create the entire universe with billions of stars, planets, all creatures of the earth and sky, man, and all plant life in six revolutions of the earth? What about the angels? Then too, what about some of the fundamental problems that exist with an entirely recent creation?

For instance, take the question of how can light travel billions of light years while still being seen by a person standing on an earth that was only created six thousand years ago? Could God have created it in that state? Sure. Did He? Not from a biblical standpoint. A critical study of the biblical passages has already shown that there are too many contradictions to support the earth being created in six literal rotations of the earth. "For God is not the author of confusion, but of peace" and He wants all "to come unto the knowledge of the truth" (1 Corinthians 14:33, 1 Timothy 2:4).

Establishing a time frame for the creation of the earth is quintessential to understanding Genesis. Confusion in the timing of creation has caused divisions and resulted in unnecessary commotion towards understanding God's creation. Unquestionably, several retractors have tried to find flaws with a longer-aged earth, by saying that it is simply an attempt to reconcile the earth's age with current scientific theory. This could not be further from the truth.

Simply put, people have questioned the logic behind a short time frame of the earth, but often, spiritual dogma has quelled any other ideas. Whether their ideas about God's timing of creation were right or wrong, they were rarely allowed to surface and held little weight in the mainstream thoughts of their generation. Essentially, their ideas were ridiculed into non-existence, without ever being allowed to explore the depth of other creative Scriptures.

A longer-aged earth is not an attempt to reconcile Scripture with current scientific theory, but rather admiring the complexity of the creation and questioning the logistics behind a more recent creation. Then, while exploring the Scriptures, different conclusions are cemented about the length of time depicted in Genesis chapter one. Since God cannot lie, it is impossible for the Bible to contradict itself. Therefore, the only explanation for the seeming contradiction of the earth's age is a misinterpretation of the passages by the reader.

Creation had a beginning point and that beginning is documented in Genesis 1:1, when the Lord introduces humanity to its history. It is a starting point between time (creation) and eternity (God), which has been shown to be at some point prior to the days of creation mentioned in the first chapter of Genesis. Further extrapolation of this will be continued in depth in the coming chapters; starting with an analysis of Genesis 1:1, which says that in the beginning God created. But who is God?

CHAPTER 3

God

God

For he that cometh to God must believe that he is... (Hebrews 11:6)

The primary premise of all the words written on these pages is that God is the Creator of all things in the universe. This is a given in a book about creation, but for some individuals this may not be a foregone conclusion. For a person inundated with secularism and bombarded by media, it can be hard to wade through the sea of opposing ideas and principles. Certainly, the fundamental belief of Him as Creator is second only to belief in Him as Savior. Unfortunately this basic tenet has been lost in translation and impiety. Therefore, it is imperative to take a minute to discover more about the Maker and Creator of humanity and the rest of the universe. Of course, the primary source to understand more about Him is through His own depiction of Himself.

The Bible literally has hundreds of different names for God, which are all employed in an effort to describe the indescribable. The list of His attributes is endless and it seems almost trivial to try and bring to light Who He is with written words. "For the deep things of God cannot be understood on tables of stone but in the fleshy tablets of the heart. For the letter kills but the Spirit gives life" (2 Corinthians 3:3, 6). Nevertheless, touching on some of His characteristics mentioned in the Bible will hopefully make known His love for His creation and help us to further ascertain who He is.

First, He is a timeless being. (Deuteronomy 33:27.) He created the known physical universe and conjunctly created time itself. Creation cannot come into existence by something made from the same substance as its Creator. It requires a being outside of its physical constraints to design and implement it.

In the same respect, since everything in the physical universe has a point at which it was created, it requires a being outside the constraints of time to dictate a time frame. Thus, since the entire universe was created during the beginning, then there had to have been some outside entity that conjured up the original elements. That entity would not only exist before the universe, but would also exist before time. Since time is measured by revolutions of the heavenly bodies, if these bodies did not exist then time would not exist.

Therefore again, since He was the Creator of the heavenly bodies, He would also be the Creator of time, which means that time is irrelevant to Him. Henceforth proving that God is an eternal God, unconstrained by the frame of time that He created. Of course, the Psalmist stated it best when he plainly declared that, "before the mountains were brought forth, or ever thou hadst formed the earth and the world, even from everlasting to everlasting, thou art God" (Psalm 90:2). Before He caused one physical thing to come forth, He existed.

The Bible often makes reference to the Lord as a God of old. (Psalm 55:19.) He inhabits eternity. He always has been and He always will be. He is past, present, and future all at once. Yet He created a universe based on time and an earth where events happened in sequential order. He is not constrained by His own creation. Through time the human body deteriorates and diminishes, but the Lord operates outside of this decay. He occupies another time that is best described as eternal or spiritual.

Therefore, for Him to start the creation process millions or even billions of years ago would not be outside of His capabilities. The amount of time that has elapsed in the creation process would be of no consequence to Him. To mankind's understanding, this would be an almost inconceivable amount of time, but to God it is all the same, for He is eternal and immortal. (1 Timothy 1:17.)

In addition to His timelessness, the Bible shows that He is holy and righteous. (Psalm 145:17.) This is attested by the angelic hosts who have circled His throne for possibly billions of years and remain continuously astounded at His works as they cry out "Holy, holy, holy, is the LORD of hosts" (Isaiah 6:3). Being holy, of course, equates to the fact that He cannot tolerate sin; the very nature of mankind. (Habakkuk 1:13.) Yet in the face of sinful mankind, He is merciful, gracious, and slow to anger. (Psalm 103:8.) And it is this merciful stance that allows His abundant nature to flow. (Ephesians 3:20.)

Certainly, His abundant and gracious nature is seen in His creation. Even with billions of people on the planet, the earth remains virtually untapped in the amount of resources He has provided for its inhabitants. Then, by simply picking up a telescope and gazing out into the vastness of space, one begins to realize the untold enormity and endlessness of it all. His abundance cannot be measured.

Yet, it is certain that no matter how much the human race comes to understand His power and majesty, it will always be a mystery. In Romans 8–11 Paul tries to put a perspective on the God he serves. These chapters are chalked full of wonderful insights into the majesty of the Creator and His concern for mankind and His creation. Still, by the end of chapter eleven, Paul realizes he has come up far short of God's splendor and concludes that His mysteries are too much for human comprehension. He ends by stating that the best He can do is to simply praise Him.

> O the depth of the riches both of the wisdom and knowledge of God! how unsearchable are his judgments, and his ways past finding out! For who hath known the mind of the Lord? or who hath been his counsellor? Or who hath first given to him, and it shall be recompensed unto him again? For of him, and through him, and to him, are all things: to whom be glory for ever. Amen. (Romans 11:33–36)

In this "age of information," mankind can only scratch the surface and gather perfunctory information about the insurmountable majesty of God's creation. Man's quest to further gather scientific insight will never end, because God's creation is too far beyond our understanding, "Which doeth great things past finding out; yea, and wonders without number" (Job 9:10). His thoughts are higher than our thoughts, His ways are higher than our ways, and all of the marvelous things that He does are innumerable. (Isaiah 55:9, Job 5:9.) Nevertheless He cares endlessly for His creation and responds to them by their belief in Him. (Romans 1:17.)

In this same respect, just as God is a God of faith, mankind is called to believe on Him by faith, even though they do not know or understand all the facets about Him or His creation. "But without faith it is impossible to please him: for he that cometh to God must believe that he is, and that he is a rewarder of them that diligently seek him" (Hebrews 11:6). The writer of both the New and Old Testaments understood this and allowed the Holy Spirit to direct their actions, revealing only what was revealed to them and nothing more. Although they added their own writing style, they did not add their own understanding on something they could not understand. God chose those men because He knew they could be entrusted to state the facts about Him without offering their own interpretation.

The word of God was given by inspiration of God Himself. (2 Timothy 3:16.) So when He speaks, He is defining His many facets. These different character defining innuendos can be seen in each of the different titles that He provides in the Bible. For instance, the first name attributed to Him in the Hebrew Bible is *Elohim*; in the beginning God (Elohim).

Elohim is generally translated to refer to God the Creator, but coincidentally it also means God the Judge. Of course, this very first descriptive name of God used in the Bible represents the two things that were happening in the first two verses of Genesis; God as the Creator and the Judge. Obviously, the fact that He is the Creator has been established and His judgment will be looked at in greater detail in later sections. Throughout the Bible, the names used to describe Him are always relative to the situation at hand and assist in developing His nature and character.

To help ascertain some appreciation for the depth of God's name in the Bible, Adam Clarke stated the following:

> "A general definition of this great First Cause, as far as
> human words dare attempt one, may be thus given: The

eternal, independent, and self-existent Being: the Being whose purposes and actions spring from himself, without foreign motive or influence: he who is absolute in dominion; the most pure, the most simple, and most spiritual of all essences; infinitely benevolent, beneficent, true, and holy: the cause of all being, the upholder of all things; infinitely happy, because infinitely perfect; and eternally self-sufficient, needing nothing that he has made: illimitable in his immensity, inconceivable in his mode of existence, and indescribable in his essence; known fully only to himself, because an infinite mind can be fully apprehended only by itself. In a word, a Being who, from his infinite wisdom, cannot err or be deceived; and who, from his infinite goodness, can do nothing but what is eternally just, right, and kind. Reader, such is the God of the Bible; but how widely different from the God of most human creeds and apprehensions!" (Clarke, Adam. [1977] Genesis 1:1. *Clarke's Commentary*. (Volume 1, p.27.) Nashville: Abingdon)

Mr. Clarke wrote this concerning his first encounter with God's name (Elohim) in the Bible. Certainly his definition helps to shed light on some of the hidden meanings of the first name of God mentioned in the Bible, but it still falls short of all of His majesty. Hence, the Lord took the liberty to use hundreds of other descriptive names throughout the Bible to portray His goodness to mankind. And embedded in each one of those names are more implied meanings of the incomprehensibility of the Maker of the universe.

One other item that is also revealed in the definition of Elohim is His plurality. Generally in the Hebrew, a word that ends in "im" is plural and masculine. It is not an admission that He is a pantheistic being, but rather one who exists on another plane. Other Scriptures help bring this to light, by showing that He has three sides that are all encompassed in one person; physical, spiritual, and emotional.

God is Three Parts

But when the Comforter is come, whom I will send unto you from the Father, even the Spirit of truth, which proceedeth from the Father, he shall testify of me... (John 15:26)

So, from the first mention of His name, the Bible shows that He is multifaceted and occupies more than one office. As previously mentioned, He also occupies more than one realm of existence. This is confirmed in several passages of Scripture, but one of the most blatant is in Genesis 1:26 when He creates man. He says, "Let us make man." That is, let us, the Godhead plural, make man. In Matthew 28:19, Jesus mentions the three parts of the Godhead: the Father, the Son, and the Holy Spirit.

Each one is distinctly identified as an individual in various portions of the Bible as they are each addressed with personal pronouns, He or Him. In other words, each portion of the Godhead stands apart from the others, yet all work together as God. Admittedly this is a difficult concept to understand, yet it is an integral part of attempting to understand who He is and allowing insight into His creation. Each entity of God is an individual, yet all three are one God. Hopefully looking into the other parts of the Godhead will help to unravel this puzzle. Following is a short synopsis of the three parts of the Godhead.

First, God the Father is a Spirit. (John 4:24.) Something cannot come from nothing, but something can come from God. In order to call something into existence, that thing or being must exist outside of the realm that is being created. God the Father exists in another realm; that is the spiritual realm. He is outside the limits of time and space. He is the Creator of time and space. He is an eternal being that has always been and will always be. (Deuteronomy 33:27.)

The Bible portrays Him as having all the characteristics of mankind; He has a face, hair, a beard, hands, feet, etc. Consequently, that means that he also has a shape in the spiritual realm. To wit, mankind is made in that very image. So, if one was able to peer into the spiritual realm and look at the Father, He would look just like any other person.

He is omniscient (all knowing "Job 37:16"), omnipresent (everywhere at once "Psalm 139:7–8"), and omnipotent (all powerful "Isaiah 40:28"). He does not change. (Hebrews 1:12.) His ways are perfect. (Psalm 18:30.) Since the beginning He has not reneged on any single word He uttered. If He would have, He would not be God, for God cannot lie. (Titus 1:2.) Therefore the Words that He spoke at the beginning of creation are true forever. He is holy (Isaiah 6:3) and righteous. (Psalm 116:5.) His wisdom is exceedingly great. (Proverbs 8.) And He is a God of love. (1 John 4:8.)

The second office of the Godhead is Jesus. Jesus was the beginning of the creation of God, the very manifestation of His Words. In the beginning God spoke and Jesus is that Word that He spoke forth. (John 1:1.) He was the beginning of the creation of God. (Revelation 3:14.) He came forth from the bosom of the Father, and shortly after this, the rest of creation began to spring forth by His words. Not only was He a witness to the creation, but He is the very word and physical culmination of creation, spoken forth just prior to all of the physical creation of God.

Also, in Revelation 3:14, Jesus is called, "the Amen, the faithful and true witness." He is the only faithful and true witness to the creation because the rest of God's creation is flawed by its sin-filled nature. Only God can obtain such a pure and noble salutation, because there is nobody else that compares to Him. When the Lord drew a covenant with Abraham, since He could swear by no other, He swore by Himself. (Hebrews 6:13.) In other words, He was calling Himself the only true witness, all other beings falling short of the truth that is the Lord, including the angelic host.

Of course, there would be no reason for God to reveal a physical dimension to Himself, if there was no place for Him to occupy. So, by faith after He separated Himself, He called into physical existence things which are seen, but not made of things which do appear. (Hebrews 11:3.) Jesus was the culmination of His Words and through Him (His Word) by faith came all the other physical elements of the universe.

Hence, shortly after His separation, at the beginning of the creation, the Lord spoke into the nothingness and the creation of the heaven and earth sprang forth and began to spread and stretch across the nothingness that is now called the universe. He was the beginning and by Him and for

Him all things were created at the very beginning of creation. He is a part of God, which fully makes Him God. (Philippians 2:6.) But He is also His son, because He came from God and this is why Jesus always deferred to His Father as being greater. (Luke 4:41, John 14:28.)

Thus, Jesus is God in the physical sense, but takes direction from God in the spirit. He is the Word, because He encompassed everything that was spoken forth from the beginning and throughout time. Everything that came forth was from Him and by Him. "For in him dwelleth all the fulness of the Godhead bodily" (Colossians 2:9).

So, in turn, He too must be perfect, and He proved this when He came to earth in the flesh and lived a sinless and holy life. (John 1:14, 2 Corinthians 5:21.) He was perfect because He is the very culmination of the perfect Word of God. Upon His death, He ascended up into heaven where He currently dwells in and rests in the very bosom of God the Father in the throne room. "The only begotten Son, which is in the bosom of the Father, he hath declared him" (John 1:18).

Finally, God is the Holy Spirit. Just as God the Father is a Spirit; His third attribute is also called a Spirit, because He exists in the spiritual realm. This is certainly a confusing concept, because two parts of the Godhead are also called spirits and both exist in the spiritual realm.

The Holy Spirit is God's soul. It is God's will, emotion, and desires. Just like the other parts of the Godhead, He is a person. Paul's words were true as he continuously refers to the Holy Spirit as a person. (1 Corinthians 12:11, Acts 13:2, Acts 15:28.) The Holy Spirit is a real entity, like the Father and Jesus; and as such, He deserves His own personal pronoun.

The Holy Spirit can be vexed (Isaiah 63:10), grieved (Ephesians 4:30), and quenched. (1 Thessalonians 5:19.) These are all attributes of a person and He is the same person that draws a man to the Lord. He is referred to as the endowment of power and it is this power that is available to all who call upon the name of the Lord. (Luke 24:49.) He is the Spirit of truth and a guide. (John 16:13.) The Amplified Bible expounds upon His title of Comforter by calling Him the "Counselor, Helper, Intercessor, Advocate, Strengthener, and Standby" (John 14:16).

When Jesus left the earth, He told His disciples that it was expedient for Him to leave so that another one could come. (John 16:7.) What could be better than the actual physical presence of Jesus? Christ said that the Holy Spirit is better and that same Spirit comes to live inside of every believer. (John 3:5.) When Paul was writing to the early believers in the Corinthian church, he told them they had the mind of Christ, meaning that they had the Holy Spirit dwelling within them. (1 Corinthians 2:16.)

The Bible shows that the Soul (Holy Spirit) and the Father are so closely joined that without the Word (Jesus), they could not have been separated. "For the word of God is quick, and powerful, and sharper than any twoedged sword, piercing even to the dividing asunder of soul and spirit, and of the joints and marrow, and is a discerner of the thoughts and intents of the heart" (Hebrews 4:12).

In other words, Jesus is the only reason that the Holy Spirit is separated from the Father. God the Father spoke the Word and divided the Spirit from the Soul. Without Jesus, the Soul and Spirit are bound together. Since the Father removed Jesus from Himself, through Jesus the Holy Spirit can also be removed. This is seen throughout the New Testament when the Holy Spirit is sent to the earth, while God the Father remains in heaven on His throne. (John 14:26, Psalm 47:8.) Jesus' separation from the Father at the beginning of time, allowed the Holy Spirit access to the entire creation; which was a necessary step to fulfill His agenda of administering council to His creation. The Holy Spirits is separated from the Father, yet so closely tied to Him it is difficult to discern the difference between them.

The Scriptures relay that the only time the Spirit actually assumed a shape was when Jesus came up out of the waters of Jordan immediately after His baptism. It says that, "the Holy Ghost descended in a bodily shape like a dove upon him" (Luke 3:22). Luke does not say that the Spirit came to earth in the shape of a dove, but rather that He came upon Jesus in a bodily shape like a dove. This indicates that in this instance He did indeed don a visible shape in the temporal realm.

Other Scriptures refer to Him as water. (John 7:38.) On the day of Pentecost, when the Holy Spirit was released into the earth, it says that, "there appeared unto them cloven tongues like as of fire, and it sat upon each of them" (Acts 2:3). Here He is portrayed as a flame of fire. So, it is apparent that the Holy Spirit can and has been witnessed in several different forms.

Understanding the differentiation between members of the Godhead is an important discussion because it sheds light into the creation of man. Mankind is made and created in the image and likeness of God. Like God, humans also are a three part being: body, soul, and spirit. On earth mankind only sees the physical body, but upon death the spirit and soul goes on to the afterlife while the body remains on the earth. This will be discussed much further in chapters nine and ten which take a deeper look into the creation of man; although for now it helps to bring to light the nature of the Creator and his intimate link to His greatest current creation.

Eyewitnesses of God

No man hath seen God at any time; the only begotten Son, which is
in the bosom of the Father, he hath declared him. (John 1:18)

Obviously, Jesus is the physical form of the Godhead that walked the earth and was seen in the flesh, but in John 1:8, he clearly states that God the Father has never been witnessed in a physical form. This suggests that no man has seen God the Father, yet there are dozens of recorded instances in the Old Testament prior to the birth of Christ where people encountered God in the flesh. For instance, God is seen in the garden with Adam (Genesis 3:8), Abraham invited God for supper (Genesis 18:1–5), Jacob wrestled with God (Genesis 32:24–30), and Moses saw the Lord (Exodus 3:6). If John says that the Lord has never been seen, then who did these men come in contact with?

There have been dozens of explanations regarding the apparent discrepancies of the ability to see God or not see God. Some state that each of these instances is a misinterpretation and that they were actually encountering angels. Another theory is that God has different levels of glory, and reveals Himself in various glorified levels to certain people at certain times. While it is true that there are different levels of the glory of God (from glory to glory), it is perfunctory to ascertain whether in all of the passages that men encountered God, if it was God the Father or not. (2 Corinthians 3:18.)

The real cause of the confusion can be found in the biblical use of the name of God. As has been seen, in English the name of the Lord has lost its vigor and become watered down. In the original Hebrew there are subtle nuances embedded in His various names that provide clues to what He is being referred to in various instances. These subtleties have often been lost in translation and replaced with a couple of all-encompassing names for God in the English, such as Lord or Savior. Though most people understand the context, often times the hidden details contained in the names in the Hebrew help to uncover deeper meaning within the passage.

Thus, when the word God is used in the English it could be referring to any one of the persons of the Godhead. Since He is a Trinity (Father, Son, Holy Spirit), when the Bible says God it often makes it sound like it is God the Father. In many instances this may be the case, but in other situations it is not. If the passage is referencing the physical presence of God, then it has to be Jesus. So although He was more formally introduced to biblical readers in the gospels, this does not mean that He was never on the earth prior to that. After all, Jesus is the culmination of the Father's words and the Maker of all things. (Colossians 1:17.)

One story in particular that brings this to light is found in Daniel 3. When Nebuchadnezzar the Babylonian king besieged Jerusalem, he threw Shadrach, Meshach, and Abednego into a raging fire to punish them for not recognizing Nebuchadnezzar as god. They were unharmed because of their faith in God, but while they were in the midst of the fire, Nebuchadnezzar proclaimed that there was a fourth person in the fire with them and He was like the Son of God. Even an uncircumcised Babylonian king was able to recognize the Son of God in the midst of a raging fire. What he saw was God's physical form on earth; Jesus the Son of God. (Daniel 3:25.)

In this same vein, when the early patriarchs saw God, each one of them were seeing the physical manifestation of God; which is Jesus. For instance, when the Bible says that Abraham encountered God, it says that the Lord appeared unto him in the plains of Mamre. (Genesis 18:1.) Obviously, Jesus hadn't been born on earth at this point in time, but the Bible calls Him the first born of all creation and the very reason that all things were created. (Colossians 1:15–16.) Certainly, it is not a stretch of the imagination to say that the Creator took a form on earth prior to His actual birth into the earth as a man. That is to say, any physical manifestation on the earth of the Godhead has to be Jesus, regardless of whether the encounter happened in the New Testament or the Old Testament (though technically He would not have been given the name of Jesus until His physical birth). Therefore, this means that when the Bible says "No man has seen God at any time," it has to be referring to God the Father (1 John 4:12).

When God appeared to Abraham in the plains, Abraham perceived that He was more than just a man or even an angel, but rather the Son of God. Recognizing Him as God, he rushed to meet Him and bowed before Him. Again, Jesus had not been physically born into the earth at this point, but it is apparent that He took a form similar to man; yet one that distinguished Him from both man and angel.

So, as it can be seen, some Old Testament passages such as Genesis 18:1–2 make it easy to determine that the person Abraham met was Jesus, because He was specifically referred to as a man. Other passages, such as Genesis 17:1 makes it a little less apparent, because He is referred to as the Almighty God; a title that is usually reserved for God the Father. Setting aside tradition, one can clearly see that calling Jesus the Almighty God is not outside of the biblical scope; because "he is before all things and by him all things consist" (Colossians 1:17). So to say that He is not the Almighty God would be contrary to the power attributed to Him in other passages.

On the other hand, there are instances where individuals did experience the presence of God the Father, however they never saw His shape, but rather a physical representation of Him. Normally, a person can only see through their physical eyes. Occasionally though, God will allow the eyes of men to see into the spiritual spectrum of light. This happened in the book of Exodus, when Moses asked to see God the Father. The Bible is clear that Moses and the Lord spoke face-to-face as one would talk to a friend. (Exodus 33:11.) Of course, during these instances, he had to have been talking with Jesus.

Moses perceived that there was much more though, and he asked the Lord to open his eyes so that he could see all of His glory in the spiritual realm. "Blessed are they which do hunger and thirst after righteousness: for they shall be filled" (Matthew 5:6). Moses' thirst for the Lord was so great that God was obliged to comply with the request of His friend.

So in Exodus 33:23, God the Father grants Moses' request by covering his eyes so that as He passed by, Moses would be able to see His glory or goodness. "And I will take away mine hand, and thou shalt see my back parts: but my face shall not be seen." If one were allowed to peer into the spiritual realm, God the Father does have a shape (one that is in the image of man). In this passage though, something else is happening because it doesn't say that Moses could see His physical back, but rather His "back parts."

The word used for back in this passage is not equated with a physical part of one's anatomy. It means that Moses was able to see the latter part of God's glory. When the Lord opened Moses' eyes he saw only the trailing parts of God's glory, but not His form or face. So not only is a human being unable to see the spiritual shape of the Lord, it is also apparent that humans are not able to see the fullness of His glory. (John 5:37.) Here, Moses was essentially allowed an angelic glimpse into His goodness and it changed him in the natural. (Exodus 34:30.) This shows that there is truth to the idea that people can see different levels of the Father's glory while being unable to see His actual figure or features.

So again, this encounter between God the Father and Moses shows that in every instance when God takes a shape and is witnessed by men, they are seeing Jesus. Jesus is God on the earth, pulled from the very Father Himself. Christ often chastised His disciples when they asked Him to show them the Father. His response was, "he that hath seen me hath seen the Father" (John 14:9).

Even though Jesus was not born into the earth until the gospels, He still is the creator of all things physical. Jesus is not mentioned in the Old Testament, because Christ's earthly name was not revealed until the angel declared it in Matthew 1:21. Rather He is declared as a deity. The physical part of the Godhead created all that is physical. It is not a stretch of the imagination to say that He would want to walk with Adam in the cool of the morning and enjoy His creation. After all, the earth will be His permanent abode in the near future. (Revelation 21:2.)

Creative Names of God

The next appearance of the name of God is *YHWH*. (Genesis 2:4.) Which means, "He who will be," portraying Himself as not only a God of the past and present, but also the God of the future. Although the original pronunciation is unknown, in Hebrew He is called Yahweh, while in English it is translated Jehovah.

When the Lord first called on Moses to lead His people to the Promised Land, Moses asked the Lord whom he should tell them had sent him? "And God said unto Moses, I AM THAT I AM: and he said, Thus shalt thou say unto the children of Israel, I AM hath sent me unto you" (Exodus 3:14), essentially telling the Israelites that He is everything, He is everywhere, and He knows all.

God reveals several more of His well-known names in the first book of the Bible: *El Shaddai*, "the Almighty God" (Genesis 17:1); *El Elyon*, "the most high God" (Genesis 14:18); *El Olam*, "the everlasting God" (Genesis 21:33); and *Adonai*, "Lord GOD" (Genesis 15:2).

In this life, we have only scratched the surface of the depths of His being. He is the limitless God of eternity and nothing is impossible for Him. It is not a sin to ponder the supernatural wonder that is the Maker of the universe. In fact, He beckons humanity to draw near and in turn He will reciprocate. (James 4:8.) He is a God of mystery and intrigue and most definitely there are unlimited facets to His being that believers will have an eternity to discover and uncover.

In addition to some of His more well-known titles in the Bible, God also uses other descriptive names to give mankind a glimpse into His glory. There are literally hundreds of additional names that deal with His benevolence, grace, mercy, redemptive properties, and His relationship to mankind upon the earth. All of them give a deeper understanding of who He is and why He brought forth this magnificent creation. Of course, all the names of God espoused in this temporal creation point to the temporal manifestation of God which is Jesus. The following are some of the names attributed to Him from a creative standpoint:

"The God of the whole earth" (Isaiah 54:5); "the everlasting God, the LORD, the Creator of the ends of the earth" (Isaiah 40:28); "Before Abraham was, I am" (John 8:58); "I am Alpha and Omega, the beginning and the ending, saith the Lord, which is, and which was, and which is to come, the Almighty" (Revelation 1:8); "For by him were all things created" (Colossians 1:16); "And he is before all things, and by him all things consist" (Colossians 1:17); "the life" (1 John 1:2); "This is the true God, and eternal life" (1 John 5:20); "he that liveth" (Revelation 1:18); "the true Light" (John 1:9); "the light of the world" (John 8:12); "the bright and morning star" (Revelation 22:16); "the dayspring from on high" (Luke 1:78); "the forerunner" (Hebrews 6:20); "he is Lord of lords, and King of kings" (Revelation 17:14); "the beginning of the creation of God" (Revelation 3:14); "the faithful witness, and the first begotten of the dead" (Revelation 1:5); "the head of every man" (1 Corinthians 11:3); "the Deliverer" (Romans 11:26); "Lord both of the dead and living" (Romans 14:9); "Lord over all" (Romans 10:12); "the Prince of life" (Acts 3:15); "him that filleth all in all" (Ephesians 1:23); "the Word" (John 1:1).

Almost every title shows that He is good, abundant, and displays His mercy and grace. Each one gives a deeper understanding of who He is and why He brought forth this magnificent creation. His plan has always been a grand plan of peace and salvation. And His plurality is undeniable and seen throughout the Scripture, even from the very first mention of His name, Elohim. So although God makes it plain that during this dispensation, mankind will never know all the intricacies of who He is and what He does, He does give insight into His greatness through the revelation of His creative names.

CHAPTER 4

Created the Heaven and the Earth

Created

*For thus saith the LORD that created the heavens; God himself
that formed the earth and made it... (Isaiah 45:18)*

From the very first words in the Bible to the very first reference of His
name, He is identified as the Creator of all that is seen and known. Belief in
God is the belief that He is the all-powerful Creator. It is the fundamental
tenet of Christianity. Unfortunately, an undercurrent of misunderstanding
in mainstream Christianity has reared its head and is attempting to destroy
this basic creative directive.

   Whether it is caused by erroneous teaching or stubborn hard-headedness,
in many instances it has leaked into people's thinking and swayed many
people's belief in a God that has the ability to create the universe. This
misbelief has caused some to say that God was not involved in the creation
process at all, while others say that while He may have had a hand in the
making of the original elements, the rest of it just sort of appeared by evolution
or some other "natural method." Still others insist that God is only a partial
Creator, because He was only involved in certain parts of earth's history
when it needed a hand in restarting the process of life. Undoubtedly there are
dozens of man-made ideologies and concepts that are often a conglomeration
of both the church and scientific teaching.

The truth is, belief in God as the Creator of everything is no different than accepting many of the seemingly impossible events the Bible purports to have happened. These principles would include, but are not limited to: the virgin birth, miracles, the spirit realm, heaven and hell, and of course, the ultimate Christian doctrine that Christ the Savior was crucified, buried, and rose again from the grave; which is the very reason for existence of the namesake of Christianity. Without Christ as Savior, Christianity does not exist. All of these and many more things are explicitly mentioned throughout the Bible. They are doctrines of the Christian faith and without belief in them the Bible is nothing more than a collection of stories.

In the same regard, Christ as the Creator is another maxim in the articles of faith cataloged in the Bible; and a quintessential belief of Christianity. Unfortunately, it seems that in today's modern society of dereliction to all things God, this fundamental truth has been discarded. Make no mistake about it, from the first sentence to the last, the Bible is explicit in detailing that all things were created by Him and without Him nothing would have been made that was made. It did not arrive here by mere luck, but by a controlled and deliberate design. Succinctly showing that from the universe, to the planet, and even down to the smallest of cells there is purpose and intent in His creation.

Biblical ideas

When the Lord speaks, His creation listens. Certainly, there are many of the creationary how's and why's that are unknown and will remain so throughout this age. "For now we see through a glass, darkly; but then face to face: now I know in part; but then shall I know even as also I am known" (1 Corinthians 13:12). A day is coming though, when all will be revealed. In the meantime, there are plenty of truths in the biblical annals that He did reveal.

Some of these truths were spoken forth long before humans had an inkling of their veracity. They were planted there long before the science existed to back up their relevance, even though today many of these scientific truths are taken for granted. These include the fact that the earth is round

(Isaiah 40:22), that living organisms grow and reproduce (Genesis 1:11–12), that human flesh is composed of earth elements (Genesis 3:19), and that blood has miraculous unknown powers to bring life to the body. (Leviticus 17:11.)

Other biblical principles include the concept of fluid dynamics when it states that wind has weight. (Job 28:25.) It also speaks to the hydrological cycle of water throughout the earth. (Ecclesiastes 1:7.) It explains how mental health is closely correlated to physical health and vice versa. (Proverbs 14:30, 17:22.) It shows how planetary bodies move and affect the earth. (Job 38:31–33.) It addresses the infiniteness of the universe (Genesis 22:17), and along this line, it speaks to its expanding nature by comparing it to an ever-expanding bedspread being stretched across a never ending bed. (Job 9:8.)

There are many more scientific revelations found in the Scriptures, but there also remain many that have yet to be discovered. It would be interesting to know how many more truth's about the creation are hidden within the pages of the Bible, but remain unknown simply due to our lack of understanding in various fields yet to be discovered. Of course, only time will tell.

All of these scientific facts from the bible mentioned above have long since been adopted as modern day scientific principles within the past several hundred years, but they were originally spoken forth when the Lord revealed them to the authors of the Bible. Many of them are now accepted as fact, even though the principles behind them are mind-boggling even among the people in those particular fields of study.

Certainly one of these baffling concepts is how is it that the universe continues to expand. TIME magazine mentions this when it states that, "The universe has expanded vastly since its earliest days -- but it isn't that galaxies and other objects are flying apart. Rather, it's that space itself has been stretching -- a difficult concept even for a physicist to grasp, but which must be true according to the equations of relativity" (Lemonick, Michael. "How the Stars Were Born." TIME August 27, 2006 pg 48).

Out of nothing

The word created in the original Hebrew is *bara*, which means to be brought out of nothing. From nothing came something. It is used only three times in Genesis one: 1:1 (heavens and earth), 1:21 (sea life and fowl), and 1:27 (humanity). By definition, it gives being to something new, the commencement of the existence of a thing, from non-entity to entity. This verb is only used when an original creative act takes place and God is always its subject. In other words, it is only used as a verb in a sentence where God is the noun. When God created the heaven and the earth, all the elements and science involved were called into being from nothing. Where previously there was nothing, now there is something. There is only one God and He is the Creator of all, who "calleth those things which be not as though they were" (Romans 4:17).

Thus, by this definition; mankind is incapable of truly creating anything on the earth. Although create is often used in the modern vernacular as an action performed by mankind, its use is misappropriated. For instance, one may complement an artist by calling a picture a beautiful creation. But based on the biblical definition, using the word creation in this instance is not accurate. The artist who drew the picture used substances already existing in the earth; such as paint and canvas. The artist did not call forth the elements composing the paints and canvas into existence from nothing, only God can do that.

Since mankind is incapable of creating anything, the artist can only make or form existing elements into a different shape or design. By using existing elements, a new and beautiful picture can be made, but that artist cannot create or call into existence the elements needed to make the picture.

Make and form are a couple of other primary verbs used in the Genesis account. In addition, there are a multitude of other actions God performed during the "creation week." He divides, brings forth, lets, blesses, calls, and rests. Each verb brings insight into God's activities during this early time frame and all the actions that God performs in this first creation week bring understanding of His creative activities. Each one helps to shed light on exactly what events are happening during the creation and helps to fully grasp the implications of the passage. (Several of these will be looked at in detail in upcoming chapters. Generally though, the three verbs; make, form, and let, along with create will be looked at in greater detail to help build a cornerstone of understanding into the activities of the creation.)

God, on the other hand, called the original elements from which the paints and canvas were made into being from nothing; that is creation. Undoubtedly, the Bible sums it up best by saying that, "we understand that the worlds (universe) were framed by the word of God, so that things which are seen were not made of things which do appear" (Hebrews 11:3).

He created it not in vain, but rather for a purposeful intent to be used in its appointed season. (Ecclesiastes 3:1.) All things created are designed for an exact moment at an appointed time. That is that period of history, when He calls it forth to be used within the realm of that period's creationary plan.

The original plan was never designed to be changed, but due entirely to the actions of His created beings, His plans have been changed on several occasions (the conduct and behavior of which will be discussed in later chapters). Certainly, the gist of the problem is sin which has caused deterioration and destruction to come upon the earth and His creation. Nevertheless, God did not give up on His creation. In fact, it is just the opposite, because the Bible states that, "While the earth remaineth, seedtime and harvest, and cold and heat, and summer and winter, and day and night shall not cease" (Genesis 8:22). Since the days of Noah, through today, and continuing into the eternal ages these promises in the earth will not stop.

In fact, the Bible purports an earth that will never end. (Ecclesiastes 1:4) In other words, throughout all eternity, there will continue to be days and nights, hot and cold, summer and winter on the earth. Even though the Bible shows that at the end of this age the heaven shall be rolled up as a scroll, and God will call forth a new heaven and a new earth (Isaiah 34:4; Isaiah 65:17), the aforementioned earthly functions will not cease.

Curiously there has been some thought given to the idea that the now expanding universe will one day collapse back in upon itself, returning to its original state just prior to the big bang, only to erupt again across the background of time. Of course, this is not exactly what the Bible predicts, but it is similar. The earth's future will most definitely bring about spectacular changes to the very physical nature currently dictated. Nevertheless, certain aspects will remain unchanged: the earth and its pivoting on its axis and its non-stop rotation will continue from now and throughout all eternity. This is one of a multitude of biblical promises the Lord gives to mankind as a whole. Praise the Lord!

One other thing to note about Genesis 8:22 is that it does not say, "As it has always been," but instead that this was a promise from the days of Noah forward. There is no indication that there has always been day and night or hot and cold, which implies that at previous points in the earth's history there may have been periods of disconnect between night and day. In other words, the implication is that there are events in the earth's past that disrupted its continual rotation and caused breaks in the earth's essential functions of day and night, etc. If there had not been any disruptions in the earth's movement in previous ages, it would seem unnecessary for the Lord to make this specific promise concerning the earth's perpetuity.

So, in the beginning, God established the bounds, laid the foundation, and created a system for the earth to thrive. For the most part, this is also the manner of God's current creation: a measured progression of day and night, summer and winter, seedtime and harvest. He established the foundation and set it in motion, there is no more need to tinker with the things that have been created and made.

Of course, this is not to say that He is not currently involved in everything that happens throughout the earth, but merely that the physical laws governing the earth have already been established. There is no more need to fidget with physical laws. This does not mean God has removed His power and presence from the earth, rather it is just a statement to the fact that He is finished with His creative prowess during this dispensation.

His power and life-giving light is always a necessary ingredient to make all things grow, develop, and thrive. Jesus proved this out when He said that the Father is indeed vigorously employed in the happenstances of the earth. "My Father worketh hitherto, and I work" (John 5:17). God is involved in all the activities of the earth, as well as the activities of mankind on the earth, but the creation of mankind, the earth, and all of its components were completed on the sixth day.

Then again, His workload changed one more time, when sin and death entered into the world. His creation was complete, but His involvement in it changed. God had to adapt. A perfect God is able to look upon a perfect creation and delight in its excellence, but a sin stained creation causes God to cringe. To even look upon the creation as it is, God has to humble Himself. (Psalm 113:6.) So the earth continues on its plotted path and will continue to do so throughout eternity. The only time God will allow a change to come to the internal workings of its predetermined orchestration is by the requests of one of His creations, but He still will never fully stop its operation. (Joshua 10:12–13.)

The Earth

My help cometh from the LORD, which made heaven and earth. (Psalm 121:2)

The Hebrew word for earth is *erets*. The word is used 2,502 times in the Old Testament including 15 times in the first chapter of Genesis. It means: earth, ground, country, or lands. Its definition is given by the Bible shortly after its introduction when it calls the earth dry land (Genesis 1:10). By definition, when the Bible uses the term earth, it represents the physical planet that rotates around the sun.

Thus, the definition of earth is straightforward and pertains to the physical planet. A second word that holds some significance in this discussion and that is occasionally mistranslated for earth in the Bible is the word "world." When the Bible uses this term, it is a completely different concept from the dry land of the earth. In fact, it has several definitions, and they are a little more difficult to decipher because there are several different words in the Hebrew and Greek that are translated world; though none of them are defined as dry earth.

For example, Hebrews 11:3 says, "Through faith we understand that the worlds were framed by the word of God." The Greek word for world is *aion*, which is where the English word eon is derived from and in the Bible it is defined as such. So this passage may be better translated as, "Through faith we understand that the ages of time were framed by the word of God," referring to a particular dispensation of time, which in this case was an indeterminate amount of time that God spoke forth the creation of the earth. It may have been the original creation or it may have been the re-creation or everything in between. Thus the word aion evokes a sense of perpetuity or possibly timelessness. It is often translated as ever and frequently combined with "for" to denote an endless perpetuation; forever. (Hebrews 5:6.)

Also from the Greek is the word *kosmos,* which is the most frequent occurrence of the word "world" in the New Testament and a more pertinent specific definition in this context. Obviously, this is where the English word cosmos or universe is derived, but its meaning is not the same. In the New Testament, the word kosmos is a reference to the system of authority that mankind has upon the earth. One example of this can be found in Paul's writing when he said, "This is a faithful saying, and worthy of all acceptation, that Christ Jesus came into the world (kosmos) to save sinners; of whom I am chief" (1 Timothy 1:15). Obviously, Paul was referring to the world as the system of mankind in the earth, not the actual earth or universe. In this same vein, John said, "And he is the propitiation for our sins: and not for ours only, but also for the sins of the whole world (kosmos)" (1 John 2:2). Jesus didn't come to save the earth; rather He came into the world to save people from their sins.

So, when the word world is used, although it may be used to represent an epoch of time; it largely is defined as a system of government, or hierarchical structure of mankind on the earth. It is not the physical earth, but rather mankind on the earth. It is the people and their respective governments that take residence on the face of the planet.

Invariably, there has been ample confusion surrounding the definition of earth and world, as occasionally each has been substituted one for the other in various passages. For instance, earth (erets) is translated four times as world into English, but an analysis of those verses shows that the phrase dry land could easily be substituted in each of those passages. One of these instances can be found in Psalm 22:27, where it says that, "All the ends of the world shall remember and turn unto the LORD." Instead of world, the passage could just have easily read that all the ends of the earth shall remember and turn unto the Lord, just like the large majority of other instances where it is defined as dry land, ground, or county (a piece of land). In the same respect, the other three instances could have also been translated as earth.

So again, occasionally the distinction between world and earth can get lost in the English translation, but the Greek and Hebrew texts show there is a clear divergence between the two. If earth is used in the passage, it means the physical planet or land and if the word world is used it generally represents mankind's authority over the earth, but it could mean a period of time depending on which root word is utilized.

Following are a few more verses to help bring further clarification to the apparent difference between world and earth. "For he saith to the snow, Be thou on the earth (erets); likewise to the small rain, and to the great rain of his strength" (Job 37:6). Obviously snow and rain are physical accoutrements of the earth. The earth being, as the Bible describes it, the dry land. In contrast, Ephesians 1:4 says that, "According as he hath chosen us in him before the foundation of the world (kosmos)." That is, prior to setting mankind on the face of the planet, God called humans to be his children. It does not say that God chose mankind before the creation of the earth, but only prior to the foundation of the world, or prior to the creation of mankind upon the earth, for It was at that point that the world was established. In other words, mankind was not necessarily an original part of the plan of God for the earth (although he may have been). Hereby, this once again proves that there was an extended span of time that occurred between the creation of the earth and the creation of man on the earth, otherwise the Lord would have used erets.

In parallel with this, the Bible reveals that when Jesus came, He came into the world, not the earth. (1 John 4:9.) He was sent to redeem all of the occupants of the earth, not the earth itself. The redemption of the earth will not happen until after His second return when He establishes His Kingdom on the earth. At which point, Satan will be removed from both the world and earth.

Other examples reinforce these truths: "For God so loved the world" (John 3:16). "For what shall it profit a man, if he shall gain the whole world, and lose his own soul" (Mark 8:36)? "That was the true Light, which lighteth every man that cometh into the world" (John 1:9). "And the devil, taking him up into an high mountain, shewed unto him all the kingdoms of the world in a moment of time" (Luke 4:5). "Blessed are the meek: for they shall inherit the earth" (Matthew 5:5). During the days of Noah's flood the Bible shows that the flood waters were on top of the face of the earth not on top of the world. "And it came to pass after seven days, that the waters of the flood were upon the earth" (Genesis 7:10).

Additionally, there are several passages throughout the Bible that bring further clarity to this truth, because they contain both the words earth and world in the same passage. Each one holds true that the earth is the physical planet and the world is the system of government upon its face. "For then must he often have suffered since the foundation of the world: but now once in the end of the world hath he appeared to put away sin by the sacrifice of himself" (Hebrews 9:26). "…for the pillars of the earth are the LORD'S, and he hath set the world upon them" (1 Samuel 2:8). "…for he cometh to judge the earth: he shall judge the world with righteousness, and the people with his truth" (Psalm 96:13). "The earth is the LORD'S, and the fulness thereof; the world, and they that dwell therein" (Psalm 24:1).

Keeping these two definitions in mind helps clarify many of the timelines currently under contention regarding the early history of the earth and helps to illuminate some of the time frames detailing the events of creation. For example, Romans 5:12 says, "Wherefore, as by one man sin entered into the world, and death by sin; and so death passed upon all men, for that all have sinned." This verse has caused considerable consternation amongst creationists because it is often viewed as proof that the earth had to be created on a recent timeline. For it specifically says that it was man that brought sin into the world and therefore sin could not have been present prior to humans walking the earth.

However, the use of the word world in this passage shows that it was not referring to the original creation of the earth, but rather was a product of mankind on the earth. Adam's fall brought sin into the world and caused death to come to mankind. That is, Adam brought sin into the world or the system of authority that mankind has over the earth, not into the earth (although a curse was also extended to the earth because of Adam's actions, but it did not involve death). In other words, Adam brought destruction upon mankind and man's infrastructure on the earth. If Romans said sin entered into the earth, then it would be assured that man was here when the earth was created, but that is not what the text states.

In this same vein, the Bible states that, "In the beginning God created the heaven and the earth." It does not say that He created the world in the beginning, if it did then the days of creation mentioned in Genesis would also be the beginning of the universe. Thus, the Bible once again proves out that Genesis 1:1 is not an overview of the creation days, but rather an event unto itself that transpired at some point in the distant ages past.

And Heavens

But who is able to build him an house, seeing the heaven and
heaven of heavens cannot contain him? (2 Chronicles 2:6)

So the earth is the physical sphere that rotates around the sun, but what is the heaven? The Hebrew word for heaven is *shamayim*, and is defined as sky, abode, heaven, air, firmament, or stars. Of course, like many other parts of Scripture, there has been some consternation about whether heaven is singular or plural in Genesis 1:1. Some versions of the Bible refer to the heaven as singular, such as the King James Version and some mention it as plural, such as the American Standard Version.

The Bible shows there are actually three different heavens. These are; the atmosphere including all the air encircling the earth; space or the universe, and the third heaven or the realm of God. Of course, the proof of these different "degrees" of heaven comes from Scripture.

First, heaven is the area above the actual terra firma of the earth. It includes the outer reaches of the earth's atmosphere and all the space in-between, stopping at the next layer that is generally called space. It is referred to as the sky or the place of clouds. "For as the rain cometh down, and the snow from heaven, and returneth not thither, but watereth the earth, and maketh it bring forth and bud, that it may give seed to the sower, and bread to the eater" (Isaiah 55:10). This famous verse clearly shows that heaven is the area directly above the surface of the earth or the earth's atmosphere; the sky. It is where rain and snow originate. Jeremiah 4:25 describes it, saying, "I beheld, and, lo, there was no man, and all the birds of the heavens were fled." Here Jeremiah is specifically referring to heaven as a place where birds fly.

Second, heaven also refers to outer space, or the home to all the celestial bodies outside of earth. It is the rest of the universe. God mentioned it when He spoke with Abraham about his inheritance. "That in blessing I will bless thee, and in multiplying I will multiply thy seed as the stars of the heaven" (Genesis 22:17). God spoke this to Abraham to tell him that he will become a great nation on account of his faith. Even though Abraham was advanced in years and did not have any children, God said that his offspring would be like the stars of heaven. Of course, the stars of heaven are the stars seen in the night sky. It is the realm of the planets, constellations, the sun, and the moon and it came into being in Genesis 1:1.

Finally, heaven is also defined as God's home. (Matthew 5:16.) Paul says he knew a man that was caught up into the third heaven. (2 Corinthians 12:2.) It is also known as the heaven of heavens and is the current realm of God. Most people recognize it as the location of God's throne, the current location of Jesus, and the place where believers will go when they die. The Bible speaks much about the beauty and majesty of this area; it is a place of peace, health, streets of gold, mansions, and eternal life. Imaginations are allowed to run wild as people try to pinpoint the resplendence and grandeur of what lies ahead in the heavenly afterlife.

All three of these definitions of heaven are called to proof in Deuteronomy 10:14 where it says, "Behold, the heaven and the heaven of heavens is the LORD'S thy God, the earth also, with all that therein is." Here all three heavens are disclosed in the same verse; there is the heaven (stars, constellations, etc), the heaven of heavens (God's dwelling place), and all that is therein (atmosphere). This verse encompasses the whole of God's heavenly creation and helps to uncover the fact that there are indeed three separate heavens mentioned in the Bible; all of which are owned and created by God, for the heaven even the heavens are the Lord's. (Psalm 115:16.)

To determine which heaven the Lord was speaking of in Genesis 1:1, one must remain cognizant that this verse encompasses all of the creation in the physical realm. Presumably then, God would not be referring to the third heaven since He was before all things and by Him all things exist. He would have been presiding there when He created the rest of the physical realm, and it is from this realm that the whole of the physical was created. "So that things which are seen were not made of things which do not appear" (Hebrews 11:3). That is, they do not appear in the physical until God calls them forth from the unseen spiritual realm; the third heaven. So, that leaves the other two heavens, which are the rest of the universe and the atmosphere directly above the earth as having the potential for being created in the original push.

In truth, the recreation account found in the rest of Genesis chapter one reveals very little about the expanse of the universe. The only day that mentions anything about the heavens is day four and they are essentially mentioned as ancillary objects to the earth.

> And God made two great lights; the greater light to rule the day, and the lesser light to rule the night: he made the stars also. And God set them in the firmament of the heaven to give light upon the earth, And to rule over the day and over the night, and to divide the light from the darkness: and God saw that it was good. (Genesis 1:16–18)

If this refers to the original creation of the universe, then there is precious little information about the complexity and enormity entailed in its creation. It is as if by sneezing God sprinkled the stars in the night sky, which gives them the appearance of a secondary creation. "Whoops. Hey look … stars." The fact that this passage is not referring to the original creation and the details surrounding the events that transpired on the fourth day of creation will be covered in chapter eight.

Overall there is very little information about the creation of the universe as a whole in Genesis chapter one or any other part of the Bible, but there is much more detail and information regarding the creation of the earth. The intricacies of the design found in the massive expanse of the universe seem to get second billing to earth's construction. In part, this can be attributed to the fact that the primary focus of the Genesis account has to do with the introduction of mankind on the physical earth, rather than his place in the universe. Everything in this current dispensation is orchestrated for mankind, so it stands to reason that the emphasis would be on the earth and mankind's place in it. Again, this is confirmed in Psalm 115:16 where it says that the heaven, even the heavens, are the Lords; but He concludes His thought by saying that the earth hath He given to the children of men.

Basically, everything from the atmosphere to the outer reaches of space is the Lord's, but He has given everything on the earth to mankind to use and administer. Since mankind is not part of the administration of the rest of the universe, there is no need to reveal all of its inner workings to His created beings. Humanity's duty is to tend to the earth and utilize its bounty. If it does not directly affect the path of mankind on the earth, then there is little need to report information about its functionality in the Bible. Of course, this does not mean there is no information; just that it is not the foremost intent of the book.

So the question still remains, was the atmosphere of the earth created in the initial surge of creation? That is, should the heaven of Genesis 1:1 be printed as singular or plural? The answer lies in several different passages, some of which are quoted here. First, the Psalmist states that, "Of old hast thou laid the foundation of the earth: and the heavens are the work of thy hands" (Psalm 102:25). That is, heavens plural were created in times of old, an action that took place during the initial onset of the creation. Then again, just as the Lord spread out the whole of the universe, the Bible also states that in this same fashion He spread out the atmosphere over its surface. "Thus saith God the LORD, he that created the heavens, and stretched them out" (Isaiah 42:5).

These verses plainly reveal that the heavens are indeed plural and were created during the same time reference as the rest of the universe. The Psalmist calls that period of time "of old." However, Genesis refers to it as "the beginning." Thus it can be stated that in these passages and several others that the earth, its atmosphere, and the rest of the universe were initiated during an indeterminate, yet quantifiable amount of time called the beginning.

Undoubtedly, the first verse of the Bible is very dynamic. In short, it has established a time frame, and announced a creative eternal all-powerful God. It introduced the action verb of the sentence, which defined exactly what was created. In the subsequent verse things appear to be starkly different to His creative activities. In fact, things become downright ominous.

CHAPTER 5

Verse Two

Discord

And the earth was without form, and void; and darkness was upon the face of the deep. And the Spirit of God moved upon the face of the waters. (Genesis 1:2)

From the very onset of the Bible's second verse it can be seen that something happens that is contrary to the beauty and pristine perfection found in verse one. The tone of a powerful creationary exuberance has changed to one that paints a gloomy, desperate picture of an earth in turmoil. The earth is without form, it is void, there is darkness, and a vast wasteland called the deep is covering some or all of it. Certainly, all of the descriptive words mentioned in this verse's first sentence are contrary to the very nature of the Creator.

In no way does it resemble the ideas of a thoughtful, resolute God beginning His expansive, beautiful, flourishing, and creative process in the first verse. Rather, verse two is the polar opposite. The scene is one of a wanton, reckless, and chaotic creation; without the power and devoid of the glory. As anyone can see, there is a discord between verse one and verse two. The author of this passage is making an obvious and blatant statement that the earth is a destitute lifeless sphere hanging in space. It is an earth that is incongruous to the very nature of God.

Without a doubt, something happened between the first two verses of Genesis one and it is right here that millions of people have stumbled. They allow the seeming contradictory influences of the passage to cast doubts on the credibility of the entire book. Even those who hold on to a more traditional view of the timing of the creation encounter riffs amongst their own ranks over Genesis 1:2. Though they believe that verse one is an introduction to the rest of the text, it is difficult to come to terms with the dark and gloomy picture espoused in this passage. It certainly seems to be a disjointed part of the creation account. So what happened exactly?

The truth is the Lord's ways are not a mystery when it comes to His creative process. He did not establish it in hopelessness and futility, but He formed it with a definitive purpose in mind. His intent for creation is clear. "The LORD hath made all things for himself" and "he formed it to be inhabited" (Proverbs 16:4, Isaiah 45:18). He formed it for His glory and this creative glory is a theme seen throughout the Bible. For "The heavens declare the glory of God; and the firmament sheweth his handywork" (Psalm 19:1). It was for this same reason that mankind was created, so that "we should be to the praise of his glory" (Ephesians 1:12). When the word glory is given to creation it pertains to its perfection. It is the Lord's divine perfections or excellence that is radiated in the creation. Everything that God has created is perfect because He is perfect; it is the very definition of His glory. (Psalm 18:30.)

Since He is perfect, then accordingly everything He does must also be perfect. "He is the Rock; His work is perfect," which means that when He originally created the earth, it was a vision of perfection (Deuteronomy 32:4). Once the earth was ready for habitation, everything would have worked in complete harmony: there would have been no death, all vegetation would grow in perfect abundance, and there would be no weeds, no violent weather, or any other natural catastrophes. It was idyllic in every sense and perfectly situated for its inhabitants to live a peaceful and tranquil life.

Undoubtedly from a modern viewpoint, it is difficult to imagine an earth not subject to some of the calamitous activities that it experiences today. The Bible makes it clear, that because of the Lord's perfect nature, the earth at its inception would have to have been perfect; designed to be without spot or blemish throughout all eternity.

Often there is a jump to conclude that when God says it is good, He is referring to a perfect state, thereby concluding that this is His original creation. This is not the case though; when describing a physical creation, the word good does not relay a sense of perfection, because good falls short of the very nature of God. Webster's dictionary defines "good" as: "complete or sufficiently perfect in its kind; having the physical qualities best adapted to its design and use."

Good is not bad, it is just the best qualifier that could be used given the circumstances. By definition, it is sufficiently perfect but not quite. It is the best design to be used for its intended function, but it is not perfect, and good is the description that he leaves the reader with at the end of each of the creation days. In other words, it falls short of God's standard of perfection. Thus, it is clear, if the Bible would have elaborated on the original creation, the use of the word perfect would have been commonplace.

To further add vinegar to the discussion; God puts a qualifier on good by calling the entirety of the act of creation on the sixth day as very good, reflecting once again that good is not perfect, but rather that good can be qualified by having various shades of goodness. (Genesis 1:31). All of which fall short of His standard, which is perfection.

Perfection, on the other hand, does not need a qualifier; it is a complete work that needs not change. Nothing can be added or subtracted from it. Webster's defines perfect as: "Finished; complete; consummate; not defective; having all that is requisite to its nature and kind; as a perfect statue; a perfect likeness; a perfect work; a perfect system." The word perfect is never used in the creation narrative.

The Lord uses the word good throughout the Genesis story to show His approval of the events that are transpiring via His handiwork. Certainly good is not subpar, but rather, it conveys a sense of abundance, profitability, excellence, moral correctness, benevolence, and a general state of well-being. God's use of the word good in Genesis one embodies all of these qualities and much more. What it does not convey is a sense of perfection.

A God that is perfect, and in turn does everything to that same perfect standard, would not be associated with the making of a formless, dark, and void earth found in verse two. Therefore, it is correct to say that there is discord found in the second verse of Genesis. The once perfect creation revealed in verse one has been marred and distorted.

The reason the earth is portrayed in this state of disharmony is due to events in the earth's past that had already occurred and established a foothold in His original creation. These events will be looked at in depth later, but needless to say, their effect was disastrous. Thus, anything that He created or made after those activities would have been brought into a system that was already flawed, thereby reducing His creative activities to a state of sub-perfection. That is to say, since prior activities in the earth were not up to the Lord's standard, the earth was now imperfect. Hence, any new creative activities in the earth would have been brought forth from a blemished substance. Therefore, good or very good was the best the Lord could do because of the deteriorated status of the earth.

Without form and void

Those who prescribe to a more recent creation argue that the phrase without form and void merely shows that the earth started out as an unformed blank slate that the Lord used as a launching pad for the rest of His creation. Others have stated that a formless and void earth proves what deep space observations are uncovering today; that the earth started as a wasteland of molten rock, and through time it coalesced into the planet that we see today. Both are interesting theories, but the Bible proves that the words used in this second verse point to something much more sinister that had choked the life out of the earth.

In Hebrew, the word for formless is *tohu* which means desolate, worthless, waste, useless, incapable of being utilized, or unformed. In Isaiah it is translated several times as confusion and vanity. Similarly, in the Hebrew, void is *bohu* which means empty or devoid of existence. Bohu is found only three times in the Old Testament; two times it is translated as void and once as empty.

Again, this is quite the opposite of the perfect standard one would envision for a perfect Creator. Using the definition of perfection above, it can be said that the earth was incapable of being a desolate wasted ball, devoid of existence, sitting in the waters and surrounded by darkness. A perfect

God would not create an earth that was initially intended for habitation and then during the creation process purposefully leave it in a state of vanity and emptiness. (Isaiah 45:18.)

In Jeremiah 4:23–28, the phrase without form and void exactly mirrors Genesis one. As it has been seen, formless and void are not common words in the Scriptures, so it is easy to decipher their exact meaning. Here is the only time outside of Genesis one that the Scripture uses both the words void and formless together.

> I beheld the earth, and, lo, it was without form, and void; and the heavens, and they had no light. I beheld the mountains, and, lo, they trembled, and all the hills moved lightly. I beheld, and, lo, there was no man, and all the birds of the heavens were fled. I beheld, and, lo, the fruitful place was a wilderness, and all the cities thereof were broken down at the presence of the LORD, and by his fierce anger. For thus hath the LORD said, The whole land shall be desolate; yet will I not make a full end. For this shall the earth mourn, and the heavens above be black: because I have spoken it, I have purposed it, and will not repent, neither will I turn back from it. (Jeremiah 4:23–28)

Throughout the book of Jeremiah, the book's namesake gives various prophecies concerning the future of the nation of Israel. In this chapter, he was prophesying to the people of Israel concerning a period of impending destruction that was about to take place on account of their wicked deeds. Unlike many of the other prophets, Jeremiah's prophecies are not in chronological order. In like fashion, here Jeremiah inserts this vision that he had concerning the earth.

Undoubtedly, the impending destruction Jeremiah is referring to in this chapter did happen during the Babylon assault on Jerusalem. History confirms that the Babylonian conquest during this era was quite complete. The dilemma though is whether or not this this particular vision fits within the parameters of the Babylonian reign. The fact is, there are several reason why it does not fit within the framework of Israel's future. Rather, it is likely that Jeremiah obtained this vision at some point during his life and placed it here because of the similarities between the vision and Israel's future.

There are there several key phrases within the passage that indicate his vision was looking backwards into the earth's past rather than Israel's future. First and most significant is that he uses the word earth. Of course, the definition of earth was covered in the previous chapter as referring to the whole of the physical globe. While the Babylonian empire throughout several generations was quite large, it did not encompass the whole of the earth. So to say that their regionalized activities would cause such tumultuous ramifications throughout the whole earth would be a misstatement.

A further disjunction between the whole of the chapter and the vision within can be seen in the fact that the activities listed within the vision do not correlate to any other events that have happened since the onset of mankind or that will happen in the future. In other words, there has never been or will be a time in the history of mankind on the earth when the Bible calls the land desolate, formless, and dark. It is these descriptive events that ties this passage back to the second verse of Genesis; the only point in earth's time line where it can be placed.

Thus, it is apparent that the use of the phrase, "without form and void" is more than just happenstance. Jeremiah's vision is referring to the earth as it was in Genesis. However, he adds quite a few interesting details that are not found in Genesis, and which will largely be covered throughout this and the next chapters.

...and darkness was upon the face of the deep

So the earth went from a perfect sphere, stretched out like a canvas over a frame at some point in the distant past to a wasted ball of emptiness floating in space, devoid of existence. Jeremiah continues his description of the earth of that time by proclaiming, "and the heavens, and they had no light" which he reaffirmed in verse twenty eight when he says that "the heavens above be black." Genesis also concurs with this statement when it says, "And darkness was upon the face of the deep."

The two key concepts introduced here are darkness and deep. Both give off an air of foreboding, cohesively corresponding and bringing additional clarity to the phrase without form and void. It is apparent that this is more than just a cloudy day. Here the earth was blocked from being able to see the light of the distant stars or even the sun.

The presence of darkness is the opposite of everything the Lord did during the original creation and is about to do in the Genesis sequence. One does not have to look far in the Scriptures to determine that there is a stark difference between light and darkness. The Bible defines the absence of light as being the antithesis of everything that is the Lord. (John 9:4.) Darkness is associated with evil (John 3:19), hatred (1 John 2:9), disorientation (John 12:35), vanity (Ecclesiastes 6:4), wickedness (Proverbs 4:19), death (Luke 1:79), and an absence from God. (John 1:5.)

Contrarily, God is light and light is associated with life. (John 1:4–5.) Creatively, it was God that commanded the light to shine out of darkness and it is light that causes all things to grow. (2 Corinthians 4:6.) Interestingly, the antithesis between light and dark, right and wrong, and good and evil is encountered right here in the second verse.

This theme of good versus evil is carried on throughout both Testaments and is one of the primary themes of the Bible. For instance, the Old Testament spends several books talking about the seemingly constant struggle that the Israelites waged against their enemies; both externally and among their own ranks. Not only were they continually battling armies of men, but the Bible purports they were frequently battling other spiritual enemies; such as idolatry and fornication. These latter enemies represent the moral struggle that the Israelites continually battled with from within their own ranks.

The Israelite's struggles are just one biblical example; this continual conflict between right and wrong, light and darkness continues throughout the pages of the Bible. The culmination and ultimate struggle between good and evil is this struggle between God and the devil (Acts 26:18); an age-old conflict that wages on in the spiritual realm and is first introduced in Genesis 1:2.

It must be stated that physical darkness is a natural part of the creation. (Isaiah 45:7.) But an earth completely blacked out is not the essence of God, who is light. (1 John 1:5.) His light represents the entirety of who He is; understanding, knowledge, wisdom, power, creativity, revelation, abundance, life, holiness, purity, etc. Light is the excellency of God and His illuminated perfection carried over from the first moment of the physical creation.

In the second verse of Genesis a physical darkness has now cloaked the earth and this particular darkness equates to something much more nefarious. Although darkness is a part of the creation, a complete blackout of the earth is not a work of God.

At the moment of the original creation when God spoke forth the universe, an immense amount of heat and energy was released. As the universe began to spread across its canvas, the initial light was also dispersed across the universe as it was stretched over vast distances. The space in between was unable to compensate for the stretching and parts of the immense expanse's darkness were left. Nevertheless, it is still reasonable to say that from any point of the creation, light is visible even in the smallest of increments. Currently on earth, light from distant planets and from the sun can be seen even on the darkest cloud-filled night. Absolute physical darkness is an anomaly that is not witnessed from the earth's surface.

In verse two, darkness is not only present, it is dominating the scene and the earth is completely encompassed by it and devoid of light. Of course, a lightless earth implies dereliction, imperfection, ignorance, distress, and sin. Without light it is impossible to sustain life and a place devoid of life is contrary to the very essence of God. Total physical darkness is the antithesis of God and equates to a spiritual darkness that is present. Of course, spiritual darkness is the reverse of God, who is light.

Obviously then, at this point in history, the earth is a picture in direct opposition to the beauty of the creation portrayed in verse one. To further clarity the situation, the Bible also makes note of an area it calls the deep.

Deep

The word deep has several definitions and relays many different concepts throughout the Scriptures. For example, it conveys a sense of profoundness, "thy judgments are a great deep" (Psalm 36:6). It expresses a meaning of something hidden or not obvious, "He discovereth deep things out of darkness" (Job 12:22). It also relays a sense of philosophical thought beyond human comprehension, "thy thoughts are very deep" (Psalm 92:5). It portrays a bit of quiet solitude or something that should not be disturbed, "And the LORD God caused a deep sleep to fall upon Adam" (Genesis 2:21). And it depicts the depth of a body of water, such as the ocean, "He maketh the deep to boil like a pot" (Job 41:31).

Undoubtedly this is not a comprehensive list of all the meanings of the word deep, but these definitions help to communicate the diversity of this one word in the Bible. From the standpoint of Genesis 1:2 it is the last definition that reveals the affairs that are transpiring on the earth. Here the word deep is a reference to an enormous amount of water that was covering its surface. Today, deep is defined as seas and oceans, but it will be seen that in Genesis 1:2 there was actually more water than what was just in the oceans; there was enough to cover the entire planet.

In this same vein, it also alludes to the second definition. Just like darkness exudes a menacing aura, so also does the word deep. The Lord uses the seas or the deep as a way to represent evil and sin. Psalm 69:14–15 says, "Deliver me out of the mire, and let me not sink: let me be delivered from them that hate me, and out of the deep waters. Let not the waterflood overflow me, neither let the deep swallow me up, and let not the pit shut her mouth upon me." Here the Psalmist compares the deep with sinking in mire, being overcome with the hatred of others, and being swallowed up in the pit.

Paul shows that when Christ was crucified He first descended into the deep before ascending to be with God. (Romans 10:7.) Job calls the deep things darkness, but the Lord brings to light this death. (Job 12:22.) This of course makes sense because the deep is devoid of light. Also, Job points out that this darkness is equivalent to death. This is why the Psalmist called upon the Lord to deliver him out of the deep waters. "Save me from sinking in the mud; keep me safe from my enemies, safe from the deep water" (Psalm 69:14 GNB). It was not a place that he wanted to be; he wanted to be in the light, away from death and the sin-drenched darkness of the deep.

The Bible goes on to show that the depth lacks wisdom. "The depth saith, It (*wisdom*) is not in me: and the sea saith, It is not with me" (Job 28:14). Of course, this is the polar opposite of God who is the source of all wisdom, and wisdom is the principle quintessential thing, the very essence of God. (1 Timothy 1:17.) For it was by His wisdom that the universe was created. His word is wisdom and hence anything that is not from the mouth of God is void of wisdom. In the eighth chapter of Proverbs, wisdom opens its mouth and begins to speak about the wonders of the Lord and His creation. It says that "wisdom is better than rubies; and all the things that may be desired are not to be compared to it" (Proverbs 8:11). It goes on to say that it was by wisdom that the heavens and the earth were created. "When he prepared the heavens, I was there... when he appointed the foundations of the earth: Then I was by him, as one brought up with him: and I was daily his delight, rejoicing always before him" (Proverbs 8:27, 29–30). All parts of His creation can be attributed to His wisdom; there is no part of creation that can escape the wisdom of God.

The Bible is clear that there is no wisdom in the waters of the deep, and even they themselves call out and say that wisdom is not in them. A place without wisdom is a place without God, and if God is no longer a part of His creation, then it speaks of the judgment of the Lord; a judgment similar to the judgment found in the days of Noah, where the Lord flooded the earth. Of course, judgment from the Lord only comes from wanton disobedience. (Isaiah 1:20.)

Thus, due to the fact that deep waters and darkness are present on the earth, it is evident that there was an evil of some kind that forced the hand of the Lord to turn His back on His creation. A perfect creation would have no reason to be judged or destroyed unless rebellion was found. This judgment came upon the earth in the form of water, just like in the days of Noah.

Water and the Earth

Although it is obvious that deep waters on the surface of the earth denote a lack of God, it was not always that way. To be sure, water is a quintessential part of life. In fact, water plays an enormous role in the creation of the earth and life. Indeed, nobody would argue that water is a refreshing gift that is needed when the palate is parched. The human body is made up of nearly 60% water and human blood is almost 95% water. Since the Bible says that the life of the flesh is in the blood, then by extrapolation it can be said that water is at least partially attributed to the life of the flesh. (Leviticus 17:11.)

The uses of water are virtually endless because water is an integral part of everyday life and health on the planet. It is the water in rivers that is often used to delineate the boundaries of lands on a map. Rain water causes plant and animal life to grow and wash away impurities by cleaning and refreshing the earth. Water is used for construction, sanitation, washing, re-creation, and on and on. When scientists look for life on other planets, they start by looking for evidence of water, because it is one of the main building blocks of life.

So although deep water is used by the Lord as a means of judgment and it are equated with perdition, other references to water are equated to purity. It is through water baptism that mankind can symbolize the washing away of their sins. Symbolizing a cleansing of their past rifts and denoting a dedication to the Lord. Flowing, circulating waters; such as rivers, springs, and streams are a symbol of the Lord, both in the earth and in the believer. The Bible informs us that water on a spiritual level is what causes the people of God to grow. (Psalm 1:3.) Of course, this type of water is the Holy Spirit and this same cleansing watery theme is used throughout the Bible.

For example, in John 4:14, the Holy Spirit is likened to "a well of water springing up into everlasting life." Then in 1 John 5:8 it says, "And there are three that bear witness in earth, the Spirit, and the water, and the blood: and these three agree in one." Jesus is the blood, the Spirit is God the Father, and the Water is the Holy Spirit. In the same vein, if one is filled with the Spirit, the Scriptures say that, "out of his belly shall flow rivers of living water" (John 7:38). In other words, the Holy Spirit, or the water of the Lord, will fill up that individual and out of their spirit will flow a new life.

Likewise, the Bible equates flowing refreshing water with peace. "For thus saith the LORD, Behold, I will extend peace to her like a river, and the glory of the Gentiles like a flowing stream" (Isaiah 66:12). Rivers, streams, and springs are small but powerful water sources and are used throughout the Bible to speak of God's cleansing purifying power. Time and again, the Lord uses the imagery of flowing waters as a cleansing agent that rushes over men and nations, bringing peace and regeneration. "Thou visitest the earth, and waterest it: thou greatly enrichest it with the river of God, which is full of water" (Psalm 65:9).

Of course, water was an integral part of the original creation. When God originally created the earth, He established it upon water. (Psalm 24:2.) Its foundational beams were erected upon water, and the Bible says that He stretched it out above the waters. (Psalm 104:3, Psalm 136:6.) This analogy of spreading out the earth is the same analogy He uses to spread out the heavens. (Job 9:8.)

Just like a canvas is stretched out over a frame, so also was the earth's surface stretched out over a watery base. The implications of this are enormous, because it shows that during the original act of creation there were no large bodies of water on the surface of the earth. In other words, during the original creation, the whole of the globe was covered with land stretched out over the watery deep.

Deep waters were not intended for the surface of the earth, but rather came about as means of judgment. Undoubtedly, given all of these depictions of the earth at the point of the original creation, it proves that the earth was completely covered in dry land and the only water on its surface was flowing, refreshing streams and rivers that littered its landscape.

However, on the second day of the creation narrative the scene is starkly different. The Lord calls forth the dry land out of a watery grave and named it earth. (Genesis 1:9–10.) He is not stretching it out as the Psalmist says, rather on the second day in Genesis, He is calling it forth. Not only did the earth have water on top of it, it was completely covered in water because the Lord called the dry land to come forth from the water, once again showing that the waters from verse two were not an event of the original creation. During the original creation God established the earth upon the water and stretched out the land over vast seas of water, but the events of the re-creation show that the earth was already covered in water and were instead called forth out of the water.

Certainly, the idea of the earth being built upon a massive sea of water is starkly different than the scientific ideas regarding the earth's origin. Most postulate that the largest amounts of water contained in the earth are on its surface. This is largely due to the fact that current scientific methods of research have not yet discovered massive amounts of water under the earth's surface.

In general, the scientific consensus is that the earth is comprised of three layers: crust, mantle and core. Each is believed to be composed of different materials. When looking at the composition of the earth, the crust is a mere thread of the total composition of the earth. On occasion, it has been compared to the skin on a peach. Notwithstanding, it is a relatively miniscule area as compared to the rest of the earth's volume, but to this day, it has yet to be pierced, even at its thinnest points under the ocean. Drilling equipment has been close, but it still has not yet breached into the second layer, called the mantle, which means that no one has ever seen the interior of the earth.

Because of this, in order to determine the earth's composition, scientists use a variety of indirect measuring techniques. These include, but are not limited to; seismic activity, radiation, geological observations, and melting points of different elements. Also, they look to the heavens and use external analysis of the universe at large, such as observations of newborn planetary systems and comets to give them further ideas about its interior structure. Comets are largely believed to be offshoots of planetary beginnings and therefore, through theoretic extrapolation, an analysis of them would help to understand the earth's composition. The premise being that if other planetary systems can be observed in their developmental stages, then it is likely the earth would have formed in this same fashion. All of these different methods are used in an effort to try and understand the composition of the earth.

For the most part, one of the main ways the composition of the earth is determined is based on earthquake activity. As seismic activity happens, compression waves traveling through the earth can be measured on the other side of the globe. The conduction and path of these waves react differently when traveling through water than if travelling through a solid mass.

Scientists have generally concluded from these readings that there are no significant reservoirs of water present in the earth's interior. Instead it is believed that nickel and iron alloy compromise much of the earth's core, based on these compression waves and observable facts found in meteorite remnants discovered on the earth. These same internal heavy metals are attributed to the magnetic field that surrounds and protects the earth from cosmic radiation. Certainly the idea of internal heavy metals causing a magnetic field around the earth seems plausible, but are heavy metals the only thing comprising the earth's core and mantle?

Certainly it can be stated that observation of the earth's interior is limited, due to the fact that human efforts are only able to penetrate a minute fraction of the earth's crust. Further, laboratory modeling cannot fully guarantee accuracy because conditions in the interior of the earth are impossible to replicate. So, the question that remains is, will the scientific estimates of the amount of water under the earth be applicable in the laboratory given radioactivity, pressure, and many other forces that are not observed and can only be tested in a controlled environment? Nobody truly knows. Obviously, some of the science can be manipulated in a laboratory, but as it has been seen, much of what is believed to be under the crust has been gathered from surface geological observation and scientific theories that are translated into subsurface theories. The same is also true of comets, how much of a role they really played in the development of the earth is purely theoretical.

Unquestionably, the Bible paints a completely different picture about the interior of the earth than the current scientific model, because it says that water is a prime ingredient in the earth's interior composition. Not only is water the basis of all human life, it is also the foundation of creation. Without it, no life would exist. So, it is not a far stretch of the imagination to believe that the earth itself was created from a watery base. This conclusion presents another question though: is the water currently on the surface the same water that was used during its creation or was there more water?

Voluminous

The total volume of water on the earth's surface seems massive, but in fact, it is only about one ninetieth of the total volume of the earth. Even though oceans cover nearly two thirds of the earth's surface, and at some points are several miles deep, there are still massive amounts of area under its crust due to the large circumference of the earth. So to say that the earth's surface water is the total amount the Lord used to establish the foundations of the earth seems unlikely, though not impossible.

Recently, in the scientific community there has been some speculation that there are indeed large amounts of water under the earth of potential oceanic proportions, but this theory proposes that these oceans of water are saturated amongst the surrounding terra firma (Than, Ker. (2007, February 28). Huge 'Ocean' Discovered Inside Earth. *Livescience.com*. Retrieved July 18, 2013, from http://www.livescience.com). In other words, the water is mixed in with the surrounding elements (rock in this case) in the earth's interior. While this is most definitely an interesting theory, if this is the case, how much water would this amount to?

It would certainly seem possible that different elements could be mixed with water in some form of cohesion to produce a soupy type of elemental rich water that the Lord created at the beginning that has never been seen by mankind. This is not the primordial soup of evolution theorized by scientists as happening on the earth's surface billions of years ago, but rather a watery base found in the earth's interior and still in existence today. Though this may be the case, the Bible never mentions anything mixed in with the earth's foundational water.

Certainly, it may be that the water on the earth today is truly a majority of the water He used to create the earth. That is to say, the watery base now covering approximately two thirds of the earth's surface may have been the only water He used to build the earth's foundations. He is the Creator and His thoughts are high above man's thoughts. If He says that the earth was established upon water, there are millions of different scenarios He could have set up to bring it to pass. Undoubtedly, if this was the only water used to establish the foundation, then there is either currently a void in the earth's interior or it was filled in with some other elements. The reality of an empty space in the center of the earth will be further looked at in a subsequent chapter.

The validity of the earth's watery base is confirmed in 2 Peter 3: 3–7:

> Knowing this first, that there shall come in the last days scoffers, walking after their own lusts, And saying, Where is the promise of his coming? for since the fathers fell asleep, all things continue as they were from the beginning of the creation. For this they willingly are ignorant of, that by the word of God the heavens were of old, and the earth standing out of the water and in the water: Whereby the world that then was, being overflowed with water, perished: But the heavens and the earth, which are now, by the same word are kept in store, reserved unto fire against the day of judgment and perdition of ungodly men.

Herein is another passage that has caused considerable consternation amongst biblical scholars. On account of water being mentioned, many have tried to pin these activities on the events of Noah's flood. The interesting thing is that Peter begins by calling these people not only ignorant of the prophetic future, but says they are turning a blind eye to the past events of the creation of the earth. He goes on to say that the people of the latter days will be scoffers; saying that events in the earth's history will be viewed as starting with Adam. But, it continues on by saying that they are willingly ignorant of the facts of earth's early history because they believe that this current dispensation of mankind is all that the earth has ever known.

He calls those who don't believe in an older earth, scoffers, walking after their own lusts, and not the truth of the Scriptures. He quickly points out that they are willingly ignorant of creation events because they continue to believe that the earth only existed from their prescribed beginning to the death of the earliest fathers (Adam, Noah, etc.). This is a clear-cut misstep in their thinking because he says that they rectify their error by deciphering the creation events on their terms. He goes on to say that the truth is, "the heavens were of old, and the earth was standing out of the water and in the water."

Of course, this verse once again confirms that the earth was created prior to the creation narrative that began in verse three of Genesis one. It starts by saying that the heavens were of old. The word old in the Bible is difficult to place in a specific time frame because, although God is often called the God of old who rides upon the heavens of old, so also are men described as old. (Psalm 74:12, Psalm 68:33, Acts 2:17.) Thus, use of the word "old" makes it difficult to pin down the time frame referenced in the passage. Nevertheless, the rest of the verse clearly states that the original creation happened at an undefined point in time and can only be considered dateless.

Peter continues by saying that the earth was standing out of water and in the water. In other words, the earth was originally laid on a foundation of water, but the surface was spread out on top of a watery subsurface. In this one statement, he confirms that the earth was indeed originally spread out on a base of water and that the foundations deep in the earth were also established in water.

Then in verse six, Peter continues by saying that the earth was flooded and destroyed, "Whereby the world that then was, being overflowed with water, perished." This is not the flood of Noah, because clearly the entire context of the passage is a reference to the events of the original creation and its destruction. Peter flat out reveals that at the time of the original creation, the earth was spread out above the water and not the other way around. Then at a point afterwards, it was flooded and destroyed or as Peter puts it, "the world that then was, being overflowed with water, perished." Of course, the entire world did not perish during the flood of Noah, instead Noah and his immediate family were saved, once again affirming that this passage is referring to a different flood. Peter concludes in verse seven by saying, "But the heavens and the earth, which are now." In other words, the heavens and the earth that we currently see about us are different from the heavens and earth mentioned in the previous verses. The current heavens and earth are the ones God established during the re-creation that begins in Genesis 1:3 and continues throughout chapter one and the beginning of chapter two.

When Peter states that "the world that then was ... But the heavens and the earth, which are now" he is saying that there was a change in both the heavens and the earth. It is correct to say that both the heavens and the earth were changed during the re-creative process of the earth found in Genesis one. Unequivocally, it would be an incorrect statement to say that the heaven and earth we see now are in some way different due to the flood of Noah. (Further discrepancies between the two floods will be looked at in greater detail in chapter seven on the third day of the re-creation.) Therefore, this passage in Peter must be referring to the earth prior to the events of the re-creation depicted in Genesis. If this passage of Scripture is interpreted in a different fashion, it would be in direct contradiction to the events depicted by Peter, the Psalmists, Genesis one, and several other passages.

In fact, Peter specifically warns people to beware of those who flippantly disregard the plain truth regarding the creation of the earth by becoming one of the scoffers of the events of creation. Assuredly then, it can be seen that the earth is founded on a watery bed and the dry land was spread out above it during His original creative actions. "For he hath founded it upon the seas, and established it upon the floods" (Psalm 24:2). Then later, as Peter shows, it is overpowered by at least a portion of the very water it was founded upon. Whether this flood involved the entirety of the water in the earth's interior is unlikely, but unknown.

Ocean-less

Even though deep waters in the Bible are largely associated with death and darkness, it was not always this way. As has been seen, large amounts of water were instrumental in his original creative thrust. As a matter of fact, the foundational waters the earth was established on were restrained by gates and never meant to see the light of day. (Job 38:8.) During the course of time, they became a method of judgment, thereby becoming associated with evil. The mere fact that these deep waters are still upon the earth shows that the deep is still a place of perdition and validates the fact that a presence of evil was on the earth prior to the events in verse three of Genesis (much more on this in later chapters).

Using some deductive logic and relaying this train of thought back to the original creation, shows that the earth was initially created devoid of large masses of water. When combining Isaiah 44:24 with Job 38:8, we see a portrait of an earth that was initially stretched out over the foundational water masses, with those masses being withheld under the earth by doors. "I am the LORD...that spreadeth abroad the earth by myself...who shut up the sea with doors". So at the moment of original creation, there were no large accumulations of water on its surface, only the flowing refreshing rivers and other smaller bodies of water that the Lord originally created.

Though many would postulate that without large bodies of water it would not be possible to produce life on the planet, this is not a deterrent from the biological hypotheses of the earliest life forms on planet earth. A sea-less beginning does not throw a kink into much of what the scientific community have based their hypotheses of early biological life on the planet earth.

Obviously, the earth and all that is contained within are dependent upon the life-giving attributes of water. Giant seas of water are prevalent in the paleontological record that is constantly being unearthed. Daily, fossilized remains of enormous sea creatures that once roamed ancient seas are unearthed in areas on dry land; which mean that in past epochs of time, massive quantities of water covered the earth at various places around the now exposed landscape. The fact that the Lord supplied these oceans with life given their odious background, speaks to His unending creative prowess in the earth.

However, the Bible is clear that at the point of the original creation of the earth, there were no large bodies of water on its face; which again alludes to the fact that between the original creation and today, there were events in both its distant and more recent past that caused these watery masses to rise and recede.

Archaeological records point to the fact that life came to the planet much later than the initial point of creation, and certainly from both a biblical and scientific standpoint, water is a necessary component of creation. But by definition, the word "create" means out of nothing. In other words, in order to create life on the planet, the Lord was not required to use water from the surface of the earth, because He called His creation into existence from things which are not seen.

Exodus 20:11 explores this phenomenon. "For in six days the LORD made heaven and earth, the sea, and all that in them is". For many, this verse is a confirmation that the Lord created the earth in six literal days, but that is not what the verse says. It says that He "made" the earth and sea in six days. Moses used the verb "made" to show that he was specifically referring to the events of the re-creation. It is not indicative that these were the first seas, only that there are now new divisions to their boundaries. This has to be the case, otherwise why would Moses mention it? Wouldn't the making of the heaven and the earth in the original creation encompass the sea also? It does not. Thus Moses confirms that the sea was made and established on the third day of re-creation due to the flooding found in Genesis 1:2. When the waters that were covering the earth receded, only some of the water was removed, leaving a portion of the dry land; that is the land mass we witness today.

One final affirmation about the ominous presence of deep waters covering the earth, and the fact that they are not destined for its surface comes from Revelation. In the future, when the Lord returns to establish His Kingdom upon the earth, the sea will no longer exist; which, of course, will return the earth to its original appearance. (Revelation 21:1.) The removing of the seas happens after His millennial reign; a point in time when sin will be eradicated from the earth, an obvious symbol that God does not want to be associated with the constant reminders of the earth's past. The sea was a means to His judgment, and when He establishes His kingdom on the earth, this constant reminder will be extradited back to its original home under the earth.

A Creationary Overview

Obviously, water plays an integral part in the creation. God used water to establish the earth and then locked it in its place under the earth (Job 38:8). Then at a point later in time, He revokes His prerogative and released the waters under the earth to cover its surface.

As a final ratification of these early events in the history of the earth, Psalm 104 confirms the events that have transpired so far. This Psalm is often called the creation Psalm, because it recounts an accurate chronological picture of the sequence of events from the original creation through the Genesis creation.

> Who coverest thyself with light as with a garment: who stretchest out the heavens like a curtain: Who layeth the beams of his chambers in the waters: who maketh the clouds his chariot: who walketh upon the wings of the wind: Who maketh his angels spirits; his ministers a flaming fire: Who laid the foundations of the earth, that it should not be removed for ever. Thou coveredst it with the deep as with a garment: the waters stood above the mountains. At thy rebuke they fled; at the voice of thy thunder they hasted away. They go up by the mountains; they go down by the valleys unto the place which thou hast founded for them. Thou hast set a bound that they may not pass over; that they turn not again to cover the earth. (Psalm 104:2–9)

Chronologically, this passage corresponds exactly with the events that transpired in Genesis 1:1–2, providing a nice confirmation and recap of the events that happened early in the earth's history. The passage begins by talking about God using light as an article of clothing. Of course, light is the quintessential part of His creative acts. He immediately shows that He stretched out the heavens (plural), laid the foundational beams of the earth in water, and forever established the foundation of the earth. This is an exact depiction of the events of Genesis 1:1, which is corroborated by many other Scriptures we have already seen. Then the Psalmist confirms that the earth was consumed with water and abandoned as a dark-lifeless-watery-floating ball left in waiting for further instructions.

In verse seven, the Lord rebukes the waters. This confirms that this cannot be referring to the flood in Noah's day, because the Lord did not rebuke the flood of Noah. Instead, He sent a breeze and the waters receded over a period of time. (Genesis 8:1–2.) By contrast, the waters prior to the re-creation are rebuked and moved hastily back to the place the Lord founded for them under the earth. Verse nine says that the Lord restrained the waters back to their predetermined place to prevent them from once again covering the earth. Notice that He does not promise these waters will never return, but only mentions the fact that they are not intended to cover the earth. The promise that God will not flood the earth again comes during Noah's day and is confirmed with a promissory rainbow.

Unnecessary Analysis

Additional scrutiny of Genesis 1:2 has caused some to go to extreme lengths in an attempt to prove that their particular view of the creation is correct. In fact, considerable debate among biblical scholars has arisen while attempting to translate the verb "was" in the verse, "And the earth *was* without form and void". (Emphasis added) Some feel that the Hebrew verb *hayah,* or "was," is better translated in the pluperfect, "had become." In this same vein, they also point out that the conjunction "and" at the beginning of the verse is better translated "but."

Thus they would read the text as, "In the beginning God created the heaven and the earth, but the earth had become without form and void." Indeed, there have actually been whole books written about this one verb conjugation and the proper translation of the conjunction. Needless to say, the excruciating tedium to analyze every instance that the Bible uses the word "and" and "was" is beyond the scope of reason. Arguments can be made from both camps about the legitimacy of their claims simply because of the sheer volume of occurrences of these words in the Bible. Although these claims would certainly prescribe to the premises on these pages, it is difficult to prove given the nature of the words under investigation.

Albeit, it is not a necessary or prudent argument, for an elementary glance at the text shows that something was clearly awry between verse one and two. Glory turned to desolation, the likes of which is contrary to the very nature of the Lord Himself. People that have even the most rudimentary understanding of the God of creation know that He is all powerful and perfect. A worthless creation points to disaster and calamity. It does not point to a masterful creative God. Furthermore, the events that did transpire are evident and proven in several different places throughout the Scriptures.

And the Spirit of God moved upon the face of the waters. (Genesis 1:2)

Undoubtedly, the second verse of the Bible paints a bleak picture of an earth in desolation. It sits in a sort of blackened stasis, almost like it was frozen in time, functioning but forgotten. It is apparent that with darkness covering the earth, God had turned His back on His creation and left the earth. Not only was it physically dead, it was also spiritually dead. Without God's presence, spiritual darkness reigned supreme and the earth was "functioning" in a state of chaos and physical darkness ensued; the physical manifestation of which was apparently a dark cloud that had cloaked the earth in complete physical darkness.

The sun's rays were apparently not allowed to penetrate the blackness, so it is likely that its surface was largely frozen from the deep waters now covering its surface. Had somebody been observing the planet from outer space at the time, they may have passed right by it and not even recognized it as a planet, because it had been reduced to a black ball of nothingness floating in space.

Whether or not the earth stopped spinning on its axis and rotating around the sun is difficult to ascertain from the Scriptures. The promise that the Lord gave to Noah that the earth would never stop in its rotation around the sun alludes to their being periods in the earth's history where it may have come to a standstill. (Genesis 8:22.) Geological observations of this phenomenon have been well documented in the strata of the Grand Canyon and other places around the globe (called the Great Unconformity). In these places where rock formations have exposed millions of years of the earth's history, there are periods of layering in the rocks that suggest breaks in the earth's normal functions. It is as if the earth simply stopped functioning.

Scientists have been largely unable to determine a reason for these segments in the earth's geological recordings, suggesting that over these millions of missing years there was either no stratification or it took place but eroded away.

The Bible gives a more sure explanation of this spectacle; it was brought about by the judgment of the Lord. Though the Bible really only mentions one such occurrence of earthly discord prior to the arrival of mankind; the earth records that there may have been many others. Also, the major unconformities found in the Grand Canyon are difficult to ascertain whether they fall within the timeline of events of Genesis 1:2 and the restoration of life in Genesis 1:3 or not. Nevertheless, the Bible purports that during this time frame, the earth was in a period of judgmental darkness and unable to sustain life.

Praise the Lord, for it at was at this darkest of hours that He decided it was time to begin His restorative work. Genesis 1:2 concludes with the Holy Spirit, who is seen moving over the face of the waters. The word waters are plural because it includes the water left under the earth as well as the water currently on top of the earth. Additionally, it would include the water above the earth, or what remains of the atmosphere (re-creation of the atmosphere happens on the second day). There is no definitive answer as to how long the Spirit was brooding over the water; He may have been hovering over the ruined creation for months, millennia, or even millions of years. Certainly, the geological record suggests that it was a substantial amount of time, but biblically no time frame is given.

Fortunately, the Lord states that He was not willing to wash his hands of the earth and its processes, "The whole land shall be desolate; yet will I not make a full end. For this shall the earth mourn, and the heavens above be black: because I have spoken it, I have purposed it, and will not repent, neither will I turn back from it" (Jeremiah 4:27–28). It is not the end. He will rebuild and restore. He will recreate. He purposed it and He will not retreat from His sayings and that is exactly what He did starting in Genesis 1:3.

CHAPTER 6

The First Day

Creation Events

Thus saith God the LORD, he that created the heavens, and stretched them out; he that spread forth the earth, and that which cometh out of it; he that giveth breath unto the people upon it, and spirit to them that walk therein... (Isaiah 42:5)

The first two verses in the Bible disseminate a lot of information regarding the earliest events of creation. Verse one exposed an all-powerful God that created the heaven and earth at a particular point in the dateless past. That was followed by the second verse, which reveals a dark and chaotic earth, being closely watched by the Spirit of God who is seen hovering over it while contemplating its future. Beginning in verse three, God begins speaking to His desolate creation and thus begins an account of the events of the re-creation; events that are broken up into seven periods called days. During the first six days the Lord is at work, which can be witnessed by the many action verbs that the text proclaims, "And God saw," "And God called," "And God divided," etc. Then on the seventh day, all of His activity is wrapped up, when He declares a day of rest from all the work that He had completed.

A Creation Day

*For in six days the LORD made heaven and earth, the sea, and
all that in them is, and rested the seventh day: wherefore the LORD
blessed the sabbath day, and hallowed it. (Exodus 20:11)*

Though there are many contested and questioned ideas about the creation account in Genesis, none is more disputed than the use of the word day. This single word has caused more division among Christians than possibly any other concerning the creation. Of course, a day as mankind knows it encompasses a period of 24 consecutive hours, or one complete revolution of the earth on its axis. Given the realities that the scientific community has uncovered in recent years, it is seemingly impossible that the earth could have been created in this time frame. Of a truth, the previous chapters have also revealed that by biblical standards the earth was indeed not created in six revolutions of the earth, but was originally created over a span of time in the dateless past called the beginning.

So then, what about the six days of the re-creation? Are these six subsequent days when the Lord recreated the earth truly six revolutions of the earth? The answer lies in the definition of the word day. Frankly, there are too many contradictions in the events of the re-creation to allow for the Lord to have recreated the earth in six literal earth days. Therefore it is imperative to review the definition that the Lord prescribes to a day.

In the original Hebrew, the word for day is *yom*, which generally is translated as a day or one 24 hour period. In many instances though, this same word is also rendered as a longer period of time. For example, in Genesis 26:8 it is used to denote an unspecified period of time that is definitively longer than a day. Then in 1 Samuel 27:7 it is used to represent a specific extended period of time: one year and 4 months. Then again in Leviticus 25:29 it definitively states that a day is one year. Thus the Bible gives relevance to several different definitions of the word day.

One final convincing instance of its multiple definitions is found in the creation account itself. At the end of the six creation days, God uses "yom" to encompass all of the creation events. "These are the generations of the heavens and of the earth when they were created, in the day that the LORD God made the earth and the heavens" (Genesis 2:4). So, at the end of the Genesis creation, He says that the whole of the works of the re-creation were completed in one day. Thus, it is evident that the use of the word day has various meanings in the Bible and the most obvious incongruence is found in the creation account itself. Obviously, with all of these various meanings for a day, it would seem that a strict definition during the re-creation would not necessarily be relevant.

To add further confusion, in both modern and biblical instances, use of the word day is sometimes used in a colloquial fashion. For example, one might say, "back in the day, I remember when…" This is not a reference to one specific day, but refers to a period of time when they were in school, or they were younger, or less experienced, etc. "Back in the day, we used to vacation with our family at the lake, but now it has been a while since we've been there." Of course, this is obviously referring to a period of years when they vacationed in one specific spot, not one particular day.

The Bible uses this same phraseology in Zechariah 14:1. Here, Zechariah is prophesying about a future time for Israel and says, "Behold, the day of the LORD cometh". The inference in this passage is not one specific day, but a time when generations of Israelites would be overrun and placed in captivity. Certainly, this colloquial use is what the Lord is evoking at the end of the Genesis creation mentioned above. Otherwise, how could the whole of the six days of creation have been referred to as one day?

The creation narrative also institutes one final use of the word day that is particularly interesting. It is found in Genesis 2:17, "But of the tree of the knowledge of good and evil, thou shalt not eat of it: for in the day that thou eatest thereof thou shalt surely die." God tells Adam not to eat of the tree, for in that day death will come. Did Adam die on that particular earth day after he ate of the tree? No, he did not physically die within the time frame that we currently call a day, but he did die within the time frame that God calls a day.

Adam lived a long life of 930 years; one of the longest recorded in the Bible. (Genesis 5:5.) Of course, this falls short of Methuselah who is the oldest person mentioned in the Bible who lived 969 years, nevertheless it is a long time compared to our modern day life expectancy. (Genesis 5:27.)

Interestingly, nobody in the Bible lived more than 1,000 years. Herein lies the answer, for it was within that day that Adam died. Not a day as it is prescribed by current convention, but a day as the Lord defines it; which means that there has to be a disconnect between the definition between mankind's meaning of day and the Lord's definition during the sequential Genesis account.

In 2 Peter 3:8, God defines what He calls a day, "But, beloved, be not ignorant of this one thing, that one day is with the Lord as a thousand years, and a thousand years as one day." This verse concludes a thought that was covered in the previous chapter, where Peter told his readers that the previous world perished by water. Now Peter is finishing his thought process by cajoling the reader not to be ignorant of the fact that God is on a different timeline than humanity.

One day to the Lord is as a thousand earth years. The ramifications of this verse are multifaceted because it affects many of the biblical timelines. It provides glimpses into future prophetic events, and it reveals current situational timelines, but in particular, it uncovers the timing of the events of the creation and re-creation. Most other instances use the word day as referring to one revolution of the earth, but Peter confirmed that during the re-creation, God was on a different timeline.

The resounding truth that Peter is trying to unveil about the creation is that each day of the Genesis creation account happened within approximately a one thousand year time frame. Of course, God is not bound by the confines of time, but gives this approximate reference to help mankind understand the earth's timelines. When Adam was in the garden, sin had yet to enter the picture. So just like God, Adam was eternal and unconstrained by the wiles of time. His reference of time was the same as the Lord's; one day was as a thousand years. Once he sinned, the dispensation of men took over and shortly thereafter the definition of time needed to be changed. Adam caused a rift between himself and God and the consequence was that God had to separate Himself. Once this happened, Adam's time frame was no longer defined in the eternal paradigm of the Lord, but switched to a more temporary definition.

The result of Adam's sin was that humanity began to die physically. Life was still abounding on the earth, but due to man's sin, God's only choice was that everyone born into the earth would have to physically die. In the first couple of chapters of Genesis after the garden, mankind is seen living several hundred years. Though this has perplexed many, the answer as to why their life was so long compared to today's standards is because they were still on God's timing. God had not yet defined the length of a day. A day at that point was still one thousand years. When the Bible says that Adam died on "that day," it was not a reference to one revolution of the earth. Rather he died within the time frame that the Lord defines as a day (1,000 years). This later changes in the sixth chapter, where God repositions the duration of man's life on the earth and shortens it to 120 years. (Genesis 6:3.) It is from that point on that revolutions of the earth are referred to as days.

Thus, the earth and heaven were originally created at a point in the dateless past, which was followed by events that left the earth in a place of chaos, and devoid of the Lord. This was then succeeded by a period of re-creation and each one of the creation days were around 1,000 years long. The truth is that this original biblical timeline leaves enough time for the earth to accept and adapt to the changes the Lord was implementing during the days of the re-creation, thereby alleviating some of the seeming inconsistencies of the six day creation event. Following is a breakdown of the days of the re-creation and a basic recap of the events that materialized:

Day one - Light
Day two - Firmament (atmosphere)
Day three - Plants, trees, vegetation
Day four - Sun, Moon, Stars
Day five - Marine life, birds, fish, reptiles
Day six - Animals, man
Day seven - God rests

Day One

And God said, Let there be light: and there was light. And God saw
the light, that it was good: and God divided the light from the darkness.
And God called the light Day, and the darkness he called Night. And
the evening and the morning were the first day. (Genesis 1:3–5)

As was previously shown, the verb created was defined as an action that only the Lord could perform. He alone is the Creator, and only He can call forth something out of nothing. Now on the first day of creation, He uses a distinctly different action verb to call the earth into action: let. He said, "Let there be..." Let is used almost 1,500 times in the Bible and is never associated with a new creation. Rather it is an act of permission, allowing that particular act to be set in motion.

In the first chapter of Genesis alone, the word is used 10 times and usually preceded by "God said." In essence, when the Lord uses let in Genesis one, He is commanding His creation to take action, either to animate or resuscitate it. Throughout the creation story, He does this with light (vs. 3, 14, 15), the firmament (vs. 6), (vs. 9), the earth (vs. 11, 24), water (vs. 20), the birds (vs. 22), and Himself in the creation of man. (vs. 26.) He is speaking forth an act of permission and telling that object or person to take action.

Here on the first day He begins using let when He speaks to the light by calling it out. "Let there be light." An indeterminate period of time has lapsed after the calamity of verse two, and it is now time for a once dormant light to be reactivated. It is not a creative act; He is simply telling something that was at one point vibrant and existing, it would now be allowed to continue in its former path. When Moses cried out to pharaoh to "Let my people go," he was telling Pharaoh to allow the people of Israel to be released from their servitude (Exodus 5:1).

In much the same way, the earth was in a state of bondage and God wanted it to begin anew. Thus God begins by speaking to the light and commanding it to bring to pass that which was left to naught. Through this act of faith, He starts the re-creative process. It was this quintessential life-giving light that the earth was in desperate need of to survive. It was not a physical light, but something that was infinitely more powerful. It was the word of God that initiated the Light; and it was the Word of God that is Light. (John 1:1, 5.)

In the Bible there are several different definitions of light. Light can come in the form of a revelation, a candle, daybreak, or it can represent the oil in a lantern. It is light that causes all life to spring forth and grow and it is light that brings heat to warm the earth. With the right amount of light things grow and prosper, without the right amount of light things die and freeze. Compare the flourishing-light enhanced Earth to the icy surfaces of Pluto at the outer reaches of the solar system. Pluto is a chunk of rock covered in ice that is completely devoid of life. Unable to obtain enough light from the sun, it will remain in this state unless changes in its orbit bring it closer to the sun.

Light causes affluence and increase and it is necessary for the success of all living things that populate the earth; from planets to animals to humans. Without light the earth would be much like Pluto; a lifeless ball floating in space. Just like it was in Genesis 1:2. With no viable source of light the earth was a dark, lifeless ball, engulfed in an ice age. During that time, there is no biblical indication that the inner workings of the earth had stopped, but with the cloak of darkness and water covering its surface, everything would have been dead and in need of the live-giving qualities of light.

Generally speaking physical light has two qualities; it is both a wave and a particle. That is to say, physical light travels in waves, and those waves are made up of particles called photons. When the sun rises in the morning and brings heat and energy to enliven the earth it is a physical light. It can be seen, felt, and experienced. The outcome of its warmth and properties are evident in almost all areas of life.

In addition to physical light, the Bible also reveals that there is spiritual light and it is liberally placed in unsuspecting areas. For instance, it was a spiritual light manifested in a physical light that illuminated the night sky and led the Israelites through the wilderness. (Exodus 14:20.) Though some have tried to put a definition to it, there is no natural explanation of a cloud that illuminates the night, except that it was supernatural light that flowed from God.

The most common word for light in the Old Testament Hebrew is *or*, which portrays both the physical and spiritual aspects of light. In the Greek New Testament, the equivalent word for light is *phos*. In the Bible, there are many other things that are mentioned as either producing or receiving a separate source of light from God. Following are a few passages from the Bible that mention some of the differing kinds of light. There is the light of the word (Psalm 119:130); the light of the law (Proverbs 6:23); the light of Israel (Isaiah 10:17); the light of life (John 1:4); the light of the gospel (2 Corinthians 4:4); children of light (Ephesians 5:8); the light of the wicked (Job 18:5); the light of the eye (Matthew 6:22); the light of the living (Psalm 56:13); the light of my countenance (Job 29:24); the light of His countenance (Psalm 4:6); and the light of God. (1 John 1:5.)

Of course, there are more, but this is just a quick introduction to show that there is more than one thing that the Bible mentions as either receiving or dispersing light. Some of the lights mentioned are physical and some lights are spiritual. Many of the lights referenced in the Bible would probably never be considered as producing their own light and are difficult to perceive as true sources of light.

The truth is that all of the lights mentioned would not be possible without the spiritual light that is generated from the Father. Certainly, it is biblically clear that humans do produce their own source of light, though it would be difficult to make a case that human light is solely dependent upon their own volition. (Psalm 56:13.) Rather, any light that a human produces comes from the Father of Lights. (John 1:4.)

In this same vein, the Bible says that the righteous have a light that shines upon them. "Light shines on the righteous, and gladness on the good" (Psalm 97:11 GNB). It is not that the righteous necessarily produce their own light, but rather that a spiritual light from God shines upon them. "Unto the upright there ariseth light in the darkness: he is gracious, and full of compassion, and righteous" (Psalm 112:4). They have a burning quality of righteousness that envelops them and is evident to those around them. It is more than just spiritual; because the spiritual shines out into the physical and causes change.

Of course, all of the lights produced upon the earth would not be possible without the original light producer Himself. God is the originator of righteousness and light is a quality that God exhibits. Interestingly, the Bible also shows that the Creator wraps Himself in light. (Psalms 104:2.) How is it that He can have light on Him and yet be the light? This phenomenon in confirmed in First John where it says that God is light (1 John 1:5), yet a couple of verses later, it states that He is in the light. (1 John 1: 7.) This mystery is unwrapped in the revelatory function of His Godhead. As it has been mentioned, God is three parts, as such; there are three different lights that emanate from the Godhead.

First, the light of the Father is a spiritual light that mankind is called to walk in. Isaiah calls to the house of Jacob to change their ways and tells them to come and walk in the light of the Lord. (Isaiah 2:5) It is a spiritual light that emanates from the Father Himself.

Second, there is the light of the Holy Spirit, a spiritual light that shines in a dark place and brings illumination to a darkened mind. (Luke 2:32.) Physically, He is shown to take the form of a cloven tongue of fire. (Act 2:3.)

Finally, there is the light of Christ. He is the light of the world. (John 8:12.) "In him was life; and the life was the light of men. And the light shineth in darkness; and the darkness comprehended it not" (John 1:4–5).

Thus, each part of the Godhead produces its own light. That is how He can both be the light and be in the light. Each of the lights of the Godhead is intimately entwined in the others to produce a far more illuminating light. The Father is covered in the light of the Holy Spirit and Jesus and vice versa. This is how God can be light and yet wrap Himself in light, because He wraps Himself in the material light of Jesus and the spiritual light of the Holy Spirit. Each member of the Godhead produces an overflowing abundant signature amount of righteous light. In addition, it is therefore true that He could certainly wraps Himself in any of the dozens of other lights that the Bible mentions; much like the light of righteousness. Since He created them all, He could use any one of them for a covering of His one true light.

Elongation of light

Therefore, it can be said all the sources of light mentioned in the Bible flow from and are created by God, the Father of lights. (James 1:17.) This would include lights that were originally made by God, but were changed into something else by human choice. (Job 18:5.) Additionally, there are several other aspects that are associated to being the Father of lights. In First Timothy 1:17 it proclaims that He is the King eternal, immortal, and invisible. All three are intimately intertwined to the reality that He is the one true light. This verse speaks to the inter-dimensionality of God. For He exists on a different spiritual dimension, yet at the same time, He occupies the known physical dimension.

He is the invisible God who dwells in a dimension that is referred to as the spiritual realm and therefore produces light in that dimension. That light in turn affects the physical realm, and its qualities are intimately linked with the physical and spiritual aspects of time and space, it speaks to the Lord's immortality and eternal existence. Remember, that for God, time is not an issue; there is no beginning or end for Him. The past, the present, and the future are all the same to Him. (Hebrews 13:8.) He is, He was, and He always shall be. He remembers all things equally, as if it was that moment, yet He still has the ability to communicate with humanity on a linear time line.

The implications of the physical properties of light were originally promoted by Albert Einstein in the 1930's. Einstein disagreed with the theories of his predecessors about the qualities of light. They believed that light was a perpetual constant in the universe; because it had been mathematically proven that the speed of light was a constant 186,282,397 miles per second.

Einstein did not disagree with this constant but he had difficulty coming to terms with the idea that if humans were able to travel at the speed of light, they would be able to catch a beam of light. Instead, Einstein proposed something different by saying that if a person were to travel at or close to the speed of light they never would be able to catch that beam because there was actually another factor that was changing; time. He proposed that if a person were to approach the speed of light, the less amount of time that would elapse. In other words, he conjectured the idea of time dilation. He suggested that once a person reached the speed of light they would actually become light.

For instance, if an individual looks into a mirror, they see themselves because of the light of their reflection is bouncing off the mirror and reflecting their image. Now if that person were to pick up speed and begin to travel at the speed of light, the light that is reflected off of them would be traveling at the same pace as the individual. That person would no longer be able to see themselves in the mirror; they would become light themselves. It is, at this point, that time itself no longer exists. They would become invisible and travel on the same plane as God.

The closer that one gets to the speed of light, the slower that time becomes. Once the speed of light is reached, Einstein said that it could only be equated to eternity. Time in and of itself would cease to exist. This of course, is why the Bible calls God "the King eternal, immortal, invisible" (1 Timothy 1:17). He is the invisible Creator, who travels at the speed of light, He is light. He is not limited by time: He is time. Time does not exist for Him. He is immortal.

One additional example of this phenomenon can be seen in a spaceship picking up speed on its journey through space as it begins to travel closer and closer to the speed of light. As things in the physical realm are sped up, they become energy; it is what the entire universe is based upon. The closer that the ship travels to the speed of light the slower time becomes. As it continued to pick up speed, one day on the ship would eclipse several days on the earth. And as the ship continued its increasingly faster journey, one day on the ship would turn into several years on the earth. Once they got right up to the threshold of crossing into eternity, one day would be the equivalent of one thousand years on earth.

So as the ship increases in speed it come to a point where it travels into a different dimension. Time is stretched the faster one moves towards this point, at which point eternity is discovered. The "end of light" is the spiritual realm: the dimension of God. When one reaches this point, the realm of the physical ceases to exist and becomes the spiritual. Therefore, the physical then exists as an extension of the spiritual realm and it benefits from it because it was manifested from it.

This documented phenomenon of time dilation helps to further confirm the timing of the creation days of Genesis one. "For a thousand years in thy sight are but as yesterday when it is past, and as a watch in the night" (Psalm 90:4). When one dwells in the light as He is in the light, a thousand years on earth may pass, but it is biblically only as one day for the Lord. Again, this was also the case with the re-creation. There are six days mentioned in Genesis, but they are six one thousand year time periods on earth because this passage of time was on "God's clock." Mankind was not on the earth yet, so any mention of time would have to be biblical definition of God's time; a thousand years are as a day.

From a scriptural standpoint, the ramifications of this for humans are astounding. In the physical, the speed of light does not change, neither does God. He is the same yesterday, today, and tomorrow. God is a Spirit, but God is also light. He exists on a different timeless plane than natural humans. Spiritually humans also have a spirit because they are created in the image of God. Human spirits exist on the same or similar plane as the Spirit of God. In order to create the physical realm, He essentially slowed down light so that the physical domain was created. Once the physical was created it also allowed for time to be measured because of the new qualities of light that God prescribed. In other words, God, the very source of light, changed the quality of spiritual light to create the physical.

One example of this phenomenon is witnessed in reverse with Enoch. He walked so close to the light of the Lord that he was translated out of the earth. As he drew nearer to the light, He became more enlightened himself. He lived on the earth for 365 years (a short time for those days), but even while he was on earth, his days would have been much longer because the closer that he walked with God the more spiritual light that he received and time become elongated for him. Then, one day as he was walking in the light of God, time stretched so much that he just stepped over into eternity. (Genesis 5:23–24.)

Solomon relayed this truth when he said, "For length of days, and long life, and peace, shall they add to thee" (Proverbs 3:2). This verse mentions two phenomenon's about life on planet earth. Not only can one enjoy a long life or a life filled with many days and years, but also the length of those days can be increased. As one walks closer to the light of Christ, time is elongated and a day can be stretched to handle more earthly tasks and enjoy more time with the Lord.

Enoch was no more, because he moved closer to the light. God removed him from his sin-ridden body and gave him a new glorified body so that he could truly approach unto God in the spiritual realm. This is most likely what will happen at the end of this dispensation. A new glorified body will be issued, one that is closer to the spiritual than the physical, because it will have the ability to walk close to the Light. Time will become almost non-existent.

The word almost is used because even eternity is short of the true light of God. Only God dwells in the true plane of eternal existence. He is the One who dwells in the light for He is the Father of all lights. All other planes of existence are an extension of His light and certainly His spiritual lights mentioned in the Bible may only be a few of the dimensions of light the He occupies. "He alone has endless life and lives in inaccessible light. No one has ever seen him, nor can anyone see him. Honor and eternal power belong to him! Amen" (1 Timothy 6:16).

It is impossible to obtain unto His standard of Light. Although, angels and ultimately mankind will all dwell in eternity, it is still a product of His light. One thousand years are as a day and a day is as one thousand years; one day is still a measure of time. Mankind and angels are never called to be light, they are called to draw close to the light and dwell in the light. (James 4:8, 1 Peter 2:9.) Creation is an extension of His life and light. "In him was life; and the life was the light of men" (James 1:4). It can never become His light and hence men and angels will eternally be awed yet fall short of the Father of Lights.

Light on the First Day

In First Corinthians 15:40–41 it states that the glory of one celestial body is different than another. "There are also celestial bodies, and bodies terrestrial:

but the glory of the celestial is one, and the glory of the terrestrial is another. There is one glory of the sun, and another glory of the moon, and another glory of the stars: for one star differeth from another star in glory." The glory of the moon is different than the glory of a star. Of course, the glory that it is referencing is the light that it is giving off. The Lord is saying that there are different lights in the heaven and each one is significant in glory or light.

Paul continues by saying that planetary bodies are like physical bodies in glory. They are covered in weakness, but are raised in power, which means that earthly bodies also have a modicum of glory. (1 Corinthians 15:43.) Enoch was a prime example of this, because as he walked closer to the one true light, he changed into a more glorious form of light.

That life-changing, light-giving glory began with Jesus, when God spoke the physical into existence in the beginning. Christ came forth and the rest of the physical creation began to take shape. He is the initial light, and His light gives life to men and lights up the world. (John 1:4, John 8:12.) John said that "the light shineth in darkness; and the darkness comprehended it not" (John 1:5).

This glorious light of Christ is unlike any other light. In the Christmas story, when the angel spoke to the shepherds in the field, it says that, "the glory of the Lord shone round about them: and they were sore afraid" (Luke 2:9). Apparently the light was so bright that it frightened them. John speaks of Jesus in His early ministry and says that they, "beheld his glory, the glory as of the only begotten of the Father" (John 1:14). The people saw His glory, it was present upon Him and bright enough to be recognizable. Then again, on the Damascus road, Paul had an encounter with Jesus where he was blinded by the glory of that light that came down from heaven and surrounded him. (Acts 22:11.) This is the very glory of His presence that emitted a light that was visible in the physical realm, and it was so strong that it blinded Paul.

The Book of Revelation reveals that once the dispensation of man on the earth is finished, the Lord is going to set up His kingdom on earth. When that kingdom arrives physically in Jerusalem, the city will have no need for the sun or the moon to shine, "for the glory of God did lighten it, and the Lamb is the light thereof" (Revelation 21:23). His glory is so great that it actually physically manifests itself by illuminating the entire city.

From these few examples, it is obvious that the Lord allows various degrees of His glorious light to be seen in different situations. The light needed for a whole city was given in a different portion than the light that was present when the disciples encountered His glory.

Taking this back to the re-creation of the earth, it has generally been assumed that the light on day one is the light of the sun, but the Bible does not say it was the sun that was reanimated to begin bestowing life upon the planet. It only says that God announced, "Let there be light" and then he divided the light from the dark and named the day and night. (Genesis 1:3–5.) The same Hebrew word for light is used for both day one and day four of the creation, but day four speaks of heavenly bodies whereas day makes no mention of heavenly bodies, only that light is called forth. It does not specify that the light on day one is the light of the sun nor does it specify what type of light it was; only that He was telling it to shine.

If the light on day one was a release of the light of the planetary bodies reaching the earth, it is certainly confusing that the same thing seems to happen on the fourth day of the re-creation. Further, how was the earth protected from the damaging rays of the sun without a fully recovered atmosphere in place, which wasn't reanimated until the second day?

When God called the light to come forth on the first day, it was not a creation of light. Nowhere in the Bible does it specifically say that God created light; rather it says that He is the Light and all things were created by Him. The light that comes from any part of the Godhead cannot change, because God is unchangeable. But He can be revealed or released in varying amounts. In other words, God forms or configures the perfect type and amount of light necessary for His plans. (Isaiah 45:7.) In this case His plans were toward the earth. The right amount of light is absolutely necessary for the formation of His creation. If you have too much light then life is unsustainable, and if you have too little light then life fails to spring forth. God had a plan for the earth at the moment of the re-creation and He released just the perfect amount of light for the situation. So the question remains, "What is this light on day one, and if it is not coming from the heavenly bodies, where is it coming from?"

Psalm 74:16 gives some insight into this illuminating quandary when it says, "thou hast prepared the light and the sun." Notice that the light is mentioned as being a separate entity than the sun. Although the sun emits light, it is evident that the Psalmist is also referring to a secondary more prominent type of light. It is a light that has been prepared. It is a light that shined into the dark places when He created the universe. It is a not the physical light of the sun created by God to cast light upon the earth, but it is apparent there is also another light that has the ability to illuminate the earth. And since all lights ultimately emanate from the Father, this light is no exception.

In the beginning of the gospel of John is a description of Jesus that mirrors and gives insight into the power and process of the creative work of God. While it is specifically referring to Jesus' time on earth, it also reflects back to the time of earth's restoration. "In the beginning was the Word, and the Word was with God, and the Word was God. The same was in the beginning with God. All things were made by him; and without him was not any thing made that was made. In him was life; and the life was the light of men. And the light shineth in darkness; and the darkness comprehended it not" (John 1:1–5).

Most of this verse has already been determined to be referring to the original creation because it mirrors Genesis by utilizing the phrase, "in the beginning." In verse four it moves forward to the re-creation when it mentions mankind. Then in verse five it references the light of the re-creation when it says, "And the light shines in the darkness; and the darkness comprehended it not." The earth was cloaked in darkness and a light began to shine that the darkness did not comprehend. In other words, during the re-creation, a light burst forth and the darkness was unable to understand its presence.

John makes it clear this was a spiritual light. It was a light that was first initiated by the Father of lights. That light is Christ. Since He was before all things and by Him all things exist, this light would have to emanate from Him. He is the inspiration and the required element for both the creation and the restoration of the earth. He is the physical light of God on the earth. Without the light of the Christ in God, darkness would prevail. Without the light that is Jesus, nothing physical could have been created. The Word of God (Jesus) enlightens the darkness that is/was in the earth. The physical light that touched all of creation and brought forth life is the same light that brings forth spiritual revelation. It is the light of God's glory and it possesses both physical and spiritual qualities.

The question still remains, is this the same light that shined in the dark places on day one? The sequential verses in John suggests that the light mentioned here and the light on day one were one and the same, but digging deeper into other passages shows that there may be more to the story.

In Second Corinthians 4:6 Paul lays out the crux of what this light was: "For God, who commanded the light to shine out of darkness, hath shined in our hearts, to give the light of the knowledge of the glory of God in the face of Jesus Christ." Paul shows that it is not the same light but it is similar, for certainly it originates on account of the true light: it is the light of the knowledge of the glory of God in the face of Jesus Christ. This light is not from the glory of God, but is simply the knowledge of His glory. It is the light of the knowledge of the glory of God in the face of Jesus Christ.

There are literally dozens of lights mentioned in the Bible, but during the re-creation the very knowledge of the glory of God was enough to start the restorative work in the earth. It is this creative light that shined in the darkness and started the rejuvenating process on day one of creation and continues to shine on the earth today. Without this light, the world would be lost and the creation would not have been reanimated. It was the necessary first ingredient that reinitiated the creative process and it is this light alone that has enough power to enlighten the whole earth. Praise God.

This light of Christ was absent from the earth and quit transferring its life-giving nourishment during the events of Genesis 1:2. Destruction had been complete and darkness cloaked the planet. In fact, it was so complete, that even the light of the sun and other heavenly bodies were unable to penetrate the darkness that was first spiritual in nature. The earth was in a holding pattern and the Holy Spirit was hovering above it, awaiting the next step.

Of course, God never wanted to leave the planet in such a state of disarray. He called out to that missing light in verse three and said let it be.

That is the light of the knowledge of the glory of God in Christ Jesus and its restorative powers were necessary for the revival of a destitute earth.

Verse four of Genesis one says that God divided the light from the darkness. "And God saw the light, that it was good: and God divided the light from the darkness" (Genesis 1:4). It was a tangible light that could be seen by the Lord in the spiritual realm and it was a light which could be manipulated and separated from the darkness. It was a byproduct of His glory and it came about by His very nature. It is generated on account of the glory of the spiritual, but had the ability to change into the visible realm. Even today, it emanates from the spiritual realm and has a grandiose effect on the natural realm.

As this light erupted upon an earth that was virtually devoid of life, the earth became expectant and hopeful of a thriving reconstructive end. Sure enough, that's when God showed up with a new plan. As the earth became enlightened by the knowledge of His word; things began to change. The frozen, upside-down planet began to rejuvenate and the rebuilding process commenced. The darkness was cast out and life began to spring forth, not by the light of the sun, but by the light of the knowledge of the glory of God in the face of Jesus Christ.

A light brought about by the word of the Lord would seemingly and of necessity need to be perfect. For certainly everything that comes from Him is perfect. Of a truth, this light is a reflection of His very being. It is a product of the knowledge of Him, which means it also has to be perfect. Therefore, since the events of day one were a product of this light, it would seem that the classification of good would fall short of being the proper adjective to describe what happened on this first day of the re-creation.

Any light that emanates from God is perfect, and that light affected the earth in profound ways, but the outcome of its properties could only be described as good, because of the state of the earth. In other words, the verse can be read like this, "And God saw the light, that it (the results and benefits of the light on the earth) was good." It was not the light itself that was good, but rather what it was doing to the earth that was good. When God looked at the earth, it still fell short of His glory because it had fallen from the perfect standard of God. Perfection is a standard that could no longer be met. So, due to the earth being in a fallen state and remaining that way until death is abolished, perfection could not have been a way to describe the outcome. (1 Corinthians 15:26.)

Sin had brought judgment and death upon the earth, and death is the last thing that will be removed, but it will not happen until after this current dispensation. Therefore, even during the re-creation, the outcome of his activities could only be classified as good and not perfect. The very fact that the earth was flooded, and partially still is, proves that it was and remains in a fallen state. Second Corinthians 4:7 continues this premise by saying, "we have this treasure in earthen vessels, that the excellency of the power may be of God, and not of us." This is obviously referring to the sin-filled nature of mankind, but in this same fashion the earth cries out for its own redemption.

The earth is the original earthen vessel, and an innocent bystander that became wounded in a territorial battle. Once the light of the knowledge of His glory began to shine upon a broken earthen vessel, it changed the earth and the recreation began, but still fell short of His true perfect standard, until death has been abolished (there will be more on the reasons why death was in the earth in subsequent chapters). On account of death, the best that the perfect light of the knowledge of God in Christ Jesus can do to the earth can only be classified as good.

In this same vein, during the re-creation, God gave mankind a spirit and soul, and it was God that brought it to life. (John 1:4.) The same or similar glorified creationary light God used during the re-creation is the same light that is necessary for human life. It is this light that gives life to the spirit and soul of mankind. Isaiah declares that mankind has its own light by saying, "Then shall thy light break forth as the morning...the glory of the LORD shall be thy rereward" (Isaiah 58:8). Throughout this chapter, he is calling upon Israel to renew their covenant with the Lord and call on His name. When they do, he says their light shall break forth and the glory of the Lord shall be their reward, or rear guard. Again, the glory of the Lord gave mankind a soul and the light of His glory is able to re-enlighten that same soul.

In the same manner that His light brings forth life, His Word also gives illumination and revelation to a man's soul. Unfortunately, that light can become obscured by the darkness of the world. (John 9:4–5.) Those who believe on His name will be renewed by the light of life. For those who choose not to believe in His name, the light of the glory of Jesus cannot be conveyed to their spirit. In John 11:10, Jesus said that a man that has no light walks in darkness and they will stumble. They have no light to shine upon their path, they are blinded to the truth and stumble in their own darkness. Once the light of Jesus is asked to show the way, they are changed from darkness to light and the True Light now lights their path. Jesus is the light that is shining in a darkened world. Those who call on His name will be filled with this same light. Those who ignore the call of God will stumble along in darkness.

The light that gives life to all things physical is the same light that gives life to all things spiritual. His light shined forth to bring the initial spark to the souls of men, but sin brought darkness that severed His life restoring light. Jesus' light can be called upon to again enlighten the hearts of men and cause a renewing able to regenerate even the stoniest soul. Once changed, the new Christian is then called to be the light that shines in the midst of a darkened world. (Matt 5:14.)

So again, various, untold and numerous lights emanate from the Lord and each one has its own significance. For the fallen man, light comes from His word. (Psalm 119:105.) On day one of the re-creation, it was light of the knowledge of His glory that brought about change to the earth and prepared it for the expanse of life that was about to erupt. On that first day, He turned His face back toward the earth and changed its bleak resolve into hope. In turn, the earth awakened in expectation of its next mission. Casting off the throngs of darkness, it began to walk in the newness of light once again. It was ready for what was about to happen; life was going to be returning to the earth.

Once His light that shined in the face of Jesus came back to the earth, the darkness cloaking the earth was eradicated and the natural processes could once again be recognized, "and God divided the light from the darkness. And God called the light Day, and the darkness he called Night" (Genesis 1:4–5). So the light of the first day was not a natural physical light, but rather a spiritual light. For without the presence of God, darkness reigns and no life can come about. Truly, His mind was on His earthly creation because

His Spirit is seen hovering over the waters, and once His light was released, things began to change.

The evening and the morning

And the evening and the morning were the first day. (Genesis 1:5)

Each creation day (except the seventh day) in Genesis concludes with the phrase, "and the evening and the morning were." Just like most of the rest of the creation account, there is untold scrutiny and division over the exact meaning of this phrase. Certainly, the evening and the morning are definite points in a day; which once again proves that each creation day denotes a specific period of time. Since the first chapter of Genesis is written from God's perspective, then what would be an evening or a morning from God's point of view? Is God subject to a night and day timeframe?

In the modern vernacular, we commonly use the words "morning" and "evening" to refer to a general time frame. For instance, one might say, "at the dawn of the Industrial Revolution," or "the eve of civilization." In each of these instances, it is obvious the words are referencing a general timeframe rather than one particular day. Carrying this same train of thought to Genesis chapter one, morning refers to the beginning of an age, while evening is referencing the end of that age.

This same vernacular can be witnessed in the Bible, "In the morning it flourisheth, and groweth up; in the evening it is cut down, and withereth" (Psalm 90:6). Crops are not planted and harvested in the same day, so it is quite obvious that the morning and the evening being referred to represent an entire planting season. Similarly, in Daniel the timeframe of morning and evening increases even more, "And the vision of the evening and the morning which was told is true: wherefore shut thou up the vision; for it shall be for many days" (Daniel 8:26).

Daniel had a vision that foretold the fate of hundreds of future generations and summed them up into what he calls, "the vision of the evening and the morning." He then further states that this vision shall be for many days.

Gabriel later comes and tells Daniel the meaning of the vision, explaining to him that the timing of the vision is many thousands of years, yet its description remains that same as "the vision of the evening and morning." Clearly the phase evening and morning is used as an idiom, and is not to be taken literally, but rather as a starting and ending point to the specific orientation of time in the reference. In the same respect, God's account in Genesis is also idiomatic, referring to the beginning and end of the particular events of that period.

A person standing on the face of the earth has one point of reference for that entire day; they are going to experience one night and one day. God, on the other hand, is not constrained by the physical rotation of the earth. For Him, time is inconsequential. Nor is he subjected to the rising and setting of the sun. A morning and an evening from His perspective would be different than a person living on the earth. By adding an evening and a morning to the text, God is giving a definite construct to the time involved in the re-creation. He is showing that there was a beginning and end to each of the creation days.

It is intended to be a point of reference for humanity to know that each of those days was not an indefinite period of time. The fact that there was a morning and evening, or beginning and end to the creation days of Genesis shows this was not a figure of speech, but actually a definitive timeframe that was established in other Scriptures as being approximately one thousand years. It also signifies that particular phase of construction being completed. There was nothing else to do; all the tasks set forth in that period were completed.

Interestingly, the seventh day is the only day where the Lord does not use the phrase evening and morning. Many believe it was purposefully left out to show that He is still in the seventh day of rest. This would certainly seem to make sense, since He is not quantifying the seventh day by adding the phrase, "the evening and the morning," it shows that the seventh day is still in progress and has not ended.

Without adding the phrase evening and morning, God is saying that the seventh day does not have a definitive time frame, nor are all of the tasks of this particular day completed. It is an open-ended, unspecified amount of time. Depending upon what God's reference is, He may not even be into the dawning of the seventh day, or He may be closing in on the evening with the end of this age quickly approaching.

The only other activity He performed on the seventh day apart from resting was to bless His creation. This is the very activity He still bestows upon His creation to this day and throughout the rest of time, which further proves that this day is still ongoing.

One final note about the first day of creation: in almost every version of the Bible "Day" and "Night" are capitalized. Grammatically, this is not a necessity. There are no unwritten laws of language that require new definitions to be capitalized. So why are they capitalized? It would appear that God recognizes them as unique creatures. Just as a person's name is capitalized because it is a proper noun, the Lord adheres to this same standard for these proper nouns (Day, Night, Heaven, and Earth). In and of themselves, they are life giving. This is especially true of the earth, which will be explored in greater detail in the next chapter when we discuss the third day.

Thus, day one of the re-creation dealt with the light of the knowledge of God in the face of Christ Jesus and defining the time frames involved. That is, bringing the spiritual back to the natural, so that His light can be initiated again in the earth. "And God said, Let there be light: and there was light. And God saw the light, that it was good: and God divided the light from the darkness. And God called the light Day, and the darkness he called Night. And the evening and the morning were the first day" (Genesis 1:3–5). The next few days go on to build the physical constructs of necessary to support life on earth.

CHAPTER 7

Days Two and Three

Day Two

And God said, Let there be a firmament in the midst of the waters, and let it divide the waters from the waters. And God made the firmament, and divided the waters which were under the firmament from the waters which were above the firmament: and it was so. And God called the firmament Heaven. And the evening and the morning were the second day. (Genesis 1:6–8)

On the first day of creation, a light arose on the earth due to the very expectation of what was about to transpire. That light was the knowledge of God's glory and wisdom in the face of Christ Jesus. It is a spiritual light that reached into the darkness and prepped the earth for the changes that were about to erupt. Without spiritual light from the Father of Lights, nothing would be able to grow and prosper. The earth was now ready to support the life that God had planned.

He begins these changes on the second day by reconstructing the atmosphere to one that would be more compatible to the life of its future inhabitants. He does so by speaking to the waters of the earth, and dividing the water under the firmament from the water above the firmament. The waters of the earth that covered its surface would have been thawed by now on account of the activities of the first day. Due to the eruption of spiritual light and the dissipation of spiritual darkness, the earth was now primed for life to spring forth, however this would not be possible without a viable atmosphere.

The destructive events that happened during the second verse of Genesis also brought about the deterioration of the earth's atmosphere. There is no indication during that time period that the earth was ever without an atmosphere, but only that its atmosphere was in need of repair.

Complete destruction of the earth's atmosphere during verse two would have likely brought about catastrophic events, such as bombardment by space debris and a lack of protection from cosmic radiation. Events such as these would have caused noticeable despoliation and pockmarking to the earth's surface which would still be noticeable today.

Furthermore, the various gases needed to support life would have dissipated into space. Without the pressure of the atmosphere pushing on the earth, some or all of its water content would have likely floated off into space. The pull of gravity by itself probably would not have been enough to hold the water in place.

Genesis 1:2 does not paint a picture that would support this premise. In fact, it definitively shows there was water on top of the earth and not floating away. Moreover, there is no geological record that anything of this magnitude transpired during the history of the earth. Thus, during that destructive event, it appears that the atmosphere was not completely destroyed but was in a state of flux. This is further confirmed by His actions on the second day when it says that He made the firmament. Made is not just another way of saying that He created the atmosphere. It is a different verb with a different meaning, one that confirms that an atmospheric template was already in place.

To make

In chapter four, the verb to make was briefly touched on as being unique from the verb *create* in the Genesis narrative. Indeed it is different, for in Hebrew the word for make is *asa* and it literally means to produce, manufacture, or fabricate. Of course, this is a different concept than creating. To create is to call something out of nothing, whereas making is utilizing existing elements to construct something new.

From the standpoint of the restoration of the atmosphere, use of the word *make* provides proof that the Lord manipulated an already existing atmosphere. Asa is used only four times in the Genesis account; 1:7 (atmosphere), 1:16 (stars), 1:25 (animals), and 1:26 (humans); each time showing God using the existing elements that He previously created and putting them into His newly desired order.

Just like the artist who paints a picture by applying paint to the canvas to make a design, although that picture may be a one-of-a-kind, they are still using existing products (paint and canvas) to formulate a new painting. Although it is often called a new creation, they have not created anything new, but have simply painted a picture and made a new design on the canvas. It is not creation, but rather a manipulation of the utilities to make something new; which is exactly what the Lord did on the second day. He made the firmament by using the existing template and reconstructed it to make it more compatible for humanity. "Things which are seen were not made of things which do appear" (Hebrews 11:3). Things which are seen were created of things which do not appear and once they are present, they can be made into something else that is relevant for God's design and purpose at that moment.

Remember, Moses stated that the seas were made and not created by the Lord in Exodus 20:11. The psalmist reiterates this by saying, "The sea is his, and he made it" (Psalm 95:5). The waters of the oceans that are seen covering the earth in Genesis 1:2 were never a part of His original plan. He made the seas and oceans we see today at a point later in the history of the earth; it did not come about at the point of creation in Genesis 1:1. So in this case, the Psalmist shows that it was the oceans that were made at a time outside of his original creation.

So the use of the word make on the second day confirms that He was using existing elements to reform the atmosphere. He was not creating a new one, because part of it was still in existence following the destruction that happened in Genesis 1:2. He was merely redesigning it to fit into His new plan, which needed it to be compatible for His new administrator: humans. He concludes by calling it heaven.

Heaven

With three distinct regions above the earth's surface being referred to as *heaven*, it can be difficult to ascertain exactly what region of the universe the text is referring to when it uses the word heaven. On the second day, the Lord uses the word firmament to clarify exactly which division of the heaven He is referencing. "And God said, Let there be a firmament in the midst of the waters, and let it divide the waters from the waters" (Genesis 1:6).

Firmament in Hebrew is *reqiya*, which means a region or a reach and it implies a stretching, extension, or an expanse. Giving a physical aspect to something that is ephemeral; much like air, which can't be seen, but we are able to witness in the wind that blows and the clouds that form and move.

The Bible says, "He hath made the earth by his power, he hath established the world by his wisdom, and hath stretched out the heaven by his understanding" (Jeremiah 51:15). In the same fashion that He stretched out the universe in the first light of creation, He also stretched out the atmosphere over the surface of the earth. The word firmament is mentioned on two separate occasions in the Genesis account. First, it is seen here on the second day and later it is witnessed on the fourth day.

On this the second day, He calls on the firmament to come forth in the midst of the waters, qualifying which expanse He is referring to by saying it is in the midst of the water. "Let there be firmament in the midst of the waters" (Genesis 1:6). Since it was not there in its full capacity, it needed to be reinstated. Thus, He stretched out the atmosphere above the earth and recreated the hydrological cycle of water on the earth, making it once again compatible with life.

On the fourth day, the firmament is already established and God calls the lights of heaven to shine forth from it. "Let there be lights in the firmament of heaven" (Genesis 1:14). That is space. The vast reaches or the stretch of space was already in existence, but now the lights of the heavenly bodies are once again allowed to influence the earth. He had already stretched it out during the original creation, now He is simply calling these lights to shine forth from it. So two different things are happening on these days, but in both cases the firmament represents the physical manifestation of "invisible" concepts, which are respectively the atmosphere and space.

The earth's atmosphere is an enormous structure, with its exact dimensions being generally unknown. Current classifications have placed it into several distinct regions, extending up to a region designated as the exosphere that ends approximately 500 miles above the earth. Of course, the atmosphere is an integral part of life on the planet. Changes in the atmosphere of a planet can cause drastic changes to its surface and the life therein.

Certainly, there is every indication that atmospheric pressure changes can have enormous ramifications on the environment. Without the proper amount of pressure in the atmosphere it is impossible to sustain life on the planet's surface. Retrospectively, it is believed that a greater atmospheric pressure than exists today may have been one of the contributing factors for the scaled up size of the plants and animals on the earth during previous eras.

Without a doubt, the earth's landscape remains littered with the remains of gigantic paleontological and fossilized records from previous eras. One scientific idea promulgated to account for this phenomenon is that the atmospheric conditions of those days were considerably different than now. Undoubtedly, this is one of the reasons why during the re-creation found in Genesis, the Lord made a new atmosphere to support the type of life that He had in mind. He made an atmosphere that would be compatible for the upstart of humanity by taking their size and needs into account. This means that the whole of this current dispensation was designed to accommodate the needs of humanity.

More Water

The last half of both verses six and seven say respectively, "let it (firmament) divide the waters from the waters," and "(He) divided the waters which were under the firmament from the waters which were above the firmament." Some questions have arisen as to which waters the Lord was dividing, because there are several waters that could have been divided. Building on the knowledge foundation laid in the previous chapters; these questions are easily put to rest.

Many have tried to add unnecessary interpretations to the obvious events of the day by complicating the simplicity of the circumstances. Some have speculated that the divisions of waters the Bible is referencing are the waters found in the nether reaches of the universe and not the waters found in the atmosphere. In other words, some have cogitated that God was somehow separating the waters of the earth and giving water to space; thereby creating further hypotheses that since water is the building block of life in the universe, He was extending the gift of life to other planets and galaxies. While water has been found on comets and other interstellar objects, its existence has yet to be documented on a large planetary scale outside of the earth; making the interpretation of the verse somewhat more compelling, but still inadequate since there are no other verses to back up this hypothesis.

Others have taken these portions of the verse to mean that God is taking the waters on the earth and in the universe, and then separating them from the waters in heaven (God's home). Undoubtedly, the third heaven has water in it, for God is a God of flowing refreshing rivers and streams and these rivers are seen flowing from the throne room of God. (John 7:38, Revelation 22:1.)

Taking it one step further, some scholars believe this division of waters is actually the sea of glass that is before the throne of God. (Revelation 15:2.) Most have quoted the Psalmist who said, "Praise him, ye heavens of heavens, and ye waters that be above the heavens," to prove that there is indeed water in the heaven which is God's home and this is the water referred to during the re-creation (Psalm 148:4).

The truth is, this last verse is simply in agreement with the fact that there is water in heaven and that it is praising the Lord. This has nothing to do with the events of the second day and indeed it is quite a stretch to draw this into the activities on day two. There is no other biblical evidence to show that the sea of glass in Revelation is somehow the water of Genesis. Furthermore, the water in heaven exists on a different plane. Since it is in the throne room of God, it would of necessity exist in the spiritual realm, so it would not need replenishing from the physical realm.

Although some have tried to read into the events of the second day and developed some intriguing theories, their postulations are not within the scope of events that transpired given the activities that have already materialized. Conclusively, the division of waters is God speaking to the atmosphere of the earth rejuvenate itself. He is simply calling out for the atmosphere of the earth to be rebuilt so that the earth can sustain His next creation. The atmosphere responds in kind by separating the waters covering it from the waters that are in the clouds. In other words, the Lord is restarting the hydrological cycle of the earth.

Again, all the events of the Genesis creation are specifically focused on the earth. There is no reason to believe that the Lord is now using these events to affect the rest of the universe. When destruction came upon the earth, it was localized to our planet. There is no evidence that the rest of the universe was destroyed or affected in any way. Thus, there is no biblical evidence on the second day to support anything other than the establishment of a viable atmosphere to prepare the earth for the imminent events coming during the next four days of re-creation.

Hence, the whole of the events on the second day is the Lord recreating the atmosphere and dividing the waters in the sky from the waters remaining on the earth. Of course, without a viable hydrological cycle, the earth would not be able to bring forth life. Once established, it allowed for the rest of the re-creation events to take place: plants, animals, and mankind. Certainly, the earth is still void of many of the essential elements of life, namely sunlight and actual planetary life itself, but without a viable atmosphere nothing on the earth could function, so it was the next logical step.

Interestingly, this is also the only day in the actual creation account that God does not call good. Every other day in the sequence of the creation narrative concludes with God calling the day's events good. Several theories have been construed as to why the second day is not given this positive affirmation, and frankly, after all the speculation, there does not appear to be a valid reason why the Lord did not use this qualifier. Though it seems unlikely that it was an oversight or lost in the translation, it is also of little consequence to the rest of the events that occurred on the second day or any other day. The re-creation of the atmosphere was necessary and by all measures good, whether it was mentioned as such or not.

Day Three

And God said, Let the waters under the heaven be gathered together unto one place, and let the dry land appear: and it was so. And God called the dry land Earth; and the gathering together of the waters called he Seas: and God saw that it was good. And God said, Let the earth bring forth grass, the herb yielding seed, and the fruit tree yielding fruit after his kind, whose seed is in itself, upon the earth: and it was so. And the earth brought forth grass, and herb yielding seed after his kind, and the tree yielding fruit, whose seed was in itself, after his kind: and God saw that it was good. And the evening and the morning were the third day. (Genesis 1:9–13)

On the first day of the creation narrative, God illuminates and warms the earth with the Light of the knowledge of His glory. On the second day He reestablishes a working atmosphere. Now on the third day, He begins again by speaking life back to planet earth. All the actions of the Lord thus far have been called forth, allowed, or made. Since the re-creation began, He has yet to actually create anything, but rather He has called back into action what was already there.

On the previous two days, God said, "Let there be light" and there was light, or "Let there be a firmament" and there was firmament. He was speaking to something that was there, but not yet activated. Here again on the third day there are no creative acts, because all of the Lord's actions are described as "let."

So on the third day, it is time for the dry land to appear and for the vegetation to spring forth. The text does not say that God created the dry land and called it earth. Instead it says that He allowed what was once there to now come forth and be visible again.

God said, "Let the waters" and "Let the dry land." The waters and land, in turn, respond by doing exactly what the Lord had requested; the waters gather in one place and the earth brought forth grass, herb yielding seed, and the tree yielding fruit; once again showing that the varied objects of God's creation have the ability to hear and respond to the Lord. Certainly, it was God's own faith-filled words that called the earth to respond and it responded favorably to the Lord and brought forth vegetation. By obeying His command it was blessed.

This is the reason Earth is capitalized in the Genesis account; it is a proper noun, it is a living creation. Since it is living, it listens to the Lord and life comes from it. This is in no way a declaration that the earth is itself a creator, but rather that it is capable of understanding the guidance of the Lord. Nor is it a testament that the earth has a living spirit like a human, but only that it has the ability to hear and respond to the Lord. In the same fashion that the earth responded to the words of the Lord, human life is based on the fundamental elements in the earth and therefore can be manipulated by faith-filled words. (Mark 11:22–24.)

So too, just like on the second day, on the third day the Lord speaks to the water and it responds to His commands by being gathered into one area under the heaven, revealing the dry land. He places a boundary upon it so that it will not come any farther. By exposing the dry land from this water it once again shows that the earth of Genesis 1:2, and throughout the second day, was flooded.

As mentioned before, with two distinct floods noted in the Bible, it can be difficult to ascertain which flood is being mentioned because there are analogous similarities to the better known flood that happened during the days of Noah and the flood of Genesis verse two. Thus it behooves us to take one more moment to revisit the distinguishing events that differentiate each flood. Although both floods were global in reach, they are different in several aspects.

One primary difference between the two is the way the Lord handled the waters that were prevailing upon the earth. During the days of Noah, they were essentially forced back underground. In Genesis eight it says that, "God made a wind to pass over the earth, and the waters assuaged; The fountains also of the deep and the windows of heaven were stopped, and the rain from heaven was restrained; And the waters returned from off the earth continually: and after the end of the hundred and fifty days the waters were abated" (Genesis 8:1–3). The Lord used a wind to push the flood waters back under the earth.

However, on the third day of creation there is no mention of wind. God simply spoke to the waters and as they did as they were instructed and returned to their established place where they could come no further. There is no mention of a wind as in the days of Noah, but rather a decree from the Lord to return to their prescribed place.

A second noted distinction is the life, or absence thereof, that could be witnessed during each event. In the flood of Genesis 1:2, there is no life and the planet is in desolation, which includes the absence of all vegetation, fowls, and human life on the earth. "I beheld, and, lo, there was no man, and all the birds of the heavens were fled. I beheld, and, lo, the fruitful place was a wilderness" (Jeremiah 4:25–26). There was no life on the planet; it was a viable wasteland after the flood waters receded. It took another decree from the Lord for the vegetation of the earth to spring forth.

Contrarily, with Noah's flood there was a contingency of life left on the ark that included both animal and human life. Additionally, the vegetation quickly sprang back to life once the waters dissipated from off the earth. (Genesis 8:11.) The Lord did not need to call it forth; as its seed was already in the earth. So once the floodwaters receded, life began to spring forth again. After the flood of Genesis 1:2 there was absolutely no life left, but the same could not be said of the flood of Noah because of the contingency of human and animal life that occupied the ark and the quick emergence of organic life once the waters abated.

One place

Continuing on with the activities of the third day, it is clear to see that when these watery boundaries that prevailed on the earth were set, they were all gathered into one specific location. "Let the waters under the heaven be gathered together unto one place," and they are collectively called seas. If all of the seas during this time are in one area, then all the dry land must also of necessity be congregated into one area; which means that during the time of re-creation, the surface of the earth consisted of just one landmass instead of several continents.

Obviously, this is contrary to the landscape of the earth today, but scientific theory has postulated the idea that at some point in the earth's history the earth was indeed one landmass. It is believed that over a span of time the tectonic plates of the earth slowly shifted and caused the continents to drift apart. This theory is relatively new, but is generally accepted and well documented in the geological findings. This idea of one landmass is the exact picture of the earth on the third day (the relevance and timing of this will be explored further in chapter nineteen). Needless to say, it is significant to note and introduce the biblical fact that at this point in the earth's history all the land was gathered in one place.

Hence, by the middle of the third day the Lord had established most of the inner workings of the earth, as evidenced in verse ten where He gives two more definitions: Earth and Seas. Previously He defined Night, Day, and Heaven and now He concludes with the final two definitions of creation. Four of the five definitions are necessary components to support life: they are light, air, earth, and water. Without these, the earth would not be able to support life. The fifth definition, Night, also indirectly points to life, given the fact that God designed His creation to have times of rest. All of God's created beings require a time of rest and nighttime is generally associated with resting and sleep. Rest is something that even the Lord prescribes to and therefore it is also considered a function of the earth.

Vegetation

Thus, by the third day the Lord had established all of the fundamental elements necessary to support life on planet earth and the bringing forth of life is exactly the next step the Lord initiated. Thus, His next act reestablished the grasses, herbs, and fruit trees. It does not say that all vegetation began to grow, but only the plants and trees of the forest that grow wild and generally do not require human cultivation. Those that are grown in tillable soil are called the plants of the field and are not mentioned until chapter two of Genesis.

One common misnomer about the plants on the third day is that they were brought forth to maturity in a matter of days so the animals would be able to consume them on the fifth day. Remember that the time frame of the creation account is the Lord's, so each day is roughly one thousand years. The earth had two thousand years to maturate the new plant life, allowing plenty of time for it to bring forth the vegetation mentioned in the third day.

When the Lord calls forth the vegetation on the third day He uses the phrase, "after his kind," to describe His actions. This phrase has become a point of contention for many, but the simplicity of it need not be befuddling. By using this phrase, He is simply saying that this type of plant life had already existed in the earth, at a point in time before the account of the six days of re-creation, and now a similar species is being brought forth again.

He is simply modifying the previous design of plant life that was already contained within the earth. The re-growth of plant life is not the exact same design seen in the earth previously; but it is similar, it is after its "own kind," which refers to a slight change in the manner of something that was once present in the earth. In this case He is saying that the trees, seeds, and grasses that were once present in the earth can come forth again, but this time in a redefined manner. A more design specific type of foliage better suited to His upcoming creation: humanity.

Something cannot be made after its kind, if there had been no other kind previously present on the earth. It is the only logical and simple explanation for the creative method of the Lord. He is calling forth to the earth to reproduce the greenery that was already prevalent on its surface during a previous era, in a new modified manner. From a re-creation standpoint, this phrase fits perfectly, because it again proves there was life prior to the seven days of creation described in Genesis.

The phrase "after his kind" is used three times in the creation narrative; here for the vegetation (Genesis 1:11–12), then again on the fifth day for marine life and fowls (Genesis 1:21), and finally on the sixth day for the animals that dominate the earth (Genesis 1:24–25). During the seven creation days, there are eight categories of organic life that are called forth after its kind: grass, herbs, fruit trees, marine life, winged fowl, beasts of the earth, cattle, and crawling animals. Each of these various categories can all be found in fossil records prior to the re-creation, showing that the current creation is of a similar mold to a creation that previously existed in the earth. Mankind was the only creation that was never said to be made after their kind. For humanity, God was not following a previous mold, but rather when He created Adam, he was the original cast of a new mold.

CHAPTER 8

Days Four and Five

Day Four

And God said, Let there be lights in the firmament of the heaven to divide the day from the night; and let them be for signs, and for seasons, and for days, and years: And let them be for lights in the firmament of the heaven to give light upon the earth: and it was so. And God made two great lights; the greater light to rule the day, and the lesser light to rule the night: he made the stars also. And God set them in the firmament of the heaven to give light upon the earth, And to rule over the day and over the night, and to divide the light from the darkness: and God saw that it was good. And the evening and the morning were the fourth day. (Genesis 1:14–19)

The events of day four involve the reintroduction of physical light from the sun and the rest of the stars. The atmosphere had been reestablished and vegetation is abounding on the earth, it is now time to complete the natural order by allowing the light of the sun to penetrate the atmosphere of the earth.

The darkness the earth was experiencing during the time frame of Genesis 1:2 was both a spiritual and a physical darkness. This spiritual darkness was resolved on the first day, when the Lord called forth the light of the knowledge of the glory of God in Christ Jesus. Now, He is allowing the lights of the heavens to penetrate down to the earth's surface in their prescribed allowance.

Of course, the sun has been shining since the very beginning of creation, but darkness had enveloped the planet and snuffed out its life-giving heat prior to the re-creation. One of the reasons for this darkness was due to the fact the earth had deviated from its rotational standard.

Undoubtedly, when the Lord created the earth, He intended for it to remain in its place forever. (Psalm 104:5.) However, activities and circumstances that happened prior to the re-creation forced the Lord's hand, and it was pushed out of its orbit. There are several mentions of these historic activities in the pages of the Bible (the circumstances surrounding this event will be looked at in subsequent chapters).

Job 9:6 says that the Lord, "shaketh the earth out of her place, and its pillars thereof tremble." The Psalmist goes on to confirm this historic disruptive event by saying that, "they know not, neither will they understand; they walk on in darkness: all the foundations of the earth are out of course" (Psalm 82:5). Paul again confirms these activities by stating that during at least one time in the earth's history, He did indeed shake the earth, but in the future He will shake not only the earth, but heaven also. (Hebrews 12:26.) Several other passages also refer to this future disruption. (Isaiah 13:13, Revelation 20:11, Isaiah 24:19–20, Haggai 2:6–7.)

These verses prove that sinful activities prior to the re-creation were so tremendous, and God was so angry that He shook the very foundation of the earth out of its place, which means that at the beginning of the recreation, the tilt of the earth's axis and its orbit were not perfectly aligned with its original axis tilt and orbit. This interruption occurred during the destruction of Genesis 1:2, when the Bible says the earth was without form and void, and darkness prevailed.

How far it moved outside of its orbit is not clear, but it was far enough that the light of the sun was unable to be seen and the constellations were not within their prescribed boundaries. Most definitely, it was disconnected from the moon, because it states that when it was reestablished, God made the lesser light to rule the night: the moon. Notice it does not simply say that He made the lesser light (moon); rather it says that He made the lesser light to rule the night. In other words, He did not make, form, or create the moon or stars, but instead He moved the earth and its moon back into its rotational pattern. He made the lesser light to rule the night, and the greater light to rule the day. Once there, then all the constellations and the light and darkness are again seen in their normal arrangements.

Without question, there are other events that would have caused some form of physical darkness to cloak the earth during that era, but an orbital disruption would likely have been the most significant. Other physical events that were happening during that age will be covered in subsequent chapters. For now, it can be established that the earth and the moon were moved back into pattern and the rest of the heavenly bodies were once again visible from their pre-appointed place; thereby returning the earth to its orbital standard and reestablishing the lights in the heaven to divide the day and night, and uncloaking the light of the sun to once again reach the earth.

Before this day summarily concludes, there is one other item of infinite significance that is mentioned that must be addressed. Once again that item is light, but this time it is a different light than the light from the first day.

Light

The Hebrew word for light in this passage is *maor*, which denotes the physical light coming from a lamp or planetary body. (On the first day the Hebrew word for light was *or*). In the New Testament, Paul reveals a little more information about the light of heavenly bodies when he says that, "There are also celestial bodies, and bodies terrestrial: but the glory of the celestial is one, and the glory of the terrestrial is another. There is one glory of the sun, and another glory of the moon, and another glory of the stars: for one star differeth from another star in glory" (1 Corinthians 15:40–41).

Each planetary body has its own glory or light, and each one differs in glory from another. At the beginning of the re-creation, the earth tapped into the forthcoming anticipation of the creative activities of the Lord and used it for illumination and heat. Of course, the light of the knowledge of the glory of God in the face of Jesus Christ has not disappeared; but it is now accompanied by the light of the sun, which is one of the essential components for the existence of life on planet earth. Certainly the Lord could have sustained the earth without the physical light of the sun throughout all eternity, but that is not the way that He established the order of the universe. It was necessary to return the earth to its prescribed path, thus reintroducing the light of the sun. For, "everything the LORD has made has its destiny" (Proverbs 16:4 GNB).

Since the destruction uncovered in verse two of Genesis was a localized event, affecting only the earth, the universe at large continued along on its path. It was not halted, but the lights of the various heavenly bodies were restricted from penetrating to the surface of the earth. Once again, we know this because in verses 14 and 15 of Genesis one, the Lord spoke to the earth's atmosphere using the word let. "Let there be lights in the firmament of the heaven." This was not a creative event, but simply an instruction to the earth to come back into alignment and allow the light of the sun to penetrate what was left of the dark shroud encompassing it. So here on the fourth day, both the spiritual and physical darkness have finally been eradicated.

With the earth back in its place, the light of the sun and other planetary bodies can be seen in their prescribed orbits, and the earth has once again become a fully functioning physical entity. It is returned to its designed natural intention of "self-existence." This does not mean that the Lord is not involved with His creation; rather it is merely a statement that God's original design was perfection and did not need any additional tweaking or influence for it to exist.

That being said, without the presence of God in the universe, life ceases to exist. Therefore the scriptural truth is that the light of the knowledge of the glory of God in Christ Jesus and the light of the sun work in unison to provide protection and illumination and will continue to coexist throughout all eternity. Without the light of the knowledge of the glory of God present in the earth, chaos would ensue, as was seen in the earth's past, and without the light of the sun the earth would be unable to return to its full former glory. That there are two distinct sources of light evident in the earth today is confirmed in Psalm 36:9, "For with thee is the fountain of life: in thy light shall we see light." This is further corroborated again in Psalm 74:16, "The day is thine, the night also is thine: thou hast prepared the light and the sun."

These verses validate the fact that there is indeed a distinction between the light of the sun and the light of His glory. God first brought His creative light to the desolate earth and it is through His light that the light of the sun is now able to penetrate through to the previously darkened earth. For it says that the Lord prepared the light *and* the sun, it does not say that the Lord prepared the light *of* the sun. The sun has light, but it is not His Light. Without the Light of the Lord, life on planet earth would be impossible.

Thus, the Lord returned the earth to its former state of existence by allowing the light of the sun to perform its necessary function. So it can be seen that both lights, spiritual and physical, are essential for life on the planet and the fact that they were prepared shows that both lights were tweaked to an exact measure in accordance with this current creation. In other words, the light of the sun and the light of the knowledge of God are perfectly suited for the existence of mankind on the earth. There was just enough glory released in each to produce the desired result.

Then in verse sixteen of Genesis one, the Lord changes from the affirmative verb "let" to the more active verb "made", thereby confirming with the Psalmist that the light was manipulated during this moment of history. "And God made two great lights; the greater light to rule the day, and the lesser light to rule the night: he made the stars also" (Genesis 1:16). One important thing to notice is that the text does not say that God made the sun and moon. It says that He made two great lights, the greater light to rule the day and the lesser light to rule the night. That is, He changed the qualities of the light that was reaching the earth. Remember, making is not creating.

Making involves a change in the qualities of something already created, and here He is not making planetary objects, but rather He is making light. The light that was previously reaching the earth was different than the light that the Lord set forth upon the earth during the re-creation. Isaiah shows that the Lord forms, or molds the light into the shape that He wants. "I form the light, and create darkness: I make peace, and create evil: I the LORD do all these things" (Isaiah 45:7). Only God, the Creator of light, can form and change its properties into something conducive to the current creation.

Sunlight

Physical light is truly one of the continued mysteries of the universe, and so little is known about its properties. Sunlight brings illumination, it generates heat, it is a wave, it is energy, it is powerful, and it is quintessential for life. Still, the how's and the why's are of it are largely unknown. There is a whole division of physics dedicated to the study of light and various theories about the properties of light have been adopted in an effort to better define and understand its properties. Still, most of what is surmised about light is merely theoretical, as it is difficult to ascertain all of its qualities.

As new theories arise, old theories are modified and the body of knowledge continues to change. These theories include, but are not limited to, the particle theory, the wave theory, the electromagnetic theory, the special theory of relativity, the quantum theory, and others. In an attempt to understand light's properties, most of these theories have been established to some degree, yet some of them contradict the other theories when attempting to establish their definition. The reason for its continued perplexity is due to light having so many different aspects to its nature.

Without a doubt, each theory has been important in gaining a deeper insight into the properties of light, but all-in-all humanity is still a long way from discovering its final definition. It can reasonably be stated that a final definition will never be obtained because as has been seen, in order to truly understand light, one would have to move into the realm of God.

Nevertheless, in an effort to grasp its unique qualities, it is interesting to examine light from the way it is processed by the human body. As light enters the eye, the human mind and body has the ability to process the overwhelming amount of information carried on that light wave: color, depth, intensity, and speed. Light travels into the eye via electromagnetic waves, which come in many forms (radio, x-rays, electromagnetic radiation, etc.) after permeating the atmosphere and then ultimately the human body possibly dozens of times per second. The waves received into the eye form a very small portion of the electromagnetic spectrum's total wavelength. The eye then separates the light into its various aspects and it is processed by the brain.

Most of the light that the body processes comes from the light of the sun that was made on the fourth day. Sunlight reaches the atmosphere packing a whopping charge of one kilowatt per square meter. This energy is so powerful that without the protection of the re-created atmosphere on the second day reducing the power of this bombardment, life would not be possible. It is truly a powerful force that positively affects the earth and aids in the generation of life; too much or too little of it and that life is terminated. Praise God for the light of day one that regulates all our planetary functions and ensures their compliance.

Looking into God

Coincidentally, another force that has characteristics similar to light and is also believed to travel in waves is gravity. The force of gravity on earth is weak, so weak in fact that there are no instruments that are able to measure it, yet its effects are definitively recognized in the earth. Thus, much like light little is known about it, yet it is a quintessential physical property and without its force life would float off into space.

Gravitational forces in the earth coincide with the multidimensionality of God. Both God and mankind are three dimensional, with each possessing a spirit, a soul, and a body. Each portion exists in its own dimension. Gravity, much like light, is believed to travel through these various dimensions on waves known as gravitons. As gravitons travel through these other dimensions, they pick up strength and speed, possibly up to ten times the speed of light, yet still remain a massless force.

The concept of dimensionality and gravitons are theories of the scientific community, but the evidence of their existence is compelling and "proven" by quantum theory. The interesting qualities of gravitons are the resemblance they have with light; both are particles (waves) and travel in virtually immeasurable speeds. There is every indication that light used to travel at the speed of gravitons but has since decreased in speed to its current level. Yet gravitons are believed to travel at speeds much greater than the speed of light. Who or what can travel at speeds greater than the speed of light?

Once again, science has stepped in and given us a glimpse into the very nature of creation and the Creator. Needless to say, the qualities exhibited between light and gravitons look a lot like the qualities of God and His creation. He is a multidimensional massless being, who has the ability to travel at the speed of light and faster. He is not a created being; therefore He is not subject to man's theories which state that as an object moves closer to the speed of light the more massive it becomes. Since God is a spirit, He is not constrained by the properties of the physical; rather He is the Creator of the physical. It is not a far stretch of the imagination to say that He exists in dimensions far beyond that which can be speculated by men, and that He travels at speeds greater than the known speed of light.

This delves into the very nature of God, who exists on dimensions that man can only dream of. But it helps to understand a God who is so far beyond human comprehension that it makes words like omnipresent, omniscient, and omnipotent almost understandable. He does not travel on physical photon energy, but rather in forces unseen and only speculated by mankind; travelling in a division of light unperceivable to the human eye. Imagine the realm of God as energy and information that is far beyond the range of electromagnetic waves. Gravitons are likely only the beginning; imagine a "particle" capable of travelling billions of times faster than a graviton. Travel through space and time would then be unlimited and unconstrained by time, and able to see and respond to everything at the same time.

Thus putting God into His own category: a Spirit that exists in His own dimension, which is a dimension of light unbeknownst to mankind. Timothy confirms that indeed He is an unknown source of light when he said that He "dwells in unapproachable light, whom no one has ever seen or can see" (1 Timothy 6:16 ESV). He is in the light and He is the light. James described Him as the "Father of lights" (James 1:17). He travels in light through multiple dimensions which give Him the ability to be in all places and know all things at the same time. His light carries on in our dimension unbeknownst to mankind, yet He also slows it down and creates the physical. When Christ came to the earth, Matthew described His arrival as a great light that enlightened the people who sat in darkness. (Matthew 4:16.)

Jesus is the physical manifestation of the light of God, which is why Jesus frequently deferred to God. He is one part or dimension of a much larger multidimensional being. It was through Him and by Him that all physical things were created. He is the physical part of the Godhead. When God changed the characteristics of His light, the physical was birthed. That extension of God is Jesus. He is equally a part of the Godhead, but only a portion. The Godhead exists in the spiritual dimension, from whence comes support, function, and direction for the physical.

Likewise, this carries on down to humanity. Jesus is the head of the body and the church reports up through Him. (Colossians 1:18.) "And not holding the Head, from which all the body by joints and bands having nourishment ministered, and knit together, increaseth with the increase of God" (Colossians 2:19). The hierarchical structure of the church is patterned after the Godhead. Along the same line, if "one member suffer, all the members suffer with it" (1 Corinthians 12:26).

Imagine the struggle that must have existed during the destruction of the earth. The physical entity that is Jesus created the universe, and part of that creation, the earth, gets caught in the cross-hairs of rebellion causing it to be destroyed under a load of sin and despair. How it much have pained Jesus to see His own creation in ruin. No longer an extension of His perfection, but tainted and withered. Praise God, He had a plan for its reconstruction, one that brought life back to the earth; one that will not allow any more schism in the body, because all the members have the same care one for another. (1 Corinthians 12:25.)

He is everything and everywhere in dimensions mankind will never understand, yet He has taken a portion of Himself (light) and slowed it down to a perceivable visible level which has the ability to support life. "In him was life; and the life was the light of men" (John 1:4). And in His life we see light. Oh the unending, never ceasing wonders of God. Is it any wonder that angels encircle his throne crying, "Holy, holy, holy, is the LORD of hosts: the whole earth is full of his glory" (Isaiah 6:3). For billions, possibly trillions of years, they have been and are still astounded at His achievement and wonder at His majesty, all due to the mysterious qualities of light, which even these spiritually created beings fall infinitely short of understanding. Thank God for the ability to glimpse into some of the science of the creation, while at the same time allowing us a revealing look into the realm of the spirit.

The Light of life

This entire thought processes is perfectly in line with the activities of the Lord on the fourth day. As we have shown, the physical light from the sun is not possible without the spiritual light of the Lord. Just as there are many unknown facts about the light of the Lord, likewise there are many unknown facts about the light of sun. Therefore, when the Lord made two great lights, it simply meant that He changed the properties of the physical light that was now permeating the earth. The light that was reaching the earth prior to the re-creation was different than the light now reaching the earth. Though indeed, just as many of the current properties and abilities of light are unknown, a perceivable change in the qualities of sunlight would also be unknown.

Speculatively though, since light produces life, a change in its characteristics could certainly cause a change in the characteristics of life. A couple of ways this can be witnessed is by examining the size of plants and animals from the previous creation. Geological records show that creatures and vegetation prior to the re-creation were substantially larger. Dinosaurs were enormous creatures, some of them larger than a blue whale, which is currently the largest living creature on the planet. Of course, it is no coincidence that plant life also mirrored this increased size. Along with atmospheric changes, this could also be explained by the many unknown properties of light and the fact that the Lord changed its properties at the re-creation.

Additionally, the increased lifespan of the early saints could be attributed to these same varied properties of light. Those living in Adam's day were constrained by the Lord's declaration of what He considers a day in earth years. Later in human history, light properties were again altered when the Lord changed the length of man's life to 120 years (Genesis 6:3). "In Him was life and the life was the light of men." Less light brings less life. He is the cause of the light and the one that makes and forms the light, as well as enables and changes its qualities.

Any manipulation of its properties would bring about major changes on the surface of the earth and its inhabitants, and these changes in human longevity occurred due to a declaration of the Lord during that time. This same type of change in light's qualities will be seen again in the future when the Lord establishes His kingdom upon the earth and dispenses eternal life to all who believe.

Wrap Up

Since the dawn of the creation, the light of the sun and the rest of the heavenly bodies in the universe have continued on their path. However, the earth was removed from its celestial influence for the period it was cloaked in darkness and removed from its prescribed orbit. On the fourth day of the re-creation, the earth was put back in its place and the heavenly bodies were once again realigned and able to be seen from its surface. Day and the night returned to being ruling models on the earth, a covenant that He later made with Noah to govern the earth for all eternity. "While the earth remaineth, seedtime and harvest, and cold and heat, and summer and winter, and day and night shall not cease" (Genesis 8:22). The earth will continue spinning and be tilted on its axis forever. Never to be shut down again, the life giving physical light of the sun will continue to permeate the earth throughout eternity.

This is further ratified by Jeremiah where he states, "Thus saith the LORD, which giveth the sun for a light by day, and the ordinances of the moon and of the stars for a light by night.... If those ordinances depart from before me, saith the LORD, then the seed of Israel also shall cease from being a nation before me for ever" (Jeremiah 31:35–36). The Lord established a covenant with David that one of his seed will reign as king throughout all eternity. That seed, of course, is Jesus Christ. He is the eternal King of Israel. (2 Timothy 2:8.) Just as Jesus will eternally be the Lord; so too will the sun, moon, and stars never fail to cease shining upon the earth. The Bible specifically declares that neither the earth nor the world will ever end

(Ecclesiastes 1:4, Ephesians 3:21). God does not change and neither will His system of government, it will extend throughout all eternity on the physical earth. Just as His kingdom will eternally exist, so too will humanity, although not in the same vessel.

At the end of this dispensation John said he "saw a new heaven and a new earth: for the first heaven and the first earth were passed away" (Revelation 21:1). What does that mean exactly? Will He destroy the universe and recreate it? No, as it has been shown, this is not the case. Instead, a new earth will emerge from the existing earth, but it will be governed by a new set of physical laws. This is the principle behind the Lord saying, "They shall perish… And as a vesture shalt thou fold them up, and they shall be changed" (Hebrews 1:11–12).

Perish does not mean extinction, but rather a change into a new form. When a piece of fruit perishes, it takes on a new form. It disintegrates into the dirt and that same dirt is used to nourish and produce the next generation of fruit. The old branch is clipped and removed so that a new branch can grow. (John 15:2.) It will be a change in the physical principles of the earth, the old will be folded up like a blanket and the new will be established upon a new set of physical laws. This means that light manipulation will once again play a major role in this new kingdom.

Isaiah prophesies of a future day in which, "Moreover the light of the moon shall be as the light of the sun, and the light of the sun shall be sevenfold, as the light of seven days, in the day that the LORD bindeth up the breach of his people, and healeth the stroke of their wound" (Isaiah 30:26). Isaiah clearly states that the light of the sun will be seven times greater and the light of the moon shall be as bright as the light of the sun is now.

Frankly, with today's understanding of sunlight, it is doubtful that our atmosphere would be able to withstand that type of intensity from the sun. But that is based on today's understanding of light. Just as in the past, it is apparent that in the future God is going to once again manipulate the light of the earth. The implications of this new sunlight are going to be an unequivocally powerful, healing type of light, enveloping the earth with glory. This is just the light of the sun. Imagine the Lord also turning up the power of the light of the glory and knowledge in the face of Christ Jesus on the spiritual side, with a force that is seven-fold its current intensity. Oh, praise the Lord, the Maker and Creator of the universe!

Even without this sevenfold increase in creative power prophesied by Isaiah, a once dead earth was rejuvenated back to life during the first four days of the re-creation. He called it good and concluded it by saying that the evening and morning were the fourth day. At the end of this age, the word good will no longer be an adequate qualifier of God's creative acts. For when He starts afresh with a new heaven and earth, death will have been abolished and the new earth and heaven will be based on new rules established in His perfection. (1 Corinthians 15:26.)

So through the first four days of the re-creation, God established all the physical functionality of earth, including planting some of its vegetation. Now, on the fifth day, it is time to introduce some of the intelligent life that roams the earth.

Day Five

And God said, Let the waters bring forth abundantly the moving creature that hath life, and fowl that may fly above the earth in the open firmament of heaven. And God created great whales, and every living creature that moveth, which the waters brought forth abundantly, after their kind, and every winged fowl after his kind: and God saw that it was good. And God blessed them, saying, Be fruitful, and multiply, and fill the waters in the seas, and let fowl multiply in the earth. And the evening and the morning were the fifth day. (Genesis 1:20–23)

The events of the fifth day are really straightforward: the Lord creates all the birds of the air and the fish of the sea. Undoubtedly, the magnitude of the creatures the Lord brought to life on the fifth day was a daunting task. Even with untold thousands of species that have become extinct since the re-creation, there are still countless tens of thousands of creatures currently roaming the air and sea. Some large and some microscopic, but each one is part of the mass of biodiversity that covers the air and sea.

There are so many creatures that populations of them still remain undocumented. The sheer magnitude and range of the created species are absolutely astounding. Needless to say, this was an awesome feat and one that could only be completed by God. "That they may see, and know, and consider, and understand together, that the hand of the LORD hath done this, and the Holy One of Israel hath created it" (Isaiah 41:20).

Here again, on the fifth day, water plays an integral part in the earth's re-creation, just as it has been mentioned in three out of five of the re-creation days. On the fifth day the whole spectrum of the creation comes forth from the water, for it says that they were all brought forth abundantly out of the water. He does so by once again speaking to both the earth and the waters, which in turn, hear and respond to the Lord's instruction.

Additionally, the Lord says that this was all accomplished by an act of creation, which means all of the creatures were an original model. "And God created great whales, and every living creature that moveth, which the waters brought forth abundantly, and every winged fowl" (Genesis 1:21). All the species created on that day were an entirely new creation.

He wraps up the passage by again using the phrase "after their kind," meaning the entire creation of the fifth day was made from a pattern established during the previous creation that populated the earth prior to the destruction of verse two.

According to fossil records, there are believed to have been at least five major death and rebirths of life in the earth's history. The one accounted for in Genesis is the latest rearranging of species on the planet. Currently there are estimated to be between 5 and 30 million different species occupying this planet of which only about 1.75 million have been documented. A large number of species on the earth remain unknown due to most of them consisting of tiny invertebrates and microorganisms; with insects comprising about half of the documented species.

The current populations of species on the earth are believed to consist of only one tenth of one percent of the total populations that have existed on the earth since its beginning. In other words, when the Lord says after its kind, there is an enormous pool of life with which to mirror from in the earth's annals; though it is largely apparent that many of the species came from a later, more recent design.

Of course, creation of any one of His creatures is an easy feat for the Lord. The Psalmist points to this simple truth when he stated that when God wants to create something He merely sends forth His Spirit and they are created. (Psalm 104:30.) He did not spend eons of time deliberating and crafting their design, but rather spoke forth what was already in His mind, creating untold diversity within that one single day.

Without a doubt, this flies in the face of current scientific theory, because the idea of after its kind is the antithesis of modern biological evolution. Of course, evolution involves a gradual change in a species as it adjusts to environmental pressures over the course of time. It cannot be seen in the lifetime of one creature, but rather it takes thousands and even millions of years for a species to adapt and change into another species. The Bible is quite clear that the idea of evolution is not a process of creation.

The time frames involved in a day of creation have been proved to be one thousand years, rather than millions. Even though, there are millions of species on the earth today that were patterned after millions of species from the distant past; the species that roam the earth today are a new creation, modeled those that previously populated the earth. Simply put, all of the creatures that have roamed the earth since the re-creation have been directly designed and created by God. To propose any other ideas would be to detract from His exact words which say, "And God created great whales, and every living creature that moveth, which the waters brought forth abundantly, after their kind, and every winged fowl after his kind" (Genesis 1:21).

In this same fashion, He created all species of creatures that have ever walked the earth throughout time. He is the Creator and He does not change. He created and designed this subset of creation, and in the same fashion He created all of the species throughout the ages. "But when you give them breath, they are created; you give new life to the earth" (Psalm 104:30 GNB).

Intermediary species purported by evolution to have been discovered are merely another creation by the Lord. If these various species were to have evolved, there would have to be hundreds and possibly thousands of intermediary species between each creature. The basic premise of evolution is called natural selection. The idea is that as cells mutate to adapt to new environments, only the creatures with good mutations will continue to thrive, while the others will die as they fail to adapt to their ever-changing environment.

Without going into the fact that "good mutations" are virtually impossible in nature, one creature that has an added fin or tail does not prove that all of the creatures evolved from one another. Albeit it is an interesting theory, but it flies in the face of God creating all things. The truth is, "God giveth it a body as it hath pleased him, and to every seed his own body. All flesh is not the same flesh: but there is one kind of flesh of men, another flesh of beasts, another of fishes, and another of birds" (1 Corinthians 15:38–39). In other words, a fish did not become a mammal through eons of time, because they are from a different kind of flesh. Each classification of species has its own flesh and each creation within that species has its own seed.

Only God the Creator can design a massive ecological system capable of supporting all the vast diversities of life in one millennium rather than millions of years. Clearly, the Bible does support the idea that current species were deliberately put together from the blueprint of former life forms, which accounts for the similarities between the fossil record and modern day creatures.

In conjunction with this, science purports that some creatures from past eras were able to survive in the harshest of conditions that existed during the destruction and re-creation of the earth. It is believed that these creatures can still be found on the earth today. These include, and are not limited to, a couple of species of fish, alligators, and a species of crabs. Certainly it would seem that the latter two species would likely be able to withstand some of the harsher conditions that occurred during the event surrounding the destruction witnessed in Genesis 1:2, due to their exoskeletons and other characteristics.

The biblical truth is that the events of day four do not allow for this, because it says that all life created on the fifth day was a new creation. "And God created great whales, and *every* living creature… and *every* winged fowl" (Genesis 1:21). Prior to their creation, the earth was truly without form and devoid of life. These species may closely resemble some of their predecessors, even more so than other species, but the fact remains that the destruction of the earth in Genesis 1:2 was total. So when the Lord brought forth new life after the destruction, it was a whole new creation.

Interestingly, in verse twenty one, the Lord singles out whales as the only species in the animal kingdom to rate a special mention on the fifth day. Why? It seems odd that the whale is the only creature mentioned amongst hundreds of thousands of different marine and waterfowl species. The truth is, God's plan from the beginning has always incorporated a hierarchy of authority. All of His creation runs on a structure of authority, similar to the different ranks in the military. For example, God is the head of Christ, Christ is the head of the church, and man is the head of the household. (1 Corinthians 11:3.) There is an authoritative structure to His creation.

So too, this hierarchical structure carries down to all the creatures in the earth and sea. The Bible mentions this phenomenon regarding the animal kingdom in Ezekiel 32:2 when it says, "Thou art like a young lion of the nations, and thou art as a whale in the seas." Just as the lion is the king of land animals, the whale is the master of the seas. This verse goes on to allude to the fact that their dominion is small and usurped by another. Of course, in this scenario, that would be mankind, who is charged by God to subdue the earth, including all the species in the animal kingdom and in the seas. (Genesis 1:28.)

So, the bottom line is that whales are the generals of the ocean. Just as humans control the whole of the earth and its entire population of creatures, the whale is the purveyor of the oceans; the great ruling class of the seas. Job 7:12 shows that God knows the movements of the whales. Job asks, "Am I a sea, or a whale, that thou settest a watch over me?"

In recent years it has been discovered that whales have large migratory patterns that traverse enormous expanses of ocean. Obviously, being the generals of the oceans, they are required to oversee their realm and report back to God. Knowing the reason why the waters are on the earth, helps to give light to the reason the Lord mentioned them as a separate creation. Certainly, there are activities still transpiring in this dark underwater realm that need to be supervised (much more on this in chapter seventeen).

Blessing

God concludes the fifth day by blessing both the fish and the fowl, instructing them to be fruitful and multiply. His only other blessing comes on the sixth day, when He blesses man. Of course, God is a blessing God. The very fact that He is resurrecting the earth proves His benevolence. He wants to prosper and bring about good for all of His creation. Often times when one reads the phrase, "be fruitful and multiply," it is arbitrarily skimmed over and passed off by saying, "sure God wants good to come to His creation." But it is certainly more than that. God bestows a blessing on a new class of creature, one that is different from all of its other creations in this dispensation. Therefore, since He calls the new creation good, His blessing would mean that He bestows upon them the ability to increase and be free of lack and disease.

All food and water sources would be plentiful, meaning that these creatures would enjoy enough to eat and drink whenever they needed or wanted it. So when God says, "be fruitful and multiply," he is instructing them to do more than just populate the earth (although reproduction is a definitive part of his plan). He is giving permission to His new constituency to prosper in every aspect of their new life. "The blessing of the LORD, it maketh rich, and he addeth no sorrow with it" (Proverbs 10:22).

In today's world, it can be difficult to envision a life with this much blessing, because mankind's fall has brought about a drastic change to the present structure of the earth. When man sinned, the things that were blessed became cursed. That curse of sin carried over to all of the recreated life; both plant and animal and it affected the earth itself. Weeds now grow to choke the life of various plants, and death has come to all of the creation. This was not the design for this new creation, but it was changed when sin entered into the equation. God will not leave the earth stranded. Blessings will return to the earth and reign supreme in the eternal future generations, and the rest of creation is waiting for the final redemption of mankind. "For the earnest expectation of the creature waiteth for the manifestation of the sons of God. For the creature was made subject to vanity, not willingly, but by reason of him who hath subjected the same in hope, Because the creature itself also shall be delivered from the bondage of corruption into the glorious liberty of the children of God" (Romans 8:19–21).

CHAPTER 9

The Sixth Day

Day Six

And God said, Let the earth bring forth the living creature after his kind, cattle, and creeping thing, and beast of the earth after his kind: and it was so. And God made the beast of the earth after his kind, and cattle after their kind, and every thing that creepeth upon the earth after his kind: and God saw that it was good. And God said, Let us make man in our image, after our likeness: and let them have dominion over the fish of the sea, and over the fowl of the air, and over the cattle, and over all the earth, and over every creeping thing that creepeth upon the earth. So God created man in his own image, in the image of God created he him; male and female created he them. And God blessed them, and God said unto them, Be fruitful, and multiply, and replenish the earth, and subdue it: and have dominion over the fish of the sea, and over the fowl of the air, and over every living thing that moveth upon the earth. And God said, Behold, I have given you every herb bearing seed, which is upon the face of all the earth, and every tree, in the which is the fruit of a tree yielding seed; to you it shall be for meat. And to every beast of the earth, and to every fowl of the air, and to every thing that creepeth upon the earth, wherein there is life, I have given every green herb for meat: and it was so. And God saw every thing that he had made, and, behold, it was very good. And the evening and the morning were the sixth day. (Genesis 1:24–31)

Animals

On the sixth day, God made all the animal and insect life that is prevalent on the earth today from the dust of the ground. For God said, "Let the earth bring forth the living creature after his kind, cattle, and creeping thing (insects)," calling the dry land to bring forth the terrestrial creatures. Whether they were called out of the water or dry land is inconsequential to their makeup, but rather refers to their purpose. On the previous day, all the life forms were called forth out of the sea and the Lord connects the fowl of the air with the fish of the sea. The fish live in the water and the fowl live in the atmosphere, which is dictated by the hydrological cycle. Subsequently, on the sixth day He speaks to the dry land to have it produce the animal and insect populations, thus making all of the terrestrial creation.

As was mentioned previously, just as all creatures are comprised of water, all creatures are also carbon based. Carbon is the very building block of all life on the planet, and all of the animate creation is built upon various elements of the earth. Of course, this is in no way a testament to evolution or any other branch of science. The text does not say they emerged from the sea and evolved into another creature. No, they were thoughtfully meditated upon and specifically designed to fulfill a divine purpose on the earth. They were created each one after his kind, showing that there was a preexisting template consisting of created creatures that previously lived in the earth.

On the sixth day, He begins by mentioning the beasts (which would entail all wild animals inhabiting the earth), then cattle, and finally insects. It would seem important that the Lord mentions cattle as a separate line item, because most people consider cattle to be a subset of the rest of the animals created on the sixth day. There are literally thousands of species of animals, yet cattle get their own mention in the creation account. Why?

Undoubtedly, God had a plan for their existence that involved His final creation, man. When God led the nation of Israel out of Egypt, He made it abundantly clear that cattle occupied a special place in their routine. (Numbers 18:17.) This would include, but not limit their usefulness for sacrifices, clothing, tools, or food. Cattle were designed to be used as a tool for humanity. (Psalm 104:14.)

So much like the fifth day of creation, His placing of animals on the earth is pretty straightforward. In this one thousand year time span, the Lord placed an enormous amount of diverse terrestrial creatures on the earth, as there literally tens of thousands of creatures in untold numbers that populate the earth. His next, and final creation, would be the pinnacle masterpiece and concluding action of the six days of the re-creation.

Humanity

For ask now of the days that are past, which were before thee, since the day that God created man upon the earth, and ask from the one side of heaven unto the other, whether there hath been any such thing as this great thing is, or hath been heard like it? (Deuteronomy 4:32)

Without a doubt, God's creation of man was the greatest event in all of the re-creation. In fact, here in Deuteronomy four, God asks all of heaven if any of the other species were as wonderful as the creation of mankind upon the earth. Humanity is the crowning achievement of this creation. It is the very reason for all the events of the re-creation up until this point. Great care and skill was put into the design of humans; not only in the physical aspect, but spiritually, and emotionally as well. Humanity's physical attributes are so elaborate and detailed that most of our intricacies are still undiscovered; causing scientists and laymen alike to ponder the wonder of their own design.

And God said, Let us make man in our image, after our likeness: and let them have dominion over the fish of the sea, and over the fowl of the air, and over the cattle, and over all the earth, and over every creeping thing that creepeth upon the earth. So God created man in his own image, in the image of God created he him; male and female created he them. (Genesis 1:26–27)

Indisputably, man is a separate created being. He does not have any ancestors and he is not a descendant from the animal kingdom. He is a new creation made in the likeness of God on the sixth day of the re-creation. Any attempt to read this verse in any other fashion is simply untenable.

The creation of mankind in Genesis one shows that God acted in three distinct ways: He let, He created, and He made. Three completely separate action verbs are bestowed upon His final creation. First God made man from the existing elements of the earth. Everything that the human body is made of can be found in the elements of the earth. Much like the animals and other creatures that inhabit the earth; the human body is carbon and water based. Though each individual is characteristically unique, every human is physically created as a product of the terra firma.

In the same respect, everything that humanity needs to survive is produced and obtained from the earth and will ultimately return to the earth. Human bodies need to be continually supplied with elements that are grown out of the earth in order to eat and protect themselves. In other words, replenishing from the earth is required of both food and water; a constant reminder to all creation of the link between humanity and the earth. It is an amazing feat of God that He designed a system that is essentially self-sustaining.

Second, contrary to the animal kingdom, humanity was not made from a previous mold, because the phrase after its kind is not used. Man was a completely new creation; his only template was God Himself, designed as a three part being and made exclusively in His image. The creation of mankind on the earth is the culmination of everything He had been making over the previous five days of creation. The stage was set and now all the elements of the earth were in place to support mankind.

God had the idea of man before the foundation of the world, but until the sixth day of the re-creation, the earth was not prepared to support him. "According as he hath chosen us in him before the foundation of the world, that we should be holy and without blame before him in love" (Ephesians 1:4). One interesting thing about this verse that flies in the face of current convention is that it uses the word world instead of earth. "According as he hath chosen us in him before the foundation of the world ..."

In other words, humanity was not necessarily planned prior to the creation of the earth, but the notion of man came around some time after the original creation. Remember that the use of the word world is indicative of a system of government that dominates the earth. In this dispensation that would be the government of mankind. In other words, God had a system on the earth prior to man, but once that system was destroyed, God devised a new way. He then devised the creation of man and built the rest of the infrastructure around him. This whole idea came about between the original creation and the re-creation, but not necessarily before the original creation in the dateless past.

Finally, He used the verb "let" to call together the other portions of the Godhead to take action in the creation of man. "And God said, Let us make man in our image, after our likeness" (Genesis 1:26). This verb was previously used by the Lord when He was speaking to either the earth or the water to bring forth life. Now He is telling Himself to take action. This is important because mankind is a new creation and each part of the Godhead has a part to play. "Let us make man."

The article that He uses to refer to Himself is plural. The Father is talking to the Son and the Holy Spirit. He is saying that He wants to give His new creation the same attributes that He possesses; that is, three unique parts. He is calling on each part of the Godhead to individually create mankind with each of the same distinctions that they individually represent: a spirit, a soul, and a body.

Therefore, just as the Lord is a three part being: the Father, Son, and Holy Spirit, so also is mankind. Jesus is obviously the physical dimension, but the Holy Ghost and God the Spirit also have a form in the spiritual dimension. So although the human physical body is the part that is witnessed by other humans, mankind also has a form on the level of the soul and the spirit, just like the Creator. Isaiah confirms that the human spirit is given by God when he says, "Thus saith God the LORD, he that created the heavens, and stretched them out; he that spread forth the earth, and that which cometh out of it; he that giveth breath unto the people upon it, and spirit to them that walk therein" (Isaiah 42:5). Mankind is created in the image of God, a three part being.

The Bible shows that God assumes a shape on all three planes of His existence and each dimension has a form or body. Therefore, in this same fashion, each dimension of man's existence must also have a form and the Bible points to the fact that the difference between the physical and spiritual is barely discernible. Paul alludes to this when he says, "I knew a man in Christ above fourteen years ago, (whether in the body, I cannot tell; or whether out of the body, I cannot tell: God knoweth;) such an one caught up to the third heaven" (2 Corinthians 12:2). Paul said the man was caught up into heaven and whether he was in his body or out of his body he did not know. In other words, the human spirit and soul each take a shape in the spiritual plane and look just like the physical.

In this same respect, just as God is the head of the trinity, so also is man's spirit the head of his trinity and can be driven by his spirit. Thus, it is pertinent to mention that humanity is first and foremost a spirit, then a soul, and finally, a temporal body. It is this distinctive spiritual element that is part of man's creation that differentiates humans from animals. It is the very definition of being created in His image, because the ultimate aspect of God is that He is a Spirit. It is from this spiritual plane that humanity is called to be constantly cognizant of while on the earth.

Of course, Jesus is the perfect example of following after His Spirit. While He was on earth, He was always looking for direction from the Father. In His own words He said, "The Son can do nothing of himself, but what he seeth the Father do: for what things soever he doeth, these also doeth the Son likewise" (John 5:19). Jesus was attuned to the direction of the Lord and always put the Father first. He is the penultimate example for mankind here on earth. He realized the symbiotic relationship that was necessary between Himself and the Father and through His example He calls for all people to establish this same relationship with the Father through their own spirit.

While in these physical bodies the Lord calls people to be more cognizant of the spiritual. It is here that human spirits are fed by God with direction and understanding that translates into physical manifestations. (Galatians 5:16–25.) Humans are the only beings created with a spirit and it is the spirit that makes human beings unique in all of creation. It is humanity's tie to the Creator because the human spirit is in direct communication with the Spirit Himself. That is why the Bible teaches that God is never far from His creation, because He is constantly communing with His human creation at the spiritual level. (Acts 17:27.) If this foremost dimension of God's creation is ignored, fellowship between man and God can be destroyed. (1 John 1:6–7.)

Of course, there is one more component to God and man. It also takes a soul to relay and comprehend the messages that are being sent from the spirit to give guidance to the physical. The Bible shows that the human soul is intimately intertwined with the spirit; in fact they are so close that they are virtually inseparable. (Hebrews 4:12.)

The word for soul in the original Hebrew is *Nephesh* and it is used about 750 times in both the Old and New Testament. It is the thinking aspect of ones being; it is their mind, will, reasoning, emotions, attitude, likes, dislikes, demeanor, ideas, thoughts, etc. In the Godhead this office is occupied by the Holy Spirit.

Most of the time, when it is used in the Bible, it is used to describe man. But on several occasions it is also used to describe animals. Both man and animals have a soul, but mankind is distinguished from the animal because humanity also possesses a spirit. This is why the Bible is clear that God places much more worth on humanity than He does on several animals mentioned in the Scriptures. (Luke 12:7.)

Throughout the creation account when God mentions life, He is referring directly to their soul. For instance in Genesis 1:20, "Let the waters bring forth abundantly the moving creature that hath life (Nephesh)" (Also seen in verse 21, 24, and 30 of the creation account). The life that God is referring to is the life of the soul. The physical needs a soul to survive. For, without the mind giving direction and intention, physical life would be impossible.

Once the flesh (body) dies, the soul (intellect) will continue on with the spirit into the spiritual realm. This is known from Abraham's conversation with the rich man in Luke chapter sixteen. Abraham was in heaven, speaking with a rich man in the bowels of hell. Both were discussing the situation on earth that landed the rich man in hell and the rich man was requesting of Abraham to send water to help relieve his torment, if only for a moment.

> The rich man also died, and was buried; And in hell he lift
> up his eyes, being in torments, and seeth Abraham afar off,
> and Lazarus in his bosom. And he cried and said, Father

Abraham, have mercy on me, and send Lazarus, that he may
dip the tip of his finger in water, and cool my tongue; for I
am tormented in this flame. (Luke 16:22–24)

This story reveals much about the afterlife, notice that the rich man did
not lose his memories of earthly things, nor did he lose his ability to reason
cognitively because he was petitioning Abraham to send Lazarus to help his
family make the right choice in an attempt to prevent them from ending up
in hell. Both not only recognized each other on the spiritual level, but the
story also proves that they had cognitive abilities to reason and remember
their time on the earth. When the physical is dead, both the spirit and the
soul move on to eternal life and the soul carries the memories of the physical
into the afterlife.

The choice that one has to make while on the earth is to accept Christ
or not. That decision dictates the eternal state of one's spirit and soul. (Luke
12:8–10.) In Jesus's story of the rich man He is referring to a time before His
resurrection, a time when the law of the prophets was to be followed. So as
the story goes, the rich man did not make the right choices in his life and
forsook the teaching of the prophets. Subsequently, upon his death he went
to hell, leaving his body to decay on the earth. While in hell, he calls out for
a taste of water to quench his unending thirst. This is interesting because
what good would water do for a man who does not have a physical body to
satiate his thirst? Of course, the text is referring to another type of water.

The rich man had passed from the physical life into the spiritual, so
the water he is referring to is spiritual water. He was not being tormented
in flames that could only be quenched by water on a physical level. Instead,
since the rich man was asking for water and knowing that mere physical water
would not remedy his situation, the text must be referring to a spiritual type
of water. The water he was referring to is the Holy Spirit. As was previously
mentioned, throughout Scripture water is associated with the Holy Spirit. (1
John 5:8.) So when the rich man was crying out for relief from the torment, he
was asking Abraham to cool his tormented mental state with the refreshing
power that can only come from the Holy Spirit.

For the rich man, he had the teachings and examples of his ancestors to follow and he made the choice to forsake those teachings while on the earth. (Luke 16:29.) Unfortunately, he chose against that wisdom of the prophets and wound up in hell. Since his physical body was dead and left on earth, then everything that was happening in the text was referring to his spirit and soul. Hence, common sense proves out that the torment he was experiencing was a spiritual torment. He was being tormented by the sins of his past life, because he chose against the remitting of sins, which comes by believing in the Son of God or in his case by following the word of the prophets. (Acts 2:38.)

He will forever be tormented, as if by flames, by remembrance of his past life and unremitted sins. In Psalm 103:12 it says that the Lord remembers your sins no more, "As far as the east is from the west, so far hath he removed our transgressions from us." This is an Old Testament truth about the human spirit and soul that Christ nailed home with His redeeming work on the cross. Without belief in Christ, sins can never be remitted and upon death that person is forever tormented by the sins of their past life, being continually under the law and never receiving forgiveness. (Hebrews 9:22, 10:17–18.)

The word is clear, time and again, that believing is the road to salvation. After the death and resurrection of Christ, only accepting the cleansing blood of Christ will allow one to pass into heaven. Man can never overcome the sins that he has committed without the blood of Christ. In 1 John 1:7, it says that "the blood of Jesus Christ his Son cleanseth us from all sin." It is the necessary ingredient, in the eyes of the Creator that each individual accepts the atoning work of our Lord and believe in His Son, or in the case of the rich man who was under the old covenant, to believe the words of the prophets.

If one is to take that step as belief in Him as Savior, then of necessity they must also believe on Him as Creator. There would have been no reason to sacrifice Himself and put an end to death if He was not the Creator of it all. Death is the final enemy of the creation to be destroyed. (1 Corinthians 15:26.)

CHAPTER 10

In the Image of God

In the image of God created He him

And God said, Let us make man in our image, after our likeness: and let them have dominion over the fish of the sea, and over the fowl of the air, and over the cattle, and over all the earth, and over every creeping thing that creepeth upon the earth. So God created man in his own image, in the image of God created he him; male and female created he them. (Genesis 1:26–27)

So far, several events of the sixth day have been addressed; in particular man's multidimensionality and the connection to the spirit realm. Now, looking into the physical creation of man introduces another intriguing development found in the activities of day six. In Genesis 1:27 it says, "So God created man in his own image, in the image of God created he him; male and female created he them." Obviously, this verse addresses the image or trinity of God and man, but looking further into the text exposes how and who God originally placed on the earth.

One of the main points being looked at in this chapter is the way the personal pronouns are used. For the verse says that He created him (singular); followed by the statement that He created them (plural). Of course, he is an individual and them refers to a group of people: two or more, which means that two completely separate acts are transpiring here. However, the general consensus amongst biblical scholars about this passage is contrary to this viewpoint. Generally, it is conceded that this verse is portraying that the Lord was creating one man and the personal pronouns show that he essentially instantly split into man and woman. Undoubtedly, that would seem to be the truth, but there is much more happening in this passage.

Generically speaking God called His new creation man. Adam was the first man. (1 Corinthians 15:45.) In fact, his name means man, though when he was first created, it may have been better to state that this new creation was human.

Certainly, one of the primary reasons for calling His creation man was to establish a hierarchy in the kingdom of God. "But I would have you know, that the head of every man is Christ; and the head of the woman is the man; and the head of Christ is God" (1 Corinthians 11:3). Therefore, just as Christ is the head of the church, so also is the Father God the head of Christ. In this same fashion, man was created in His image and he is the head of his household.

Obviously, one question that arises from this passage is the establishment of gender roles. Not only with Adam, but also with God since Adam was created in the image of God. Hence, the first question to look into concerning gender roles is whether God is a man or a woman. Simply stated, the Bible is quite clear that God defines Himself in the masculine and never in the feminine. However, this does not mean that God confines Himself to a specific sexual orientation or any other definition of what modern vernacular defines as a man. Rather He establishes Himself as the head of the Kingdom.

In this same fashion, Adam is called the first man because he is positioned at the head of all other created things. That is to say, Adam was neither male nor female based on how the current gender roles are defined, but rather he was created in the image of God. And God is not confined by a modern definition of gender roles; rather He is the Creator of gender roles.

He is the, "One God and Father of all, who is above all, and through all, and in you all" (Ephesians 4:6). He is truly the consummation of all things, as He is all things to all people. When called upon by Moses to tell the Israelites who sent Him, He simply said to tell them that "I AM hath sent me unto you" (Exodus 3:14). There is truly no definition that fully describes Him.

This is not some sort of bizarre transgender confession of who God is, as mankind would imagine it, rather it is showing that He is the "God which worketh all in all" (1 Corinthians 12:6). He is everything and He is the ultimate fulfillment of both genders. Not constrained by gender roles, but the Creator of the sexes, and He is the fulfillment of all things to all people. And Adam was made in His image.

There is no reason for Adam to be designed with a particular sexual orientation if there is no one else of the opposite gender to consummate the union. Therefore, just like God, when Adam was created he was called the first man, because he was the patriarchal head of all of creation. He was not confined by gender roles until Eve was separated from him in the garden; an event that did not transpire at the moment of creation but at a point that was much later in time, in the Garden of Eden (the timing of the events in Genesis chapter two and their outcomes will be looked at in greater depth in chapters 11 and 12). It was there that God separated one person into two and established sexual orientation for the human race it is known today.

Thus, for man's sake in the garden, God removed the woman from Adam. God's purpose was twofold: both for companionship and so that man would have a helper. This can be seen in Genesis 2:18, "And the LORD God said, It is not good that the man should be alone; I will make him an help meet for him." So God made woman from man. That is, Eve was not a separate creation but rather she was a byproduct of the creation of Adam; she was made. (Genesis 2:22.) If woman came out of man, then she had to be a part of man. And Adam confirms this by saying, "This is now bone of my bones, and flesh of my flesh: she shall be called Woman, because she was taken out of Man" (Genesis 2:23).

The removal of Eve from Adam did not happen at the moment of His creation but instead was an event that transpired after Adam's original creation. Adam was not created in the garden, but rather the Bible shows that he was moved to the garden after the events of the original creation; not on the sixth day, but on the seventh day. (Genesis 2:8.) It doesn't make sense to say that God created Adam and then instantly realized that He should have created two separate individuals. Instead, the Bible is clear that Eve was removed from Adam sometime after the sixth day of the re-creation: after Adam was moved to the garden.

God separated them for reasons of companionship, recreational, and physical duties. (Genesis 2:18.) They were then returned to each other so that they could again be one flesh. This means that when a man and a woman come together in marriage, they form a bond that complements and completes the other. That is why God says the two shall become one flesh. (Genesis 2:24.) Yet for reasons of final hierarchical decision making, the man was established as the head of the household. "For the husband is the head of the wife, even as Christ is the head of the church: and he is the saviour of the body" (Ephesians 5:23).

God calls them man and wife and immediately God saw the union as a marriage. "Therefore shall a man leave his father and his mother, and shall cleave unto his wife: and they shall be one flesh. And they were both naked, the man and his wife, and were not ashamed" (Genesis 2:24–25). Adam and Eve came from the same flesh and they returned to each other in the marriage relationship, which was designed by God since their separation.

In reality men and women are very similar physically: two eyes, two arms, hair, a nose, etc. However, in other areas men and women are diametrically and entirely different: different abilities, different sex organs, different desires and needs, etc. In truth, there are certain things that a man is and does that a woman is not and there are certain things that a woman is and does that a man is not. While each party can develop the physical and mental strength to complete the needed task at hand, this is not the plan of God. His plan was for the two individuals to find one another and become one flesh; to complement and complete the other.

Of course that does not mean that a person is not a complete individual if they are not married. Christians have a covenant with God that says that He will never leave nor forsake His children. He is "a father of the fatherless" (Psalm 68:5). If allowed, He can be everything to everybody, "the fulness of him that filleth all in all" (Ephesians 1:23). God can always complete the circle when He is called on to do so.

In the New Testament, Paul was a good example of this because he understood the covenant relationship that he had with the Lord. "I say therefore to the unmarried and widows, It is good for them if they abide even as I" (1 Corinthians 7:8). He called upon his readers to remain as he was (unmarried) because of the relationship that he had with the Lord and that relationship was more than enough. He did provide an option for the rest of the population though, when he said that if the desire for a spouse is too great, then by all means those two people should be joined in marriage. (1 Corinthians 7:9.)

In summary, Adam was created in the true image of God; which means that He was not constrained by gender roles. Ultimately, it was God's desire that Adam would not remain alone, and He recognized Adam's need for companionship. Eve was miraculously separated from Adam after the original creation, when Adam was placed in the garden. She was not a new creation but a copy of the template set forth in Adam. Then the two came back together to form one flesh.

Male and female created He them

Again, the separation of Eve happened at a point in time after Adam was moved to the garden. In verse 27 there is one more thing to note about the events surrounding the creation of man. Adam was not the only individual created, God also introduces a second group which He called "them."

"So God created man in his own image, in the image of God created he him; male and female created he them." (Genesis 1:27)

While God was creating him (Adam), the text shows that He also created a group of individuals that He refers to as them, who were separately created as male and female. Specifically by using the pronoun "them" it shows that there were indeed additional beings created on the sixth day during the time that God created the first man Adam and that those being were created as separate genders.

"Them" cannot be used to describe Adam and Eve because God did not create Adam as two separate individuals; they were separated after the original creation. Therefore God only created him (Adam), He did not create "them" (Adam and Eve) during the original creation on the sixth day. When verse 27 uses the word "them," it is apparent that God created more people that were evidently already divided into separate genders.

Undoubtedly they were physical humanoid-like creatures with bodies and souls, but it was likely they were not spirits. The Bible shows that only Adam was created in the image of God, these others were a separate thought and as such they were probably not created in His image because the passage separates the two creations.

Certainly, God created Adam in His image but the group He describes as "them" were only created as male and female. Therefore it is likely that they did not have all the attributes that were given to Adam, most notably a spirit. Since they were created as male and female they could procreate and perform all the tasks necessary for life, but without a spirit or direct connection to God they would have been more animal-like in nature and subject to death.

Archaeological records report that this was indeed the case. Scientists have uncovered dozens of different humanoid-like creatures that roamed the earth in eons past. Many of these earlier humans have been given names like Cro-Magnon, Neanderthal, and Homo-erectus. These are all commonplace names in the scientific community and most lay people are aware of the existence of these and other groups of people on the earth many thousands of years ago, whose existence is speculated as predating mankind.

Of course, the Bible shows that they did not predate the original man, but instead were created and existed simultaneously with Adam. Theories and dating methods put their existence anywhere from 70,000 - 50,000 BC, although some estimates place it as occurring much earlier, like 200,000 BC. Still others believe that some of these humanoid species date back several million years. Findings of these early people have cropped up in various regions of the globe, but they are mostly clustered in proximity to the Mediterranean Sea and Africa. Archeologically, there is no indication that modern man existed prior to these other humanoids, but the Bible states that this was not the case. The Bible is quite clear in stating that indeed one man was created just prior to these other humanoids. That man, of course, was Adam.

There is no archaeological record of Adam's existence alongside of these other humanoids, because a single man by himself would have left an insignificant archaeological or fossil footprint on the earth. Obviously, there would have been no skeletal remains as he was created to live forever.

He was all alone and the ability to procreate was not granted until he was moved to the garden where Eve was formed from his rib. Then after he was evicted from the garden, he began to procreate and his first child was born shortly thereafter.

Human remains have shown that this all happened approximately six thousand years ago; which is in agreement with the scriptural account. Henceforth, modern day humans began to populate the earth after all the other humanoid species were already pushed to extinction. Of course, since death was already in the earth, it is evident and proven that these other species were living and dying just like all the other creatures on the earth. That is, except Adam, because he was given a spirit and a choice for life and death (more on this later). The reasons and timing of the extinction of these other humanoids is largely theorized.

The scientific community takes a different stance on the existence of these other humanoids and states that modern man evolved from these earlier ancestors and they have spent considerable time and resources in an attempt to prove this idea. In fact, over the last couple of centuries they have quested to find the "missing link" between the two as it would be a definitive bolster to the evolutionary premise. According to the Bible, the two species are not relatives. God created two different types of humanoids in the beginning of creation. First God created "him" (Adam) and then He created "them" (other humanoid like species). Both were created at the same time, but they are not the same.

This fact holds true scientifically because there are very minimal DNA matches between modern humans and early mankind. Indeed God created these individuals when He created Adam and they roamed the earth with him, but they are not what the Bible calls the first man, even though they may have some minimal DNA resemblance.

Generically speaking, all of the individuals created on the sixth day were called man or Adam. "Male and female created he them; and blessed them, and called their name Adam, in the day when they were created" (Genesis 5:2). Adam means man, so it can be difficult to determine exactly when Adam was first used as a proper noun and when it was used to describe a group; though it seems apparent that the change took place at some point shortly after the first man Adam arrived in the garden. This is evidenced in the New Testament where Adam is defined as the first man. "And so it is written, The first man Adam was made a living soul; the last Adam was made a quickening spirit" (1 Corinthians 15:45). It was from this man that God removed Eve.

Biblically, it is apparent that throughout the early creation account these other humanoids were treated equally and given the same commands to subdue the earth and have dominion over it. "And God blessed them, and God said unto them, Be fruitful, and multiply, and replenish the earth, and subdue it: and have dominion over the fish of the sea, and over the fowl of the air, and over every living thing that moveth upon the earth" (Genesis 1:28). They were all given a blessing and instructions to control and multiply on the earth.

Nevertheless, only one man was chosen to be placed in the refuge of the garden. That is the individual who was created in the image of God and who later obtained the proper name of Adam. He was the first man because the Bible shows that he came first, "So God created man in his own image, in the image of God created he him." That was the creation of Adam, then there was a secondary creation at the same time that were created as separate genders that the Bible describes as, "male and female created he them."

Undoubtedly the concept that God purposefully created other people that walked the earth is a difficult concept to grasp. Church tradition has been clear that there was only one man and one woman that promulgated the entire world we see today. Certainly it is true that the entire human species came from only two individuals, but it is also true that there were additional creative activities that coincided with the creation of humans that walk the earth today. Even Jesus called this out when he was questioned about marriage and divorce. "Have ye not read, that he which made them at the beginning made them male and female" (Matthew 19:4)? It does not say Adam and Eve but rather "them." He concurred using the exact phrase that is found in Genesis 1:27.

One point that many people have trouble hurdling over is the problem of sin entering into the world. If one man brought sin into the world and death through sin, then how could other early humans have died prior to the sin of this one man? Remember that it was through Adam that sin entered into the world not the earth. Adam was the beginning of the world system, which means that death would have been brought through Adam because of his sin and subsequently to all of Adam's descendants.

For those other species, they were subject to death that was already in the earth; already witnessed in the earth by the life and death of the plant and animal life. Only Adam was given a spirit and designated by God for a greater purpose. He was set apart and avoided the wiles of death that were still resident in the earth until he was moved into the garden where the Lord formed him and gave him a choice.

So although they are referred to as men, these other species that the Lord created alongside of Adam were not under "Adam's world." So it stands to reason that since Adam was considered the first man, only he could bring sin into a world that was born of him. All of the rest of creation was born into an earth that had already been marred with sin. This would include the other groups of individuals that were created alongside of Adam, which the Bible refers to as "them." Thus, the Bible proves that not only were there other individuals during the re-creation; it once again proves that death and possible extinction were brought about by sin that existed in the earth prior to their creation. Of course, this same phenomenon is also evidenced in the animal species that were created on the fifth day.

Why create mankind?

God's ultimate purpose in creating man was to commune with Him. The first and most obvious example of this takes place in Genesis, when God takes time to walk with Adam in the garden. (Genesis 3:8–9) God enjoys the fellowship with those who seek Him. (James 4:8.)

That communion was subsequently broken with Adam's act of disobedience. Since then there have been multitudes of laws established by the Lord to establish boundaries for humanity in the now sin-dominated world. Most of these came about during the days of Moses, when the Lord defined what His standards were by stating what was acceptable and what was contemptible. "For until the law sin was in the world: but sin is not imputed when there is no law" (Romans 5:13).

During those days of Old Testament legalism, it was a difficult task to commune and draw near to the Lord. Precious few were allowed to enter into a personal relationship with their Creator. Only the priests, prophets, and certain chosen men and women of God could hear from the Lord. This, of course, was abolished with the death of Jesus, "And, behold, the veil of the temple was rent in twain from the top to the bottom; and the earth did quake, and the rocks rent" (Matthew 27:51).

The veil of the temple was a symbol of Moses' law being confined within the synagogue or church. The tearing of the veil is symbolic of the fact that the Spirit who was previously hidden behind the veil was now ready to be released into men's hearts; thereby allowing the Lord to come to all who called on His name. (Acts 2:21.) When Christ left the earth, believers no longer needed to see a priest or a prophet for direction, but could find direction from the Lord within themselves. "Neither shall they say, Lo here! or, lo there! for, behold, the kingdom of God is within you" (Luke 17:21). God now lives in all those who call on His name and His Holy Spirit comes to dwell in them and provide them with daily direction.

No longer was God to be some ephemeral being that was seemingly inaccessible. With Christ, He now lives within man's spirit and provides the direction both in the eternal, invisible realm and in the real physical everyday life. Believers can now walk with God, just like Adam did in the garden.

Believers today can walk in the cool of the garden as Adam once did and fellowship openly with Him; partaking freely from the tree of life that Adam chose against. "To him that overcometh will I give to eat of the tree of life, which is in the midst of the paradise of God" (Revelation 2:7). On account of Christ's sacrifice all people can choose to partake of this gift (more on this in chapter seventeen). But it can only be done by faith. Just as God created the universe by faith, mankind is called to believe and fellowship with Him by faith. (Hebrews 11:6.)

The ability to worship and have a relationship with God is believed to be one of the main differences between man and animals. Recently though, some religious relics were uncovered alongside the remains of the bones of early man. Prior to this, there was some question as to whether these early humans had the capacity to worship God, but these artifacts prove that these early humans did indeed worship the Lord.

Worship of the Lord would potentially imply that they had a spirit, but the Bible does not say that these early humans were made in the image of God, but that only Adam was made in his image. "In the image of God created He him, male and female created He them." (Genesis 1:27) Again, Adam was created in His image, but the Bible does not specifically state that these other early humans were created in His image, and thus they likely did not have a spirit.

Having a spirit is the one unique thing about humanity. It is the connection between God and man. Without a spirit, one would be more animal-like in nature, but absence of a spirit does not necessarily imply that one would not be able to worship the Lord. Worship of the Creator can be done though ones intellect or soul and this is seen again and again throughout the Scriptures. "The fear of the LORD is the beginning of knowledge" (Proverbs 1:7). Knowledge of a situation does not necessarily predicate a spirit. Knowledge is a byproduct of having a soul, because the soul is ones intellect. So worship of the Lord can be done solely through ones intellect and not on a spiritual level.

Undoubtedly, as it was stated earlier, the whole of creation is a result of His glory and has the ability to worship Him, which is why it says that the rocks of the earth would cry out to the Lord if humanity stopped its adoration. (Luke 19:40.) Even inanimate objects have the ability to worship the Lord. "Mountains, and all hills; fruitful trees, and all cedars... Beasts, and all cattle; creeping things, and flying fowl: ... Let them praise the name of the LORD: for his name alone is excellent; his glory is above the earth and heaven" (Psalm 148:9–10, 13). In James it says that the rust of earthly objects shall be called upon to lay testament to ones works on the earth. (James 5:3)

Thus the ability to worship the Creator was not necessarily dependent on having a spirit, but rather all of creation has a built in predisposition to worship the Lord. Since mankind was given a spirit, it allows for a much more intimate relationship with the Creator to be developed. "The spirit of man is the candle of the LORD, searching all the inward parts of the belly"

(Proverbs 20:27). On account of the spirit, mankind is now called the sons of God and can freely walk in the presence of the Lord. (1 John 3:1, Hebrews 4:16.) Therefore, even though early man was able to worship their Creator, it does not mean that they were given a spirit. Adam, on the other hand, was unique and created in the image of God, which allowed him to have a much deeper spiritual relationship with the Lord.

Timing

Adam was the first man and he appeared just prior to these other humanoid species, but when did these events transpire? Of a truth, the Bible does not give any definitive answers concerning the timelines during these earlier eras. Therefore, it is pertinent that dating methods are used to help determine some of these historical timelines. Many of the earliest humanoids are generally identified by the fact that they walked upright, which is considered by the scientific community to be the contributing factor in determining their link to humanity, and this certainly may be the case because bipedalism can really only be linked to humans.

Retrospectively, some of the earlier humanoids were believed to have walked on two legs but their cranial size and appearance was likely more ape-like then that of a man. Therefore, they would potentially more closely resemble an ape-like species and not humanoid. Some dating methods have put these earliest humans on the earth over four million years ago. Others, that are considered more human-like due to their upright stature and cranial features were believed to have populated the earth around 200,000 to 35,000 years ago.

Since Adam was created just prior to the earliest man, then of necessity he would have been on the earth for tens of thousands to potentially millions of years prior to his arrival in the garden. Certainly if the archaeological records are allowed to bear witness and based on a more conservative definition of bipedalism, Adam would have been created in the range of tens of thousands of years to a couple of hundred thousand years ago. Other prior species that have been considered humanoid by some in the scientific community would really then be nothing more than animals.

From a realistic perspective it may seem impossible that Adam was on the earth for anywhere near a length of time that borders on hundreds of thousands of years or greater. After all, all men die even though biblical death was not a part of Adam's creation until He made the choice of partaking of the tree of the knowledge of good and evil after he was moved to the Garden of Eden. Though other humanoids were dying around him, Adam would have been exempt because he was created for a different purpose.

So although, it may be difficult to comprehend that Adam was on the earth for a seemingly massive amount of time, remember that he was walking in the presence of God as witnessed by the time spent with the Lord in the garden. (Genesis 3:8.) Of course, the closer one walks in the presence of the Lord, the slower the perceived time on the earth because time eclipses quickly in the presence of the Lord. Although an extremely long amount of time may have passed in literal earth years, it may have felt like only a couple of hundred years or less to Adam.

Of course, God's original intent for the creation of mankind on the earth was to spend an eternity here. Certainly an eternity spent in the presence of God is the expectation for all believers of the afterlife. Fortunately, after Adam ate from the tree of knowledge, he was stopped by the Lord from eating of the tree of life so that he would not have to spend eternity in a sin-filled body after partaking of the tree of the knowledge of good and evil. (Genesis 3:23–24.) So, in light of eternity, the fact that Adam may have been on earth for tens of thousands to hundreds of thousands of years or more does not seem impossible.

Undoubtedly, eternal life has always been God's expectation, but it was put on hold when sin entered the picture. Therefore, it should not be baffling to think that Adam may have been on the earth for potentially hundreds of thousands of years prior to the establishment of the garden. The endgame then is that the exact timeline for Adam prior to his time in the garden is unknown, but it certainly may have been in the tens of thousands to even hundreds of thousands of years.

Replenishing

And God blessed them, and God said unto them, Be fruitful, and multiply, and replenish the earth, and subdue it: and have dominion over the fish of the sea, and over the fowl of the air, and over every living thing that moveth upon the earth. And God said, Behold, I have given you every herb bearing seed, which is upon the face of all the earth, and every tree, in the which is the fruit of a tree yielding seed; to you it shall be for meat. And to every beast of the earth, and to every fowl of the air, and to every thing that creepeth upon the earth, wherein there is life, I have given every green herb for meat: and it was so. And God saw every thing that he had made, and, behold, it was very good. And the evening and the morning were the sixth day. (Genesis 1:28–31)

So God granted authority and influence over all the earth and its creations to mankind by giving specific instructions for Adam to put it under his dominion. By definition, dominion is the power or right of governing and controlling. It is God telling Adam to have sovereign authority over the earth and all of its creatures. Mankind was put on the earth to survive on the earth's abundance and in order to do so they have to take control of it and manipulate it to do their will.

Unquestionably, the survival of the species is based upon the abundance that the earth produces both plant and animal. Fortunately, the Lord has enabled more than enough provision for all the humans on the planet and so much more. Designing a system so diverse that even the most remote creatures thrive in what would be considered the harshest of conditions. And at the pinnacle of it all, the earth's plenty is man, who is called to be its supreme ruler. In recent times the line on humanity's authority has become somewhat grayed, but the Bible is clear that the earth was designed to serve mankind, not the other way around.

In these verses then, it seems apparent that the Lord is instructing humans that they are to eat only seeds, fruits, and herbs and these are to be their meat. For it says, "Behold, I have given you every herb bearing seed, which is upon the face of all the earth, and every tree, in the which is the fruit of a tree yielding seed; to you it shall be for meat" (Genesis 1:29). Then he speaks to the animals, "and to every beast of the earth, and to every fowl of the air, and to every thing that creepeth upon the earth, wherein there is life, I have given every green herb for meat" (Genesis 1:30).

Based on these verses many purport that God originally created men to be vegetarians and that the human body was not designed at that time to process the flesh of animals. He also did the same with animals by telling them that they could only eat green herbs for food. Then later the Lord lifts this restriction for Noah and all future generations and calls for animals to be used as a food source. "Every moving thing that liveth shall be meat for you; even as the green herb have I given you all things" (Genesis 9:3). Speaking this directly to Noah, it does not mention anything about the animals being able to use one another as a source of food.

This argument that humans were not designed to be meat-eaters, stems from the belief that animals were also created to live forever. Subsequently then, the argument is that physical death was also extended to them when sin was introduced into the world by Adam. Again the primary verse that is used to exploit this idea is found in Romans 5:12, where it says that, "by one man sin entered into the world, and death by sin; and so death passed upon all men, for that all have sinned." This premise is then extended to the carnivorous animals, saying that at this same time they must also have been changed to be meat-eaters. But this idea does not coincide with the re-creative events witnessed in Genesis. The whole reason that the earth was recreated was because it was destroyed, as witnessed in Genesis 1:2. Of course, the Lord would never have allowed the earth to be destroyed unless there was sufficient cause necessitating its complete and utter destruction.

The truth is that the earth was already steeped in millions of years of death and destruction that resulted in the events found in Genesis 1:2. Furthermore, although Romans specifically states that death was passed to all men; there is no mention of animals in the text. When the restriction was supposedly lifted in Genesis nine, there is no mention that the members of the animal kingdom could then become carnivores. If it was lifted for Adam at that point in history, then when were the carnivorous animals allowed to eat meat?

Of course, the answer is ambiguous since death was still in the earth and it will continue to be until it is destroyed. (1 Corinthians 15:26.) It was the reason that creation was limited to the word good and not perfect. The animals, being made after a previously carnivorous mold, were already under the laws of the earth and death was in the earth. Therefore, on the day of the re-creation of the animals, God created some as carnivorous and some as herbivores.

So too, when God granted dominion over the earth to mankind, that dominion would include the consumption of animal flesh. By definition the word meat found in Genesis 1:29 is a general term used to describe nourishment or food, which would obviously include the flesh of animals. Merriam Webster's Dictionary primary definition calls meat, "food; especially: solid food as distinguished from drink." Secondly it states that it is, "the edible part of something as distinguished from its covering (as a husk or shell)"

Additionally, Genesis 1:29–30 does not say that man cannot eat the flesh of animals; it merely states that fruit and wild plants are one source of food. It does not have to be the only source of nourishment. Certainly then, the meat of animal flesh could be another source of nourishment. Timothy clearly states this truth by saying that, "every creature of God is good, and nothing to be refused, if it be received with thanksgiving" (1 Timothy 4:4).

Interestingly, one of the first things the Lord did just prior to expelling Adam and Eve from the garden was to cover them with animal skins. This incident occurred prior to the Lord's supposed edict that man could eat animals. (Genesis 3:21.) If the Lord used animals as a method of covering, then most certainly humans would have also been using animals as a tool for survival.

Thus from the context established, the fact is that mankind was created to be meat-eaters. Nevertheless, both viewpoints are hotly contested. Indeed, the outcome of the argument is inconsequential to the overall framework here, but it is a rather interesting side note.

The sixth day concludes with direction from the Lord for mankind to take charge over the earth; to subdue it and eat from the bounty that the Lord had provided. The Lord also mentions that Adam is to be fruitful and multiply, which clearly shows that the Lord had a plan for his future.

In the meantime, all the other humanoids fell under the directive to replenish the inhabitants of the earth; alluding to the fact that there were inhabitants of the earth prior to the re-creation. The prefix "re-" dictates that the events are being duplicated or done again. Replenishing cannot take place unless the earth had at some point in the past been "plenished" in the first place. Here again, in the course of the six day creation narrative, the Lord confirms that the destructive events of Genesis 1:2 were necessary to eradicate prior sinful activity in the earth.

When the Lord is finished with this final step in the creation/re-creation He concludes the day by saying, "it was very good." On all the other days of the creation events He merely calls the creation good, but here He added the word very to the text as an additional qualifier on the final creative day. Again proving that since the good can be qualified; it falls short of His standard of perfection. His works could only be classified as good and very good, since the earth was still tainted with past sins.

CHAPTER 11

The Sabbath

The Seventh Day

Thus the heavens and the earth were finished, and all the host of them.
And on the seventh day God ended his work which he had made; and he
rested on the seventh day from all his work which he had made. And God
blessed the seventh day, and sanctified it: because that in it he had rested
from all his work which God created and made. (Genesis 2:1–3)

The earth and everything that had recently been created and made is now
finished and God rests. Ecclesiastes sums up the rest of God as pertaining to
the creation and beyond by saying, "The thing that hath been, it is that which
shall be; and that which is done is that which shall be done: and there is no
new thing under the sun. Is there any thing whereof it may be said, See, this
is new? it hath been already of old time, which was before us" (Ecclesiastes
1:9–10). All of the creating during the previous six days was complete, and
nothing more needs to be done. He has reestablished it and placed man upon
it to subdue it and rule over it; all the natural laws, science and physics are set
in motion. All the physics, mathematics, and chemistry have been established
and do not need to be changed.

In other words, the earth is now governed by the laws which the Lord
established during the re-creation and all of them exist for the benefit of
mankind. By doing so, He is prescribing to His word that seedtime and
harvest, day and night, hot and cold, will continue while the earth remains.

At the end of the sixth day, nothing needed to be added or subtracted; all things were and continue to be on the earth that is necessary for human survival. In the future, He will once again rearrange the physical laws that the earth is established on and design a new heaven and earth based on these new laws, but the earth will remain in its orbit and on its rotational pattern forever. (Genesis 8:22.)

The same thing holds true for animal life. Although there continue to be new species discovered virtually every day, they are still a part of the original creation that took place during the six episodic days of Genesis. From the end of the sixth day and forward God was done creating, and this fact can be confirmed in the declining number of species in the earth. It is a documented fact that animal species are continually becoming extinct and there are no new species springing up to replace them. Praise God, for His creative power that was so massive and diverse that the extinction of a species is hardly a noticeable event in such an enormous biodiversity.

For now, the Lord was finished with His creative activities and it was time to sit back and enjoy His new creation. And the Bible shows that to this day the Lord is still in a state of rest from the creative activities. The fact that the Lord is still resting is found throughout the pages of the Bible.

The Psalmist recalls how the Israelites were chastised for their errant ways and the Lord did not allow them to enter into His rest. "Forty years long was I grieved with this generation, and said, It is a people that do err in their heart, and they have not known my ways: Unto whom I sware in my wrath that they should not enter into my rest." (Psalm 95:10–11) God is still in a state of rest from His creative activities. Paul points out that He calls Christians to enter into His rest. "Let us labour therefore to enter into that rest, lest any man fall after the same example of unbelief" (Hebrews 4:11). He could not invite them into His rest if He was not resting Himself and continuing to rest even unto today.

Rest from the creative activities of the previous six days does not mean that He has stopped working in the earth. Certainly, He was done with His creative activities but He has not turned his back on His creation. Some might say that death and turmoil in the earth would indicate differently, but the Bible says that God still cares for His creation. (Ephesians 2:4) In John

5:17 Jesus said that, "My Father worketh hitherto." He is not done. God didn't recreate the earth with all the plants, animals, and mankind, and then suddenly decide to abandon them. No, God is a loving God who cares for His creation and He responds to the requests of mankind. He is still working in the earth; He is simply not creating anything new in the earth.

His continued work in the earth can be witnessed in His miraculous activities that He performs on a daily basis. His continued power can be witnessed in the smallest things to the greatest. In other words, the light on the first day continues to shine upon the earth; bestowing power, mercy, and unending grace.

Examples of this can be seen everywhere in the earth, for daily He performs miracles in the lives of expectant mothers and the lives who need deliverance and healing when they call upon Him. The mere fact that Jesus came to this earth through the virgin birth shows His continued miraculous power. Once here He confirmed His Word with signs and wonders and upon His death, He conquered the grave. His hand is not diminished because He has not changed. Oh, the miraculous, all-encompassing, powerful hand of God that continually looks "throughout the whole earth, to shew himself strong in the behalf of them whose heart is perfect toward him" (2 Chronicles 16:9). He truly cares for His creation and wants all men to come to the truth. (1 Timothy 2:4.)

The last part of John 5:17 says "And I work." That is Jesus' work. His blood cleanses the sins of all and His body provides the healing touch to many that are desperate. God actively supplied His Son to redeem people from the sin-filled works of the world. He came to the earth and gave His life to work in the lives of all people. "Christ also hath loved us, and hath given himself for us an offering and a sacrifice to God for a sweetsmelling savour" (Ephesians 5:2).

Later in John, Jesus states again, "For I came down from heaven, not to do mine own will, but the will of him that sent me" (John 6:38). By sending His Son in human form, He provided the avenue for humans to enter into his rest. "For he that is entered into his rest, he also hath ceased from his own works, as God did from his" (Hebrews 4:10).

For those that believe this and draw near to Him, He will even forgo the laws of nature to answer their requests. When Joshua was fighting the Amorites, he called upon the Lord to stay the sunlight so the Israelites could finish the battle. (Joshua 10:12–13.) The Lord complied by allowing the sun to stand still for an entire day. In verse 14 it says, "And there was no day like that before it or after it, that the LORD hearkened unto the voice of a man." The Lord will go to great lengths to help those who call upon Him, even to the point of stopping the rotation of the earth. That work continues today through the ministry of the Holy Spirit who is endlessly working in the hearts and lives of individuals in an effort to draw them closer to the Father.

Further proof of the continuing hand of God in the world comes in the verbiage of the seventh day, for it is the only day of the creation account that is not concluded with an evening and a morning. All the other sequential days of creation were ended with the phrase, "And the evening and the morning were the (number of the day)."

For centuries, people have debated as to why this was left out of the text. It is often believed that the reason this was excluded was because the Lord is still "resting" to this day. As it has been seen this is most definitely the case. Without bracketing a day with the phrase day and night, it changes the definition of a "day" set forth in the previous creation days. It now becomes a broader term and it is not restricted to one evening and one morning. Here again showing that the word "day" in the Bible can be a colloquial phrase that is unrestricted by time. Praise the Lord for His continued work in the earth amongst His creation.

Thus, the six days of creation are complete in Genesis 2:4. Genesis 2:5 and on, are all new and sequential events. First though it is necessary to delve into the concluding verse of the creation narrative, which has encased within it several pieces of factual information about the creation narrative and the rest of Genesis.

A Summary of the Re-creation

These are the generations of the heavens and of the earth when they were created, in the day that the LORD God made the earth and the heavens... (Genesis 2:4)

The fourth verse of Genesis two reveals a multitude about the events of the creation week, beginning with the fact that it uses the past tense verbs "were" and "made" to show that both the creating and the making are now finished works, which brings the creation to a close. Second, although punctuation is not a part of the original text, here it is correctly used by inserting a comma and dividing the text into two parts. The first part speaks of the generations of the heavens and earth when God originally created the earth. That is, the earth and heavens that were created at a point in the dateless past.

Then the second half of the verse tells of the day that the Lord God made or recreated the heavens and the earth, at a point in time much later than the original creation. It uses the verb made to confirm that the events that transpired were indeed a reconstruction of the infrastructure of the earth and heavens. Only the added accoutrements of the earth (not the earth itself) were created: plants, animals and mankind. Of course, this once again gives testament to the validity of Genesis 1:1; that the earth was originally created at a date in the distant past, and the rest of the chapter goes on to explain the more recent re-creative events.

Third, it alludes once again to the timing of the creation and the re-creation by using two distinct words to reference the amount of time that transpired. The word day is found in the re-creation part of the verse which has been extensively reviewed in an effort to prove that a day referenced in these passages of Scriptures does not represent one full rotation of the earth in its orbit. Rather, the six days of the re-creation have been noted to be on God's time. That is one earth day for the Lord is actually one thousand years. And since the account of creation was prior to man, it is pertinent to use the Lord as a point of reference for the amount of the time that had transpired.

Here, Genesis 2:4 once again throws a wrench into the strict 24 hours of creation, because it sums up the entire re-creation text by saying that the whole process was essentially completed in one day. "In the day that the

LORD God made the earth and the heavens" showing one final time that the use of the word day can also have a colloquial meaning. In this case it represents a period that covers a broad era or span of time.

How could the entire six day Genesis account be summarized in a single day? The word day in this text quite obviously refers to an era of time. Like saying, "Back in the day, we used to …" A literal translation of the word day here would mean that God created the earth and all the heavens in one day. This would fly in the face of the entire previous chapter, which said that it took the Lord six days to create the earth.

Generations

Genesis 2:4 also introduces a second reference to an amount of time that has passed which is found in the first part of the verse when it uses the term generations. "These are the generations of the heavens and of the earth when they were created". A generation is an amount of time and here it is in reference to the time that has elapsed since the original creation of the earth at a point in the dateless past. Therefore, since it is a specified amount of time, it shows once again that there was a specific point in history that the earth was originally created. It happened "in the beginning" of the generations mentioned here. Biblically speaking, there is no precise definition of a generation. In fact, the definition changes with the author.

In some instances it refers to their life prior to them having children, but in other cases it is their entire lifespan. It is never documented to be less than one year, but in Matthew a generation is used to represent the entire dispensation of mankind on the earth. (Matthew 24:34.) Generally though, throughout the Bible a generation is used to represent some portion of the life of a man. Needless to say, it is difficult to pin down an exact amount of time for a generation in the Bible; except to say that it is an extended amount of time, usually within the life of any one man.

Thus, to try and summarize the entire account of the creation as a generation of time does not correspond to even the loosest of definitions of a generation. The fact is that the text says that multiple generations of time had passed, not just one generation. From a general biblical and human standpoint this would be several generations of a family, generally extended out to grandchildren or possibly great grandchildren.

One thing to note is that this part of the verse is still not written from a human standpoint. These are all the generations that elapsed as a part of His original creation in Genesis 1:1. So this entire period would have to be defined as generations of God's time. Since one day is as a thousand years with the Lord, then it is evident that potential eons of time had eclipsed in the first verse of Bible.

For instance, if one generation represents 120 earth years (this is a number that the Lord gave as a generation of man after the expulsion of Adam and Eve from the garden); then from God's timing, one year of 365 days would be 365,000 years of time. This would then be multiplied by 120, which the Lord designated as one generation of mankind on the earth, for a total of 43,800,000 years. So, one generation of the Lord would be 43,800,000 years in the corresponding years of mankind's timeline. This is assuming that a generation of the Lord represents 120 years.

Of course, it is unknown exactly how long a generation is for the Lord. The early patriarchs lived to be much older than current generations. If one were to use a generation of time of the early vanquishers of the garden, a generation would be even longer. Many of the early patriarchs did not have children until they were 200 years old or older and most of them lived several hundred years. Obviously, the extension of a man's life would definitively increase the amount of time that a generation encompasses if a generation were to be defined within the constructs of a man's life.

There is more, because He states that there were several generations that elapsed during His original creation. He does not expound exactly how many generations passed, but certainly there was more than one and there may have been several hundreds or even untold thousands of generations squeezed into the first verse of Genesis. If these earlier patriarchs life spans were used as a generation for the Lord, which is likely more accurate, than the earlier estimate of 43,800,000 years could be multiplied by a factor of seven conservatively. Thus at least one generation for the Lord would be around 306,600,000 years.

Continuing this thought process backwards in time, it is certainly plausible that the original creation comprised a dozen generations; making the timeline of the original creation more than 3.6 billion years ago. Of course this is just an example based on an extrapolation from Scriptures pertaining to mankind of how long a generation is for the Lord. However a generation is determined in the original creation, it would change the expanse of the time of the early earth. The obvious question then is exactly how long was that?

Unfortunately the Bible does not specify how long or how many generations were included in Genesis one, nor does it say exactly how long mankind has been on the earth. Therefore, it is applicable to use current geological information and scientific methodology in an effort to determine its span. Scientific determination currently estimates that the earth is around 4.5 billion years old, confirming with the Bible that the original creation happened several generations of the Lord's time ago; prior to the creation of mankind.

Authorship

There is one final construct to Genesis 2:4 that will help bring to light some interesting clues concerning its authorship and additional insight into its timeline. It does this by identifying its writers and in turn giving clues to the timeline of the entire book of Genesis. Tradition has it that Moses is attributed with writing the first five books of the Bible. Certainly, the last four books largely fall within the timeline of Moses's life and would have been written by him. But since Moses was not born until after all the events of the book of Genesis occurred it is largely speculation on how he obtained the information for the book of Genesis.

The general consensus is that God gave Moses the information and timeline contained within its pages. After all, he did have several extended encounters with the Lord in various locations. Of course, his most famous encounter was when he obtained the Ten Commandments and was absent from the people for 40 days. (Exodus 24:18.) Additionally, the Bible records many other times that Moses is seen communing in the presence of the Lord, so many believe that that there would have been ample time for God to present to him the accomplishments of his ancestors. Therefore, most scholars agree that at some point during these encounters Moses transcribed the entire book of Genesis.

This, of course, is all speculation, as there is no indication in the Scriptures that Moses is the author of Genesis, but he is attributed with authorship primarily because it is believed that writing was not a skill that people possessed prior to Moses' generation. Outside of a couple of pottery fragments and glyphs, there is little definitive archaeological evidence that written language was used prior to Moses and his generation. Of course, this is only what archaeological findings have unearthed to date. The Bible relays a different story, for it can be seen that written language is a skill that dates all the way back to Adam's generation.

This is known because in ancient Aramaic, when writing a biography about you and your ancestors it began or was concluded with the phrase, "the generations of," an expression that appears 12 times in the book of Genesis. This phrase tells the reader who was the author of the preceding or subsequent passage or section. For instance, in Genesis 6:9, it says, "These are the generations of Noah." meaning that Noah is the author of all the information contained within that section of the Bible from the previous mention of, "the generations of." (Faid, R. W. (1993) *A Scientific Approach To Biblical Mysteries.* Green Forest, AR: New Leaf Press, Inc.)

Then in Genesis 6:10, immediately after Noah recounts his generational line, Shem, Ham, and Japheth are introduced as the authors of the next section which continues until Genesis 10:1. Obviously, they would be the most qualified to recount the stories of them and their father, since they were eyewitnesses and partakers of the events that transpired during Noah's time on the earth. This holds true for all of Genesis. Moses then takes over as the author of the next four books that he experienced.

Thus, in this case of Genesis 2:4, the previous author mentioned was Adam, cited in Genesis 5:1, "this is the book of the generations of Adam," proving that Adam was the author of everything from Genesis 2:5 to Genesis 5:1. Undoubtedly, this was a period of time that he was acutely aware of and able to communicate about because he was alive, an eyewitness, and a main character in the events that transpired.

Hence, each of the twelve authors of Genesis were giving an autobiographical portrait of their time on earth. It is a built in generational break which tells the reader who the author of the passage was throughout that section of the book. In general, Genesis is separated by each one of its major characters or their children, who kept the generational timeline intact. The Bible does not relay stories about the lives of every age, but it does keep an accurate historical family tree intact to pass on to future eras. So, since this is the case for all of Genesis, who then wrote the passage from Genesis 1:1 to Genesis 2:4?

Certainly, Adam was the author of everything from Genesis 2:5 through Genesis 5:1, but he was not present on the earth until after most of the events that transpired in the first chapter of Genesis were completed. Plus, Genesis 2:4 clearly shows that there was a break in the authorship by closing out the re-creation account with the phrase, "these are the generations of the heaven and earth."

Therefore, the first author of Genesis would have to be someone or something that was present during that time frame: an eyewitness. The obvious answer would be God Himself, for who else would be better equipped to portray the events of the creation than the Creator Himself? It is likely then that He simply told Adam, who in turn transcribed it.

Since the Lord freely walked and talked with Adam in the Garden of Eden, there would have been plenty of time for the Lord to tell Adam of the events of the re-creation that happened prior to his recollection. As had been discussed, there were tens of thousands to possibly hundreds of thousands of years that Adam globe-trotted the earth in the presence and protection of the Lord. Of course, for Adam who was directly communing with and walking in the presence of the Lord, it was perceived as a much smaller amount of time.

Although this would seemingly be the most plausible scenario, this does not follow suit with the rest of the generational accounts. Certainly God is the overall author of the entire Bible, but when it comes to the use of the phrase, "these are the generations of," it is always somebody that was a witness to those events. Second Timothy 3:16, says that "all scripture is given by inspiration of God." In other words, the Lord is not directly the author of any section of Scripture but rather He is the one that inspires each biblical author to transcribe His words.

Of course, in the Genesis narrations each author of that section refers to himself in the first person. For example, in Genesis 6:9, Noah concludes his genealogy by referring to himself in the first person as the generation of Noah. The first generational break in Genesis refers to the Lord as the Creator, but not as the author. The text reads, "These are the generations of the heavens and of the earth when they were created" (Genesis 2:4). If this section were to follow suit with the rest of the segmentation of Genesis, than this portion of Scripture would have been written by heaven and earth. Of course, who better to reiterate the re-creative actions that transpired than the earth itself?

Obviously this sounds strange by today's standards, but this is certainly not beyond the realm of the capabilities of God's creation. As it has been seen, the Bible is chock full of descriptions of the earth having a voice. In Romans 8:22, it says that "the whole creation groaneth and travaileth." In Isaiah 55:12, it says that the mountains and the hills shall break forth in singing. Even Jesus tells the rulers of His day that if the people hold their peace in praise toward Him, the stones would have to cry out in worship to Him. (Luke 19:40.) Then again, throughout the creation account, the Lord speaks directly to the earth to heed his commands, in which the earth listens and responds accordingly.

So instead of the Lord speaking, it is obvious that it was the earth itself who wrote the first chapter and Genesis. Certainly then, it would not be a far stretch of the imagination to say that Adam may have transcribed the events dictated to him directly from the earth. Imagine as Adam is contemplating the beauty of the creation in the cool of the afternoon and a nearby hill suddenly speaks up and tells Adam all of the logistics and timing of the re-creation. Or a passing comet erupts into a song about the magnitude of the creation that is perceivable by Adam.

Though it may seem implausible, Adam was already used to having discussions with the Creator Himself in the cool of the garden. It is not a far stretch to say that the earth would also have been in communication with

Adam. Of course, this train of thought only makes sense, since the earth was a witness to its own creation and re-creation. It saw all the majesty of the Lord's right hand at work during its critical redevelopment in preparation for the arrival of man. In praise to the Lord, it described to Adam the events that materialized through God's faithfulness.

Or it may be that Adam was unaware of the many voices of the earth, but one day the Lord opened Adam's ears to perceive what the earth was already saying about its creation in its everyday jobs. For instance, the wind blowing is testament to the goodness of the Lord and is continuing praising Him just by doing what it was designed to do. In order to perceive what was already being said, the Lord allowed Adam to perceive the truth that was already around him and he in turn wrote down what the earth recapped and gave credit to the true author.

Of course, this is not directly documented in the Scripture, but it can be extrapolated from the way the previous authors left their signature at the end of their documentary. (Sidebar: Knowing that the creation account was likely documented by the earth itself, it will most definitely be an incredibly glorious experience to one day read the earth's transcripts of God's creation since its inception. Possibly the earth itself will just respond to all those who inquire about its beginnings or while strolling by a rocky outcropping, it opens up one day and begins to tell of the wondrous glory of God during its awesome original creation.)

The fact is that one author did not write the entire book of Genesis. It was written by several different generations of people, who observed firsthand and wrote down the events that transpired during their lifetime. Giving testament to the truth that each generation spoke about events that happened during their particular generation, explaining only events that happened in the earth while they were alive. In turn, this helps to consummate the fact that the events of Genesis are in chronological sequence according to the individual doing the talking.

In the end, Genesis 2:4 recaps the account of creation, and reveals a multitude of information about both the creation and re-creation of the earth. First, it verifies the authenticity of the previous account and by dividing the creation into two sections which shows that indeed there was an original creation and proves that the earth was recreated. This can be seen by the action words that the text uses (created and made) and by using reference words for the amount of time involved.

It continues its recap by using the colloquial expression of the word day when it says that the entire re-creation of the earth happened in one day. Truly the earth was recreated in six days, but here the Lord also uses the word day to show that a strict definition does not need to be followed when looking at the whole act of re-creation.

It also uses the word generations to show that a specific amount of time had transpired during that original span. From the standpoint of the creation of the heavens and earth, mankind was not present, so any timelines that are depicted would have to be on the Lord's time. Of course, the Bible is not specific as to how long a generation of time is for the Lord, so it is difficult to fully quantify it. Nevertheless, using the fact that one day is as a thousand years for the Lord, it has been estimated that multiple generations for the Lord could potentially be billions of years, which has been substantiated by scientific methodology.

Finally, it introduces the separation of authorship in the creation narrative by using the phrase, "these are the generations of the heaven and the earth." Testifying to the fact that it was the earth that received inspiration from the Lord to speak of its creation and that Adam transcribed it.

Seven days

Another interesting item about the timing of the events of the creation week is that there are seven days. The number seven in the Bible is a significant number for the Lord; it denotes completion and perfection. There are literally dozens of instances of the number seven being used in creation and in nature. There are seven days in a week. There are seven musical notes. Jacob agreed to work seven years for Rachel. (Genesis 29:18.) Joshua marched around Jericho seven times for seven days and then seven priests blew seven rams horns. (Joshua 6:4–5.) Naaman washed seven times in the Jordan River. (2 Kings 5:14.) When Joseph interpreted the Pharaoh's dreams, He predicted seven years of plenty and seven years of famine. (Genesis 41:25–31.) When the seventh angel poured out his vial, a voice from heaven came out of the throne room to say that it is done. (Revelation 16:17.) So it is easy to see that seven is a significant number in the biblical landscape.

From an overall biblical perspective many scholars concur that the seven days of creation are in direct parallel to the seven thousand years of man's time on earth. During the creative narrative of Genesis one, there are six days of creation events with a seventh day of the Lord resting. During mankind's reign on earth, there are six one thousand year time segments followed by a one thousand year period of rest that is often referred to as the millennial reign. They are parallel pieces of time; seven thousand years for creation and seven thousand years for man. In other words, the timing of the creation narrative is a foreshadowing or prophetic telling of the time that mankind is on the earth, which begins at the point that Adam and Eve were ejected from the garden.

Again, everything that happened from Adam's creation through the point of his eviction from the garden was on the Lord's clock, an amount of time that is generally unknown. Most people put Adam's arrival in the garden and his sin so close together that they are virtually indistinguishable. It is as if Adam is placed in the garden and walks over to the tree of the knowledge of good and evil and partakes of it. There is virtually no time lapse or it is no greater than a couple of weeks, maybe a month or two.

Of course, the Bible does not give an exact reference for the amount of time that eclipsed in the garden, but it is likely that the amount of time from Genesis 2:4 until the end of Adam's time in the garden is substantial. During that time, Adam was required to name all the animals, Eve was made, they had to become familiar with one another, and they had to find the tree, etc. So it is likely that he had spent a considerable amount of time there prior to his eviction; several years, possibly hundreds or even thousands. Once he was removed from the garden the timing of mankind's generations on the earth starts because God is no longer in direct control and the sinful nature of man has started a new clock. It was from this point on, that the human dispensation will last an equivalent amount of time as the re-creative narrative.

In order to qualify the timing from the point of Adam's sin on is to simply count the ages of the patriarchies and other events that are expounded in the Bible until Jesus birth plus the years since His death. Detailed extrapolation by various biblical scholars have calculated all the time frames involved in the various passages of the Bible and shown that there was approximately 4,000 years prior to Christ and approximately 2,000 years since Christ. When adding them together, it comes to a total of 6,000 years of time. A direct parallel to the account of creation: God created the earth in six one thousand year periods of time and since then mankind's dispensation on the earth since Adam's partaking of the tree has been approximately a similar amount of time: 6,000 years.

A second way to confirm this is to calculate the amount of time in the dispensation of mankind by looking into the teachings of Jesus. In several cases Jesus's parables give insight into the history of mankind's time on the earth. For instance, when Jesus was called by Mary and Martha to heal Lazarus, the Lord delayed His departure for two days and did not arrive on the scene until Lazarus had already been dead for four days. (John 11.)

His delay was not unintentional, for each day is equivalent to one 1,000 year period of time until Jesus. In other words, the Lord waited four days until His arrival. Four days for the Lord equates to four thousand years on the earth. There are approximately 2,000 years from Adam to Moses and 2,000 years from Moses to Jesus. The later period between Moses and Jesus is referred to as the law, because it is when the law was given by God to Moses and the people were under continual condemnation in an effort to fulfill the law.

So Jesus' waiting for two days is representative of the two thousand years prior to the law from Adam to Moses. Then, His traveling time (working) for two days is representative of two thousand years of death by the law. When Jesus told them to roll away the stone of Lazarus's tomb this is symbolic of putting away the law; the unforgiving stone representing the law. It was time for the age of grace, ushered in by the very man that resurrected Lazarus; which is also foreshadowing of the events that were about to transpire with Jesus' own resurrection from the grave.

The final two thousand year period is illustrated in the parable of the Good Samaritan. (Luke 10:30–36) It is a pertinent picture of Christ and the new age of grace. Most people are familiar with the story. A man is beaten and stripped by robbers and left for dead. Both a priest and a Levite passed by the man and do nothing. The priest is symbolic of the law and the Levite was in charge of the blood sacrifices, showing that neither had any capacity to change the situation.

It took a Samaritan on a journey to pick up the man, treat his wounds, and take him to safety at the local inn. The beaten man is representative of mankind upon the earth and the Samaritan, of course, is representative of Jesus. The important thing to note for this commentary is that the amount of money that the Samaritan gave to the local innkeeper was two pence. A pence in the days of Jesus was equivalent to a day's wage. The Samaritan or Jesus gave the innkeeper two days wages or two days to allow the man to recuperate. Those two days in the Lord's timing are 2,000 years, which parallels the amount of time that the redemptive work of Jesus will be in the earth before He returns again. The Samaritan finished by giving the innkeeper specific instructions that he will return again; a prophetic telling of his own return to the earth at the end of this age.

So there were approximately 4,000 years before Christ and there are approximately 2,000 years since Christ. The final 1,000 years is brought to life in Revelation, where it prophetically speaks about a 1,000 year time frame referred to as the millennial reign or the time that Christ will rule the earth. (Revelation 20:1–6.) From a creative standpoint this is the seventh day or the day of rest.

These events shown in Jesus' parables detail the dispensation of mankind upon the earth. They also parallel exactly the creation events and show that the six days of creation are matched with six one thousand year periods of man upon the earth. Both periods are followed by a time of rest.

It would appear evident that the reason for this parallel is to give humans an inclination into the amount of time that the Lord is going to give to man upon the earth before He comes and sets up a new heaven and earth governed by new rules which He previews in Revelation and other portions of Scripture. In other words, the seventh day is about to begin for mankind and after that the Lord will establish a new set of rules for the earth and the universe. Of course, the Bible says that nobody will know the day or the hour, but it does reveal that mankind's dispensation in the earth is rapidly drawing to a close. (Matthew 24:36.) It also proves, once again, that the creation days of Genesis were indeed six periods of one thousand years each.

CHAPTER 12

Genesis Chapter Two

The Creation Story Continued?

And every plant of the field before it was in the earth, and every herb of the field before it grew: for the LORD God had not caused it to rain upon the earth, and there was not a man to till the ground. But there went up a mist from the earth, and watered the whole face of the ground. And the LORD God formed man of the dust of the ground, and breathed into his nostrils the breath of life; and man became a living soul. (Genesis 2:5–7)

Beginning in verse five of the second chapter of Genesis and continuing through verse twenty-five, the Lord begins to explain man's activity upon the earth. Unabashedly, it is one of the most misunderstood parts of the creation account. Almost all scholars agree that this portion of Scripture is a retelling of the creation of Adam and Eve from Genesis one, but in greater detail.

Since it is a common misconception that Moses was the author of all of Genesis, then this idea really becomes confusing because many of the events in this passage seem to contradict many of the events of the creation described in the first chapter. If Moses was the author of the entire book, why would he recount the events of the creation of man again? Undoubtedly he wouldn't, which again points to the fact that there is indeed a separation of authors after Genesis 2:4. Of course, a separation of authors means that each respective author only spoke of things they witnessed during their life.

Thus, following this train of thought concerning the authorship of this portion of Scripture, the next passage was written and lived by Adam. He was the autobiographer of all the events after Genesis 2:4 until the next author begins in Genesis 5:1 where he is recognized as the true author at the end of the passage where it states, "This is the book of the generations of Adam."

Again, these various authors only write about events that transpired within their day. Here in Genesis 2, Adam would not have used the next few verses to recap the creation narrative; especially since he was likely the one transcribing the earth's rendition of the creation. Which means that everything after Genesis 2:4 are new events that transpired in the life of Adam and on through his generation. This autobiographical chronological journey of various authors continues on through the rest of Genesis and ends with the death of Joseph.

So, although it is apparent that the events that transpire in Genesis chapter two are similar to the events that happen in Genesis one, there are some fundamental differences. These differences expose the fact that Genesis two is not a revised retelling of Genesis one, but rather a continued chronological account of the narrative. Taking a closer look at some of the events of Genesis two will help to further bring this fact to light.

One of the first things that trips people up when deciphering this passage is the lack of rain. "And every plant of the field before it was in the earth, and every herb of the field before it grew: for the LORD God had not caused it to rain upon the earth, and there was not a man to till the ground. But there went up a mist from the earth, and watered the whole face of the ground" (Genesis 2:5–6).

God definitely had already established the hydrological cycle on day two of the re-creation, but here in verse five it clearly says that it had not rained yet. If Genesis two is not a retelling of the creation account, then how is it that here it states that God had not caused it to rain? Obviously, mankind was on the earth at this point and without rain the earth would not be able to produce the abundance of foliage created in Genesis one. Additionally, it seems logically impossible that the Lord would recreate the atmosphere on the second day by dividing the waters and not allow it to rain on the earth.

A second area of contention is the mention of the formation of mankind. "And the LORD God formed man of the dust of the ground, and breathed into his nostrils the breath of life; and man became a living soul" (Genesis 2:7.) In Genesis one it states that he was already created and made. Obviously, this begs the question, "Isn't creating and making Adam the same as forming him?"

Since, God is not the author of confusion, it must be concluded that even though God finished the sixth day with the best salutation of all the days by saying it was very good, there must be more to the story. Adam makes it apparent that indeed God was not finished with His entire plan. So, since the author has changed, the story is continuing to recount the events from Adam's perspective.

Rain

And every plant of the field before it was in the earth, and every herb of the field before it grew: for the LORD God had not caused it to rain upon the earth, and there was not a man to till the ground. But there went up a mist from the earth, and watered the whole face of the ground. (Genesis 2:5–6)

Since the premise is that this is a continuation of creation account, then these events are at a point that is much later than the re-creative events from the previous chapter. The King James makes it seemingly apparent that at this point in history the Lord had not allowed rain to fall upon the earth, which would make it sound like it has not rained for at least the past four thousand years. Of course, both animal and human lives are dependent on the rain for its cleansing and life-giving power in order to survive. The Hebrew verb to rain in this instance is *matar*, which is generally used to describe rain falling to the earth, though it is important to note that matar is not always indicative of rainwater.

For instance, when the Lord was speaking to Moses about the provisions He was going to provide the Israelites in the wilderness He said, "Behold, I will rain (matar) bread from heaven for you", obviously not a rain of water, but still a very physical action of raining bread (Exodus 16:4). Then again in Job, Zophar is speaking with Job and uses rain to describe the wrath of God, "When he is about to fill his belly, God shall cast the fury of his wrath upon him, and shall rain (matar) it upon him while he is eating" (Job 20:23). Here depicting the wrath of God as a rain being sent upon this individual. Not a physical type of rain, but rather a picture of a man that is overtaken with the wrath of God.

Still, in the underlying text, the King James Version and most other translations of Genesis make it apparent that the Lord had withheld physical rain from the earth until after the re-creation. Taking a look at the Young's Literal Translation helps to decipher exactly what is transpiring though, "and no shrub of the field is yet in the earth, and no herb of the field yet sprouteth, for Jehovah God hath not rained upon the earth" (Genesis 2:5 YLT).

The literal translation brings to light the missing piece of the puzzle, because it says that it was Jehovah God that had not rained upon the earth, meaning that it is not a rain caused by God but it is a rain of God. In other words, it is not a rain of water, but a hyperbole for a different type of rain; like His wrath. This type of rain would bring about a distinctly different result. It is a rain that could cause a change in the earth to a greater degree than just water. Of course, the next question is what exactly is this rain from God?

Isaiah 45:8 gives additional insight into another type of rain from God, "Drop, ye heavens, from above, And clouds do cause righteousness to flow, Earth openeth, and they are fruitful, Salvation and righteousness spring up together, I, Jehovah, have prepared it" (Isaiah 45:8 YLT). The word prepared here is the same word that is used by Young's translation in Genesis 1:1, "In the beginning of God's preparing the heavens and the earth--" (Genesis 1:1 YLT).

So combining these two verses brings to light the events of the third passage in Genesis 2:5–6. In the beginning God was preparing the earth to be a place of habitation for His creation. Then in Isaiah He reveals that a part of the preparation came to fruition shortly after the creation of mankind in the earth. It specifically says that there was not only a rain that fell, but there was also some that sprung up from the earth. There was a rain of righteousness, which in turn caused the earth to open up and produce a mist of salvation and righteousness that was fruitful on the earth. In other words, in Genesis 2:5–6 the Lord sent forth a rain of righteous that brought about a change to the earth.

Other versions render a different translation of the misting event by essentially saying that underground aquifers erupted to water the earth. "But streams came up from the earth and watered the whole surface of the ground" (Genesis 2:6 NIV). How is it that physical streams could rise up and water the whole face of the earth? As it has been seen, the hydrological cycle was already in place, which in conjunction with the existing groundwater would have been more than enough water to cause the plants to grow. Again though, looking to Isaiah 45:8 it is obvious that the streams (mist) that arose from the earth were not physical but spiritual because it says that the, "Earth openeth, and they are fruitful, Salvation and righteousness spring up together, I, Jehovah, have prepared it" (Isaiah 45:8 YLT).

God prepared the earth and part of the preparation entailed a flow of righteous from Him, which caused the earth to open up and be fruitful. The rain of Genesis 2:6 is a rain of righteousness that flowed from God to the earth and once that rain struck the earth it mixed with a mist of salvation that brought fruitfulness to the earth.

This glorious powerful redeeming action from the Lord has been seen throughout the creation account. In the beginning, when the Lord originally created (prepared) the heavens and the earth He poured out a portion of His glory on the earth to bring it into existence. God is all powerful, He did not expend the extent of His power on any one portion of creation, but rather there are unlimited resources still available.

Then when He recreated the earth another portion was released. With the re-creation it was determined that it just the mere knowledge of the glory of the Lord in Christ Jesus that sustained the earth for several creation days. Even after all the righteousness and revelation that was released at this point in history, it is only a fragment of his overflowing love and righteousness that He has in store for the earth and man. So, in Genesis two, after the seven days of the re-creation, the Lord releases just a little more righteousness that dropped from the clouds and brought forth another level of abundance in the earth. That rain of righteousness changed the course of human life. Even after all of His creative acts in the earth up to and during that point in history, it is still just a minute fraction of His unending power.

Rain can come in many different forms, but rain that comes from Him is a force that changes the earth in a moment. (Psalm 78:24, Psalm 11:6.) This ever-changing phenomenon of His power is witnessed throughout the Bible, culminating with the rain that fell in Genesis two. There was no need for a physical rain, as it was already happening in the earth. Here, the righteous power of God came down from above and caused an eruption of salvation in the earth, that changed its course. Why? Because He was about to bring about a change in the human condition, that would forever change the course of human history!

Plants of the Field

Delving into the impending changes, the Bible begins by making mention of the earth's vegetation. To wit, there is a significant difference between the re-creation events of day three and the events that are transpiring in Genesis chapter two. On day three it says, "Let the earth bring forth grass, the herb yielding seed, and the fruit tree yielding fruit after his kind, whose seed is in itself" (Genesis 1:11). Obviously, He is bringing forth plants (grass, herb yielding seed, and fruit trees) that provide shelter to wildlife, nutrients for the soil, oxygen for the air, and berries.

The residents of the earth that were created on the sixth day survived on these berries, fruits, and nuts that could picked from a tree or gathered from a shrub. Since they had dominion over all the animals, they also hunted the animals from the fifth and sixth day. Thus, all the people on the earth prior to this point were hunters and gatherers.

One thing to note about the vegetation of the third day is that it does not say anything about the harvestable plants of the field, such as tomatoes, eggplants, carrots, etc. God had not yet caused these crops that are such an integral part of human life today to grow during the re-creation of the earth. These crops were added to the earth in Genesis two when it says, "And every plant of the field before it was in the earth, and every herb of the field before it grew" (Genesis 2:5).

The difference is that herb yielding seed on the third day is separate from herbs of the field. The same thing is true of the plants of the field and fruit trees which are not plants of the field. There were not even seedlings planted as of yet because Genesis 2:5 says that the Lord had not put them in the earth yet. They were placed there after the six days of creation when He transferred Adam to the garden.

Prior to this, early man would have stayed close to water sources where the hunting was good and fruit trees were plentiful, leaving large areas of wilderness uninhabited. There would have been little reason to venture into an area of wilderness that was not supportive of their life. These areas were devoid of nourishing plant life and inhabited by dangerous wild animals.

Again confirming that immediately after the creation of man, they were indeed scavengers for berries, nuts, and herbs and given dominion over all the creatures of the earth to use as food. This was good, but there was more to the Lord's plan that is introduced in the days after the re-creative account of Genesis one. "And the LORD God planted a garden eastward in Eden; and there he put the man whom he had formed" (Genesis 2:8).

He takes Adam and transports him to a new location that He had recently planted for his enjoyment and gives him charge over it. Just prior to his arrival, God caused the earth to spring forth harvestable vegetation. That is why in verse five it says, "and there was not a man to till the ground" (Genesis 2:5). All of the earliest humanoid species were hunters and gatherers including Adam, but the Lord had a special plan for Adam; he became the first farmer.

He was called by God to harvest the newly planted crops of the garden. Job confirms Adam's account of these early days when he says, "To cause it to rain on the earth, where no man is; on the wilderness, wherein there is no man; To satisfy the desolate and waste ground; and to cause the bud of the tender herb to spring forth" (Job 38:26–27). There has been some confusion as to where these verses affix themselves in the history of the earth, but a sequential reading of Genesis solves the issue and completely supports the events that were transpiring in the earth during this period in its history.

In conclusion, this is a short but important verse in the chronological history of the re-creative narrative. The re-creation of the earth was completed in Genesis 2:4, but there was more to the Lord's plan. The earth gets watered with a mist from the Lord, and that mist causes an outbreak of salvation the swept across the whole of the land. When the Lord did this it filled up the wilderness areas that were covering the earth with harvestable vegetation and in the same breath gave the earth its first farmer. Now Adam is set up for the next stage of his life; that is the ability to harvest and replant the plants that were now growing. In order to do this, he would need the cognitive ability to plant and harvest the crops produced.

A New Man

And the LORD God formed man of the dust of the ground, and breathed into his nostrils the breath of life; and man became a living soul. And the LORD God planted a garden eastward in Eden; and there he put the man whom he had formed. (Genesis 2:7–8)

When God originally created and made man, He gave him a spirit, a soul, and a body. The entire infrastructure was there and available. He had knowledge of his Creator, the ability to worship Him, and He was essentially self-sufficient, being able to feed himself and tend to all of his needs.

This was not the final resolve for Adam, because the Bible shows that the Lord deemed it necessary to perform two final steps that separated him from his counterparts. Shortly after his arrival in the garden, the Lord took Adam and transformed Him into the human species that walks the earth today. By doing so, He changed his appearance and his mental capacity.

This is known because in verse seven it says that the Lord formed the man. Of course, in Genesis one the Lord is seen creating and making man in the image of God. He was a new creation. Here, the verb formed is a new entry in the descriptive verbs category that has been encountered in the creation narrative.

It is evident from the use of this new verb that something additional is happening at this point. He is evidently fine tuning and changing the shape of Adam into something that is more recognizable now. The Hebrew word for form is *yatsar*, which means to mold or squeeze into shape like a potter. When translated into English there are several other descriptive words that are used to display its meaning; such as, fashioning, framing, and pottering. (Isaiah 44:12, Isaiah 29:16, Jeremiah 18:2–4.)

It also has a built in assumption of destiny and predestination. "And now, saith the LORD that formed me from the womb to be his servant, to bring Jacob again to him, Though Israel be not gathered, yet shall I be glorious in the eyes of the LORD, and my God shall be my strength" (Isaiah 49:5). Here, Isaiah had the revelation that he was formed from the womb for a special purpose.

The same is true for all of humanity and it began with Adam when the Lord changed his shape. He squeezed him into a new mold, one that gave him an appearance that is recognizable today. His original appearance was probably more the look of a Neanderthal or one of the other early human-like life forms that appear in the geological record. Of course, Adam was one-of-a-kind and his exact features at that time may never be known, but it is certainly within the realm of possibility that he had characteristics similar to the many other humanoid species that roamed the earth.

Undoubtedly, Adam was the first to be created, but just after Adam's original creation, the Bible shows that there were other created beings that also walked the earth. Therefore, it is certainly likely that Adam looked similar to the other humanoids that walked the earth when the Lord originally created him. In order to distance him from the others the Lord deemed it necessary to change him. Part of that change was a physical manipulation of the way that he looked.

Archaeological finds have uncovered the fact that early man was considerably different in appearance than present day mankind. One particularly noticeable feature was the shape of the cranium. For instance, the Neanderthal cranium was much more elongated and pointed and their faces protruded much more definitively. Certainly, by today's standards these early humans would have been strange looking.

Science once attributed changes in skull size to climate adaptation. Without question there have been significant climate changes even in recent millenniums, so the theory was that their bodies adapted to colder weather to protect themselves. Now the thought process has changed and the scientific community calls this change in cranial structure "genetic drift"; meaning that the change was completely random.

The truth is that Adam was a creation of God that probably looked very similar to the other species on the day of creation. The difference is that the Lord had predestined him for something else. He was then separated out and formed into modern man. Not as a gradual change but rather, he changed in a moment of time by the hand of God into today's more modern recognizable shape. Certainly, it is much more plausible to believe that a loving Creator established the standard of beauty when He formed man just prior to moving him to the Garden of Eden than it is to believe that random genetic mishaps changed an entire species.

The Lord also performed this same type of manipulation to many of the animal species that were on the earth at this time. The animals of the post-re-creation / pre-formation of man were significantly larger in stature than their current predecessors. The same forming that the Lord conducted on Adam happened to the animals shortly after Adam was singled out and placed in the garden. "And out of the ground the LORD God formed every beast of the field, and every fowl of the air" (Genesis 2:19). They too were formed to be more compatible with the changes that the Lord made to Adam during this time frame. It was not all created creatures, but only the beasts of the field and the birds of the air.

Additionally, there was one final ingredient that was required beyond changing the physical shape of Adam to convert him into modern man. It was the one task that truly distanced Adam from his early counterparts that walked the earth. That is, He breathed into his nostrils the breath of life. Without a doubt it is the one qualifying act of God that definitively changed Adam, for the Bible says that it was at that point that Adam became a living soul.

A Living Soul

Of course, all creation requires air to breathe and by the breath of the Lord the infrastructure of the earth changed. David says that a blast from His nostrils splits the seas and reveals the foundations of the world. (2 Samuel 22:16.) Certainly it is by the words of His mouth and the breath in His lungs that He created the heavens and all their hosts. (Psalm 33:6.) In this same respect, His breath gives life and breath to all humanity; making it apparent that without the breath of the Lord upon the earth, all flesh would undoubtedly perish. (Acts 17:25.)

Evidently then, a blast from His nostrils that is pointed in the right direction is a powerful force that brings change to the earth and humanity; which is exactly what happened when the Lord breathed into the nostrils of Adam. Something changed. It brought life to Adam's soul though his spirit and he became a physical living soul connected to a spirit; a new creature that was now set apart from the rest of the creation; implying that prior to this point, there were pieces of Adam's psyche that were missing. When the Lord's Spirit or righteousness is poured out upon the flesh of men, life springs forth. That is, revelatory life-changing light came and filled up the soul of Adam. It connected all the pieces (spirit, soul, and body) and elevated his level of functioning.

Without question, there are levels to the modern human psyche that sets humanity apart from all other creatures on the earth. Humans are emotionally and spiritually deep, they believe in the sanctity of life and have an embedded moral compass that guides them through life. Contrarily, there is evidence that most of the early humanoid species were very primitive and lacked much of the higher level cognitive and emotional maturity we see in modern man today. They were unable to function on the emotional and spiritual level that modern mankind functions on. They were almost more animal-like in their demeanor.

Adam was somewhat unique, God had definitely given him a spirit, a soul, and a body and he was the one chosen to bring all the pieces together by receiving the breath of life. Some insight on this can be garnered from the first chapter of John. In verses one through five, it deals with the creation, but specifically verse four talks about the creation of man. It says that, "In him was life; and the life was the light of men."

God gave Adam a new level of life when He breathed into his nostrils. That life was from Jesus and it enlightened Adam's spirit. Just as God is Light and God is a Spirit, God gave man that same spirit, and initiated it in Adam by breathing life into him. It connected all the pieces of the creation and brought revelatory light to his soul. As has been discussed previously, there are multitudes of light sources flowing from the Creator. Here, the Lord institutes a new level of light to Adam's spirit that rearranged his being and changed the whole course of humanity.

John 1:4 corresponds with Genesis 2:7, because once He dispensed light or revelatory knowledge to man's spirit, it overflowed to his soul, causing him to have a desire to further seek and understand the things of God and his surroundings. Of all the creatures and creations only man has this ability, and it is brought about by God's gift of a spirit to man and His awakening of it after he was moved to the garden.

Verse nine of John chapter one further proves this when it says, "That was the true Light, which lighteth every man that cometh into the world." This life changing light came through man's spirit by God's Spirit and enlightens the whole person. That light is wisdom, revelation, knowledge, and physical life. Not only does the Lord's breath give physical life, but it also gives revelation light. When the Lord breathed into Adam's nostrils, a darkened unknowing soul was awakened to revelation and understanding. Adam's soul, his intellect, will, and emotions began to interact with his spirit and in turn his body.

Proverbs shows that there are three levels of intellect: the first is knowledge or a general understanding of surrounding situation. (Proverbs 2:3.) Most likely the earliest humans were thriving in this state. Although they had a simple knowledge of their surroundings, they lacked the cognitive understanding to change it. They could gather information, but they did not have the understanding or ability to better their status or situation in life. They were not able to apply particulars of various experiences to change their situation. Understanding that they were hungry, they took animal-like action to satiate their hunger, but they did not have the intellectual capacity to rise above their primitive state of hunting and gathering.

The second level of intellect is understanding, which is a deeper comprehension of the knowledge accumulated. (Proverbs 9:10.) It is the ability to gather knowledge and convert it to a conclusion. When the Lord breathed into the nostrils of Adam, immediately his eyes were opened and he was lifted out of the primitive quagmire that he was in and was given the capacity to better understand the world around him and interact with it and his Creator. The breath of the Almighty gave him understanding and an increased capacity to manipulate his surroundings and change his economic status. Of course, Genesis relays it the best by saying that he became a living soul.

In the garden, once the breath of life inflated Adam's lungs, he was immediately given a choice between right and wrong. It allowed him the ability to decipher between good and evil and to understand the consequences of his actions. That is why after he sinned, he immediately went and hid himself from the Lord. He understood the cost of his disobedience. (Genesis 3:10.)

The third category of human intellect is wisdom. Wisdom is one step beyond understanding and of course, God is the source of all wisdom for He is the God of wisdom. (Proverbs 2:6.) It is not only comprehending the why, but also the how. It is communicated by God through the human spirit and allows humans to gain deeper insight into this life and beyond. This level of insight is garnered from His word, for it is only through His word that light is brought forth and imparted by the Lord as one draws closer to Him. (Psalm 119:130.) Solomon understood this and directly asked God for it. (2 Chronicles 1:10.)

The Bible shows that this same wise privilege is available to all believers who ask for it. (James 1:5.) Access to this was accomplished by the gift of Jesus that was given to mankind in John 20:22. Jesus had already ascended to heaven after His death and then He appeared to His disciples and breathed on them, saying, "Receive ye the Holy Ghost." It is the same Holy Ghost that can now be in direct communication with the human spirit by accepting Jesus as savior. Once He is allowed to come into a person, a new level of revelatory knowledge is released, giving individuals the ability to tap into a deeper level of their Creator, which comes through His word. Adam was originally in that position and now all of humanity has the ability to experience that level of intimate communion with God that Adam had in the garden.

Adam and Eve were in the garden and already in communion with the Lord when they received the breath of life which opened their eyes to a deeper level of communication with the Lord. Unfortunately their sin severed the level of flow that they were receiving from the Lord before others were introduced to it. Once sin entered in, that communion was lost. Imagine as they freely walked with the Lord in the garden. But after their disobedience, mankind was forced to gather revelation only through His written words because the direct connection with the spirit was lost.

This changed again with the resurrection of Jesus. Now all of mankind has the ability to receive unlimited wisdom directly communicated from God, both through His written words and with a direct tie to His spirit. This is further confirmed in 1 Corinthians 15:45 where it is written that, "The first man Adam was made a living soul; the last Adam was made a quickening (living or made alive) spirit." When God breathed on Adam in Genesis, his soul (mind) was made alive, and then when Jesus breathed on the disciples their spirits were awakened with revelation. In the Old Testament this privilege was reserved for the Lord's select few. Now in the New Testament, all of humanity can call upon His name and receive this same quickening of the human spirit.

Through Jesus all things physical were made and He is the deliverer of the very breath of God. (John 1:3–4.) Jesus spoke out the words of God and His words are the very mind (Spirit) of the Almighty. "It is the spirit that quickeneth; the flesh profiteth nothing: the words that I speak unto you, they are spirit, and they are life" (John 6:63).

Just prior to the re-creation, the Spirit is seen hovering over the watery earth in anticipation of the upcoming events. The very next thing that the Scripture says is, "And God said..." In other words, the breath from His mouth restarted the creative process. His breath (voice/Jesus), combined with His intellect (Spirit) caused the creative process and restored the earth. It is this same combination of spirit and breath that activates the souls of mankind and brings understanding and wisdom.

By the breath of the Lord all things are possible, and without His breath life on the planet is quite different. Job understood this when he said "the breath of the Almighty hath given me life" (Job 33:4). He also discerned that it was the Lord's breath that gave him so much more when he said, "But there is a spirit in man: and the inspiration of the Almighty giveth them understanding" (Job 32:8). It is the breath of the Lord that gives understanding to man's soul; if it is taken away then all flesh would perish. "If he set his heart upon man, if he gather unto himself his spirit and his breath; All flesh shall perish together, and man shall turn again unto dust" (Job 34:14–15).

In the garden, God separated Adam by forming him and breathing into his body the breath of life. That breath brought life to Adam's soul, enlightening his understanding of his surroundings. He began to flourish in all ways, far outpacing his previous counterparts in all aspects of life and ability. This incrementally increased academic ability brought about by the breath of God caused him to walk on a cognitive level that was more compatible with his Creator.

Obviously, he was already walking in close communion with the Lord, which allowed him to survive so long on the earth, but this was changed to a further degree when the Bible says that he became a living soul. Allowing him closer communion with the Lord, he is later witnessed walking with the Son of God in the cool of the day. Ultimately, sin broke up that most intimate fellowship that was brought about by the breath of God, but Jesus' sacrifice allowed it to return. The created is now once again able to interact with the Creator on a greater spiritual level, which can only come from His Word and be administered by His Spirit.

CHAPTER 13

The Garden of Eden

The Garden

And the LORD God planted a garden eastward in Eden; and there he put the man whom he had formed. And out of the ground made the LORD God to grow every tree that is pleasant to the sight, and good for food; the tree of life also in the midst of the garden, and the tree of knowledge of good and evil. (Genesis 2:8–9)

So the Lord took Adam and moved him to an area on the east-side of a region called Eden. There He planted a garden and called Adam to be the gardener, thus transforming him into the first of the human race that covers the earth today. Verse nine confirms the continued manifestations of God's power in the earth after the re-creation when it says that out of the ground He caused every tree that is pleasant to the sight and good for food to grow.

Eden is defined in Hebrew as pleasure or delight. Certainly, there is every indication in the Scripture that the garden was a place of delight for the Lord. It must have been a great source of pleasure for Him to revel in the coolness and tranquility of the newly recreated splendor of the garden. It had everything that Adam could desire, and without the curse, it was literally heaven on the earth.

One question that has befuddled many over the past millennium is where is the exact geographical location of the garden? People from all over the world have spent years attempting to detail the exact location of the garden by using mathematics, archeology, historical records, and various theories.

During the past century in particular, many have spent tireless hours in an effort to pinpoint its location, largely due to better cartography and enhanced technological advances such as satellite imagery. It would seem to be fairly easy to discover compared to other ancient sites, because the Bible is relatively detailed in its description of its actual location.

> And a river went out of Eden to water the garden; and from thence it was parted, and became into four heads. The name of the first is Pison: that is it which compasseth the whole land of Havilah, where there is gold; And the gold of that land is good: there is bdellium and the onyx stone. And the name of the second river is Gihon: the same is it that compasseth the whole land of Ethiopia. And the name of the third river is Hiddekel: that is it which goeth toward the east of Assyria. And the fourth river is Euphrates. (Genesis 2:10–14)

With such detailed explanation concerning a river that branches into four heads, it should be relatively easy to find given the detailed charting methods of today. This is especially true when the names of two of these rivers are still in existence today. However, this is not the case as each biblical student that has attempted to pinpoint the garden will give a detailed interpretation as to why it is located in their particular backyard.

The truth of the matter is that no matter how well-intentioned the garden seekers have been they have all come up short in pinpointing its location. This is partly due to the fact that many of the names mentioned in Genesis are not those of currently named geographical areas. Also, although these individuals accurately use part of the Scriptures to narrow down its location, their endgame is that their proposed location contradicts other parts of the Scripture.

Therefore it is relatively easy to abolish their theories, continuing to leave the exact location of Eden a mystery. By and large, most scholars are convinced that the Garden of Eden was located somewhere in the vicinity of the Middle East because some of the names are still in use today.

Seven different proper names are mentioned in the description of Eden: four rivers and three regions. The three regions mentioned are Havilah, Ethiopia, and Assyria. Although nobody has been able to pin down an exact location, these regions have by and large been narrowed down to one area of the planet. As a general reference, Havilah is believed to be somewhere near the Caspian Sea. Ethiopia is generally confirmed to be in the same geographical location as its current day location. And Assyria is defined again and again as modern day Iran and Iraq. These all are large areas and widely separated from one another by a great span of distance.

If the east side of Eden was to begin somewhere near current day Israel it can be seen that the Garden of Eden was a massive piece of land encompassing nearly twelve of the modern day countries, generally referred to as the Middle East today. It is apparent that God's intention and blessing on Adam was not small.

Remember, this is merely a description of the physical location of a portion of the area called Eden, not all of Eden. The Bible is definitive in saying that the garden was planted in the eastward section of a region called Eden. That is, God had already designated an entire area on the earth named Eden and the garden occupied only a portion of it on its eastern side.

If the garden was as geographically large as most scholars believed it to have been, then the whole of the region of Eden would have been at least four times as large and probably larger. Since the garden was located on the east side of Eden, the area that it could occupy would be no more than one quarter of the entire area of Eden. The Bibles depiction makes it seem that the garden was only a part of the eastern side of Eden.

Let us say that the garden encompassed one half of the eastern region of Eden. Then it would be one eighth of the entire district of Eden, again proving that the entire region of Eden was enormous. If the garden occupied much of the Middle East, then the entire area of Eden would have been quite large, spreading out into portions of Europe, Africa, and possibly beyond (more on this later).

To help pin down the exact area of the garden the Bible mentions four rivers: Pison, Gihon, Hiddekel (Tigris), and Euphrates. This is where it gets tricky, because only two of these names are currently in existence today and they do not seem to be the same river, but merely named the same: the Tigris and Euphrates. Additionally, there is no place on the current map where a river splits into four heads or that four rivers converge to form one larger river.

In reality, only some of the locations mentioned in Genesis two exist today and most of those areas correlation to Biblical references are questionable. If there is an equivalent name it does not seem to match what the Bible is saying about the surrounding regions. So why does the Bible even mention a location for the garden and why has it never been pinpointed?

Since these earliest of passages were written by eyewitnesses of the events, then it is correct to say that events in the earth have since transpired to cause a change in the disposition and topography of the region. Without a doubt, it can be said that the physical geography of the earth can change in a relatively short span of time. Geological records have shown that supple, lush areas of the landscape are now covered in deserts and deserted wastelands are now lush and prosperous forests, even within the span of a few thousand years.

Undoubtedly, natural events and earth cycles can cause changes to the earth's climate in mere years. Earthquakes, volcanoes, and hurricanes are a few of the events that can disrupt the weather and topography across various regions of the earth. So it is not difficult to reconcile the stark difference between a flourishing, fertile garden versus what is now largely a desert, known as the Middle East.

Albeit, changes in the weather and natural disasters still do not explain what happened to the rivers. For rivers are not easily redirected. Even if they were, it is likely that remnants of their existence would have been discovered. Even using modern technology and satellite imagery has yet to uncover anything remotely close to the descriptions of the named regions of the Garden of Eden. Thus, it can be concluded that climate changes and cataclysmic events of the earth could be one of the reasons why the location of the garden can be difficult to ascertain.

Other considerations that should not be overlooked when trying to determine its location are the catastrophic events that transpired during the days of Noah. Of course, that event involved a flood that encompassed the globe. Certainly it is probable that when Noah and his family left the ark, they were unaware of their exact location. In all likelihood, he and his offspring would have begun to name regions and landmarks with different names than those the Lord had given them prior to Adam; thus changing the names of the regions that the former inhabitant of the earth had previously named. Though there may be some truth to this theory, the Bible gives the impression that Noah did not stray too far from his launching point because it says that he landed on an apparently familiar landmark called the mountains of Ararat. (Genesis 8:4.)

Another aspect to consider is that with a flood on the magnitude of what occurred during Noah's days its destructive force may have completely rearranged the entire topographical landscape. Certainly, it would have destroyed the foliage of the earth, but would it have resulted in enough changes to deter the course of rivers? Again, the Bible says that a river went out of the garden and split into four heads and essentially occupied the four corners of the garden. Although there are several theorists that proclaim that an earth-wide flood would completely change the landscape; it is likely that when the floodwaters receded most of the remaining runoff would return to its preexisting location.

Certainly sentiment and silt would have caused some filling in of the rivers; however elevations and topography would not have changed, which means once the floodwaters receded, the collection of waters and streams after the flood would most likely be located in the same location. The waters would have re-dredged the rivers and caused them to flow in the same direction. Thus, it is unlikely that a global flood would have caused a change in the location of four major rivers. There is one final event that took place that is detailed in the annals of the Bible that likely would have changed the course of a river. An analysis of the actual event that transpired will be looked at in detail in chapter nineteen.

Notwithstanding the rivers of Eden, the end result of the garden itself can be found in Ezekiel 31:18. "Yet shalt thou be brought down with the trees of Eden unto the nether parts of the earth". Here it is made clear that the once lush garden was engulfed by the earth itself. The Bible shows that it was an event that happened long before the days of Noah. Once Adam was evicted from the garden a curse was placed on the earth by the Lord. (Genesis 3:17–19.) Thorns and thistles were brought forth and choked out the beauty of the garden. The easy, pleasurable life of Adam became work and trouble when he was removed. A curse on the very land that he gardened and occupied would have had devastating effects. The opposite of a fertile garden is a harsh, dry desert landscape, and that is exactly what much of the Middle East looks like today.

A curse overtook the earth and the beautiful trees and lush landscape quickly became desolate and barren. A second confirmation of this fate is found in Isaiah 51:3, "For the LORD shall comfort Zion: he will comfort all her waste places; and he will make her wilderness like Eden, and her desert like the garden of the LORD." A curse is a serious thing in the Bible and here it destroyed the lush garden of Eden and turned it into a desert wasteland. Ezekiel said that the earth swallowed up Eden and Isaiah reveals that in its place was left a desert wasteland.

In fact, research has confirmed that many of the arid places of the Middle East were once a lush and prosperous garden-like area in recent millennia. Archaeological digs have unearthed that from approximately 10,500 to 5,300 years ago, portions of the Sahara were once a tropical savanna. Of course, this would be part of the area that is generally believed to be the Garden of Eden. Thus, modern-day research concurs with the biblical timeline that the proposed area of the garden was once lush and green and now is covered with sand.

Garden Life

And the LORD God commanded the man, saying, Of every tree of the garden thou mayest freely eat: But of the tree of the knowledge of good and evil, thou shalt not eat of it: for in the day that thou eatest thereof thou shalt surely die. And the LORD God said, It is not good that the man should be alone; I will make him an help meet for him. And out of the ground the LORD God formed every beast of the field, and every fowl of the air; and brought them unto Adam to see what he would call them: and whatsoever Adam called every living creature, that was the name thereof. And

Adam gave names to all cattle, and to the fowl of the air, and to every beast of the field; but for Adam there was not found an help meet for him. (Genesis 2:16–20)

The story continues, with the Lord telling Adam that in the day that he eats of the tree of the knowledge of good and evil, he will surely die. True to his word, Adam did indeed physically die within the day that he ate of the tree. Of course, when that was spoken forth the dialogue was still on the Lord's timeline. Thus, that day was one day for the Lord or one thousand revolutions of the earth around the sun. In earth years, Adam died at the age of 930, beginning when he partook of the tree, well within the biblical constraints.

Until that point, his life span had essentially not been recorded; from God's point of view it was merely moments. While it is true he would not have been an eternal being until he ate of the tree of life; it is also true that he would not have been able to die until he ate of the tree of the knowledge of good and evil. Therefore, the years of his life began once he ate of the tree of knowledge and was evicted from the garden.

Since Adam was told not to eat of the tree of the knowledge of good and evil, but that he could freely eat of the tree of life, he was given a choice: eat or don't eat of the tree of life and/or eat or don't of the tree of the knowledge of good and evil. Adam choose the later and was blocked from eating of the tree of life until God could rectify the course that Adam had initially pursued by eating of the tree of the knowledge of good and evil. God always gives a choice.

The giving of a choice is the defining moment in the relationship between God and mankind and it was initially brought about with the breath of life. Mankind now had the ability to make decisions that could change their future. This is seen in Deuteronomy 30:19 where God beseeches mankind to choose life over death, to choose the blessing over the curse, choose to accept Him or reject Him.

It is the choice that He gave Adam in the garden and that same choice is provided today under the new covenant of the shed blood of Jesus. Now, any person can choose to believe in a risen Savior, or they can choose to reject God and suffer eternal death. (Matthew 25:46.) Life is always God's best. He didn't create this expansive universe only to kill it off. Instead He created it to live and to live abundantly. (John 10:10.) God is the giver and sustainer of life, He is not the destroyer. Undoubtedly due to sin, all men are now appointed to die, but upon His death the Lord provided a way to life eternal. Praise Jesus.

The narrative of the garden continues with the Lord taking all the beasts of the field and bringing them to Adam to be named. "And out of the ground the LORD God formed every beast of the field, and every fowl of the air; and brought them unto Adam to see what he would call them" (Genesis 2:19). There are three categories of species mentioned here: the beast of the field, the fowls of the air, and cattle. These animals are not dinosaurs; these are the animals that occupied the earth following the re-creation and were formed into their current shape along with Adam. Just as the Lord formed Adam, He also used the elements of the earth to form the fowls of the air and the beasts of the field.

The birds were originally created on day four and are now formed to be more compatible with Adam's new form. The same is true for the animals, although in Genesis one they were called the beasts of the earth; here they are called the beasts of the field. This, of course, is a reclassification that came about on account of designating the garden as the field and placing Adam in it to farm. It is evident that He is molding those animals He deems as the animals of the field into something more compatible to humanity's size.

A few of the land-based animals that most people are aware of that roamed the earth while early man was here are Saber-tooth Tigers, Wooly Mammoths, Wooly Rhinoceros, Megaceras (deer-like), Mastodons (elephant-like), Auroch (cow-like), and Prehistoric Bears. Though there may be thousands more, these are some of the more well-known because of their size and predominance in the paleontological record.

All of these species were considerably larger than their modern day counterparts. The Bible is clear that God restructured these animals in the days of the Garden of Eden and formed them into the animals that populate the earth today. The original animals of Genesis one did not necessarily become extinct, they were merely changed by God into the animals of today. So although there were climate changes and cataclysmic events that may have caused the extermination of some of these early animals, the Bible shows that ultimately it was a decision by God to change their structure to make them more compatible to the eminent human occupation of the earth.

This portion of Scripture concludes in verse nineteen when all the newly formed animals and cattle are brought before Adam to be named. "And Adam gave names to all cattle, and to the fowl of the air, and to every beast of the field; but for Adam there was not found an help meet for him" (Genesis 2:20). While cataloging all of the earth's species, it is discovered that they all had mates. Unfortunately for Adam, he was unlike all the other creatures of the earth and did not have a female counterpart. So the Lord took action and gave Adam a wife.

Eve

And the LORD God caused a deep sleep to fall upon Adam, and he slept: and he took one of his ribs, and closed up the flesh instead thereof; And the rib, which the LORD God had taken from man, made he a woman, and brought her unto the man. And Adam said, This is now bone of my bones, and flesh of my flesh: she shall be called Woman, because she was taken out of Man. Therefore shall a man leave his father and his mother, and shall cleave unto his wife: and they shall be one flesh. And they were both naked, the man and his wife, and were not ashamed. (Genesis 2:21–25)

After being pulled from Adam's ribs and designed by God, Adam awakes and discovers Eve, and then he makes the proclamation that she was bone of his bone and flesh of his flesh. She truly is a part of Adam; she was half of Adam's whole being. That is why immediately after the separation, the Lord begins the covenant of marriage by declaring that the two shall cleave to one another and become one flesh. Thus, Eve was brought to life from the very bone of Adam with all the same attributes of his (a spirit and a living soul), which is why the bible says that Adam was the first man and that Eve was the mother of all living, substantiating that all people came from only two individuals. (1 Corinthians 15:45, Genesis 3:20.)

There were no other women for Adam to choose from. Only Eve and her offspring would have received the breath of life. Those without the breath of life would not have been compatible. It is the breath of God that gives life to all of Adam's descendants, and it is God who forms humans in their mother's womb. (Job 33:4, Job 31:15.) Therefore, Eve became the mother of all living by giving birth to her sons and daughters and to each individual afterwards that God has given the breath of life.

Additionally, in order for the various species to propagate, the bible is very specific that it can only happen with like-kind species. When God formed Adam in the garden, he changed his molecular makeup so that he was incompatible with any other creature on the earth. Only someone born of him would be a compatible mate. Of course, that is Eve whom Adam called "bone of my bones, and flesh of my flesh" (Genesis 2:23). In Acts it says that the Lord "hath made of one blood all nations of men for to dwell on all the face of the earth" (Acts 17:26). All people on the earth came from this bloodline, and it was out of this one line of blood that Jesus was born.

"And they were both naked, the man and his wife, and were not ashamed" (Genesis 2:25). Again the Bible is not clear how long Adam was in the garden after Eve was made, it may have been thousands of years or more. But from a chronological perspective, the knowledge of their nakedness did not last for long. Chapter three begins with them being deceived by a serpent into believing that disobedience to God would offer enlightenment. It is the path that they decided to take and once they made the choice to disobey God and eat of the fruit; their eyes were opened to their inadequacy and sinful nature. Unaware of how their lives were going to change once they partook of the tree of the knowledge of good and evil, they blatantly disobeyed the Lord.

"And the serpent said unto the woman, Ye shall not surely die: For God doth know that in the day ye eat thereof, then your eyes shall be opened, and ye shall be as gods, knowing good and evil" (Genesis 3:4–5). How is it that the serpent was knowledgeable about the consequences of partaking in the tree? How did the serpent know that their "eyes would be opened?" And why would he want them to eat of the fruit? The only way that the serpent would have been aware of the consequences of their actions would have been by his own experience in partaking of a similar act. Which is exactly the case and it is why he wanted Adam and Eve to partake.

As most people are aware from the garden account, the serpent represents the devil. Revelation 12:9 says, "And the great dragon was cast out, that old serpent, called the Devil, and Satan." He was in the garden with Adam and Eve and his deception caused them to fall from the grace of God. Since he is the one perpetrating the fraud, it is undeniable that he understood the cost of their actions; for he said to Eve that she would not die but rather that her eyes would be opened, and that they would be as gods, knowing good and evil. (Genesis 3:4–5.)

So from when and where did Satan come? It is obvious that he has been around much longer than all of humanity and he is familiar with the consequences of disobedience to the Lord. Determining where he came from and why he wants to deceive humanity requires a look back into the earth's history prior to the re-creation of the earth. From here the back story of Satan can begin to be unwound; which in turn will also unravel the mystery of what happened to the earth necessitating its recreation. In that regard it is relevant to first recap the entire time frame of the earth's existence.

Timeline

So far, several of the events of creation have been described including the original creation, the destruction, and the re-creation. The exact beginning and length of each of these periods is generally unidentified, but certain Scriptures and geological records help to prove that it has been a substantial period of time. The fact is the original creative event of the earth happened at an unknown time frame in the distant past. Its exact moment of origin may never be known in this dispensation, except to say that there was an exact point of origin.

From the biblical standpoint, little is known about the timing of the events of the earth before the reconstruction, except to say that the earth was under the timing of the Lord; that is, one thousand years is as a day. Without knowing how long a generation is for the Lord and how many generations passed in the earth prior to man, it is impossible to determine an exact span of time. Therefore it is pertinent to use the evidence produced by the earth to help discover its age. Thus the current scientific methods put the earth somewhere around 4.5 billion years old.

Earthen records reveal that life was prevalent throughout much of its history. Generally, the first single celled creatures appeared about 3.8 billion years ago. Then, approximately 600 million years ago multicellular animals began to arise. Reptiles appeared around 570 million years ago, which gave rise to the age of the dinosaurs, ending about 65 million years ago. Mankind first appeared around 200,000 years ago (possibly older), with modern man emerging about 10,000 to 12,000 years ago.

In the midst of these various ages came the rise and fall of many species. Generally these various species arose and became extinct in wave-like succession. Geological and paleontological clues left in the earth throughout the ages have been used to develop this timeline which is generally accepted and continues to be reinforced with subsequent findings in the earth's annals.

Certainly, each one of the time frames extracted from the earth's crust fits within the biblical perspective, which means that there were literally billions of years of history in which the earth went through dozens of periods of life and death. This was ultimately concluded with one final destructive event revealed in Genesis 1:2, which destroyed all life on the planet and left the earth in a darkened state.

The earth emerged from this destructive state in Genesis 1:3, with six one thousand year periods of creation in which the Lord brought life back to the planet. This eruption of life culminated with the creation of Adam and early mankind, and although they were all dubbed Adam (man) only one was created first and ultimately emerged from this group with the proper name of Adam. Immediately after the six episodic days of creation/re-creation, the Lord rested. Now in the seventh day, Adam is walking with the Lord and may have done so for an untold amount of time, possibly hundreds of thousands of years or more.

During these ages of time, the closer that Adam walked with the Lord, the more quickly time elapsed. One day in the presence of God is 1,000 earth years. So, even though several hundred thousand years or even several million years seems like an enormous amount of time from the current perspective, it may have only seemed like a couple of hundred years for Adam. At the prescribed moment, the Lord took Adam and placed him in the newly planted garden, approximately 6,000 to 20,000 years ago. He then received the breath of life and he was physically formed into a new more modern recognizable man.

During this same general time reference, God formed or changed the animals of the field and molded them into their current appearances to make them more compatible with Adam and brought them to him to be named. Adam was likely in the garden for untold thousands of years. As it was seen, it was a massive place and it may have taken him a period of years to even encounter the tree of the knowledge of good and evil. There must have been unlimited things to explore and do. Imagine a garden that was not cursed with thorns or thistles; all the while basking in the presence of the very Creator Himself.

Noticing that Adam was by himself, the Lord made a woman to be his companion. Shortly after this the two were deceived into eating of the forbidden tree and were evicted from paradise, which left a curse on mankind and the earth. That curse resulted in death, briers, and toil for humanity and this situation remains in the earth today.

CHAPTER 14

Science and the Bible

Science

The heavens declare the glory of God; and the firmament sheweth his handywork.
(Psalm 19:1)

Albert Einstein once said that, "the significant problems we face cannot be solved at the same level of thinking we were at when we created them." Sometimes the simplicity of creation can get bogged down in the details present in today's understandings. There are multitudes of unknowns concerning the early earth and its development. Unfortunately, in an effort to understand this time in history, the scientific community often fills in the gaps with speculation and theory. Although these opinions of the early earth are generally promulgated as truth, they are largely fabrications based on opinions.

To try to understand how and why God created can only come through the revelation of His word. To make science understand and try to prove God is fruitless, it has to be the other way around. Correct empirical analysis should always begin with the paradigm that God came first. Humans can only empirically judge the world around them, but within the word of God there is access to an unlimited source of wisdom and power; a wisdom and power which shows that human existence is based solely upon what is said in His word.

"In the beginning was the Word, and the Word was with God, and the Word was God" (John 1:1). This is the first piece of the puzzle: to take the word as truth and base all discoveries upon that foundation. With proper analysis it will always show that science correctly aligns with biblical principles, not the other way around. Still, at the end of the day there are always going to be unknowns in the universe because in this time frame, humans will continue to see through a glass darkly. (1 Corinthians 13:12.) In other words, humanity will never understand the full magnitude of His creation in this lifetime.

Of course, this will not stop the scientific community from continuing to broaden their understanding of the creation. Certainly it is awesome to look into the creation and how it works. Unfortunately, the reality of scientific exploration is that it generally does not take the Bible into account when analyzing its surroundings. Therefore, instead of having Christ as the cornerstone of belief, things are now reversed to where science is taken as fact and Scriptures are superimposed over these scientific facts to fit into what is known in the scientific fields of the day.

This approach, of course, has distorted many different passages of Scripture in an attempt to force them to agree with current schools of thought, particularly those passages from Genesis. Those who even attempt to question the latest scientific theory in light of God's word are pigeonholed into a category of using God as a crutch.

This is truly unfortunate, for much of this confusion is brought about by the misconception that the Bible has little to say about the history of the earth. Of course, nothing could be further from the truth. A careful analysis of the Bible reveals much about the earth's history, but this is often disregarded as other ideas have arisen and become adapted into modern culture. Today the one theory that has become generally accepted and expounded upon is evolution.

In general, the main premise of scientific thought is to determine the cause and effect of situations in the universe. It does so through observation and analysis and experimentation of the subject that we are trying to gain an understanding of. If the theory cannot be proved by repeated experimentation that results in a positive outcome, then the theory is discarded.

Evolution is given a caveat to this well-established definition because the scientific community says that the time frames involved are too large to gather the empirical data necessary for proper observation and experimentation. Therefore, it garners a stipulation, "Our theory of evolution has become ... one which cannot be refuted by any possible observation. It is thus 'outside of empirical science,' but not necessarily false. No one can think of ways in which to test it ... (Evolutionary ideas) have become part of an evolutionary dogma accepted by most of us as part of our training." (Paul Ehrich and L.C. Birch, "Evolutionary History and Population Biology," Nature, Vol.214 (1967): p 352) Although this was spoken back in the sixties, it still holds true today. Evolution is accepted because it cannot be disproved. The time frames involved are too great for mankind's limited lifetime of observation.

Hence the scientific community at large has taken the theory of evolution and established it as fact, then later filled in any gaps as more and more ideas and evidence are gathered. Of course, this is exactly the opposite of how scientific proof is usually gathered. Generally, the scientific method states that there must be observable, empirical data that can be evidenced through experimentation, thus forming a testable hypothesis. Once the hypotheses has been tested and not given any negative results, it is only then generally accepted as scientific fact.

Evolution essentially skipped this step and has become rooted in scientific reasoning, claiming that the evidence of evolution is just too overwhelming. Therefore, since it is so obviously a fact, then it must be true and other branches of science have fallen into line and adopted it as the backbone of their particular methodology. Indubitably, there are many holes in the idea, but the populous belief has tenaciously claimed that prolonged exposure to the idea of evolution has therefore proved itself. It cries out to be believed, but it falls short in so many avenues because there are so many unanswered questions.

For example, logic would dictate that massive sudden upstarts of life that are well-documented in the fossil record would most logically point to a benevolent Creator. Yet, logic often gets ignored as several man-made theories have been espoused as to why there was a sudden increase in life. All of them are based on the assumption of evolution, which states that environmental or ecological factors caused a sudden developmental change in the earth at that point. Thus foregoing the necessary timeframes needed for evolution of a species to transpire.

The fact is that any eruption of life in the earth's records speaks of the Creator. There was simply too much diversity of life to be accounted for by an incidental upswing in life on the planet. Coincidentally and similar to the events of Genesis 1:2, just prior to the Cambrian Explosion the sedimentary layers of the earth reveals that there were events in the earth's geological record that can of necessity be called a "holding pattern."

In other words, the geological record reveals that just prior to this upshot of life; there is a line in the sand that divides rocks with fossils from those with no fossils for potentially millions of years. To some these are periods of time in the earth's geological records that are unexplainable, but in reality it is the geological record that proves the Bible. Certainly, points of unconformity in the geological record and the destructive events like the one found in Genesis 1:2 are one in the same or very similar incidents. That is, gaps in the geological record and upshots of life speak of destruction and re-creation; just like the events in the beginning of Genesis.

Of course throughout the history of the earth, gaps and sudden upswings in life are closely linked together and speak to judgment and rebirth. They call out for a Creator who is continually choosing life, but has had His hand forced to pass judgment. Fortunately, each episodic period was never finished as the Lord always initiated a rebirth of life.

Thus, the only logical reason for a sudden upshot of life on the planet would be that God orchestrated it. Any change that can be observed in a species was already programmed into that species when it was created. In this dispensation, the whole of this creation is finished; God is now resting from any more creating. Macroevolution has never been observed in real time, nor will it ever be, because God said that it was finished. (Genesis 2:1–2.)

In fact, endangered species and extinction lists prove that creatures are not evolving but dying off at measurable rates. This is the exact opposite of the premise of evolution which states that populations of organisms gradually change through subsequent generations brought about by genetic mutations and are then enhanced by natural selection. The fact is that deterioration and death of the creation came about by the sin of Adam and the subsequent curse upon the earth. Thereby confirming, once again, that the entire massive eco-structure is a product God created and not a product of it having evolved naturally or even that He evolved it.

A Standstill?

Still, since before the first printing of Charles Darwin's *On the Origin of the Species*, until now, creationists and evolutionists continue to wage a seemingly endless debate in which adherents on each side presents an argument and the opposition points out valid reasons why their position is incorrect. For every argument there is an opposite and essentially equal counter-argument that garnishes the opposition's ideals. Neither team seems to ever make any headway against the other's argument because each side is so staunch in its opinion that under no circumstances will they ever agree with the other. The end result is that the two sides are diametrically opposed and will stay that way in a kind of trench warfare because of their respective strong-willed and preconceived notions.

Both sides contest that the others beliefs are improbable and unrealistic. On the most elemental of suppositions, the evolutionists complain that science doesn't need a God. If He exists, where is He now and how did He come into existence? The creationists retort that something or someone had to create the initial elements when the universe was brought forth. Otherwise, how did the initial elements come into existence? Obviously, neither camp ever sways the other camp into believing its point of view and each always has a response to contradict the ideas espoused by the other; always making the evidence fit into their particular stance.

The truth is that the end game for both suppositions is faith. For the believer, it takes faith to believe in a God, who has not given the answers to all the questions that continue to arise from the creation. It can only be by faith that one would believe in Him and stand on the fact that some things in this life will only be seen through a glass darkly, but at some point in the unknown future much more will be revealed.

For the non-believer, belief in an unknown, unseen God is hard to swallow. It takes faith to believe that some entity outside of our physical control created the universe and placed man upon the planet earth. "I've never seen it, so how can I believe it?" In this same vein, one could say that evolutionary principles are largely unproven. Thus it takes even more faith to believe that the universe and human existence was merely happenstance based on limited empirical evidence.

The bottom line is that more and more in today's society, it is becoming evident that a biblical view of the earth makes sense. Historically and presently the creation model stands up to the test; it is consistent with what is observed in its current surroundings and what is seen from a historical scientific standpoint.

Science fiction writer Ray Bradbury once said that, "We are an impossibility in an impossible universe." From a physical strictly scientific perspective, that statement is correct. The existence of the universe and all of its functionality outside of God is impossible. The intricacies that exist on a galactic level all the way down to the minutest of cells in the human body are immense. Of course, the complexity of it all is only impossible if you are human, because for God nothing is impossible.

In the final years of his life, Albert Einstein attempted to prove an idea that everything in the universe was tied together. The basic premise of his theory was that all forces in the universe are joined together into one simple formula. For example, electromagnetic forces and gravity are intimately linked together and react to one another even though they seem mutually exclusive. That same force exerts a behavior in the universe that all unquantifiable unities and bodies must adhere to, including time and space. He called the link that ties them together the Unified Field Theory.

The Bible hints at the truth of his theory in Job 38:31, "Can you bind the chains of [the cluster of stars called] Pleiades, or loose the cords of [the constellation] Orion" (Job 38:31 Amplified)? What bands and cords is the Bible speaking of? It is apparent that the Bible is trying to convey exactly what Einstein was attempting to prove in the last twenty years of his life. That is, that the universe, with all of its intricate parts are inexplicably bound together; each part being dependent on the other parts and conjoined through light, space, time, gravity, etc.

Of course, Einstein was correct but never came to the ultimate conclusion, which is that the connecting tissue that ties all of the creation together is the Word of God. "By faith we understand the ages to have been prepared by a saying of God, in regard to the things seen not having come out of things appearing" (Hebrews 11:3 YLT). Everything is all tied together by the very Words of the Lord; spoken out at the original creation and at subsequent points in history thereafter. "And he is before all things, and by him all things consist" (Colossians 1:17). The universal link that ties it all together is the very breath of God.

Enormous Complexity

Through those words the whole of the creation has been measured; from the largest of scales even to the smallest. Beginning to admire the creation on a planetary perspective is daunting. Its sheer size cries out for a Creator. God gives a glimpse at the size of the universe by saying that He would multiply Abraham's seed as the sands of the sea shore and as the stars of heaven. (Genesis 22:17.) To the naked eye the sands of the seashore are seemingly more numerous than the stars of the heaven. Yet God infers that the two are equally comparable. How awesome is His creation that there are as many stars in heaven as there are sands on the seashore.

Mankind will never truly know the size of the universe, but from what is able to be seen with the farthest reaching modern telescopes, researchers believe that there are over 100 billion galaxies and within each of these galaxies are about 100 billion stars. Yet the Bible makes it clear that it is even greater than that, because the universe is compared to the individual sands on the seashore. How many grains of sand can be seen while standing on just one shoreline? One hundred billion galaxies may only be scratching the surface. This fact will continue to come to light as telescopes reach deeper and deeper into space and continue to prove the fact that the universe is truly immeasurable.

In this same vein, looking at the creation from an individual planetary scale further reveals the overwhelming complexity of it all. There are thousands of different variables that are necessary for life to exist on planet earth. The delicate balance between life and death is really only a couple of percentage points difference. For instance, the distance, size, and make up of other planetary bodies in the solar system play an integral factor on the probability of life on the planet. If the other planets are too small or too big or if their orbits are not similar, then life becomes impossible.

Similarly, there are dozens of variables about the planet itself that are necessary for life. These include, but are not limited to, its distance to its sun, elemental content, thickness of the crust, speed of rotation, movement on its axis, oxygen levels, ozone protection, expansion rate of the universe, type of galaxy, speed of light, and size of the moon. All of these have to be in precise coordination with each other and even the slightest change would create an environment not conducive to life on the surface of the planet. In other words, the balance between life and non-existence are miniscule.

Stepping this down even further it can be seen that God is the Creator, not only of galaxies and planets, but He also works on the most finite scale. The makeup of any one living cell is incredible, because one single human cell is infinitely more complex than any man-made device ever built. And every human body has over 5 trillion cells which can be broken down into 35 primary groups that comprise the human body. These include cells that make up one's blood, liver, bone, skin, hair, etc. In every living human body, cells are dying, dividing, and replacing at a rate of up to 25 million new cells each second. Blood cells themselves regenerate at a rate of 100 million per minute!

Within each of these cells is an entire world unto itself. A single human cell is the most complex structure known to man, because inside every cell in the human body are 23 pairs of chromosomes, each one containing genes. On each one of these genes hinge the building blocks of life called Deoxyribonucleic Acid or DNA. DNA determines how that particular cell will function and develop, which ultimately dictates each person's traits.

Scientists have finished mapping the DNA of the human body and although this is an astounding feat, it has revealed even greater unknowns about the workings of the human body. That is, science has essentially provided the atlas to the human molecular code, but it has also discovered that this is only the beginning. Now the purpose is to use this information to better understand the inner working of the human body.

The quest is to take this atlas and narrow it down into a road map and finally a regional map for each particular area in the body; a task that has proven to be quite daunting for even the best laboratories given the sheer volume of DNA sequencing in the body. The high points have been marked, but the more specific sequencing has yet to be fully determined.

It has yet to be determined how each strand of DNA interacts with another strand. Experts believe that each strand of DNA has a translation package built into its structure to determine its function. Each cell needs to communicate its function with the other cells so that if it needs to be replaced or rebuilt the others will know. This is disseminated through a subset of the DNA that has been called messenger code, or RNA. Still another sect called t-DNA carries out the functionality of the cell.

Determining how cells communicate with other cells has indeed been a daunting task. All parts of the DNA have to be in perfect sequence to function properly, if any one strand of the DNA is out of order the cell will not perform its intended duty properly.

The point is that within any one cell in the human body, the intricacies of its design are immense and difficult to grasp even on the most basic level. To wit, this is only the beginning because there is evidence to suggest that cells are based on information that is infinitely smaller than the atoms that make up the cells. Even the most powerful of microscopes have been unable to determine the makeup of an electron, but it is conjectured that they do consist of some form of matter that may be less than a sixth of its size.

God truly is a God of big and small. Not only are humans unable to fully explore the expanses of the universe, it is likely that they will never be able to fully see and understand the minutiae of their own bodies.

Purpose

Still, if the sheer enormity and complexity of it all is not enough to sway ones belief in the Creator, there is one final consideration to take into account that evolution is unable to come to terms with, and that is the reasons why life arose on the planet. Why did "the universe" suddenly decide that life was essential and begin to push toward that mark? What desire did a single cell have to overcome all the impossible odds and want to develop into a life? What was its burning desire to want it to change from inorganic to organic? For what reason would the genetic code take it upon itself to spontaneously decide to increase on its own into a functioning being? Or even, what desire would say, an arm have to develop and replace a non-functioning fin that is no longer needed?

It is questions like these and many others that sheer scientific data is unable to answer. Of course, it is answers to these and many other questions that the Bible specializes in. Isaiah states that, "It is he that sitteth upon the circle of the earth, and the inhabitants thereof are as grasshoppers; that stretcheth out the heavens as a curtain, and spreadeth them out as a tent to dwell in" (Isaiah 40:22). Herein, the whole purpose of His creation is revealed, both currently and prophetically. First, this verse smacks at the concept of life itself. He sent people (grasshoppers) to the earth to oversee and reside in His creation.

Moreover, Isaiah is painting a much broader picture for His creation. It specifically says that the universe and not only the earth is where his creation is called to dwell. Without question this is foreshadowing His eternal plan for this vast creation. This creation is not meant to occupy this one little tiny planet. No, He created an unlimited ever-expanding universe for humanity to occupy. Just like He spread out the universe, His human contingency is called to spread out and occupy His creation.

At the end of this age, He will roll up the heavens and start with a clean slate. There will be a new physical law, governed by new rules and mankind will be a ruling class. (Isaiah 34:4, Revelation 6:14.) Those that believe will have unlimited access to the new heavens and earth filled with His creation. Undoubtedly, it is fun to imagine the possibilities of a whole new creation that the believer is called to administer. A new universe filled with untold numbers of planets, each with their own diverse species of plants and animals; all of which mankind is called to oversee.

Disparity

In conclusion, the following are a couple of glaring differences between evolution and creation. Evolution says that life forms evolved. The Bible says that all things were created after their own kind and have their own kind of flesh. (Genesis 1:11–12, 21, 24–25, 1 Corinthians 15:38–39.) Evolution says that man evolved. The Bible says that man was created and later was formed into his present state. (Genesis 1:26–27, 2:7.) Evolution says that woman preceded man. The Bible shows that man was created in the image of God, and then later separated into two species. (Genesis 2:21–22.)

Evolution calls sudden increases in life punctuated equilibrium. The Bible calls it creation. (Genesis 1:1.) Evolution says that life forms are still evolving. The Bible says that creation is complete. (Genesis 2:2.) Although there continues to be new documented species of plants and animals; experts agree that those species have been on the earth, but they have just never been documented. The truth is the number of species on the planet is decreasing not increasing. It is just the opposite of the evolutionary model. In fact, it is decreasing at an astounding rate. Biblically, this reduction in created species can be attributed to the fact that God said He was done creating and the curse that was placed on the earth on account of Adam's sin. (Genesis 2:2, 3:17–19.)

The end product of the whole debate is that the Bible states that all species on the earth outside of men were created after their own kind. They each have their own DNA strands, which gives them their unique traits and this is more than sufficient to show that the multitudes of species did not evolve. In all instances, they were created by God to fit the mold of the creation model of that particular era.

In addition, the geological record shows that abrupt changes took place in the fossil record. One day multitudes of animals appeared and the next day they are gone. There is no possible way these changes could be accounted for by evolution, nor is there any proof. The same holds true for mankind. The quest for the missing link is never going to be found. Modern day man came about because God took Adam and formed him into a being that was completely unique of his counterparts. Not made after his own kind from millennia past, but in the likeness of God.

The biblical truth is evident and undeniable: humans did not evolve and fossil records, archaeological finds, DNA testing, and all future methods of scientific evaluation will continue to prove these facts. Unfortunately, mankind has been duped into changing the truth of God for a lie and the end result is that the creature (evolution) has been worshipped more than the Creator. (Romans 1:25.)

James F. Coppedge sums it up when he states in his book, *Evolution: Possible or Impossible?* "This old analogy is as reasonable now as ever: We intuitively know that a watch requires a watchmaker. It has many parts that must be precision-adapted to match other parts that are useless alone. Why would anyone attempt to circumvent this principle in science?

"The conflict is basically between chance, disorder, and chaos on the one hand, and God, order, and organization on the other. Of him it is said that he "sustains the universe by his word of power." (Hebrew 1:3 NEB) Nothing else gives any adequate explanation of what we ourselves can observe. There is a type of evidence which may be far more convincing to an individual... It is the assurance which God has promised to all who will take him up on the following offer:

"He said, through Christ, "Whoever has the will to do the will of God shall know whether my teaching comes from him. . . ." (John 7:17 NEB) Such a person will be given inner assurance that Christ was who he claimed to be: the Son of God by whom the worlds were made. (Hebrews 1:2)"

CHAPTER 15

Precedence

Preceding Man

Ah Lord GOD! behold, thou hast made the heaven and the earth by thy great power and stretched out arm, and there is nothing too hard for thee... (Jeremiah 32:17)

The events of creation depicted in Genesis one entail three parts: a beginning point, a destructive event, and a re-creation. The original creation of the earth has been determined to be an event that transpired billions of years ago when the Lord spoke it forth in Genesis 1:1. This was followed by a large period of time until a destructive event in the second verse left the earth in a sort of dark stasis. Then in Genesis 1:3, the Lord once again initiated the process to bring forth life to the planet.

All of these events have been looked at in some detail by a chronological analysis that concluded with Adam and Eve in the Garden of Eden. Of course, there is much to be deciphered yet; particularly what was happening for those eons of time between the original creation and destructive event documented in Genesis?

It has been reviewed and well documented that the geologic and fossil records report that the earth was vibrant and full of life during that period, but were dotted with multiple periods of destruction. So why did the Lord place all these life forms on the earth prior to man and what were the events that lead to the destruction seen at the beginning of the re-creation? After all, the destruction that is evident in Genesis 1:2 must have been caused by something or someone.

Certainly, God would not allow things to be destroyed unless there was a reason for it. Sin and judgment have been alluded to, but there is much more to the story that has yet to be uncovered. Geological and archaeological records can only show physical events on the earth, but the Bible reveals many more things in the spiritual realm that the earth doesn't document and can only be found in the Word of God. Obviously, the millions of years of life that transpired between Genesis 1:1 and Genesis 1:2 are not fully disclosed in these two verses nor are any explanations as to what transpired during this time generally found in Genesis. Rather, like many other topics, the compilation of the Scriptures is not a chronological telling of events, but rather an exploration into its depths to discover its truths.

Therefore it is necessary to delve into its pages to uncover exactly what happened and why the Lord would turn his back on His own creation in Genesis 1:2 and at other points throughout history. The answers are there, but it requires some piecing together of various biblical authors to unearth its truth. The end result is that the Bible does give an explanation of the events that transpired from the original creation to the history of man.

Light and Darkness

Quickly reviewing a key spiritual component, which has already been discussed in some detail, will help to lay a background to the events of this period. As has been seen, just prior to the re-creation, the earth was cloaked in a darkness that was foreboding and sinister and covered in water. It was a double whammy, the earth covered in water and shrouded in darkness are both obvious indications that judgment had been dispensed. The darkness and the presence of water were of a spiritual nature as much as it was physical. This is evidenced by the fact that two different sources of light were released on subsequent days of the re-creation and the Spirit of God was seen hovering over the water.

Certainly, it can be stated that spiritual darkness is closely tied to spiritual death. Paul referred to it as "the law of sin and death" (Romans 8:2). It is introduced to the reader in Genesis 2:17, where God tells Adam, "But of the tree of the knowledge of good and evil, thou shalt not eat of it: for in the day that thou eatest thereof thou shalt surely die." His disobedience caused a separation between him and the Lord. The evidence of his actions were later seen when the Lord came to take a walk with him in the cool of the morning, but Adam responded by hiding himself. When the Lord arrived to commune with His creation, He asked, "Where art thou?" Adam's response was, "I hid myself" (Genesis 3:9–10). His sin had caused him to separate himself from the Lord. That kind of spiritual separation ultimately leads to physical death.

It is the same for the earth. The picture in Genesis one of the earth covered in darkness (spiritual darkness) is the same picture that came about from Adam's disobedience. It was a spiritual darkness that cloaked the earth during those days, and it also brought about physical death and darkness (or a curse) upon the rest of creation. Currently the earth is still in that cursed state, but it would prefer to be delivered. (Romans 8:22.) That is why when the Lord recreated the earth in Genesis; He proclaimed that it was only good and not perfect. Even though His creation was new, the earth was already marred by prior sins and therefore could only be classified as very good, which was more than adequate for the Lord.

In light of this, one of the sacred cows of religious tradition is the idea of original sin, which essentially states that Adam was the first to sin. It has thrown a wrench into many people's ideas about creation because they believe that when Adam sinned, he was the first one to do so. Of course, there is no place in the Bible that the phrase original sin is penned, but it was used by mankind to show the point in history when sin came into the world. The one verse that has brought about all of the confusion is Romans 5:12, "Wherefore, as by one man sin entered into the world, and death by sin; and so death passed upon all men, for that all have sinned." The text is clear that Adam brought sin into the world and there is no question that is exactly what Genesis teaches.

Of course, although Adam brought sin into the world, it does not mean that he brought sin into the earth. Remember that the Bible views the world as a system of government brought about by the creation of man. In contrast the earth is the physical floating ball in space. When Adam sinned, he brought death into his entire familial line. Romans goes on to say that sin brings death, and death comes to all men for all men have sinned. It is evident that this text is referring to the sin of individual men and its consequences which is death. It is not inferring any other creature or inanimate object sinning, just mankind.

The rest of the physical creation, including the plants and the animals do not have the capacity to sin. Only creatures that are given spirits and the breath of life have this ability. On account of Adam's sin the earth was also cursed. Of course, earthen fossilizations report the fact that prior to mankind the earth had already been riddled with sin.

So what happened in the earth prior to the events of Genesis one? As has been touted, the earth did not bring destruction upon itself, but sin and death were already present. Destruction is a byproduct of sentient beings. Therefore, the obvious truth is that other sentient beings must have made some mistakes. Just as mankind rebelled against God, these other sentient beings also rebelled against the Lord. These beings are referred to in the Bible as angels.

Angels

Bless the LORD, ye his angels, that excel in strength, that do his commandments, hearkening unto the voice of his word. Bless ye the LORD, all ye his hosts; ye ministers of his, that do his pleasure. (Psalm 103:20–21)

The existence of angels is well documented throughout the Scriptures, as they are mentioned in about half of the books of the Bible. Nevertheless, there are still a lot of misconceptions about angels. So, in order to dispel some of the mystery it is necessary to look at a few of these passages.

Angels are spirits and reside in the spiritual realm with the third heaven as their primary domicile. (Matthew 24:36.) They are called the sons of God because they were born into the spiritual realm and therefore have seen His glory from their beginning.

In contrast to this, mankind is referred to as the sons of men. (Psalm 33:13.) As such humans are first carnal or witness natural sinful things first and are called to seek after the spiritual. (Jeremiah 29:13.) So although mankind has a spirit and a soul, his current state of existence is in a physical body. Upon death the physical body will return to the earth and man's spirit and soul will immediately be present in the spiritual realm. (2 Corinthians 5:8.) So from an orientation perspective, mankind and angels are the opposite; mankind sees the physical first whereas the inverse is true for the angels, who first see the spiritual.

Yet in certain situations their orientation can be changed and they can also take physical form and be witnessed on the earth. (Hebrews 13:2.) This idea of an angel taking on a physical form is found prolifically throughout the Scriptures. There are literally dozens of encounters with humans and angels found throughout the pages of the Bible and largely people's reactions show that they recognize them as angels.

In Genesis 19, Lot had a meeting with some men at the gate of Sodom. Immediately he recognized that he was not standing in the presence of mere men, but rather that they were angels and he bowed himself to the ground and called them Lords. Similarly, Abraham had this same reaction one chapter earlier when he encountered them by his tent.

The Bible shows that when a human dies their disposition will be like that of an angel. (Luke 20:36.) This is witnessed when Christ walked the earth after his resurrection; He was seen doing things that no other human being had ever done. He could travel through walls and manifest himself in different places whimsically. (John 20:19.) Yet He ate and could be touched just like any other human being. (Luke 24:42–43, John 20:27.)

Upon His resurrection, Jesus received a new body and with this new body He took on a different level of physical capabilities. The angels have the same sphere of existence. They originated from the spiritual and in some situations they are allowed to be manifested in the physical realm. That is one of the reasons why the Bible says that humans will become like the angels, because when they are allowed to manifest themselves in the physical they have a larger range of capabilities.

Angels are the original sentient creation of God and they were present when the Lord called the earth into existence. According to Job, angels were an eyewitness to the Lord laying the cornerstone of the earth and they were excited about the possibilities of physical creation. "When the morning stars sang together, and all the sons of God shouted for joy" (Job 38:7).

Angelic populations are huge; so big in fact that they are called innumerable. (Hebrews 12:22.) On several occasions the Bible refers to the angelic population as stars. (Revelation 1:20; Psalm 148:3.) When God told Abraham to multiply like the stars of heaven, He may have been referring to the angelic hosts as well as the actual heavenly satellites.

Angels have a hierarchical organization just as men do. This is the way God has designed His creation. Just as Christ is the head of God and Jesus is the head of the church, angels have the same sort of hierarchy and most of the time they are cumulatively referred to in a military type of ranking. (1 Corinthians 11:3, Ephesians 5:23.) Groups of angels are called a company, an army, or a host, to mention just a few. (Hebrews 12:22, Daniel 4:35, Luke 2:13.) "Praise ye him, all his angels: praise ye him, all his hosts" (Psalm 148:2).

In addition to cumulative names, angels also have personal names. (Isaiah 40:26) The ones that are specifically mentioned in the Bible are: Gabriel (Luke 1:19), Michael (Daniel 10:13), and Satan. (Job 1:6.)

Angels are holy, but they are not God. They are not omnipotent, omnipresent, or all knowing. They are created beings, just as man is a created being. (Colossians 1:16.) Their original moment of creation is undisclosed in the Bible, but it was definitely before the creation of the earth; meaning they have been around for undisclosed billions of earth years. Angels were created to live forever and death has never been an option for them. (Luke 20:36.) Humans are in a similar situation; their existence is also eternal, but in order to reach that eternal existence they must first experience a physical death.

It is generally believed that the entire angelic population was created by God in one moment of history. "Let them praise the name of the LORD: for he commanded, and they were created" (Psalm 148:5). This would appear to indicate a one-time-creative event in the past by the Lord that established the whole of their entire population. This is certainly a possibility, but when God says that He created something it does not necessarily mean that He created the entire population in one instance.

Take man for example, the Bible continually references the fact that God created mankind, "Have we not all one father? hath not one God created us" (Malachi 2:10)? Even though all human beings are created by God, the actual process occurs through the offspring of a woman and it is continuing to happen today. Yet the verse makes it sound like it was a one-time past event. The same is likely true of angels, just because the Scriptures say that the angels were created does not mean that it was an event that only happened one time. It is quite probable that angelic populations are continuing to explode; after all they are innumerable.

To back this claim that all angels were created at one moment in time, some people reference Matthew 22:30 where it says that angels are not given in marriage. This is the only reference to angels and their relationship to other angels in the Scriptures. However, the verse in no way proves that angels do not bear children, but only that they are not given in marriage as humanity knows marriage.

With the Lord all things are possible and there are untold countless ways that the Lord could have established a growing angelic population. Our limited human understanding of how the Lord promulgates a species in the natural may not be even close to the way things work in the spiritual. Additionally, there are several references to angels breeding, which will be looked at in a subsequent chapter.

Angelic Loyalty

All angels are ministers to the Lord first. "Are they not all ministering spirits, sent forth to minister for them who shall be heirs of salvation" (Hebrews 1:14)? The word minister here is referring to their dedication to the Lord first. Then, as a part of that dedication, the next part of the verse says that they are sent forth to be ministers to mankind. They are doing the will of the Lord and ministering to Him by ministering to mankind.

A simple definition of a minister is a public servant. They are sent from God to be the helpers of mankind and this dedication can be seen throughout the Bible. It is not a compulsory servitude; it is a free will choice that God gives to all of His creation, which means that just like humans have a free will so do angels. Thus, they have a choice to follow the ways of God and during this age, they choose to minister to mankind.

One famous example of their ministerial call is seen with Jacob's ladder. Jacob tells of a dream that he had in which he saw angels moving freely up and down a ladder between heaven and earth. Their objective was to relay messages from the Lord and minister to people on the earth, providing a courier-like service between God and man. (Gen 28:11–19.) In Jacob's case he was asking for protection and assurance from the Lord that he would be safe. The Lord responded by revealing the spiritual realm to him, allowing him to see the angelic host moving back and forth between heaven and earth to reassure him that he was not alone. This was not the only encounter that mankind has had with angels. Following are a few of the many instances of angelic appearances mentioned the Bible.

When the armies of the Syria were closing in upon Elisha, his servant was fearful for their lives. Elisha prayed to God that his servant's eyes would be opened to the great multitude of the angelic host that flanked them amongst the hillsides. Elisha walked with the knowledge that angels surrounded Him all the time. (2 Kings 6:13–17.) Jesus was ministered to by an angel in the Garden of Gethsemane. (Luke 22:43.) Daniel met an angel. (Daniel 10) Moses encountered an angel at the burning bush. (Exodus 3:2.) Angels liberated Peter and other apostles from imprisonment. (Acts 5:19.) Angels are seen throughout Revelation performing multiple tasks and dispensing judgment. Abraham spoke with angels on several occasions and the birth of Christ is littered with angelic visits. Joseph, Mary, and the wise men all saw angels in advance of the upcoming birth.

Albeit, angels seem to show up at the most interesting times and it is quite possible that many people have encountered angels in their daily lives but were unaware of their presence. (Hebrews 13:2.) Since angels have access to the earth, they coexist with man to some degree. It is probable that there are angels all around us but we are unable to see them because they travel in a different realm of light and only when one's eyes are opened by the Lord are they able to perceive their existence.

There is some misconception regarding the ability of angels to travel great distances. Since angels live in heaven and come to the earth, than they must be millions of light years away on a planet called heaven. In other words, Jacob's ladder is somehow an extension of time and space millions of light years long. The Bible paints a different picture of God and heaven when it says that, "It is he that sitteth upon the circle of the earth, and the inhabitants thereof are as grasshoppers; that stretcheth out the heavens as a curtain, and spreadeth them out as a tent to dwell in" (Isaiah 40:22).

Isaiah shows that the Lord's dwelling place in heaven is actually on a circle that encompasses the earth, but its presence is cloaked as with a curtain. The obvious insinuation then is that the actual juxtaposition of the third heaven is next to the earth. Therefore, the moving of angelic hosts between heaven and earth would seem to be relatively easy. Of course, their movements are unseen by mankind because they travel in a different (spiritual) plane that is not readily seen with physical eyes; unless the Lord allows that realm to be seen, just like in the case of Jacob.

Notwithstanding, it is certainly possible that they have the ability to travel great distances in moments of time. Since they are in close proximity to the Lord, time becomes elongated. Thus it may be that angels can move at incredible speeds, essentially hopping around the universe in a moment's notice. Of a truth though, this would not seem to be necessary, as they are right next to the earth and their call is to be ministers to the inhabitants of the earth.

The Bible also mentions the fact that there are guardian angels, which are angelic assignments to minister specifically to certain individual humans. The Bible requisites that children have guardian angels, "Take heed that ye despise not one of these little ones; for I say unto you, That in heaven their angels do always behold the face of my Father which is in heaven" (Matthew 18:10). "Their angels" are referring to those that are assigned to each particular individual, an assignment that is never mentioned as being completed. In other words, all people have at least one angel assigned specifically to them, throughout their time on the earth.

The early Christian church believed in these angelic assignments. In Acts 12:15, Peter had just been released by an angel from Herod's prison and came to the door of a local believer and began to knock. When a girl by the name of Rhoda answered the door, she ran back into the other to tell them it was Peter. The occupants of the room responded that it could not be Peter but certainly it was his angel. It is interesting that they believed Peter's angel looked like him.

In other words, "guardian angels" are not a part of folklore, but are actually spoken about in the Bible. Additionally, it can also be seen that some angels do look like humans, for how else could a person come in contact with an angel and not be aware of the difference. On the other hand, there are plenty of instances in the Bible where men and women encountered angels and knew instantly that they were in the presence of an angel. So although, the Bible says that it is possible that angels may be encountered without knowing they were in the presence of an angel; in other circumstances they were immediately recognized as angels. Certainly it is possible that the spiritual eyes of these individuals were enlightened to the fact that they were in the presence of an angel. Or it may be that some angels are of a different stature than others, which is why some can be entertained by humans and remain unknown while others are instantly recognizable as angels.

Angelic Characteristics

In general, the rank and file of the angelic host is simply called angels, but the Bible does differentiate a couple of different classes of angels; including but not limited to Seraphim's, Cherubs, and Archangels. Each class is tasked by God with special assignments and each one has special characteristics. For instance, Seraphim (literally the burning ones) have six wings, frequently speak to each other about God's glory, and are continually amazed at His majesty and power. (Isaiah 6.)

Cherubs are called living creatures, have four wings, and are depicted as having a face on all sides (a man, a lion, an ox, an eagle), giving them the ability to see in all directions. (Ezekiel 10:14.) In Genesis 3:22–24 it was a cherub that protected the tree of life. They too are continually proclaiming the majesty of the One who was, and is, and is to come. (Revelation 4:6–11.)

Finally, Archangels are seen standing in the presence of God. Michael is an Archangel who has a special commission to protect God's people. (Daniel 12:1.) He is seen in Jude 9 rebuking Satan, but ultimately it is those two and their corresponding armies will do battle. (Revelation 12:7.)

From these references, it can also be seen that some angels have wings like God, but possibly only those that are closest to the throne room of God. (Ezekiel 10:5.) Other eyewitness accounts of angelic encounters do not mention wings and since the Bible says people can see them and be unaware of their presence then some of them would of necessity not have wings.

Additionally, it is apparent that when angels take on a human form they are subject to the same laws of nature as any other human. Lot called them in to eat and when they did they were filled. (Genesis 19:3.) He then invited them to spend the night and they apparently would have although this never came to fruition. So it is possible that they may have slept. (Genesis 19:4.)

One thing that is certain is that angels are stronger than men. "Whereas angels, which are greater in power and might, bring not railing accusation against them before the Lord" (2 Peter 2:11). Angelic physical prowess is renown in the Word of God. Some angels are so powerful that the Bible shows that they are able to control the wind and the earth's rotation. (Revelation 7:1.) They are often seen dispensing the Lord's judgment. (Revelation 7:2.) On one occasion a single angel killed an entire army of Assyrians totaling 185,000 men in one evening. (2 Kings 19:35.)

It was angels that destroyed Sodom and it was angels that killed Herod. (Genesis 19:13, Acts 12:23.) They were used to bring pestilence upon Israel when David transgressed the Lord by conducting a census. (2 Samuel 24:15–17.) In this same manner, they are called upon to avenge those who persecute the saints of God and at the end of a believer's life they are leveraged to escort them to heaven. (Psalm 35:5–6, Luke 16:22.)

They are not only physically superior, but the connotation of power and might give light to the fact that they are indeed more powerful than humans in courage, energy, morality, ability, force, and ruling power. Definitively the Bible says that they are wise and obedient. (2 Samuel 14:20, Psalm 103:20.)

No doubt it helps that they dwell next to His light on a daily basis and draw their strength from it. (Matthew 18:10.) It is from hence that they are endued with power by continually living close to the Light. Imagine on a daily basis living and witnessing the very face of God.

The Bible says that currently mankind is in a lower status than the angelic host, but that at the end of the age there is a common belief that the rankings will change and mankind will enjoy an elevated status above the angels in heaven. (Psalm 8:4–5.) This is a common misnomer based on 1 Corinthians 6:3 where it says that humanity will be the judge of angels. Of a truth, it does not say which angels that Christians will judge. Obviously, there is no need to judge those angels who have not sinned and there is no indication in the Bible that all angels have sinned.

Apparently then, mankind will be the judge of some angels, but which ones has yet to be determined. Therefore, it is quite possible that at the end of this age, those who believe will be elevated to a status equal to the angels. (Mark 12:25.) One thing is sure, one man, Jesus Christ took a position of authority over all men and angels upon his resurrection and is now seated at the right hand of God. (Hebrews 1.)

Since angels are created beings, just like man, they are not to be worshiped. "Let no man beguile you of your reward in a voluntary humility and worshipping of angels, intruding into those things which he hath not seen, vainly puffed up by his fleshly mind" (Colossians 2:18). Paul's instructions clearly states that humans are not to delve into the things that are not understand, thinking that God will protect them.

Angelic worship is idolatry and distorts the truth of God. In addition, if any man or angel comes preaching a gospel other than Christ, it is a lie and should not be entertained. (Galatians 1:8–9.) Propaganda brought from other sources, including angels, brings people down to their lowly human or angelic level instead of building them up to the level of Christ. Retrospectively the Bible also says that angels are not to be disrespected. (2 Peter 2:11.) Of course, it is a fine line to walk between respect and worship.

On a lighter note, it is interesting that the angels have been around eons longer than man and still the Bible says that they are curious to look into the things of man. (1 Peter 1:12.) That is to say, angels are curious about the plan that God has for man because the events that shape the earth now have direct ramifications in heaven. When the Lord taught his disciples to pray, He prayed, "Thy kingdom come. Thy will be done in earth, as it is in heaven" (Matthew 6:10). It also works in reverse, in heaven as it is on earth. It is for this reason that angels are intent on understanding the happenings of the earth.

Unfortunately, the Bible brings to light that there are some angels that have not been true to the Creator and for those who have not been faithful it is too late for them, which means that angels can also be guilty of sin. "Behold, he put no trust in his servants; and his angels he charged with folly" (Job 4:18).

Once the Lord introduces a spirit into His hierarchy, it means that He also allows that spirit to have a choice and when choice is allowed there is always a potential for rebellion. God has always allowed choice for his sentient beings. If there were no choice there would be no individuality, and there would be no rights. With the gift of a spirit, one can choose to serve God or not; one can choose life or they can choose death.

If there is no choice, then humans and angels alike are essentially forced into the Lord's service. With a choice comes responsibility, because one could make the wrong choice. Once a choice (spirit) is given, the Lord gives up his ability to completely trust His creation. It is for this reason that even the angels can be found to be in folly or rebellion. In the same respect, those angels that have remained faithful are hopeful for the coming age and the activities that are transpiring in the earth today.

Think about what the angels have seen since the beginning of His creation. Not only have they witnessed billions of years of creative acts on the earth, but most importantly the birth and death of Jesus Christ, the most significant event in the history of the universe. His blood sacrifice covers the sins of humanity for all eternity. Then in the afterlife, the Bible says that mankind will take on a form that will be like the angels. Any sin that transpires in the eons of eternity will be covered by the eternal sacrifice of Christ and since human and angelic forms will be similar, it is certain that they will also be covered by this same promise.

The redemptive power that was released to all humanity is also carried over to the angels. They understand that they too will be able to participate in His resurrection and forgiving grace. Thus, God's plan is not only for humanity, but for all sentient creatures. It is an all-encompassing plan that will never end, nor will it ever fail. The last stronghold that Christ conquered was death. All those that have been faithful will inherit His promises; on earth as it is in heaven.

Unfortunately for one angel, he made the wrong choice and brought several of his colleagues along for the ride. He is known as the chief folly-maker and is frequently mentioned throughout the Bible as Satan. He is recognized throughout all Christian religions as an opposing force that is trying to destroy the very knowledge of God's existence. Jesus encountered him just before His public ministry, and He was continually meshed in a daily struggle with his influences.

The Bible teaches that he is a real force in opposition to the works of God in the earth and it will be shown that it was his activities that brought about the devastating scene that is witnessed in the beginning of Genesis, due in part to a play he made for the throne of God. Definitively his plot of mutiny was squelched by the Lord, but the residual damage left an indelible scar on the earth. So, who is he and what caused him to be so jaded that he is continually in a fight against the positive influences of God? And what will happen to him in the future ages to come?

CHAPTER 16

Dissent

Deception

And the great dragon was cast out, that old serpent, called the Devil, and Satan, which deceiveth the whole world: he was cast out into the earth, and his angels were cast out with him. (Revelation 12:9)

This chapter and the next two will be exploring the kingdom of Satan. At the outset it is necessary to disclaim that Satan and his kingdom are defeated. (Hebrews 2:14–15.) Christians have all authority over the enemy. When Christ came to earth, He conquered all the power of the devil. (Luke 10:19.) Belief in the Son of God will always give deliverance over Satan's influence. His kingdom (the world) and power in that kingdom is still in existence, but his control over his dominion will be short lived.

So for those who have Christ, they will always reign supreme in all aspects of life; wealth, happiness, health, spiritually, etc. By His blood sacrifice, Christians are covered from all calamities brought about by the wiles of the devils. Ephesians says that Christ was raised from the dead and triumphed over all principalities, might, dominions, and names that are named. (Ephesians 6:10–18.) Colossians confirms that Christ is the fullness of the Godhead and the head of all principality and power and we are complete in Him. (Colossians 2:9–10.) Therefore, through Christ you are redeemed from all the power of the enemy; he is now under your feet. (1

239

Corinthians 15:25–27.) It is imperative to keep this in mind when talking about the devil and his kingdom.

The devil is mentioned frequently in the Scriptures and is given many different names, here are a few: Beelzebub (Matthew 12:24), Angel of Light (2 Corinthians 11:14), Anointed Cherub (Ezekiel 28:14), Devil/Satan (Revelation 12:9), Liar/Murderer (John 8:44), Adversary/Roaring Lion (1Peter 5:8), Prince of the Air (Ephesians 2:2), Lucifer (Isaiah 14:12), God of this World (2 Corinthians 4:4), Oppressor (Acts 10:38), Tempter (Matthew 4:3), Wicked One (Matthew 13:19), Serpent/Dragon (Revelation 12:9), and King. (Revelation 9:11.)

Satan is more than just a metaphor for evil. He is a created being who is set upon the destruction and thwarting of the plan of God in the earth. (Colossians 1:16.) His activities are seen throughout the Bible, but most notable from this perspective is that it was his actions in Genesis 1:2 that caused the earth to be without form, and void, and cloak the deep with a cover of darkness.

His presence in the earth is reconfirmed by the end of Genesis chapter one, when the Lord gives an edict to mankind to, "Be fruitful, and multiply, and replenish the earth, and subdue it" (Genesis 1:28). The reference is subtle but pertinent. There would be no reason to subdue a perfect creation unless rebellion already existed. Essentially God was telling mankind that there is a force in the earth today that needs to be subdued. Indeed there is a force and he is in opposition to God. Ultimately his rebellion will cause the whole thing to fall once again; for the creation was not willingly subjected to defeat, but rather it came about by the one that forced it into defeat. (Romans 8:19–22.)

By Genesis chapter three, he was already meddling with God's new sentient creation by setting a trap and attempting to deceive them into believing that they were missing out on the good life. Appearing to Adam and Eve as a serpent, he tricked them into partaking of the very thing that God told them not to do, eat of the tree of the knowledge of good and evil. They both imbibed and afterwards realized their sin and hid themselves from God, who, in turn, bestows judgment upon all three of the parties involved.

First the Lord cursed the serpent by informing him that going forward he will crawl upon his belly. He also tells him that it would ultimately be

---

through the seed of a woman that his defeat would be finalized. Then the Lord turns to the woman and tells her that she will be in subjection to her husband for the rest of her life and pain will be a part of childbirth. Finally, the Lord turns to the man and curses the ground on which he stands, saying that by the sweat of his brow he shall labor and toil to overcome it and it will bring sorrow, and ultimately death will be his reward.

Undoubtedly the penalties for disobedience were harsh. Truly he is the opposing force of all things God, for just in the first few chapters of the Bible he has already been seen several times. This pattern continues throughout virtually all of the conflicts in the Bible, because it is Satan that is directly or indirectly involved when things go awry.

Of course, these events in the earth have been detailed in prior chapters, but now it will be seen that Satan was the responsible party behind them. During the span of time between the original creation and the re-creation, he masterminded and led a rebellion in heaven that left the earth in a state of bedlam, confusion, and an absence of the Lord. On account of this rebellion, he lost his access to the earth, but when Adam sinned he regained his authority through mankind.

Nowadays his tactics are much more subtle, as he uses deception in the hearts and minds of humanity to turn them away from God. He does a good job too. His deceptions work and many are caught off-guard when he attacks because they fail to realize it is him. One of his greatest deceptions is to convince mankind that he does not exist, which in turn infers that God does not exist. Many are deceived, as his primary method of persuasion is to plant doubts and questions about the omniscience and creation of God.

Paul warns us not to get caught up in the philosophy and traditions of men and the rudiments of the world (Satan). (Colossians 2:8.) By doing so, one can lose sight of their first love and become closed off to the things of God. The Bible says that he is constantly before the throne of God, accusing the brethren of their shortcomings. (Revelation 12:10.) That is why it is imperative to gird up the loins of your mind and put on the whole armor of God. (Ephesians 6:11–18.)

Satan's Range

The Bible refers to him as the prince of the earth and because of this there is an underlying belief that he is only located on the earth. (2 Corinthians 4:4.) The truth of the matter is that he continues to have free range of motion throughout all aspects of God's creation, which means that he can not only thwart the plan of God on the earth but also in the heavens. Although he had limited access to the earth after the destructive events of Genesis 1:2, Adam and Eve's sin allowed him greater access once again. His activities in heaven as well as the earth can be seen in the answer to Daniel's prayer, found in the last four chapters of his book.

Daniel had asked the Lord for the restoration of the Jewish nation and relief from captivity. He waited patiently for an answer and fasted, but it was not immediately forthcoming. After three weeks an angel finally shows up and informs him that his prayer was heard immediately, but complications arose while he was attempting to convey the answer to Daniel. While personally delivering the answer from the Lord, the angel (messenger) tasked with delivering the response encountered some difficulty and had to call in reinforcements because He was being thwarted by the Prince of Persia or Satan. (Daniel 10:13.)

Michael (the archangel) is called into the battle to assist the angel who was commissioned to personally deliver the answer to Daniel's prayer, which was thwarted in its timeliness by twenty one days. In other words, the message was hindered because of a battle that was transpiring in the spiritual realm that was unbeknownst to Daniel and his colleagues. Satan is still active in the realm of the spirit, which is why he is called "the prince of the power of the air, the spirit that now worketh in the children of disobedience" (Ephesians 2:2).

This free range access is also witnessed in the book of Job, as he was the one who brought calamity on the house of Job. "Now there was a day when the sons of God came to present themselves before the LORD, and Satan came also among them" (Job 1:6). Although his rebellion was well known amongst all the attending parties, he was still allowed in their presence when a board meeting was called. Standing in the throne room of God, he is there to accuse the brethren day and night by using their own words against them. (Revelation 12:10.)

This is an interesting feat since one would assume that as a result of his actions in Genesis he would have also been removed from heaven. This is evidently not the case and here the Lord was the one that asked Satan to consider his servant Job, and by doing so allowed the door of destruction to be opened upon himself on account of his own fears. "For the thing which I greatly feared is come upon me, and that which I was afraid of is come unto me" (Job 3:25). Job had left himself open for attack by not fearing (reverencing) the Lord and instead fearing unknown calamity. "The fear of the LORD is a fountain of life, to depart from the snares of death" (Proverbs 14:27).

Leaving himself open for attack, Satan was quick to devise a plan to bring about Job's ruin and try to force him to open his mouth and curse the Lord. Satan's deceptive tactics stems from his own heart condition because the Bible shows that he has been sinning from the beginning. (1 John 3:8.) "He was a murderer from the beginning, and abode not in the truth, because there is no truth in him. When he speaketh a lie, he speaketh of his own: for he is a liar, and the father of it" (John 8:44). In Job's case, Satan was allowed to strike Job with all sorts of disaster and affliction but he kept his mouth closed and the Lord restored his fortune, health, and family. (Job 42:10.)

In light of what Job says about Satan's free range throughout both realms, there still seems to be some confusion. A lot of this may stem from a passage in Luke that says, "And he said unto them, I beheld Satan as lightning fall from heaven" (Luke 10:18). Though, it appears that this verse is saying that Satan was cast out of heaven. The fact is that Jesus was using a metaphor as He was addressing the 70 disciples that were sent out into the surrounding regions.

When they returned from their missionary journey they were elated that they had authority over devils. Jesus responds by saying, "like lightning falling from heaven, is how it is when you take authority in my name, I see Satan having to surrender to you." It is not a commentary on past events. It is a response to His disciples concerning the authority that they had in His name. In Young's literal translation says, "And he said to them, 'I was beholding the adversary, as lightning from the heaven having fallen.'" It is not a historical event but rather a commentary on what Jesus saw in the spirit realm. In other words, Satan is still active in the heavens as much as he is in the earth.

Beginnings

So when the Bible says that Satan was a liar and a murderer from the beginning, when was the beginning exactly? As has been seen from the rest of the creation account, the beginning is a specific point in time. It is the beginning of the universe; it is not a metaphorical perpetuity of time. So here too, when the Bible is referring to the beginning of Satan, it is referring to this same beginning point in the earth.

In the coming chapters, it will be meted out that just like all the rest of the angels that were rejoicing over the creation of the earth, Satan was one of them. Soon after, the Lord discovered that his heart was in a different place. Even before the dawn of the new creation, his murderous, treacherous, and lying ways were already evident in his heart. By that point in time (the creation of time) Satan had already hatched a plan of disobedience and it was his continued faithless ways that brought destruction upon the earth, throughout the ages, and through the generations of man.

Of course, this once again references the fact that at least a portion of the angelic host, including Satan, existed long before the creation of the earth. They were born into the eternal spiritual realm, but witnessed the birth of the physical. Therefore, they were not created with a physical aspect, but rather were granted access to the physical realm after the declaration of the physical from the Father.

Still, their creation was framed by the words of God, which means that Satan was originally created in perfection. He was not created in sin, but he became the author of it, because the Bible makes it clear that he conceived of the sin in his own spirit. "When he speaketh a lie, he speaketh of his own: for he is a liar, and the father of it" (John 8:44). This cannot be a function of God. Satan acted on his own volition, unprompted by any outside forces. This means that he is the originator of sin, not Adam as some would believe.

He is the one that was there from the dawn of man and it was his acts that caused the darkness that covered the earth at the dawn of the re-creation. It was not a created darkness that the Lord would have initiated, but rather it had a connotation of evil. It was a darkness that was induced by Satan that the one true Light could not comprehend. That light is perfect and Satan's sinful nature was unable to understand the Light of Life.

Thus the allegorical original sin came from the very father of sin himself. This is the reason that catastrophe is seen in the geological record. Satan had already been there and muddled things up. His actions are also the reason that the earth's geological record is gapped. It was Satan's misdeeds that caused God's judgment to fall upon the earth prior to the re-creation and other times in the past ages. Just as sin caused a change in the formally tranquil life of man, so also sin caused change in the early earth. So what happened during the early years of the earth that caused him to be so rebellious and evil?

The Anointed Cherub

In Ezekiel 28, some of Satan's early exploits are disclosed. The first eleven verses of this passage are prophetically referring to his future exploits as the Antichrist, but starting in verse twelve it begins to speak of the king of Tyrus. The area of Tyrus was both a region and a city, and it is documented to be a center of idolatry. Although there was an actual king whose name was Ithobalus the second, the Bible generally refers to the leader as the king of Tyrus. As with many passages of Scripture, the king of Tyrus is a double reference to both the physical and the spiritual. In this passage it is clear that the king of Tyrus is a direct parallel to Satan.

This is known because there are many items stated in this passage that cannot possibly refer to a natural king and must be referring to a supernatural being and should be interpreted as such. God uses the natural situation to address the supernatural, because both of their situations were similar. This usage of double references is seen throughout the Scriptures, and probably the most renowned instance was when Christ addressed Satan while He was talking to Peter.

Peter had rebuked the Lord for the things that Jesus was prophesying to his disciples about his impending sufferings and death. Peter took the Lord aside and said, "Be it far from thee, Lord: this shall not be unto thee" (Matthew 16:22). Peter was being used as an instrument to try to hinder God's plan. Jesus called him out saying, "Get thee behind me, Satan: thou art an offence unto me" (Matthew 16:23). Obviously, Jesus was not speaking to Peter directly, but the spirit that was influencing him. This type of double reference can be seen throughout the Scriptures and definitively in this passage, as it refers to both the natural and the supernatural. The same is true in Ezekiel where it is apparent that the passage is about Satan because many of the attributes and activities described could not possibly be human in nature.

The passage begins with Ezekiel taking a look at the physical appearance of Satan. There are hundreds of common misconceptions about who Satan is and what he looks like. Often he is portrayed as goat-faced individual with cloven feet, two horns, and a pitchfork. Or he has a long pointed tail with a flowing mane of hair, a forked tongue, and fiery eyes. These are just a few of the many characteristic that modern day society has given to him and in most people's minds-eyes this is probably how they picture him. In this passage, the Bible paints an entirely different picture about who he is and what are his characteristics.

Son of man, take up a lamentation upon the king of Tyrus, and say unto him, Thus saith the Lord GOD; Thou sealest up the sum, full of wisdom, and perfect in beauty. Thou hast been in Eden the garden of God; every precious stone was thy covering, the sardius, topaz, and the diamond, the beryl, the onyx, and the jasper, the sapphire, the emerald, and the carbuncle, and gold: the workmanship of thy tabrets and of thy pipes was prepared in thee in the day that thou wast created. Thou art the anointed cherub that covereth; and I have set thee so: thou wast upon the holy mountain of God; thou hast walked up and down in the midst of the stones of fire. Thou wast perfect in thy ways from the day that thou wast created, till iniquity was found in thee. By the multitude of thy merchandise they have filled the midst of thee with violence, and thou hast sinned: therefore I will cast thee as profane out of the mountain of God: and I will destroy thee, O covering cherub, from the midst of the stones of fire. Thine heart was lifted up because of thy beauty, thou hast corrupted thy wisdom by reason of thy brightness: I will cast thee to the ground, I will lay thee before kings, that they may behold thee. Thou hast defiled thy sanctuaries by the multitude of thine iniquities, by the iniquity of thy traffick; therefore will I bring forth a fire from the midst of thee, it shall devour thee, and I will bring thee to ashes upon the earth in the sight of all them that behold thee. All they that know thee among the people shall be astonished at thee: thou shalt be a terror, and never shalt thou be any more. (Ezekiel 28:12–19)

As can be seen, the physical attributes of Satan are vastly different from the modern Hollywood perception. This passage starts by describing his characteristics as that of perfection, because it says that he seals up the sum, or better, "In you, I have encapsulated the idea of perfection." Everything that God designs is perfect, but Satan was designed with attributes that set the standard for all the other angels to look upon. He created Him as a perfectly beautiful individual; which is not the type of beauty as man understands it, but rather this is God's definition of beauty.

He wore a tunic that was made of gigantic stones of topaz, diamond, beryl, onyx, etc. It is possible, though not stated exactly, that these gemstones were more than a covering, but they were actually a part of his body. His voice is organ-like, erupting in beautiful sounds when he speaks. Then, in verse 14 it shows why such beauty was culminated within one creature.

It says that he was blameless or without sin. He was the anointed cherub of God. Once again cherubs are a high ranking angel in the army of God. They can be seen throughout the Bible adorning the Ark of the Covenant, guarding the Garden of Eden, and near the Lord's court. (Exodus 25:19, Genesis 3:24, Ezekiel 10.) In fact, God is often described as the one who dwells between the Cherubim. (Isaiah 37:16.)

According to Ezekiel chapter ten, they both support and encircle the throne of God. With their wings they make the throne mobile and they surround it to give it protection. There are believed to be at least four cherubim based on Ezekiel 10:9, because it shows the Lord being transported in a vehicle with four wheels each supported by one cherub. In other passages of Scripture, Gabriel and Michael are two of the named cherubs, but ancillary traditional materials also mention others.

Satan was the covering cherub. He was the fifth cherub from Ezekiel that corporeally blanketed the throne of God. In other words, he occupied the overarching chief spot of all the angels; a place of authority over the highest ranking angels in the Lord's host. On top of that, he had the designation of anointed; meaning God gave him special abilities to carry out specific tasks.

In the Bible, when somebody is anointed it means that they have a special call upon their life and they are gifted to perform that call. The anointing of God can be seen throughout Scripture by the administration of oil. When a priest was called to the priesthood they were anointed with oil. (Leviticus 21:10.) In the same fashion, kings were anointed with oil by a prophet as a symbol of their Godly assignments. (1 Samuel 16:13.) When the anointing of God comes it is meant for purification to prepare one for a calling to a special purpose in their life. (Luke 4:18–19.) In Jesus' case, He is called the Christ. It is not His last name, but rather it is a reference to the fact that His entire life is anointed in all ministerial and kingly functions. So as a part of the Godhead, He has His own anointing, but in addition to that He is anointed by God the Father because He came to earth as man.(Philippians 2:7–8.)

Satan too had a special anointing on his life and since he was a cherub, he was already in a close relationship with the Lord. There is no other creature in the kingdom of God that is given the title of the anointed cherub. Certainly, there are other references to cherubs, but here he is seen as the head of the cherubs, the anointed one and it is likely that he was the highest ranking angel in the army of the Lord. Quite possibly it is the greatest designation that the Lord could have bestowed upon any of the angelic order, second only to Christ. Revelation shows that He had ruling authority over one third or more of the angelic host. (Revelation 12:4.)

Isaiah goes on to say that he was set upon the holy mountain of God. When the Bible uses the phrase, "the mountain of God," it is referring to God's government. Of course, God has a government and He is the commander in chief. His mountain is an actual mountain in the spiritual realm, but it is also symbolic of His government. (Hebrews 12:22.)

Additionally, Satan is the only other being under heaven mentioned in the Bible that occupied multiple offices (Jesus being the first one). Not only was he the anointed cherub, with the ability to walk in God's presence, he is also mentioned as a priest. Ezekiel says that he had defiled his sanctuaries and if he was in charge of sanctuaries than he would have been acting in a priestly capacity. As a priest he may have been charged with several special duties, tasks, and oversights. Certainly he was well equipped to occupy this office as he had more than one sanctuary under his supervision.

Furthermore, Isaiah 14:13 shows that Satan had a throne, which means that he had a kingdom, which means that he was a king. This, of course ties back to Ezekiel where he is called the king of Tyrus with his dominion being the leader over the region of Tyrus. Though this is a parallelism with an earthly kingdom, it is also parallels with a previous kingdom established on the earth. This is true because Ezekiel 10:20 calls cherubs living creatures; which mean that they have physical human-like bodies and the ability to walk the earth. In this same fashion, in the book of Job, when the Lord asked the devil where he had recently been, he responded by saying that he was "going to and fro in the earth, and from walking up and down in it" (Job 1:7).

The same is true of the other cherubs, who have often been seen by many saints of God. One of these sightings already mentioned was seen in Daniel 8:15–16 where the angel Gabriel appears to Daniel and explains a vision. The wording of Gabriel's presence is very particular. It says that Gabriel had "the appearance of a man." Clearly showing that Gabriel looked like a man, but there were likely some distinctive qualities recognizable by Daniel that separated him from a human. Also, it does not mention when they can manifest themselves to humans on the earth, it may be that they always have access to the earth or that it is only at the discretion of God.

Finally, Satan is a businessman, although it appears that this was brought about solely by his own hand and not at the approval of the Lord because he is called a trafficker of iniquity. (Ezekiel 28:18.) Recognizing the greatness of the power that he wielded, the upstart apparently thought that he could use his position to further his own desires. Unfortunately for him the lust of his merchandise caused him to sin, to which the Lord responded by casting him as profane out of His presence. He became so elevated in His own mind that Ezekiel says that he was blinded by his own brightness and his wisdom became corrupted. So he was not only a powerful angel in the priestly ministry, a king, and a commander in the Lord's army; but he was also an entrepreneur.

Ezekiel goes on to say that he was created to walk amidst the throne room of God, up and down in the midst of the stones of fire. There are a couple of other references to this in the Bible; one is found in Exodus 24:10, where the elders of Israel were called to meet the Lord upon the mount of Sinai. While they were there, they witnessed stones about the feet of God, which were said to have a transparent clearness to them. This verse coincides with Revelation 4:6, where it says that "before the throne there was a sea of glass like unto crystal". Satan was created to be right in the midst of God, walking in and out of the Lord's throne room. He was an integral part of God's government.

On account of his close relationship to the Lord, Ezekiel goes on to say that Satan sealed up the sum and is full of wisdom. In other words, the sum of God's creation was Satan. Wisdom encompassed him. Certainly, the concept of wisdom is a something that God holds in high esteem. He freely gives it to those that are righteous and it is revered throughout the Bible as something that men should strive to obtain. (Proverbs 2:6–7, 4:7.) Understanding and knowledge are the building blocks to discovering God, but it is wisdom that comes from God. The Bible shows that having a pure heart and a reverential fear of the Lord will increase one's wisdom. The first step is to depart from evil, and then the next step is the fear of the Lord. (Job 28:28.) So at some point prior to the creation of the earth, Satan must have met this reverential standard.

Obviously then, when tying all of this together, it shows that there was a point in angelic history that Satan was in a position of complete trust by the Lord. He was full of wisdom, a nomenclature that could only be obtained if he was thoroughly acquainted with the Lord. Since Satan was created to be in the midst of God's presence, he was constantly being filled with the Word of God and since Jesus is the Word it can be assumed that Jesus and Satan were close friends.

Additionally, he was created to have direct communion with God and worship Him, all while having access in the very courts of the Lord's throne room. Anointed and powerful in the kingdom of God, he was beautifully designed to stand out among the angels. He was the epitome of what God would call perfect and since there has been no indication that his appearance has changed, it has to be assumed that he still looks the same. The idea of a pitchfork wielding, half-human-half-animal looking creature is simply misguided. His appearance is probably quite human-like with added features of beauty as discussed above.

With his position of authority, Satan would have had command of divisions of angels at his disposal to assist and carry out his desires in the service of the Lord. It is possible that he would have been the leader of more than just one third of the angelic host, but rather the whole congregation of them. This is an assumption that is made based on his proximity to God, his priestly office, and his kingdom.

Since the Lord's government is based on a hierarchical leadership structure it can be assumed that the highest ranking angel in the order would have had possibly all of the angelic divisions under his command. This is confirmed by the Bible when it calls him the anointed cherub that covereth. Needless to say, he was a powerful being in a position of authority both in heaven and earth and at some point prior to the beginning of the earth the Lord trusted him completely with virtually His entire Kingdom.

There is every indication in these passages and others that God anointed Satan for a much larger plan for his life and this earth. With his position of authority and influence he was destined for a greatness that was unsurpassed in the kingdom of God with unimaginable power and reach. Unfortunately, an evil born out of his own heart brought about his destruction.

Satan's Downfall

Continuing on with the passage in Ezekiel, it mentions the fact that he had been in Eden, "Thou hast been in Eden the garden of God" (Ezekiel 28:13). Of course, Satan was in the Garden of Eden with Adam and Eve when he came in the form of a serpent to deceive the couple into eating of the tree. Here though, it is apparent, that this garden is a reference to a different garden in a different span of time. Since the entire passage is a flashback to a time prior to mankind being on the earth, then the garden that is being mentioned in this passage is a garden that existed prior to the re-creation.

There is a subtle but important difference in how Ezekiel refers to Eden that brings this to light. He calls it "Eden the garden of God," whereas in Genesis it is called the "garden of Eden" (Genesis 2:15). Remember that for Adam, the garden was planted in Eden to the east. (Genesis 2:8.) That is, the Garden of Eden in Adam's day occupied only the eastern portion of the area called Eden. In Ezekiel though, it says that Eden was the Garden of God. That is, the entire area of Eden was a garden.

Obvious there are two completely separate gardens that are being referenced in these two passages and both of them are in an area called Eden. Since there is no other Eden's mentioned in the Bible, this has to be the same region of the earth. Undoubtedly, the geographical location of Eden did not change but merely the reference of time, which is why it is confidently recognized in Genesis as a proper name. Eden was already named at a point prior to man and all of the area of Eden was a garden during that dispensation.

Thus the area named Eden was originally on the earth prior to the re-creation, as such when Adam was moved into the garden he was placed in an area in the eastern region that was once again converted to a garden. Also, there is every indication that the Eden prior to man occupied much of the known earth today (this will be looked at further in chapter nineteen).

Satan was in that original Eden at a time prior to the re-creation of Genesis when all of Eden was a garden. (Ezekiel 28:13.) It was God's sanctuary, put on the earth for God's enjoyment and Lucifer was allowed access. During that time he was in a position of authority over untold multitudes of angelic hosts, and subsequently he was given a greater freedom than all the other angels.

He was given the keys to the earth to tend to it and care for it; much like God gave Adam this same power over all the earth. Unfortunately, it was here, at the pinnacle of his power, that he lost it all. For it is apparent that Satan's ruling sphere of influence was on earth as much as it was in heaven. Unfortunately, Ezekiel says that iniquity was found in him and he goes on to describe these transgressions. "By the multitude of thy merchandise they have filled the midst of thee with violence, and thou hast sinned... Thine heart was lifted up because of thy beauty, thou hast corrupted thy wisdom by reason of thy brightness... Thou hast defiled thy sanctuaries by the multitude of thine iniquities, by the iniquity of thy traffick" (Ezekiel 28:16–18). All of the items that are mentioned here are physical in nature.

None of his shortcomings that are cited would have been caused by his life in heaven. This is confirmed in Isaiah 14:13–14 where it says, "For thou hast said in thine heart, I will ascend into heaven, I will exalt my throne above the stars of God.... I will be like the most High." His goal was the throne of God, but in order to ascend into heaven he had to have been on the earth. (The entire passage of Isaiah 14:9–17 gives additional insight into Satan and his demise. It too is a double reference to the kingdom of Satan, but it is in reference to the Babylonian empire. Throughout the Bible, Babylonia is analogous to debauchery and generally believed to be the axis of evil on the earth during that era.)

Pride

Ezekiel stated there was more than one reason that Satan fell from the grace of God; he makes it clear that the whole of Satan's problems stemmed from his own pride-filled condition. He conceived in himself that due to his own beauty and power, he should be in a position of greater authority. He desired to elevate himself above all the stars (angels) of heaven and with that imagined position; he believed in himself that he must be an equal with God. He became so puffed up with pride that he lost his perspective regarding his true position as one of God's servants and conceived the notion that he could take the place of God.

In other words, the created wanted to become the creator. "For thou hast said in thine heart, I will ascend into heaven, I will exalt my throne above the stars of God: I will sit also upon the mount of the congregation, in the sides of the north: I will ascend above the heights of the clouds; I will be like the most High" (Isaiah 14:13–14). Sin was already in his heart before the earth was created, but when he saw the creation of the earth and the power that he had over it, he wanted more. His pride came to a head when he believed that he would ultimately be able to overthrow God. His authority on the earth and in heaven shifted his heart and distorted his ability to decipher right from wrong. Jealousy overtook his heart and ultimately he lost sight of whom and what he was in God's grand plan. Pride truly does go before destruction. (Proverbs 16:18.)

Satan was the first, but certainly not the last to allow pride to influence their life. The Bible is full of examples of kings and leaders that allowed pride to enter into their hearts and ultimately cause their demise. One pertinent example of this is when King Nebuchadnezzar declared, "Is not this great Babylon, that I have built for the house of the kingdom by the might of my power, and for the honour of my majesty" (Daniel 4:30)? Before he even finished the sentence a voice from heaven called out, "The kingdom is departed from thee" (Daniel 4:31).

Within the hour Nebuchadnezzar was removed from the palace and lost his position as king. For seven years he became an outcast of society to eat only with the beasts of the field. It is quite a jump he made from ruling the largest kingdom on earth to being a societal outcast overnight. All because pride had built up in his heart and he would not give glory to God for putting him into that position that he enjoyed.

After seven years his reason was restored and he was elevated back to his position of authority. His heart was now in the right place as he professed, "Now I Nebuchadnezzar praise and extol and honour the King of heaven, all whose works are truth, and his ways judgment: and those that walk in pride he is able to abase." (Daniel 4:37). It took him seven years but he finally came to the conclusion that he was but a blip in the kingdom of God, and that all honor and glory goes to the one true King, the God of Heaven and Earth.

Unfortunately for Satan, he also did not turn away from his prideful heart, and millions of years of earthly despoliation brings this to light.

A couple of other prideful notable mentions include Herod, whose destruction was wrought because of a prideful heart. (Acts 12:21–23.) Then there was King Uzziah whose pride caused him to be shackled with leprosy. (2 Chronicles 26:16–21.) Of course, there are many more, but the precedent is set and still holds true that God despises pride. Paul sums it up in his letter to Timothy by letting him know that a pastor should not be a "novice." (1 Timothy 3:6.) That is, it is difficult for someone to be a young Christian and a leader in the church because they will have a tendency to be, "lifted up with pride he fall into the condemnation of the devil."

First John 2:16 teaches that the pride of life, though arguably the most ruinous, is one of three conditions that can lead men astray. The other two are the lust of the flesh and the lust of the eyes. These additional two categories are also seen in Ezekiel's depiction of the fall of Satan. The lust of the flesh is generally considered to be sexual in nature, but it obviously extends to all fleshly desires. In Satan's case his desire was towards his own self. "Thine heart was lifted up because of thy beauty, thou hast corrupted thy wisdom by reason of thy brightness" (Ezekiel 28:17). His own beauty led him astray.

The third and final act mentioned in both passages is the lust of the eyes or greed. He became puffed up because of the multitude of the stuff that he possessed. On account of his position in the Kingdom of God, he had power, possessions, and wealth. It was this stuff that caused him to turn his gaze off of his Creator and elevated him in his own mind to a level of importance and self-dependence. Ultimately convincing himself that he did not need God and even more arrogantly, he thought that he could be God.

Just like pride, the Scriptures are littered with men who fell into the same trap of wealth and material possessions that Satan had succumb. In Luke 12:15, Jesus gives stern warnings about coveting, "Take heed, and beware of covetousness: for a man's life consisteth not in the abundance of the things which he possesseth."

When he was on the earth, it was easy for him to turn his now physical being into something that God did not intend. He recognized the power that he possessed in his new body and he began to distort that power into things that God did not intend, namely the trafficking of goods and undoubtedly all kinds of debauchery against the Lord. His sin caused his eyes to be opened to all sorts of evil. It is this same knowledge that he used to entice Adam and Eve in the Garden of Eden.

A kingdom of lies

It is important to note that the Bible makes it clear that Satan used his voice to construct his own precedent. "For thou hast said in thine heart, I will ascend into heaven, I will exalt my throne above the stars of God: I will sit also upon the mount of the congregation, in the sides of the north: I will ascend above the heights of the clouds; I will be like the most High" (Isaiah 14:13–14). Just as God called the earth into existence by His words, Satan used his words to construct the exact opposite paradigm of the creative power of God. (Hebrews 11:3.)

Instead of creation he brought sin and destruction into the earth. The thoughts that had filled his heart were voiced. Corresponding action followed his words and rebellion was the result. With his words he framed the antithesis of what God had planned for creation and in the process he caused division, strife, and a war that has waged for eons.

He filled his heart with the exact opposite perspective of God and his rebellion caused a division amongst the angelic hosts. Ezekiel says that he "hast defiled thy sanctuaries by the multitude of thine iniquities, by the iniquity of thy traffick" (Ezekiel 28:18). Undoubtedly his sinful acts were attractive to a number of angelic hosts that were members of his congregation. With his position of priestly authority and dominion over an untold number of synagogues, those under his leadership were subject to his persuasive devices and fell into his cultish trap.

With his smooth tongue and deceptive trickery, some of the angelic host followed after him and the way of sin while others remained with God.

The Bible shows that a full one third of the angelic armies were convinced of Satan's tactics. (Revelation 12:4.) Due to his enviable and influential position both in heaven and on earth, they too were enticed by the temporary pleasures of sin and fell victim to their own lusts. (Hebrews 11:25.)

Those that followed Satan most definitely explored all kinds of depravity. Imagine an enormous infrastructure of angels, each occupying a particular station in their life; not unlike humans on the earth today, each competing for social status and easily susceptible to the whims of their leader. So too the angels felt a sense of pride as they climbed the social ladder and were sucked into the deceitfulness of riches and the lust of the flesh. How easy was it for Satan to influence the minds of angels to join a new order where they could potentially gain additional social status? Through Satan's example, their pride caused them to fall from God's grace and disobey Him.

The Bible shows that angels have their own will. (Isaiah 14:12–14.) So the same tricks that Satan works on the hearts and minds of individuals today are undoubtedly the same devices he used to sway the hearts of minds of the angels back then. He used his influence to trick them into believing that God was not listening anymore. They willingly turned the truth of God into a lie and started down a path that was not meant for them, much like Adam in the garden.

God understands the intention in the hearts of all men and angels and He gives all men and angels a free choice to follow Him or not. "Who changed the truth of God into a lie, and worshipped and served the creature more than the Creator, who is blessed for ever. Amen" (Romans 1:25). It is easy to see now that this verse in Romans, which can be applied to generations of humans on the earth, can also be applied to generations of rebellious angels.

God, of course, is merciful and will forgive their forsaking of His creation for an amount of time determined only by the Lord. In all cases, there are ample opportunities for them to come back to God, during which time He makes every effort to sway that individual back into the fold. (2 Peter 3:9.) "The Lord corrects the people he loves and disciplines those he calls his own" (Hebrews 12:6 CEV). It is out of love for His creation that He disciplines them, but there comes a point where He could take no more and judgment must be dispensed.

Unfortunately, for the angels, their continued sin-filled ways and thoughts produced a desire in them that cannot be quenched. They knew that they had deviated from God, but they were unable to abstain from their appetites and willfully give up communion with the Lord. Eventually they reached a point of no return, where their apostasy was sealed and they could not come back to the Lord nor did they want to. (Hebrews 10:26.)

This same phenomenon can happen in the hearts of those who have accepted Christ and seen and experienced the power of God, but have willingly turned their back on Him. Although God is always willing to forgive and accept them back into the fold, their comes a point when a person's heart has become so closed off that they will not be susceptible to the prompting of the Holy Spirit. (Hebrews 6:4–6.) "There is a way which seemeth right unto a man, but the end thereof are the ways of death" (Proverbs 14:12).

Satan had reached this point and literally millions of years of earth's history show that the Lord continued to hold out hope of his eventual return and reconciliation. Unfortunately, untold epochs of earth's history bear testimony that millions of years of mercy were not enough to overcome his willful apostasy and time and again it brought about negative ramifications and destruction to the earth. The Lord had given him every chance but he was past the point of no return and his final judgment will come in the last pages of the book when he will be cast into the lake of fire. (Revelation 20:10.)

Another human example of the Lord's far-reaching merciful attitude that he has on even the most corrupt societies can be seen when Moses led the Israelites out of Egypt after they had been there for 400 years since Pharaoh first invited them. The Israelites stayed in Egypt this long because the Bible says that the iniquity of the Amorites was not yet full. (Genesis 15:16.)

Unquestionably, the Amorites had sinned, but God determined that it would take several more years for them to reach a point where they would never be able to reconcile with the Lord. So God kept His contingency of Israelites in Egypt for a specified time that he deemed necessary. Once they reached the end game, the Lord sent Moses to remove them from Egypt and take them into the promised land of Canaan that was currently possessed by the Amorites.

In this same fashion, for Satan and select other angels that followed after Satan's pattern, they have already been charged with sin, but their full judgment is yet to come. "Behold, he put no trust in his servants; and his angels he charged with folly" (Job 4:18). Jesus goes on to say that, "the prince of this world is judged" (John 16:11). Jesus' words are past tense, it has already happened. The ruler of this world has been condemned and his fate is sealed, but his full sentence has yet to be fully executed.

In the meantime, God created another species to take their place. Of course, that species is mankind, to which He bestowed free access to the earth. Unfortunately, mankind has fallen for Satan's tricks and sin has entered into the world. Though he was restricted from the earth, mankind's sin has allowed Satan access to the earth once more to fulfill his sinful desires; this time using mankind as the vehicle for disobedience and condemning all generations of mankind to death. Fortunately for humanity, the Lord had another plan: He sent Jesus to conquer the grave once and for all and to save those who will believe. (Mark 16:16.)

So why didn't God just destroy Satan when he realized that a coup was about to take place? Certainly, if God is all powerful and knows all that is happening in the universe, then why didn't he squash the rebellion of Satan and end the ongoing problems? There are two primary reasons. First, God's plan and promise for all of creation was choice. From the beginning He has given the right to choose life or death; to choose blessing or cursing. (Deuteronomy 30:19.) Without the ability to choose between right or wrong, His unwitting sentient creation would be nothing more than slaves. Instead He allows His creation to be free moral agents and choose their own destiny.

Second, God is bound by the words of His mouth. (Titus 1:2.) His words are a contract between all of creation, and especially men and angels. Just as mankind was brought forth by the word of God, so too were the angels brought forth in this same fashion. And just as God established a covenant with man, he also established a covenant with the angels. Some of the promises that were given to the angels are found in the Bible. Others are likely found in some heavenly book that draws up a contract between God and the angels. One glimpse that God reveals to humanity is that angels are eternal. (Luke 20:36.) On account of His word then, He is unable to destroy them.

Of course, Satan knew the promises of God and attempted to use this knowledge to his advantage. He understood that God is eternal and that His word does not change. It is likely that he attempted to try and use this to his benefit by twisting and distorting the Lord's words into something that He had not said. Since he was so close to the very word of God himself, it is likely that he believed God would have no recourse for his thoughts of insurrection. Becoming disillusioned by his own grandeur, he convinced himself that he had outsmarted the Lord and his play for the throne of God would be triumphant.

In other words, Satan reasoned that due to the promises God had established, he would use these words to try and paint the Lord into a corner. Thus he believed that he was tricking the Lord, thinking that He would have no recourse against his coming actions. Reasoning that his logic was impeccable, he likely tried to trap the Lord into some kind of word play. Playing every card in his deck, he assumed that God would have to give up his throne in the face of his logic.

Unfortunately for him, he forgot one key element in his attempted coup; once he walked away from the Lord, he was giving up God's light, the very author of all wisdom. Of course the light of God is the wisdom of God and wisdom only comes from the Lord. Satan was the closest and therefore most likely the wisest being in God's angelic kingdom, but once he forsook his rank and launched his own platform, the wisdom and creativity stopped. He still retained the wisdom he had already garnered, but once he left the flock there was no longer a connection to the only true source of wisdom. Without a doubt, he underestimated what he was walking away from, for every card that Satan played the Lord had a counter-move that trumped him.

Blinded by his own pride, he overlooked this fact and believing that God's hands were tied, it is likely that he thought that there would be no ramifications for his actions. Prior to this, Satan had never seen the judgment of God. As such, he could not have possibly known God's response to such a rebellion. The Psalmist asks, "Why does the wicked renounce God and say in his heart, 'You will not call to account'" (Psalm 10:13 ESV)? But indeed the Lord did require that his account be counted. The Lord required justice.

Undoubtedly it must have been difficult for the Lord to find deceit blackening his soul. It is clear that although He knew that he was a liar from the beginning, there was a point where the Lord did not suspect that Satan's pride had overtaken him, because it says that the Lord found iniquity in him. Flabbergasted to find a traitor in His midst, it goes without saying that compassion took over, as He continued to try and draw Satan back into the fold and convince him to give up his deceitful ways. Satan was stubborn, and because of his position of authority and his own brightness, he was convinced that he could ascribe to greater things. Unfortunately for him, without the wisdom of God backing his every move, things went wildly awry and he lost his favor in the eyes of the Lord.

In Isaiah 14:12 Satan is called Lucifer; a name equated with evil and destruction. That same name has also been rendered as the Morning Star or keeper of light, and gives further tribute to his importance in the Kingdom of God. It shows that he had a light and that light shone so brightly that it illuminated the sky at dawn. No doubt he was and still is a wise being.

He was the mold that was set for all angelic beings to behold in awe and possibly inspire them to walk closer with God. Of course, now the opposite is true; not only has he ceased to walk in the light; he has become an abomination to God. He has lost his position as the Morning Star and has been replaced by a more sure light that shines in a dark place. "Until the day dawn, and the day star arise in your hearts" (2 Peter 1:19). Jesus is The Day Star, the one who is brighter than the sun.

As has been seen, millions of years of death and destruction have been the outcome, and when the Lord turned his back on his own creation in Genesis 1:2 it was the last straw. Oh how it must have grieved Him to remove His presence and leave the earth cloaked in a state of darkness, void of the life and the knowledge of Him; left in the clutches of the prince of the power of the air with no prospect of growth and in its place, death.

Of course, Satan was still endowed with all the knowledge and understanding he had prior to his removal because "the gifts and calling of God are without repentance" (Romans 11:29). Once God gives a gift to somebody, He does not take it back. At no time in the Bible is there any mention of a prophet losing his call or gifting. Their own personal attitudes and appetites may cause them to lose sight of their direction and ultimately bring about their destruction, but the gifting is still there.

In Satan's case, although his calling is still there, his heart is so blackened that he will never be able to return to the Lord. Now, he is simply surpassed by the brightness of the Lord, for it is impossible to produce fruit without being attached to the vine. (John 15:1–8.) Without Him, Satan cannot do anything that is worthwhile. All of his efforts are withered and dead to the Lord. In this same respect, while the earth was / is under the authority of Satan, it was unable to manufacture the fruit it was designed by God to produce.

Omniscient

Again, in Ezekiel it states that God found sin within Satan. (Ezekiel 28:15.) It does not say that he knew of Satan's iniquity, but rather that it was discovered that his heart was tainted. Herein lies a philosophical question that has plagued many throughout time, for if God is truly omniscient why did He allow any of this to happen in the first place? Of course, God knows the end from the beginning, but how that end is achieved is largely still up in the air, which allows for a great deal of flexibility. It means that His plan can be achieved by other methods or individuals who are willing to step up.

Ultimately, God's desire for the earth is peace and goodwill. (Luke 2:14.) Satan's disobedience threw a wrench into this outcome and God had to change the method of how His plan was going to be finalized. On account of the free will of men and angels the Lord has needed to be pliable to see the end of His purpose. Of course, the outcome will always be that His intention will come to fruition, but the individuals that are used and how it is done is up to those that pursue His plan.

Each one of His beings, whether they are angelic or human, has choices to make. Their choice will set them on a path of obedience or disobedience. If they are not walking in the best path for their life, then God may choose somebody else to complete the objective. That one so chosen may be able to change the course of history, whether it is through prayer, finances, evangelism, or any other methodology that He sees fit. God will use that individual to complete the necessary task to finish His devised plan.

So, although it is true that God knows the end from the beginning, the path He uses to accomplish His objectives may be littered with unwilling participants. Faithfully, He will continue to sequester their obedience through the prompting of the Holy Spirit and use His knowledge of their hearts to understand their intentions. Unfortunately, it is this free will choice that has caused some to be left on the sidelines and others like Satan actually end up fighting against the plans of the Lord.

Spiritually Unenlightened

Unfortunately for Satan, his fall from the grace of God was a choice made on his own behalf. The irony with Satan is that the true freedom he had with God was forsaken for the ultimate form of bondage. "For of whom a man is overcome, of the same is he brought in bondage" (2 Peter 2:19). Satan made his choice and embraced the lifestyle of sin with such gusto that he actually became a slave to the very thing he thought would bring him freedom.

Of course, that very same thing happens in the world today. The things that appear to bring peace and happiness are usually accompanied by discord and sorrow. Satan is the perfect example because without God freedom cannot be obtained. It is only dependence upon the Savior that brings freedom from the cares of the world. "If the Son therefore shall make you free, ye shall be free indeed" (John 8:36).

Unfortunately for Satan his time is at hand. Prophecies in the book of Daniel and Revelation predict an end to his reign on the earth. His final judgment is yet to come, but it begins with an abrupt end to his access in heaven. (Revelation 12:9.) This in turn will be followed by a prison term locked in hell and restricted access to the earth. (Revelation 20:2–3.) He has no recourse regarding his future. The Word of God must be fulfilled. The devil is not an idiot, but without a relationship with the Father he has lost his understanding and discernment of all things spiritual.

Proof of this can be seen when he misconstrued the significance of the single greatest event in the history of the earth: the death and resurrection of Christ. Logic would dictate that since he had thousands of years to study the prophecies, he would have understood the implications of Jesus' death. Unfortunately for Satan that was not the case. In 1 Corinthians 2:8 it says that had he known the reason for Jesus' mission on earth he would not have crucified him. Playing right into the hands of God, he murdered Christ and ultimately brought salvation to untold millions.

There are over 300 prophecies in 500 passages throughout the Old Testament that tell of the birth and death of Jesus here on earth. He had access to these books just like all the people on the earth prior to that point. In fact, he was probably there when various parts of it were written. Ultimately, without a connection to the Lord, he was just looking at letters on a page. By turning his back on God, he was unable to decipher the truth of God's word. He chose a path of ignorance to the word of God that left him spiritually blind.

It is forever a mystery to him; once closely linked to the very heartbeat of the Lord, he is now unable to even find a pulse. "But we speak the wisdom of God in a mystery, even the hidden wisdom, which God ordained before the world unto our glory: Which none of the princes of this world knew" (1 Corinthians 2:7–8). In a quest for his own selfish motives, Satan threw away the wisdom of God long ago. Truly, only a fool despises the wisdom and instruction of God. (Proverbs 1:7.)

Anyone can find themselves in this same predicament if they do not make a genuine decision for Christ. They will be left forever without the one true light. Once the decision is made to believe and follow, the blinders can be removed and the light can now enter. "But the natural man receiveth not the things of the Spirit of God: for they are foolishness unto him: neither can he know them, because they are spiritually discerned" (1 Corinthians 2:14). Without Christ, mankind is nothing more than a natural individual unable to interpret the spiritual. However, with Christ the spiritual blinders can be removed and the Spirit can be allowed to reveal the mysteries of God. Once the light of Christ's word is revealed, it can be allowed to gain a foothold into ones heart and mind.

The beginning of the end

Satan was called the anointed cherub that coverth and he was called by God for special purposes both in earth and in heaven. Unfortunately, he lost sight of the prize and his heart became so dark and twisted against the Lord that now there is no going back. Obviously God was not going to be defeated, but His way of reversing the sinfulness that Satan introduced was a mystery to all of creation, until Paul and the disciples' grabbed hold of the revelation. "And to make all men see what is the fellowship of the mystery, which from the beginning of the world hath been hid in God, who created all things by Jesus Christ" (Ephesians 3:9).

God's decision was a mystery from the beginning of the world, not the beginning of the earth (time). Satan's iniquity was not yet full, but will be at the end of this age. In the meantime, He devised a plan after the destruction of the earth to undo the sinfulness that Lucifer had introduced; a plan that was all encompassing, not only for the current occupants of the earth but also for all future inhabitants of the earth. It began by introducing a new species into the earth, with the idea that "they shall be my people, and I will be their God" (Jeremiah 32:38).

Of course, once again Satan and sin quickly entered into the picture and God needed a way to undo the ravages it would have on His creation. He did this by bringing about the remediation of sin through the shed blood of Jesus. Through the creation of man he brought forth Jesus to carry atonement for all the sin-prone creation. (Unfortunately, as has been seen, Satan and his followers' hearts were so dark that they are not interested in returning to the Lord. Even if further mercy was extended, the Bible shows that they would refuse it.)

Hence the offices that Satan relinquished in the spiritual realm had to be replaced. His gifts and callings were still a part of him, but he had lost his familial status. In Job it says that "there was a day when the sons of God came to present themselves before the LORD, and Satan came also among them" (Job 1:6). He is mentioned separately because he is no longer considered a son of God. His own choices brought about his being stripped of this title, but he still has access to the throne room and His earthly reign is not yet over.

Fortunately, since God is a God of wisdom, ingenuity, and creativity, He is always one step ahead of everybody. He knows things about the future that even the angels are astonished to see. (1 Peter 1:12.) His wisdom is never-ending; contrasted with Satan who cannot impart even one new thought, but is sequestered to unoriginal dead thinking. "Doth not their excellency which is in them go away? they die, even without wisdom" (Job 4:21). He can now only keep repeating what he already knows. The call of God will still be on His life, but he will never return to the Lord, and ultimately he will be cast into a place of perdition. The gifts that he has been given are useless for fulfilling a destiny that he has rejected.

Blinded by pride, his ego is too large to concede that he has been defeated. No matter what the prophecy says, he believes that he can overcome these mere words of insight. He is consumed by his own beauty and desires to set himself above the throne of God. Of course, setting himself on God's throne would not be good enough. To truly show his dominance, he desires to set himself above God's throne. Apparently, his view of reality has become so distorted that he believes that he is not just equal with, but greater than his Creator. Pride has caused him to lose sight of his ranking in the kingdom of God and it is this pomp that has brought him down to the grave. (Isaiah 14:11.)

His time is up. The things of the Spirit are a mystery to him and always will be. His rejection of Christ proved which side of the line he stands on. He made up his mind long ago and he is not coming back. Satan's ultimate destruction is yet to be seen, but the course is sure and the final nail is already in his coffin by the administration of the shed blood of Christ. He will be brought down to hell, a place designed especially for him and his followers. (Isaiah 14:15, Matthew 25:41.)

When Jesus rose from the grave He stepped in to occupy all of the vacated positions of Satan. Christ is the culmination of all the offices that he relinquished (prophet, priest, and king) and so much more. (2 Peter 1:19,

Luke 4:17–21, Hebrews 1:3, 5:9–10, 1 Corinthians 1:30.) In fact, He is the fulfillment of all things physical and not one word out of His mouth will pass away until all things in heaven and earth are fulfilled. (Matthew 5:17–18.) Upon His death He filled in the gap and reconciled all of the sins of mankind.

Today, all believers have the anointing of God in their life because of the price that Christ paid to unite mankind with God. (1 John 2:27.) Thus, in a well-positioned twist of fate, the very one who was allowed access to the throne has been removed and will be condemned forever from His presence. In his place another one has stepped in and allowed millions upon billions to have the same direct access to the Creator that Satan once enjoyed. This includes the entire population of the angelic host who will receive a new level of freedom provided by the blood that was previously unavailable to them and Satan never saw it coming.

Epochs

During the reign of Satan and the angelic hosts, paleontological records indicate that there were also other creatures dwelling in the earth. Of course, notwithstanding the generations of mankind, his reign encompassed the span from the original creation until the destruction of the earth in Genesis 1:2. Almost daily there are new discoveries of prehistoric life forms, the most prominent of which are dinosaur bones that are being unearthed all over the globe. In fact there are so many finds that there are scarcely enough paleontologists to document them all. So where do these dinosaurs and other paleontological life forms specifically fit into the creation?

Historically, single-celled life forms began in an era dubbed the Precambrian period which took place somewhere between 3,500 to 570 million years ago. After this came the Cambrian era, which occurred from 570 to 505 million years ago and introduced significantly more complexity to earthly life forms. During this period the paleontological records show a burst of life suddenly erupting on earth which took on many different forms: algae, trilobites, sponges, and worms. This sudden spurt of life on earth has been aptly named the Cambrian Explosion.

In an extremely abbreviated overview of the numerous eras, the Cambrian was followed by the age of the dinosaurs, which transpired somewhere between 290 million to 63 million years ago. Accordingly there are multiple eras of life and extinction during these many millions of years when the dinosaurs roamed the earth as hundreds of thousands of different species would rise up only to die off and give rise to a whole new set of species. These periods have been named the Permian, Triassic, Jurassic, and Cretaceous ages respectively.

From a scientific standpoint, little is known as to why various life forms emerged and then suddenly become extinct for seemingly no reason throughout time. Of course, there have been several theorized interpretations of the paleontological record from these periods. Among the suggested likely causes of these extinctions are temperature changes, meteorites, volcanoes, etc. Undoubtedly, the record shows that after each disruption in the timeline, life always re-emerged abundantly and quickly

Earthly records show that there has been at least five major periods of extinctions and rebirths in the early earth. The Bible agrees with these interruptions of life on the planet and gives a hint that there may have been more.

Beginning in Mark 12:1 Jesus relays the parable of the vineyard. This particular parable is largely promoted as a teaching about the kingdom of mankind since its creation in Genesis. In reality though, the timeline can also be viewed as a glance into the history of the earth from its original creation. Of course, parables are insights into the kingdom of God in heaven and on the earth. They reveal hidden truths about God, and in virtually every instance, one parable can have several different valid interpretations, as is the case here. Thus, following is the parable of the vineyard.

And he began to speak unto them by parables. A certain man planted a vineyard, and set an hedge about it, and digged a place for the winefat, and built a tower, and let it out to husbandmen, and went into a far country. And at the season he sent to the husbandmen a servant, that he might receive from the husbandmen of the fruit of the vineyard.

And they caught him, and beat him, and sent him away empty. And again he sent unto them another servant; and at him they cast stones, and wounded him in the head, and sent him away shamefully handled. And again he sent another; and him they killed, and many others; beating some, and killing some. Having yet therefore one son, his wellbeloved, he sent him also last unto them, saying, They will reverence my son. But those husbandmen said among themselves, This is the heir; come, let us kill him, and the inheritance shall be ours. And they took him, and killed him, and cast him out of the vineyard. What shall therefore the lord of the vineyard do? he will come and destroy the husbandmen, and will give the vineyard unto others. And have ye not read this Scripture; The stone which the builders rejected is become the head of the corner: This was the Lord's doing, and it is marvellous in our eyes? (Mark 12:1–11)

The story begins with a man who plants a vineyard. That man is God and the vineyard is the earth. Immediately, the Lord sets a hedge around his vineyard and digs a place for the winefat. The winefat is the juice from the grapes that were stomped out and siphoned into a vat to be fermented. The obvious connotation was that the Lord expected fruit from His new creation. It was not created in vain, but rather it was purposefully constructed to yield a bountiful harvest.

Once it was created and set in motion, he charged His underlings (Satan) to administer it. Putting all of His trust in Satan's ability He left and went His way. After a period of time He sent one of His faithful stewards (angels) to check on His harvest. Of course the caretaker was not yielding the harvest that the Lord had expected. In fact, he had become so corrupt that he beat the steward and sent him back to the Lord empty handed. Each season the Lord would check on the progress of the vineyard and send one of His stewards, and each season the angel was either wounded or killed. This happened three times in the parable and it concludes by inferring that there have been many more, saying in verse five, "And again he sent another; and him they killed, and many others; beating some, and killing some."

Each season is an epoch of life in the history of the earth. If the fruit produced in the earth is not desirable to the Lord it is cast into the fire. (Matthew 7:19.) Since the dawn of creation the earth has been producing fruit, but the caretaker (Satan) was not properly administering it and that fruit was abandoned. It was hewn down to make way for something better. In other words, during various epochs of the earth's history, God wiped out the entire living spectrum or most of the entire living spectrum and started again in a new season with a different creation. It is evident that the Lord did not feel that the transgressions of Satan had been completed and He continued to give him opportunities for restitution. Each time producing another whole spectrum of life on the planet and in each situation Satan failed to oversee it. According to this parable, this cycle happened on at least five different occasions, but leaves the number of times open-ended by saying that there were many others.

The fossil record shows that each one of these occasions is separated by millions of years. The reality of the parable is that God is upset over the administration of the earth by Satan during these millions of years. Each season he returns to look at the fruit that has been produced and each season He becomes more and more wroth at the situation. The administration of the earth is not being conducted in a manner that is pleasing to God and the administrator is mocking him by hurting or killing the servants that are reporting on its progress. In turn God responds with at least a partial judgment, which wholly affects the earth. Then again, following each season the Lord recreates the harvest in hopes that it will get better.

When the situation does not change, He eventually creates a new administrator to watch over the earth. That administrator is man, who quickly turns the reins back over to Satan. God sent one last steward to come to the earth and ask for the fruit. That steward was his own Son. He too was beaten and this time killed, with the thinking that if the only Son was killed then the inheritance of the earth would be up for grabs. Of course, the Lord had a better plan and out of His death came the ultimate abundance of life.

Basically, Satan was given every opportunity to straighten out his act, but his wickedness continued to grow worse and worse. Ultimately, Satan had reached what the Bible calls the fullness of iniquity. (Genesis 15:16.) Each time that Satan was given another opportunity, he rejected the Lord and his heart became more hardened.

A parallel situation to the hard-heartedness of Satan in the earth prior to mankind is that of Pharaoh during the days of Moses. It took Pharaoh ten signs from God before he finally allowed the people of Israel to be removed from slavery, and even after his own son died he still regretted the decision. His heart had grown hard to the things of God. There was no turning back to the Lord; and his heart was likened to stone. (Exodus 14:5.) Ultimately, his final decision left a whole host of his army dead at the bottom of the sea. (Exodus 14:28.) He had become completely defiant and unyielding to the things of God, even in the face of the Lord's continued mercy.

Undoubtedly, millions of years of death and destruction in the earth's annals are proof of Satan's continued disregard for all the things of God. He has been and continues to be the very antithesis and distorter of God's plan. One of the better documented eras of time in the history of the earth is the age of the dinosaurs. Records of their existence have been uncovered all over the earth and a wide range of diversity and creativity are exposed with each subsequent finding. Of course, Satan was present when the dinosaurs roamed the earth and he would have had administrative control over all their activities.

He is the one who comes to steal, kill, and destroy; violence is in his nature because the Bible says that "by the multitude of thy merchandise they have filled the midst of thee with violence, and thou hast sinned" (Ezekiel 28:16). His power and earthly wealth became the very object of his affection. He believed himself to be God and used the power that he had to turn it against the very creation he had administration over; distorting the very creation he was charged to oversee. Yet, over and over again the Lord deemed that his time was not yet full and He would start afresh with new life on the planet.

Satan was a liar from the beginning, so basically his sin has always been a part of the physical creation, which carries over to all generations of time in the earth. Certainly, his violent nature influenced each generation of creation on the earth and the outcome of each particular period was something that the Lord never intended. In other words, sin distorted the creation during each subsequent era and in time, the Lord respectively passed judgment on Satan's administrative abilities. Of course, paleontological finds show that during each one of these periods almost everything died, but then it was reborn in a relatively quick fashion by the Lord.

The overall final outcome of his continued disobedience was millions of years of death and disaster that were all caused by Satan's hand. Each period leading to not only the destruction of animal life on the planet, but also potentially rearranging the earth in some fashion. As the geological record shows, Satan's dispensation covers hundreds of millions of years or more and throughout these epochs not only were the biological species affected, but also the earth itself.

Earthen records reveal that during those early ages, the landscape had been rearranged time and again. Volcanoes erupted and dispersed, earthquakes ripped apart the earth's surface. Floods ravaged whole regions, and on and on. There are untold thousands of region-specific-destructive events that the earth has witnessed and suffered at the hand of Satan's rule. Geological records show that various places on the planet that are now habitable were once covered by great seas of water and vice-versa.

These events happened untold numerous times throughout the generations of the earth prior to man's appearance. In fact the entire modern day economy is "driven" by the plant and animal life of epochs past. Vast reservoirs of oil are discovered all over the planet and under the ocean, proving that at various points in the earth's past there were thriving ecosystems that covered its entire face. Not only on the populated surfaces of the earth today but also where the ocean waters cover its surface. These aptly called fossil fuels allow commerce to transpire on the earth today.

Now during this current dispensation, history is repeating itself and just as has happened numerous times in the past, it will be happening once more on the earth. This time mankind became the administrator, but still Satan wiggled his way back into the business. Fortunately, the Lord has had enough. Satan has failed every test and his days of authority in the kingdom of God are quickly reaching an end. The dispensation of mankind on the earth is his last stand and the shed blood of Christ marks the end of his authority. At the end of this age, his ultimate judgment will be dispensed.

On Earth

So now with some background of Satan's activities during the earth's earlier years, it is easy to understand how this affected the creation of Genesis. Satan was restricted from his administration in the earth, but in the spiritual realm he was still very much alive. The earth had been literally washed clean of Satan's sin, but due to the fact that there was no remission of the sin it still remained dormant on its surface. Once Adam partook of the fruit, he unearthed all of the sin that had been pent up from past ages and Satan realized that he still had authority in the earth, though not necessarily in a physical form. While mankind was sinless, his influence and authority on the earth was meaningless, but once Adam yielded to sin, it gave Satan access to the earth once again. Since he is a spirit, it is through human spirits that he now can resume his prior sinful life (though physical possession is also a possibility if he is invited in, which will be the case with the Antichrist).

Now his primary influence over mankind is through manipulation and deception to procure his ultimate plan. Humanity is an unwitting recruiting ground for Satan and his cohorts. Once Adam ate of the tree of the knowledge of good and evil, he lost God consciousness and gained sin consciousness. Hence the war continues to wage, and sin and disobedience are still in existence throughout God's kingdom, both on earth and in heaven. "For we wrestle not against flesh and blood, but against principalities, against powers, against the rulers of the darkness of this world, against spiritual wickedness in high places" (Ephesians 6:12). The wickedness happening in heaven is something that Christians battle against and are told to resist. (James 4:7.)

And so the battle wages on, being fought with subtle techniques by making individuals believe that there is no more need for God. It is truly deceptive in nature and designed to acquire additional intellectual property. One of the biggest lies that Satan has propagated in recent years is that God's creation was a farce. By slowly leaking his corrupted ideals into society, he has undermined the truth of creation and caused division amongst untold millions. It is exactly the type of deceitfulness that he wants humanity to believe.

By distorting the truth, the creature ends up becoming more worshipped than the Creator. (Romans 1:25.) "Beware lest any man spoil you through philosophy and vain deceit, after the tradition of men, after the rudiments of the world, and not after Christ" (Colossians 2:8). When this age comes to a close it will also bring about a close to the age of Satan and his rebellion. Unfortunately for those that choose the wrong path, the outlook is bleak. For without the belief in Jesus and the washing of His blood there is no remission of sins. If transgressions are not blotted out, they will have no protection against God's judgment and they will be cast out of His presence. (Matthew 25:41.)

CHAPTER 17

Paradise and Perdition

Deep

Whatsoever the LORD pleased, that did he in heaven, and in earth, in the seas, and all deep places. (Psalm 135:6)

The deep has been looked at extensively in earlier chapters, but returning to it will help expose the circumstances that predicated the re-creation. The Bible states that, "In the beginning God created ... and darkness was upon the face of the deep" (Genesis 1:1–2). Obviously, if there was a deep, then there were flooded areas, because the deep represents a watery abode placed on the earth for a particular reason by God. The Psalmist confirms this when he says that, "He gathereth the waters of the sea together as an heap: he layeth up the depth in storehouses" (Psalm 33:7). It is not an act of creation, but rather a manipulation of watery storehouses.

Second Peter 3:5–7 brings further insight into the state of the earth at this point when it says that,

> For this they willingly are ignorant of, that by the word of God the heavens were of old, and the earth standing out of the water and in the water: Whereby the world that then was, being overflowed with water, perished: But the heavens and the earth, which are now, by the same word are kept in store, reserved unto fire against the day of judgment and perdition of ungodly men.

Though many conjecture that Second Peter is depicting the flood of Noah, it is not. Rather Peter is pointing to a time prior to Adam. He is speaking about the water that covered the earth at the re-creation; the world that was controlled by Satan before mankind. Though many have tried to place this passage during Noah's generation, there are several clues in the verse that show that the flood being described is not the flood of Noah.

Peter starts by mentioning the original creation when he says that "the heavens were of old." Although it has been mentioned that there is not a definitive definition of the word old in the Bible, it can be a reference for a time prior to the creation of man. God is occasionally mentioned as the God of old. (Psalm 74:12.)

It goes on to say, "and the earth standing out of the water and in the water." In other words, during that time of old, the earth was built upon a foundation of water and its entire surface was resting upon it. There were no large bodies of water on its surface after its original creation, a fact that has been established in previous chapters.

Next, it says, "the world that then was." Of course, the use of the word "world" helps to classify which era this verse is referencing. Again, the word world refers to a system of government established upon the face of the earth; it is not a description of the earth itself. Since the introduction of mankind on the earth, there has only been one world system; that is the system of mankind which was established by God upon the earth. Anything that happened since the creation of Adam on the earth is still the same world system. Therefore the distance from Adam to Noah is not a new world system, but rather the same world. It is the world system that came about with the creation of mankind on the earth.

Thus, when Peter says, "the world that then was," he has to be referring to a world that existed prior to the existence of man. That is the world that was overflowed with water and is still largely overflowed with water today. It is referring to a world that was under a different authority; the world that was under Satan's rule. That world was different than the world that mankind inhabits, because they are two different divestitures based on two different sets of laws (one for man and one for angels). In conjunction with this when it states that, "Whereby the world that then was, being overflowed with water, perished," would be an incorrect statement if it was referencing Noah because Noah and his family did not perish. To say that the world perished would not be a correct statement if any contingency lived.

Third and perhaps most convincing, Peter says, "But the heavens and the earth, which are now, by the same word are kept in store." In other words, Peter is stating that the heavens and the earth have changed. The only time that both the heaven and earth could possibly be referred to as changing or being different would have been during the re-creation. Although there certainly could be an argument that during the flood of Noah the earth was changed, that same argument would not apply to the heavens. The only time that the Bible refers to the heaven being changed was on the fourth day, when it says, "And God made two great lights; the greater light to rule the day, and the lesser light to rule the night: he made the stars also" (Genesis 1:16). It was changed during the re-creation.

Finally, it calls God's word during the re-creation the same word. "But the heavens and the earth, which are now, by *the same word* are kept in store, reserved unto fire against the day of judgment and perdition of ungodly men." That is the words that the Lord began to speak during the re-creation, they are the words that are now. It is apparent that the Lord spoke other words to other generations of time prior to mankind, but this current period of words pertain to the same word from the Lord that changed the heavens in Genesis and put mankind upon the earth.

That same word that recreated the earth is the same word that was given to Adam, and it was that same word that Noah and all the other patriarchs in the Bible received. It was designed for mankind and it has not changed since. He first began to speak it in Genesis 1:3. It is not a word that was given to angels; they were already given a word that was designed specifically for them. That word was for a heaven and earth that have since passed (though no less poignant and likely a very similar word because God does not change, just a different word in a different time for a different generation of His creation).

So when it says the world that then was it means that there was a world that existed previously. That world was established by the same God but was a different world made for a different group of individuals. That former earth was destroyed and remains largely covered in water. This world though is destined for a different judgment, which is called the day of fire. The relevance of this is that there were two world systems on the earth and there were at least two floods: Noah's flood and another flood during the ages of Satan's rule prior to man.

Of a truth, geological records indicate that throughout time the earth has gone through many large, yet localized floods. There has also been some scientific speculation that some of the floods may have been global in their reach, but it is far too difficult to determine given our current knowledge base. Speculation aside, the Bible shows that there were at least two global floods in the history of the earth. One was the flood during the days of Noah and the other can be attributed to the Lord turning away from the earth just prior to the creation of man. It was that later one that left a remnant of water on the earth that comprise the oceans of the earth today.

Several biblical authors mention the large bodies of water that cover the earth today as places of sin and foreboding. Job says that there are mysterious and deadly things covered by the deep, "He discovereth deep things out of darkness, and bringeth out to light the shadow of death" (Job 12:22). Daniel concurs when he states that the Lord, "revealeth the deep and secret things: he knoweth what is in the darkness" (Daniel 2:22). Isaiah gives a stern warning to those who would seek to find it by saying, "Woe unto them that seek deep to hide their counsel from the LORD, and their works are in the dark, and they say, Who seeth us? and who knoweth us" (Isaiah 29:15)?

Without question, the deep is a place that many of the Old Testament writers were acquainted with by reputation. Clearly, it is not a place that should be sought after, rather it is a place of secrecy, darkness, and death. The fact is references like these conjure the exact opposite image of the manifest presence of the Lord. He is not death and darkness, He is Light and Peace. (Luke 1:79.) In Him is life and no darkness at all. (John 1:4, 1 John 1:5.) Indeed, He is a God of flowing shallow water that cleanses, refreshes, and purifies; He is not a God of deep, stagnant, and dead water.

At the end of this age, the Bible shows that the sea will give up its dead. (Revelation 20:13.) Is this referring to the people that die at sea and have their bodies cast into the ocean? Possibly, history recants tales of great naval victories that resulted in horrific human loss. Certainly, all the humans that have lost their lives at sea will be brought forth and judged with all the other men and angels at the time of judgment, but the implications here are much more.

Unquestionably, the deep is on the earth because of the activities of Satan in ages past. "For thou hast said in thine heart, I will ascend into heaven, I will exalt my throne above the stars of God: I will sit also upon the mount of the congregation, in the sides of the north" (Isaiah 14:13). Satan looked up from his earthly position of authority and desired to use his physical authority in the earth as a base of operations and use it to overthrow God's spiritual throne and eternal kingdom. An all-encompassing plan that continues throughout the ages starting from the original creation, and continuing on through the events of Genesis 1:2 as witnessed by the geological record, which is still seen in the earth today with the presence of the oceanic bodies.

He could not carry out this ambitious plan on his own, he had to have help. The Bible instructs that there were others who were on the earth with Satan. Those others were angels and it was a full one third contingency that followed after him in his rebellion. (Revelation 12:4.)

Perdition

And the sea gave up the dead which were in it; and death and hell
delivered up the dead which were in them: and they were judged
every man according to their works. (Revelation 20:13)

When the earth was flooded prior to the re-creation it was to cover up and destroy the sins that were prevalent in the earth. Those sins were brought about by Satan and the angelic host that had followed after him. So although Revelation shows that the sea will give up its dead, it is certainly referencing more than just deaths due to maritime wreckage and battles.

Just like in the days of Noah, the Lord used a flood to eradicate the sinfulness that permeated the earth; the same is true of the angelic hosts prior to the re-creation. The passage in Revelation is referring to the judgment of the angelic hosts that were destroyed prior to the re-creation. Deep water is not a function of the Lord, so when the earth was originally created there were no oceans. The oceans came about on account of the sin of the angelic hosts prior to the re-creation and those waters still cover the earth today.

It is why the Psalmist calls to God to deliver him from the hand of the deep, where people hate him. (Psalm 69:14.) If he was talking about humans that had died at sea, this verse wouldn't make sense. There is not a contingency of people that died at sea with their spirits still hanging around the oceans. Those people had left their bodies behind and are now in another place. (2 Corinthians 5:6, Luke 16:22–23.)

No, he is speaking about a contingency of people who are currently occupying the deep and who undertake hating him as an occupation. Their own selfish and wicked ways brought them there and they are fully envious and desirous to be back on the earth in the flesh. So, although the Lord has said that the angels are eternal, he did not say that they were eternal in a physical state, but only spiritual. (Matthew 25:41.)

Thus, it is apparent that the Lord used the sea as a vehicle to eradicate not only Satan, but an entire population of sin-filled angels that were living on the earth prior to Adam. The Bible makes it undeniably clear that the deep is an area that used to be an envoy of sin and that sin is still prevalent in these deep recesses. This means that the large bodies of water currently on the earth are intended to serve as a reminder and are representative of prior wickedness in the earth.

There are several chapters in Ezekiel that help to bring these facts to light, each one is a double reference to both an earthly kingdom and the kingdom of Satan. In fact, the Bible reveals that each of these earthly kingdoms were strongly influenced by Satan and he was a driving force behind their wickedness. The first one was already looked at in Ezekiel 28, but the Lord continues in the very next chapters where Ezekiel is called to prophesy against the Pharaoh of Egypt. (Ezekiel 29–32.) He begins the prophecy by saying:

> Son of man, set thy face against Pharaoh king of Egypt, and prophesy against him, and against all Egypt: Speak, and say, Thus saith the Lord GOD; Behold, I am against thee,

Pharaoh king of Egypt, the great dragon that lieth in the
midst of his rivers, which hath said, My river is mine own,
and I have made it for myself. (Ezekiel 29:2–3)

The parallelism between the two kingdoms is obvious from the first few
verses; definitively the passage is addressing Pharaoh, but allegorically it is
speaking about Satan's kingdom and the connotations are obvious. It begins
referencing Satan by calling him "the great dragon that lieth in the midst
of his rivers." Of course, the great dragon is one of the monikers assigned
to Satan. (Revelation 12:9.) It goes on to say that he "lieth in the midst of
his rivers." To say that there is more than one river in Egypt would not be
a correct statement, because the only river in Egypt is the Nile. Parallel this
with Satan's kingdom, which was found in Eden the garden of God which
was bordered by four different rivers.

One last thing to note about this phrase is that it clearly states that
the rivers are his. Certainly mankind has dominion in the earth and over
its waterways, but to state that any one human owns a river would not be
a correct statement. Satan, on the other hand, as has been seen, had more
direct power over the earth. So to say that he owned the rivers of Eden may
be a correct statement based on the passages detailing satanic power over the
earth that have been reviewed previously.

This passage goes on to further illuminate his conceit, because it says that
he was egotistical enough to proclaim in God-like fashion that he had actually
made the rivers. Obviously, the degree to which Satan's pride had elevated
himself was beyond what one can imagine. It continues on in chapter 31:

Whom art thou like in thy greatness? …a cedar in Lebanon
with fair branches, and with a shadowing shroud, and
of an high stature; and his top was among the thick
boughs. The waters made him great, the deep set him up
on high …Therefore his height was exalted above all the
trees of the field, and his boughs were multiplied, and his
branches became long because of the multitude of waters,
when he shot forth. All the fowls of heaven made their nests

in his boughs, and under his branches did all the beasts of
the field bring forth their young, and under his shadow
dwelt all great nations. Thus was he fair in his greatness,
in the length of his branches: for his root was by great
waters. The cedars in the garden of God could not hide
him ...nor any tree in the garden of God was like unto
him in his beauty. I have made him fair by the multitude of
his branches: so that all the trees of Eden, that were in the
garden of God, envied him. Therefore thus saith the Lord
GOD; Because thou hast lifted up thyself in height, and he
hath shot up his top among the thick boughs, and his heart
is lifted up in his height; ...Upon his ruin shall all the fowls
of the heaven remain, and all the beasts of the field shall be
upon his branches: To the end that none of all the trees by
the waters exalt themselves for their height, neither shoot
up their top among the thick boughs, neither their trees
stand up in their height, all that drink water: for they are
all delivered unto death, to the nether parts of the earth, in
the midst of the children of men, with them that go down
to the pit. Thus saith the Lord GOD; In the day when he
went down to the grave I caused a mourning: I covered the
deep for him, and I restrained the floods thereof, and the
great waters were stayed: and I caused Lebanon to mourn
for him, and all the trees of the field fainted for him. I made
the nations to shake at the sound of his fall, when I cast him
down to hell with them that descend into the pit: and all the
trees of Eden, the choice and best of Lebanon, all that drink
water, shall be comforted in the nether parts of the earth.
They also went down into hell with him unto them that be
slain with the sword; and they that were his arm, that dwelt
under his shadow in the midst of the heathen. To whom
art thou thus like in glory and in greatness among the trees
of Eden? yet shalt thou be brought down with the trees of
Eden unto the nether parts of the earth: thou shalt lie in the

midst of the uncircumcised with them that be slain by the sword. (Ezekiel 31:2–10, 13–18)

The Bible is clear that this passage is referring to Pharaoh and his kingdom, but the distinct similarities to Satan's kingdom cannot be ignored. It says that there was not "any tree in the garden of God was like unto him in his beauty ...so that all the trees of Eden, that were in the garden of God, envied him" (Ezekiel 31:8–9). Just as mankind is equated to a tree, here also Satan and the angels are depicted as trees. (Psalm 1.) Satan, of course, was the main tree, but it reveals that there were also other trees in Eden that were not as prominent in stature and as such they envied him. Those other trees were angels that were in the garden of God with Satan and, of course, the garden of God refers to the garden that God established on the earth prior to the onset of mankind. (It is also interesting to note that all the animals and fowl were also under his control. "All the fowls of heaven made their nests in his boughs, and under his branches did all the beasts of the field bring forth their young" (Ezekiel 31:6).)

So just like mankind is told to bring forth fruit unto the earth, the angels of those earlier days were called upon to do the same thing. They had the ability to grow tall, straight, and produce a thick shadowy canopy, which is all due to their proximity to the flowing rivers of the Lord. "The waters made him great, the deep set him up on high with her rivers running round about his plants, and sent out her little rivers unto all the trees of the field" (Ezekiel 31:4).

Drinking from the flowing water of the Lord, they could shoot up in glory and strength. Unfortunately, much to the Lord's chagrin they failed to do so, "To the end that none of all the trees by the waters exalt themselves for their height, neither shoot up their top among the thick boughs" (Ezekiel 31:14).

It is apparent that they followed after their leader's example and lost sight of their One True King. "Because thou hast lifted up thyself in height, and he hath shot up his top among the thick boughs, and his heart is lifted up in his height" (Ezekiel 31:10). Under Satan's influence they failed to produce the fruit that the Lord was requesting. The outcome was that the Lord brought about their destruction by bringing the deep upon them, causing the great waters to cover them; "for they are all delivered unto death, to the nether parts of the earth" (Ezekiel 31:14).

Ezekiel is clear that the source feeding his trespasses was the deep because it says that the "the deep set him up on high" (Ezekiel 31:4). Of course, this is the same deep that is seen in Genesis 1:2, which is the same deep that the Old Testament patriarchs mention as a place of perdition, one that is dark and secret. They are the oceans and the seas of the earth today that the Lord used to destroy a population of angels that lived on the earth prior to mankind.

Geological records show that there have been many instances of large seas covering various areas of the earth at different points throughout time. Additionally shallow seas and reservoirs dotted the current landscape in epochs past. Unquestionably, regional flooding and climate changes may have had some temporary influence on these phenomenon, but the Bible is clear that large bodies of water on the earth in times past were a method to cover and eradicate sinfulness.

Of course, without water, life does not exist; but deep menacing water is not from the Lord. He is always associated with smaller manageable amounts, such as rivers and streams. Thus, the amount of water on the earth is in direct correlation to the residue of sin that plagued the earth in ages past. Looking back again at the Satanic influence over Tyrus, it points to this same fate:

> When I shall bring up the deep upon thee, and great waters shall cover thee; When I shall bring thee down with them that descend into the pit, with the people of old time, and shall set thee in the low parts of the earth, in places desolate of old, with them that go down to the pit, that thou be not inhabited; and I shall set glory in the land of the living; I will make thee a terror, and thou shalt be no more: though thou be sought for, yet shalt thou never be found again, saith the Lord GOD. (Ezekiel 26:19–21)

Tyrus was a walled island city just off the coast of Lebanon that was known for its trade. In fact, the very next chapter gives a list of their trading partners. The list is detailed; making it easy to see why they would have been compared to Satan regarding the iniquity of their traffic. Of course, no one can serve two masters, which is why the Bible makes it apparent that the city of Tyrus lost sight of God. (Matthew 6:24.)

Certainly, the city's fate was similar to the fate of the earth just prior to the re-creation. The passage goes on to detail what that fate was, all the while revealing a little about the previous inhabitants of the earth. It says that they will go down into the lower places of the earth, places that have been desolate of old.

Researchers state that there are no large reserves of water under the earth and there never have been, but the Bible paints a far different picture. In fact, right in this verse it says that there are places under the earth that are desolate of old. The water that the Lord used to flood the earth prior to man's existence came from these places that are now desolate. In other words, the water that once occupied these places under the earth is now on its surface as an ever present reminder of sin and judgment. Its foundation is still established in water, but some of that water now covers the earth.

Certainly, these events are easily correlated with the current landscape of the globe. Remember that when God planted the garden for Adam it was in the east of a region called Eden. This was determined to be an area that encompassed most of the Middle East and possibly beyond. Ezekiel showed that originally all of Eden was a garden and since the garden encompassed most of the Middle East, the rest of Eden was an enormous area. It is probable that much of the earth's present day exposed landscape was called Eden the Garden of God. It was here that the Lord said Satan had dominion over prior to the re-creation and still has dominion over today.

Ezekiel goes on to point out that it was in the garden that other trees grew and of course, other trees means that other angels also had access to the garden. The numbers are unknown but it is likely that since it was God's Garden, only God's select were allowed access. Nevertheless, this could mean that the number reached into the hundreds of thousands or even millions of the angelic host that also walked in the garden.

Additionally there was a whole different contingency of angelic hosts that are not mentioned that are in the area now covered with the oceans. Those numbers were likely more of the rank-and-file angels and not a major part of the leadership, but still fully joined in the satanic rebellion. Combining both the area of the garden with the areas now covered by seas could put the numbers of angels well into the billions or tens of billions. Certainly, one third of an innumerable company of angels is still innumerable, so the entire size of the population will never be known.

One additional note about the angelic population on the earth is that there is no trace of angelic bodies that remain on the earth. Ezekiel describes the judgment of their physical bodies, "By the multitude of your iniquities, in the unrighteousness of your trade you profaned your sanctuaries; so I brought fire out from your midst; it consumed you, and I turned you to ashes on the earth in the sight of all who saw you" (Ezekiel 28:18 ESV). Satan's body was physically destroyed by fire and so too were the rest of his followers. His spirit was delivered unto the nether parts of the earth during the flood mentioned in Genesis 1:2. The same was the fate of all of his followers.

It does not end there, because Ezekiel states that Satan still rules from amidst these waters, "Because thine heart is lifted up, and thou hast said, I am a God, I sit in the seat of God, in the midst of the seas; yet thou art a man, and not God, though thou set thine heart as the heart of God" (Ezekiel 28:2).

Satan still believes that he has a shot at usurping the Lord, even though destruction has come upon his kingdom. Thus, his main throne or rule comes from the midst of the seas. And since Adam turned over the keys of the earth to him, he once again has access to the earth. (Romans 5:19.)

Fortunately, Job states that his kingdom is benign and mundane because, "The depth saith, It (wisdom and understanding) is not in me: and the sea saith, It is not with me" (Job 28:14). His plans are routine, predictable, and ultimately beatable. In the meantime, even though there are no original thoughts emanating from his throne, mankind is still enticed by the same old trickery. Hence the battle continues for the hearts and minds of individuals that roam the earth today.

So when the earth flooded in Genesis 1:2, all the angelic populations on the earth were burned up and covered with water, whereby they lost their home and their ability to manifest themselves physically. Then when the earth was recreated, it emerged out of those same waters, a land mass that was known as Eden. Still a large contingency of waters remained and these are the oceans of the earth today. Thereby keeping covered approximately two thirds of the stomping grounds of Satan's unwitting minions and leaving a pit or desolate place under the earth.

Since final judgment has not been expounded by the Lord, the former angelic hosts whose homes are now covered by water still take up residence in the deep in the spiritual realm. It is for this reason that the Psalmist mentions that he does not want to sink into the deep waters. He understood that there were fallen members of the angelic hosts who live there and are envious and hate filled toward those who walk the earth. (Psalm 69:14.)

Others that were occupying the Garden of God are likely the forces that Jesus frequently encountered and are still at work in the earth today. They are the trees mentioned in Ezekiel 31 as taking up residence in Eden, the garden of God prior to the dispensation of man.

Unfortunately, for all the angels during those days, they lost the title of angel and are now considered demons or angels that have fallen from the grace of God; fallen angels. Proof of this can be found throughout the Scriptures as it differentiates between angels and devils. For instance, angels are in heaven but demons are earth bound. (Matthew 28:2, 12:43–45.) Angels do not sleep but demons need to rest. (Revelation 4:8, Matthew 12:43.) Angels are messengers but demons are distorter's of God's word. (Hebrews 1:14, John 10:10.) Angels can have bodies, while demons desire to have a body. (Judges 13:6, Acts 1:10, Mark 5:1–13.) The distinction between the two is obvious, fallen angels have human-like qualities because they once had a physical form in the past and after their death they remain trapped in this same state, unable to return to their full former state of physical existence, yet they are desirous to do so. These facts are reconfirmed by Jesus when he said that,

> When the unclean spirit is gone out of a man, he walketh through dry places, seeking rest; and finding none, he saith, I will return unto my house whence I came out. And when he cometh, he findeth it swept and garnished. Then goeth

he, and taketh to him seven other spirits more wicked than
himself; and they enter in, and dwell there: and the last state
of that man is worse than the first. (Luke 11:24–26)

It is apparent that when the unclean spirit went out to look for other
spirits, he did not have to travel far, as they were present in the earth. Then
again in Luke 8, when Jesus entered into the region of the Gadarenes, a man
with a number of unclean spirits came and met Him on the shore once His
boat had docked. When He asked what their name was they called themselves
legion because their number was so great. Jesus cast the unclean spirits out,
but they besought him to not cast them into the deep. Jesus listened to the
demons and allowed them their request. In turn, they removed themselves
from the man and they went and possessed a herd of pigs, which ran down
a hill and cast themselves into a lake. (Luke 8:26–39.)

They had been in the deep before the earth was entirely flooded after
Genesis 1:2, but on account of their geographical placement after the re-
creation, they were earthbound in the spiritual realm once again. Thus they
understood the ramification of the deep and that a large portion of their
colleagues were still residing there. Knowing what the deep was, they did
not want to go back, but were aware of the fact that Jesus had the authority
to send them there.

In other words, the angels that previously lived in what is now the oceans
still reside there, apparently unable to escape its watery boundaries. So it is
apparent that the natural boundaries that are seen today would have to be
the same in the spiritual realm. That is, the physical boundaries of the earth
today are the same boundaries in the spiritual realm that the fallen angels
are forced to adhere to. Those that were on the earth when it was destroyed
were allowed to remain in spiritual form on the earth, but those that were in
the areas of the seas are confined to its boundaries. When Jesus spoke of a
devil recruiting others to go back into a person that he had just been removed
from, they would not have had to go down to the pit to recruit because other
devils were already roaming the earth.

For the legion of demons that Christ encountered in the man from the
Gadarenes, they were granted compassion for their limited remaining time

on the earth. Essentially they were allowed to remain on the earth (their domicile) and take up temporary residence in a herd of swine. (Luke 8:32–33.) Once Adam released the curse of sin back into the earth, it allowed access to the spirits who were residing in the earth access to it. Now they can gain that access through human beings, but only for those who allow it to happen. (Ephesians 4:27.)

Certainly, there is another course. Look not into their things which will only lead to death, rather look to the cleansing blood of Christ which will always lead to life. (Romans 6:13.) Their final demise has already come with the death and resurrection of Christ, but they remain free due to an extension of mercy granted by the Lord. Their time on the earth is limited and the beginning of the end will start with a trumpet and the voice of an archangel declaring the coming of the Lord. (1 Corinthians 15:52.) That is the beginning of the end, which will lead to the final enemy that will be destroyed; death. (1 Corinthians 15:26.)

At the end of this dispensation, the tide will change and judgment will come upon those that strayed from the Lord; both man and angel. The curse will no longer have a stronghold on the earth. His Light will shine throughout all the earth for eternity, eradicating the darkness before finally concluding with the removal of the seas from the earth because of what it represents. (Revelation 21:1.)

The seas and oceans that cover the earth now will be forced back underground from where they originated. The vacated desolate areas under the earth will be replenished with the water now covering its surface, and it occupants, along with the people of old time (more on this shortly), will be judged and cast into the lake of fire. (Revelation 20:14–15.) At that time, the water (rivers) of the Lord will run throughout the earth, uninhibited to do its ever-refreshing work of restoration. This was and always has been God's plan for the earth.

Now taking this information and looking back to the conclusion of the sixth day, or the re-creation, it gives clarity to the edict that the Lord gives Adam to be fruitful and multiply, and replenish the earth. (Genesis 1:28.) If there were no other sentient species on the earth prior to mankind then the Lord would merely have said to fill the earth. Instead, He makes it clear that the earth was once populated and He gives Adam charge to do it again. This obviously refers to more than just repopulating the animals; they were already reproducing on their own. This is a direct command from God for Adam to replenish / repopulate the earth with humanity because the earth was formerly occupied by a contingency of angelic hosts.

Satanic divisions

As it has been mentioned, when the Bible refers to the organization of angels it is usually in a militaristic manner. No doubt this is due to their current defensive status in their battle against the forces of evil. In much the same fashion, just as God established a hierarchy in His dominion, so to Satan has positioned his troops in the same sort of ranking, with himself as the general.

With the influence that Satan exhorted in spiritual realm, it would stand to reason that Satan attracted angelic followers from all divisions of God's kingdom. From the top of the officer corps all the way down to the lowly foot soldier, Satan indoctrinated his peers to come and join his empire. Those unwitting oafs who signed up likely occupy a similar place of authority under Satan's authority.

There are four realms of devilish authority mentioned in Ephesians 6:12: principalities, powers, rulers of the darkness of this world, and spiritual wickedness in high places. These are the four areas where Satan still has influence, both in heaven and on earth and the four areas that Christians do battle in.

Of course, when any class of devilish hierarchy is mentioned in the Bible it is always referred to as something that Christians have authority over. "For this purpose the Son of God was manifested, that he might destroy the works of the devil" (1 John 3:8). On account of the blood sacrifice of Jesus on the cross, believers have unlimited access to counter Satan's attacks. (Revelation 12:11.) Praise God for the blood.

The works of Satan in the earth are not yet fully destroyed, but the physical and spiritual infrastructure for his ultimate demise has been established. His final resting place is the lake of fire, but before that final step takes place the

Bible shows that there are actually several regions established for occupation. (Revelation 20:10.)

Three of these areas are found in Revelation 20:13, where it states, "And the sea gave up the dead which were in it; and death and hell delivered up the dead which were in them." First there is the sea, which was seen above as begin occupied by the angels that took up residence on the earth in ages past and still remain confined to a watery spiritual tomb.

The second region is death, which is the physical death of the body and is referred to in the Old Testament as the grave. Upon death, the human body remains and decays on the earth but the spirit and soul move on to their respective places. For the believer it is heaven. (2 Corinthians 5:8.) For the non-believer it is hell. (Luke 16:22–24.)

Finally, hell is the last area under the earth mentioned here. It is a temporary holding place for humanity that makes the choice against the Lord while on the earth. (Luke 16:23.) Ultimately, the angelic host and non-believing humanity will be cast into an area called the Lake of Fire; an area originally designed for Satan and his followers. (Revelation 20:10–15, Matthew 25:41.)

Hell

Depart from me, ye cursed, into everlasting fire, prepared
for the devil and his angels... (Matthew 25:41)

Much like the Sadducees who questioned the existence of hell, amazingly a lingering question of its existence remains today. It is likely that this lack of belief in hell can be tied to the false teaching that claims God would not dispense judgment upon anybody for any offence. Those that take this stance believe that no matter what a person has done, they are entitled to an eternity in heaven.

Certainly, this could not be farther from the truth; the ramifications of His judgment can currently be witnessed by looking at the oceans of the earth today. Additionally, the Bible is chocked full of instances that judgment was dispensed on various people and nations on account of their not following after the Lord. God is not going to judge the world and separate the sheep nations from the goat nations only to accept them all into eternal life. (Matthew 25:31–46.) No, the Bible is definitively clear that not only is there a hell, but it is being used for those who make a choice not to follow the Lord. (2 Thessalonians 1:8–9.) Therefore, it is imperative to bring to light some of the simple biblical truths about hell and the afterlife.

Preachers throughout the ages have used hell to scare the heaven into people and get them to believe in God. The "fire and brimstone preacher" can still be found using this style of preaching all over the earth today; forcefully urging all of their patrons to make a decision for the Creator or be cast into a place of eternal fire. Hell is described as a place of great physical torture; where 2nd and 3rd degree burns cover your body throughout all eternity. A place that is completely dark and its inhabitants are forever separated from other individuals, forever burning and wandering throughout the nether-regions of this vast landscape. This is truly an interesting concept of hell, but what does the Bible have to say about it? Indeed, some of the perceptions of hell are simply not based on biblical extrapolation, but on conjured rhetoric of the afterlife.

In the Old Testament the most prominent Hebrew word used for hell is *sheol*, which is a general term to describe a place of death that is physically located under the earth. (Psalm 63:9.) Its usage can be somewhat confusing, for as many times as it is translated as hell, it is also translated as grave. Of course, while both are under the earth, one is a physical death, while the other is a spiritual death. Thus, the definition of sheol can be somewhat ambiguous in the Old Testament and it is therefore pertinent to look at the New Testament.

The definition of hell is considerably less ambiguous in the Greek (New Testament) where the word *hades* is translated as hell. Hades is never used to describe a physical location, but rather a spiritual place. To describe a place of physical death in the Greek, the word grave is used

The bottom line is that hell is one division of an area under the earth that is called the pit or the bottomless pit. Isaiah mentioned this when he proclaimed, "Yet thou shalt be brought down to hell, to the sides of the pit"

(Isaiah 14:15). The Psalmist said, "For great is thy mercy toward me: and thou hast delivered my soul from the lowest hell" (Psalm 86:13). Obviously, indicating that if there is a lowest hell there must be a higher hell and other divisions. Finally, Solomon confirms hell's segmentation when he states, "Her house is the way to hell, going down to the chambers of death" (Proverbs 7:27).

Its current use is to house those who make a choice against the Lord. "The wicked shall be turned into hell, and all the nations that forget God" (Psalm 9:17). There is no mention in the Bible of hell being a place that demons are currently restricted to. There are other divisions of the pit where some devils are currently housed (more on this later).

Additional proof that humans are sent to the pit can be seen in the example that God provided to the tribe of Israel when Korah and his company rose up against the leadership of Moses. The Bible shows that they were swallowed up by the earth and went quickly down to the pit. (Numbers 16:30–33.) Here again the word pit is used as a parallel with hell. Certainly it is true that their path was the pit, but the division of the pit that they were compartmentalized into was hell. In this same regard, David cried out to the Lord to not be silent to him, "lest, if thou be silent to me, I become like them that go down into the pit" (Psalm 28:1).

Without question, hell is not a place that anyone would want to go, because the Bible makes it abundantly clear that those that do go long to get out, or at least warn their brethren. (Luke 16:28.) There is no order and it is a place of complete chaos and corruption. (Job 10:21–22, Job 17:13–14.) There is no praise of God. (Psalm 6:5.) There is neither work nor original thought, nor knowledge, nor wisdom. (Ecclesiastes 9:10.) It is a place of wickedness. (Psalm 55:15.) The very nature of the devil is encouraged, causing envying and strife and resulting in every evil work. (James 3:16) It is a place of torment that continues to grow as it lodges an increasing number of unbelieving dead from the earth. (Isaiah 5:14.)

Also, the Bible portrays it as a place of darkness, because the light of God does not shine into its darkness. (Matthew 22:13.) Job conveys the sense that even the slightest hint of light is darkness, "where the light is as darkness" (Job 10:22). God is there, but only because He knows the works of all of

His creation. (Psalm 139:8.) Undoubtedly, God is aware of its activities, but the light of His presence does not enter. Without His light, darkness reigns supreme and there is no good thing. It is a complete separation from the Lord, which is the exact picture of the earth in Genesis 1:2. Of course, that implies that just prior to the introduction of mankind the earth was literally hell-like. For without His presence things die and spiritual wickedness rules; it is a situation that can only be described as hell.

Certainly it can be confusing as to whether the pit is a physical or a spiritual place. The Bible makes it clear that it is both. It is a physical place located under the earth, but its boundaries are largely used as a point of separation to constrain the spirits of mankind upon death. Though there are apparent exceptions to this rule (Korah), during this dispensation it is solely used as a place to house the spirits and souls of non-believers. (Psalm 9:17.)

After this dispensation, the Bible teaches that new bodies will be distributed and those that are in hell will be reassigned to the Lake of Fire along with Satan and his cohorts. (Revelation 20:10–15.) Proof of this can be found in several Scriptures, beginning with Jesus who said, "And fear not them which kill the body, but are not able to kill the soul: but rather fear him which is able to destroy both soul and body in hell" (Matthew 10:28). Daniel agreed when he stated, "And many of them that sleep in the dust of the earth shall awake, some to everlasting life, and some to shame and everlasting contempt" (Daniel 12:2).

So what about the idea that hell is a place of fire and brimstone? Certainly, the New Testament is filled with verses that mention hell fire. "Where their worm dieth not, and the fire is not quenched" (Mark 9:44). Verses such as these make it apparent that hell is not only a physical place, but is also a place of torment. The Psalmist stated, "The sorrows of death compassed me, and the pains of hell gat hold upon me: I found trouble and sorrow" (Psalm 116:3). Jude calls the fires of hell eternal. (Jude 1:7.) Albeit, there is every indication that the torment of hell is physically real once a new body is received during the resurrection. In all truth, the Bible does not spend an inordinate amount of time on the physicality of hell. So to what degree the fires of hell impact the physical is unclear.

There is one other consideration that needs to be examined when looking at the fires of hell and that is the spiritual implications. Once one goes to hell, it's because of a choice that was made during their lifetime. If one chooses against accepting Christ as their savior, then they are rejecting His redemptive work. They are saying no to the remission of their sins. When Christ died, He died for all men and the forgiveness of sins. If they do not believe on the Savior then they are eternally separated from the Father. There is no more communication with the Father forever and their soul burns with the desire to draw near to Him to a level that can only be described as torment. It is the spiritual separation from God that is the real burning. It is a burning desire to draw near to the Lord, which is the ultimate torture: an eternity separated from the love of God.

The burning that happens in one's soul will never be quenched. God has withdrawn Himself from that person, the exact picture of Genesis 1:2 when hell was on the earth. The ultimate death is spiritual and not physical. Without God the unbeliever is forever trapped in a state of disorder and darkness, unable to receive forgiveness, they are tormented by guilt, and they long for the presence of God.

Fortunately, there is an answer. Christ speaks of Himself when He says, "I am he that liveth, and was dead; and, behold, I am alive for evermore, Amen; and have the keys of hell and of death" (Revelation 1:18). By dying to conquer both the grave and hell, He is now alive and has dominion over both physical death and spiritual death. This is further confirmed in 1 Corinthians 15:55 when it says, "O death, where is thy sting? O grave (hades), where is thy victory?" Here the word Hades is translated as grave, but it is apparent that it should have been translated hell for Christ's resurrection was for both the body and the soul. He died once for all and He leaves a simple choice for everybody: believe on Him and be removed from the disasters of hell. "That if thou shalt confess with thy mouth the Lord Jesus, and shalt believe in thine heart that God hath raised him from the dead, thou shalt be saved" (Romans 10:9).

Heaven

In the Old Testament, heaven is almost always referred to as the physical realm of the sky and stars, though on occasion it does make reference to heaven as the abode of God and angels. So for believers in the Old Testament, in addition to the ambiguity of hell, there was also essentially no reference to heaven as a place where human souls will abide. Heaven was not a place that Old Testament believers went after death and various authors make it clear that Old Testament believers were largely unsure of what the afterlife had in store.

The reason for this stems back to creation: man was created to live on the earth eternally and had Adam made it to the tree of life, existence in this earthbound state would have been the outcome. Fortunately he did not make it to the tree of life after he partook of the tree of the knowledge of good and evil. Had he also partaken of the tree of life, he would have forever been trapped in this current sin-ridden state of existence.

Since Adam did not make it to the tree of life, it is apparent throughout the Old Testament that there was a general lack of understanding of the afterlife. This lack of insight caused some Old Testament saints to search for a temporal Kingdom of God on the earth. Abraham during his lifetime is seen looking for a city of God. (Hebrew 11:10.) Undoubtedly, he would not have been looking for it if he did not believe that he would run across it while he was on the earth. He knew that there was an afterlife, but there was no clear concept of what was in store.

The fact is that the saving grace of Jesus was not yet dispensed to the Old Testament saints. They proclaimed the message of a Messiah that was going to come and change the course of history, but for the most part they were unaware of what it meant for them and their eternal souls in the meantime. So even though they were faithfully compliant to the law, they were not yet partakers of the saving blood of Christ.

On account of this, the Old Testament is awash with allusions and inferences to a resurrection and salvation for the righteous. They knew that at some point they would be delivered from the clutches of death, but they were unclear as to the how and when. Following are a few of the hundred or more references to salvation in the Old Testament. The Psalmist calls God "the God of our salvation" (Psalm 68:19), "O Lord my salvation" (Psalm 38:22), and "the rock of my salvation" (Psalm 89:26). Isaiah said that He is the "God is my salvation; I will trust, and not be afraid" (Isaiah 12:2). Old Testament believers understood the Lord's saving grace. Furthermore, they had hope for a better life after the grave. Even though their writings portray a sense of the unknown, they knew that there was going to be redemption, they just did not know when.

Reassurance for their eternal souls is found in several other passages of Scripture that show that they understood the grave was not their final resting place. "But God will redeem my soul from the power of the grave: for he shall receive me. Selah" (Psalm 49:15). Job had some introspective on the resurrection when he says, "If a man die, shall he live again? All the days of my appointed time will I wait, till my change come" (Job 14:14). He understood that there may have to be a time of waiting before he was to be received into the heavenly realm.

Indeed, even the righteous among the Old Testament proclaimed that their habitation upon death was actually below the surface of the earth. "But he refused to be comforted; and he said, For I will go down into the grave (sheol) unto my son mourning" (Genesis 37:35). As we have discussed, the word sheol in the Old Testament is largely unclear as to its meaning, but Jacob's statement here is very clear that he viewed dying as being more than just a physical death; it was also a spiritual juxtaposition that placed him below the surface of the earth.

One final proof of this comes from the book of Samuel when Saul approaches a woman who has "a familiar spirit" and asks her to bring Samuel back from the dead so that Samuel can tell him what plan of attack he was supposed to take in his pending battle. (1 Samuel 28:7–19.) The Jewish king knew that he needed direction from God to determine if he should go into the battle or not. But since Samuel had recently died Saul was unable to get clear direction, so he called upon the local sorceress to conjure up Samuel from the dead. The woman was able to find Samuel, the righteous priest of God, and he came and spoke with Saul.

The interesting part of this is that the Bible shows that Samuel came up from out of the earth. "And the woman said unto Saul, I saw gods ascending out of the earth… And she said, An old man cometh up; and he is covered with a mantle" (1 Samuel 28:13–14). Samuel, the great priest of God, was confined to the bowels of the earth. From whence he came up and prophesied to Saul about the impending battle and the immediate future of the nation of Israel. (1 Samuel 28:18–19.) The implication is that even though he was below the earth, he was not devoid of interaction with God who would be the only one that could have possibly known the outcome of the battle.

The only two times that there seems to be a contradiction with this is in the case of the prophet Elijah and Enoch. In both of these instances they were removed from the earth and directed straight up to heaven. (2 Kings 2:11, Genesis 5:24.) The interesting part of this story is that in each of these cases they never died. Their soul and body were preserved from the grave or possibly they were simultaneously changed to a new heavenly glorified body on their way up to heaven. Thus, giving the Old Testament men and women of God hope that heaven may ultimately be a place for them.

Ultimately, those that descended (which was everybody except Elijah and probably Enoch) knew that they were going to be with God, but they were unclear as to when and how. Their outlook for eternal bliss was a little less bright than our knowledge, but they understood that one day their dream of salvation from the grave would be complete. In the interim though they were unsure as to how their deliverance was going to be fulfilled.

Of course, this adds a great deal of confusion when trying to decipher the exact definition of hell. For if hell is dark and bleak and below the earth then how is it that even the believers in the Old Testament went there? And if Samuel, one of God's notable priests in the Old Testament, along with multitudes of others didn't make it to heaven, then what happened? Fortunately for the saints, the Lord allowed one other option for the Old Testament believers. It wasn't a complete reunion with God, but it also was not the same path that the sinner took, despite both being referred to as being under the earth.

The Tree of Life

When Adam was in the garden he had two choices to partake in: the tree of the knowledge of good and evil and the tree of life. He must have been too busy naming animals and enjoying the beauty of the garden and his wife, because he never made it to the tree of life. He only partook of the tree of the knowledge of good and evil and his choice caused him and his wife to be removed from the garden and a curse to be brought upon mankind and the earth.

Immediately after Adam's first disobedient act, God expelled him from the garden and prevented him from partaking of the tree of life. Again, had Adam found the tree of life and eaten from it, he would have forever been bound in a sin-filled state of existence upon the earth. Instead Adam's sin brought physical death to mankind.

Once Adam was exiled from the garden, the Lord prevented anyone from re-entering it by placing Cherubim's at the entrance so that humanity would not have access to the tree of life. (Genesis 3:24.) That access remained restricted until the death and resurrection of Jesus Christ. With His death came the plan of redemption through His resurrection. His resurrection provides a way to the tree of life eternal, not only in the afterlife but it also releases untold benefits in the here and now. Unfortunately for the Old Testament saints of God, this was not an option until the days of Christ. The only way they could reach the tree of life was after death.

That means that the tree of life is still in existence. God did not want to destroy the tree, because His intention for humanity was still eternal life. Adam was unable to find his way, therefore God needed to preserve the tree. His plan for man to live eternally has never been swayed, indeed current physiology points to the fact that mankind was designed to live indefinitely. Of course, this design was changed once Adam was expelled from the garden and mankind began to age. So he drove out the man; and he placed at the east of the garden of Eden Cherubim's and a flaming sword which turned every way, to keep the way of the tree of life.

It is interesting to note the way that Genesis describes the angels' purpose concerning the tree, it says they were placed there "to keep the way of the tree of life" (Genesis 3:24). It does not say that the angels were put in place to guard the way to the tree of life, rather they were keeping the way. Thus, eternal life for the Old Testament believers was still available on account of the preservation of the tree of life.

Since the Garden of Eden encompassed much of the Middle East and it is apparent on any topographical map that this entire area is now a desert, then what happened to the angels and the flaming sword that was used to guard Eden and the tree of life? The answer is found in Ezekiel, where he states that Eden has moved, "To whom art thou thus like in glory and in greatness among the trees of Eden? yet shalt thou be brought down with the trees of Eden unto the nether parts of the earth" (Ezekiel 31:18). Again this verse is a description of the prominence of Satan over his kingdom but it also contains a clue about the continued existence of Eden.

It says that all of Eden was swallowed up by the earth and now occupies an area under the earth. So not only are the pit and hell found under the earth, but here it is clear that the Garden of Eden had also taken up residence under the earth and what was left on the surface of the earth was a desert. Isaiah points out this same fact when he says, "For the LORD shall comfort Zion: he will comfort all her waste places; and he will make her wilderness like Eden, and her desert like the garden of the LORD" (Isaiah 51:3).

That is, at some point not long after Adam was removed from the garden, it was swallowed up by the earth and in its place was left a desert. Nowhere does it state that the garden was destroyed, but rather that it was swallowed whole into the belly of the earth; leaving in its place a deserted landscape as a reminder of the propensity of both man and angel toward sin.

It is no wonder that the Lord has an affinity for the area of Israel. It was originally named Eden and it was designed for His glory and manifestation for untold generations of time by both humans and angels. Unfortunately, neither party was able to fulfill its purpose; that is until one man stepped up and declared against all improbability that he was going to follow after the Lord. That man was Abraham and on account of him the nation of Israel was born and they became the chosen people of this now deserted landscape.

Interestingly, it is Abraham that is mentioned by Jesus in the parable of the rich man and the beggar Lazarus. (Luke 16:19–31.) The parable tells of a man by the name of Lazarus who was treated with disdain while he was on the earth. He was so poor that he longed to eat the crumbs off the rich man's table. Upon death the rich man went to hell and Lazarus went to a place called the bosom of Abraham. "And it came to pass, that the beggar died, and was carried by the angels into Abraham's bosom: the rich man also died, and was buried" (Luke 16:22).

Though some would contend that Abraham's bosom was a region in the afterlife that was before unmentioned, remember that Eden is literally translated as paradise. So in this story, the paradise that it is referring to is the Garden of Eden. Although the Garden of Eden was a physical place, it had kept its status of paradise and continued to exist in the heart of the earth. Therefore, it can be seen from this passage then that all Old Testament believers went to the Garden of Eden which is paradise. Abraham's bosom is literally referring to the fact that the man was resting on Abraham's lap. Similar to the way that John rested on the bosom of Jesus. (John 13:23.)

The continued existence of the tree of life is also witnessed in Revelation, where it says, "Blessed are they that do his commandments, that they may have right to the tree of life" (Revelation 22:14). So for those that remained faithful to the Lord, prior to his arrival on the earth, they were given access to the tree of life upon their death which had been engulfed by the earth.

In other words, for the Old Testament believers who followed the Lord, upon their death they went into the heart of the earth to partake of the tree of life that was still in the midst of the Garden of Eden. No doubt the Lord preserved the lives of the Old Testament saints in this abode under the earth for "precious in the sight of the LORD is the death of his saints" (Psalm 116:15).

They descended under the earth to a place that was formerly on the surface of the earth called the Garden of Eden. Certainly, it still remained in a physical form since it occupied a physical place under the earth, undoubtedly lit by the very presence of the Lord. Its occupants were constrained by its boundaries in their spiritual form. Their bodies remained on earth while their spirits continued on in paradise. The true benefits of the tree remain unrealized until the end of this dispensation when death is swallowed up in victory and new bodies are distributed. (1 Corinthians 15:51–54.)

Unfortunately for Satan, the humans who believed on the Lord took his place in the garden. For him and his colleagues their future course was clear, they will be going to a very real place called the lake of fire. (Revelation 20:10.) Once under the grace of God, Satan had free reign in God's garden, but he greedily decided on the wrong path and was replaced by those that chose the way of the Lord.

The Bible does not say exactly when the garden was swallowed by the earth, but since God was not going to destroy the tree of life and Eden was now under the earth, it must be assumed that the removal of Eden from the earth predated the first believers going to the grave. Abel the son of Adam would have to have been suspended there, as he was surely the first man of God to die, making it apparent that the garden had been consumed by the earth prior to this point. Additionally, the Bible shows that shortly after his death, his brother Cain went back to the area that was formerly the garden to establish a settlement; an area that would have been off limits if it still contained the tree of life. (Genesis 4:16.)

Furthermore, after Cain had killed Abel, the Bible states that the voice of Abel's blood cried unto the Lord from the ground. (Genesis 4:10.) Abel was a righteous man and his death needed to be atoned for. In the meantime, Abel followed the Garden of Eden into the bowels of the earth, though his blood would not stop calling to the Lord until the perfect sacrifice had been accomplished. So, returning to the story of the rich man and Lazarus will help to unearth a few more clues to the existence of the garden under the earth.

And in hell he lift up his eyes, being in torments, and seeth Abraham afar off, and Lazarus in his bosom. And he cried and said, Father Abraham, have mercy on me, and send Lazarus, that he may dip the tip of his finger in water, and cool my tongue; for I am tormented in this flame. But Abraham said, Son, remember that thou in thy lifetime receivedst thy good things, and likewise Lazarus evil things: but now he is comforted, and thou art tormented. And beside all this, between us and you there is a great gulf fixed:

so that they which would pass from hence to you cannot; neither can they pass to us, that would come from thence. (Luke 16:23–26)

Abraham and the rich man could see one another, but they were separated by a gulf or chasm. Imagine the picture, here we have Lazarus, a poor man who was essentially disdained and disregarded throughout his entire life is now resting in the bosom of Abraham and residing in the Garden of Eden. On the opposite side is a wealthy man of earthly riches and fame who now has nothing and is tormented because he is separated from the Lord and forever guilty of his sins. He is without hope, but he looks over and sees Abraham and asks him for some help. Abraham responds by saying that he is unable to help due to the great gulf that separates the two different areas.

So here again, for those that died in the days of the Old Testament, whether righteous or unrighteous, their spirits and souls descended under the earth. That is, when a person physically died prior to Christ not only were they buried under the earth, but their souls and spirits remained under the earth. Depending on one's choice on the earth, some went to hell and others went to the Garden of Eden. Those that resided in hell were located on one side of the bottomless pit. From the story of Lazarus and the rich man it is apparent that on the other side of the pit was the Garden of Eden. Even though the chasm was bottomless, it was not so wide as to prevent a conversation, but it was wide enough that neither the rich man nor Abraham were able to cross.

Simply put, on one side of the great gulf or pit is hell and on the other was Eden or paradise, with both being located under the earth. Those that made choices to follow after the plan of God for their lives are treated to the fruits of the garden. "To him that overcometh will I give to eat of the tree of life, which is in the midst of the paradise of God" (Revelation 2:7). For all others the wide road leads to hell.

The saints of the Old Testament are enjoying the "fruits" of their earthly walk, but their path was not yet finished. Unquestionably their new home in the Garden of Eden had all the amenities of Eden while it was on the earth, but nevertheless it was not heaven. Essentially it became a place where men and women of God who were born and died under the old covenant congregated.

While Abraham was on the earth, the Bible says that he searched for a city of God, because he understood that there was something more in store for him. It is possible that he may have believed that if he reached it, he would just cross over that veil from death to life. Through the years, other Old Testament saints had a slightly different view, "The LORD killeth, and maketh alive: he bringeth down to the grave, and bringeth up" (1 Samuel 2:6). They knew that although they were going under the earth, they also understood that there would be a day that they would rise out of the earth.

Daniel prophesies about the upcoming event by saying, "And many of them that sleep in the dust of the earth shall awake, some to everlasting life, and some to shame and everlasting contempt" (Daniel 12:2). Hereby, pointing to the fact that the grave and death would not be able to contain the spirits of men. Some people will get pushed into eternal punishment and others will go on to everlasting life.

Abraham found solace upon his death, but his true peace came at one precipitous event in the history of the earth. That event was the death, resurrection, and ascension of Jesus. Without the cleansing blood of Jesus, mankind was not able to ascend to be with God, including those believers in the Old Testament who first had to descend and reside in the garden, which was still tainted by the sins of man. Upon the resurrection of Christ, all of this changed. The shed blood of Jesus was recognized by God as a covering for the sins of mankind and it incorporated the previously cursed garden also. "But now it has been revealed to us through the coming of our Savior, Christ Jesus. He has ended the power of death and through the gospel has revealed immortal life" (2 Timothy 1:10 GNB).

The reality of this was seen while Christ was hanging the cross. One of the condemned men next to Jesus recognized his deity and asked Jesus to remember him when he entered into His kingdom. Jesus said to him, "To day shalt thou be with me in paradise" (Luke 23:43). The man made the choice for Christ just prior to his death and that choice put him in paradise (Eden). Just like all the other Old Testament saints; that man believed and made it into the garden, where he met up with the Lord again.

Of course, upon his death, the first thing that the Lord did was proceed down into the bowels of the earth for three days and nights. (Matthew 12:40.) It is puzzling that Christ would need to go down after death before He went up to heaven. Being the Son of God would seem to confer certain privileges and spending unnecessary time in middle of the earth seems frivolous in the overall perspective of what He accomplished. After all, didn't he suffer enough on the earth as a human being when he was disgraced and beaten before the Jews, His family, the Sanhedrin, the Roman government, and so many others? Furthermore, as He hung on the cross, His Father looked away as He took on all of the sin and sickness of the world. (Mark 15:34.) Surely that would have been enough.

So what could possibly be gained by also spending time in the bowels of the earth for exactly three days? The crux of the matter is found in Acts 2:27, "Because thou wilt not leave my soul in hell, neither wilt thou suffer thine Holy One to see corruption." Jesus was not about to be left in hell or the grave. In fact, it was just the opposite. He was about to show His redemptive power in the face of death.

Hence, upon His death the first thing He did was to descend into the bowels of the earth. His descent served a three-fold purpose. His first stop was the Garden of Eden where he met with all the Old Testament believers and announced the good news that He had just bridged the gap between mankind and the Father. It is likely that just as the disciples were immediately unaware of the meaning of his sacrifice, so too were the occupants of paradise, even though some of them had prophesied of His coming. Undoubtedly, once He appeared and explained the situation, their uptake was quick and it is certain that a celebration broke out.

He was not done though, because after His stop in the confines of the garden, he crossed over the chasm to the other side of the pit where he encountered the gates of hell. Hell has gates just like heaven. (Matthew 16:18, Genesis 28:17.) If there are gates then there are keys and that is exactly what the Lord's goal was in His journey to hell; it was to obtain the keys of hell and death. "I am he that liveth, and was dead; and, behold, I am alive for evermore, Amen; and have the keys of hell and of death" (Revelation 1:18).

No longer would anyone have to fear the grave because He overcame it and now owns the keys. It is why He has the authority to cast unbelievers into the confines of hell and later cast them into the pit also known as the second death. (Revelation 20:14.) He is in possession of the keys and now has authority over all of its power. In turn, He released that same overcoming power to those that believe on Him. (His third stop while He was under the earth will be looked at in the next chapter.)

Accordingly, Ephesians says that after he descended, He in turn ascended and led captivity captive and gave gifts unto men that all things might be fulfilled. (Ephesians 4:8–10.) He took those that were righteous and led them to heaven; replacing the sinful nature of Adam with the pure blood of Christ; the Second Adam. He then ascended into heaven with the believers of the Old Testament.

While He was passing from the pit to heaven with those that were captive under the earth, He made a stop on the earth; appearing to Mary and warning her not to touch Him because all of the sin filled nature of the world had been left in the grave and His perfect blood sacrifice had yet to be presented to the Father. By touching Him, Mary would have tainted His perfection with her worldly nature. (John 20:17.) One other interesting thing that the Bible mentions about this point in history is that during this brief stop on the earth, His resurrection power carried over to other people also. "And the graves were opened; and many bodies of the saints which slept arose. And came out of the graves after his resurrection, and went into the holy city, and appeared unto many" (Matthew 27:52–53). Although this verse is mentioned immediately after his death, some of the activity did not transpire until after His resurrection.

When He died, the earth shook from an earthquake which split rocks and tore the temple veil in two. (Matthew 27:51.) At that point in time, some of the graves of the men and women of God buried in the earth were exposed. Apparently the Jews and the Romans were unable to cover them back up in a timely fashion due to all the other disruptions from the earthquake. As Jesus was transporting the people in paradise to heaven, He stopped on the earth with the whole procession, resulting in some of the occupants of paradise coming in contact with their physical remains, bringing them back to life and appearing unto many in Jerusalem. Then apparently, once Christ continued on His path to heaven with the rest of the believers, their bodies were once again abandoned on the earth.

Additionally, the Bible is clear that along with the transition of the saints to heaven the physical structure of paradise was also moved, including the tree of life. Paul confirms this when he said that he knew a man that was caught up into the third heaven. "I knew a man in Christ above fourteen years ago, (whether in the body, I cannot tell; or whether out of the body, I cannot tell: God knoweth;) such an one caught up to the third heaven ...How that he was caught up into paradise" (2 Corinthians 12:2, 4). This passage interchanges paradise with the third heaven and goes on to state that this gentleman was caught *up* there.

The Old Testament believers and the garden were no longer trapped underground but were instead united with the Father in heaven. So when Jesus spoke to his fellow convict on the cross, He told him that He would see him in paradise that day because that was the disposition of paradise at the time. Christ first descended prior to His ascension. (Ephesians 4:9.) Then later, that same paradise can be found above the earth, taken up with the rest of the captivity and now resides in heaven.

This truth can also be seen several times in Revelation where the tree of life is mentioned as being located in heaven. One example places it in close proximity to the throne, "And he shewed me a pure river of water of life, clear as crystal, proceeding out of the throne of God and of the Lamb. In the midst of the street of it, and on either side of the river, was there the tree of life, which bare twelve manner of fruits, and yielded her fruit every month: and the leaves of the tree were for the healing of the nations" (Revelation 22:1–2). The tree of life is now in its rightful place in the midst of heaven, due to Christ's actions on the earth.

The waiting of the saints was over; their sin-filled nature was unable to be accepted by God until the Lord paid the price for their sins. Once He did, it was at this point that their spirits became perfect. (Hebrews 12:23.) Their imperfection and sinful state was washed clean and replaced with the spirit of perfection. In time, the tree will ultimately move back to earth one final time after the final judgment when Christ sets up His kingdom here on earth. Death will have been destroyed and all believers in Christ will have new bodies and be able to physically partake of the fruit of the tree of life; then the final enemy that will be destroyed is death. (1 Corinthians 15:26.)

God's plan for His creation was unfolded upon the death of His Son. "Forasmuch then as the children are partakers of flesh and blood, he also himself likewise took part of the same; that through death he might destroy him that had the power of death, that is, the devil; And deliver them who through fear of death were all their lifetime subject to bondage" (Hebrews 2:14–15). His death and resurrection put an end to death and fear for those who were all their lifetime subject to it.

CHAPTER 18

Life after the Garden

Life after the Garden

Therefore the LORD God sent him forth from the garden of Eden,
to till the ground from whence he was taken. (Genesis 3:23)

Once again returning to the account of Adam outside of the garden, it can be seen that when Adam was expelled from the garden he continued in his profession as a farmer, returning to the area that the Lord had removed him from prior to his transition into the garden. As a living soul, he now had the know-how to farm instead of merely gathering herbs and hunting. On their own, Adam and Eve began to have children, and from their seed the population of the earth erupted.

"And Cain went out from the presence of the LORD, and dwelt in the land of Nod, on the east of Eden. And Cain knew his wife; and she conceived" (Genesis 4:16–17). There is a common misconception that Adam's son Cain found his wife in the land of Nod, but that is not what the passage says. Instead, it says that he knew his wife in the land of Nod; it does not say that she came from the land of Nod. It is certainly possible that she came with him after he left the presence of the Lord. Herein lies one of the seemingly open-ended questions of Christianity; if Adam and Eve were the only two humans who had received the breath of life and they only had a couple of boys, then where did Cain find a wife?

When Cain killed Abel the Lord cursed him, causing him to be a vagabond upon the earth. Cain's greatest concern was that he would be found by other individuals and killed because of the curse that was placed on him. The Lord placed a seal upon him to protect him against all who would rise up to kill him. (Genesis 4:8–15.) So where did all these other individuals come from?

When Adam moved to the garden, it was not only to receive the breath of life, but also to protect him from several documented factors that caused the extinction of other early men. The garden was essentially a safe haven amidst the surrounding world. The number of his days in the garden is unknown, but may have been upwards of hundreds of thousands of years. Once Adam was expelled from the garden the biblical timeline begins, which means that this was roughly 4,000 years prior to the birth of Christ. Hence, archaeological records indicate that there were no other species of humanoids on the earth for Cain to be concerned about. Therefore it had to be his own family members that he feared.

Although it seems unlikely and frankly wrong that Cain would have had relations with one of his sisters that is really the only option. When Adam and Eve left the garden their bodies were perfect. They were designed to live forever and had they eaten from the tree of life they would have lived forever. Following the reason for their departure from the garden, death became a part of the equation and bodily defects also became a part of the curse. Cells designed to withstand disease and genetic mutations were now fair game in this new sin-filled regime.

Genetic mutations are permanent changes in the DNA sequence. From the standpoint of evolution it was positive gene mutations that are essentially the main premise of the theory. That is, if a gene were miscoded in a positive way that would be beneficial to the individual as it continued to evolve. It is really the opposite that is true; genetic cell mutations are harmful to the individual and passed on to subsequent generations and this problem is multiplied when one marries a sibling or close relative.

Once expelled from the garden, genetic cells that were created in perfection are now subject to harmful mutations that resulted in disease. These mutations would have begun in Adam's children and each generation that married a sibling would potentially encounter more problems. As the populations continued to expand, these mutated cells would continue to be passed along to subsequent generations and through time other mutations began as well. As people married other people outside of their relatives the chance for matching defective cells greatly decreases, but if they married a close relative, defective cells may be matched and cause birth defects in their offspring.

This is a well-documented phenomenon called genetic burden. People today carry dozens of genetic inadequacies in their genes. When they marry outside of their relatives it is very unlikely that their particular gene deficiencies would match, which means that their offspring would have a significantly less chance of being born with birth defects. If they marry inside of their close relatives then the chances are greatly increased that their defective cells will match their spouse's defective cells and hence their children have a greater chance of being born with birth defects.

Adam and Eve's children were the first to experience any genetic loading; therefore they were not subject to the defects in their newly created bodies. The earlier the date the fewer the amount of defects, but as time progressed the defects continued to pile up. Henceforth, the Lord made an edict in the days of Moses that a man shall not sleep with his mother or his sister, among other sexual restrictions. (Leviticus 18, 20.) The moral consequence of this still rightly emanates in people's psyche today; because by the days of Moses, the defective cellular loading would have been too great to tolerate. Prior to this there were no laws forbidding sibling relationships and "where no law is, there is no transgression" (Romans 4:15).

Hence, Cain married one of his sisters when the genetic burden was virtually nonexistent. That means that Eve's offspring were not limited to three children. Instead the Bible makes it clear that Adam had daughters. (Genesis 5:4.) Of course, the number of his siblings is unknown, but they may have had dozens of more children. How is this possible? Time is the real factor, several of the earliest Old Testament believers lived to be over 900 years old. Adam was one of these. He was 130 years old (outside of the garden) by the time that he had his third boy, Seth. The text makes it apparent that they were hopeful for a boy to replace Able. In other words, they were having children after Cain and Abel, but they were all daughters until Seth came along. If they continued to have children for several hundred years, their youngest children would have been potentially hundreds of years older than their siblings.

Therefore, given the amount of years and the population growth that would have occurred due to just one fertile family, there would have been lots of women on the earth. Cain could have married a sister or possibly a niece or grandniece, etc. In just a few hundred years, exponential population growth would have occurred. By the end of Adam's lifetime (930 years), the earth's population would have multiplied to potentially millions of people, all starting with just one couple. (Genesis 5:5.)

Also, it has been previously mentioned that Cain dwelt in the land of Nod; a place that was geographically located in the east part of Eden. When Cain journeyed back there the garden and the angel protecting the tree were already gone, spiritually sequestered to its temporary home under the earth. The exact amount of time it took for Cain to move back to the area of the Garden of Eden is unknown.

Nevertheless, it is apparent that the region had already been explored and named by someone else who called it Nod, which means that another one of his siblings had already been there; showing that his siblings or extended family were already expanding across the face of the earth and whole regions were being named or renamed. Accordingly, those names were known by others, which mean that there were enough people on the earth to communicate geographical boundaries.

Patriarchal Life Spans

In Genesis chapter five, Adam accounts for the lineage of his family. One of the most notable points of this ancestral account is that most of the early patriarchs lived upwards of 10 times the average age of modern humans. Oftentimes, their lives stretched hundreds and hundreds of years with many reported to have died in the 900 year range. Again, concurring with the

Lord's proclamation that Adam's death would occur within one of the Lord's days.

There is a lot of speculation about how these early people were physically able to live hundreds of years. Certainly from a modern perspective it seems almost funny to imagine a person living over 900 years. In order to make sense of this, many people have looked to the earth to try and decipher if there were any changes that allowed people in that generation to live for such a long spans of time.

Some of the ideas espoused include speculation about a "water canopy" which is potentially alluded to on the second day of creation when it says that there were "waters which were above." (Genesis 1:7.) Some have said that these waters were trapped greenhouse gases in the atmosphere that somehow elongated the lives of humans. Though it is an enticing theory, there are no other indications in the Bible that this is the case.

Another interesting theory is that due to less farming there would have been a higher nutrient count in the vegetables and less pollution in the water, thereby causing longevity. Again this is an interesting theory, but there is little proof that nutrient content in the soil by itself would prolong someone's life by hundreds of years.

The simple truth of the matter is that God caused a decrease in the lifespan of humanity because of their sin. "And the LORD said, My spirit shall not always strive with man, for that he also is flesh: yet his days shall be an hundred and twenty years" (Genesis 6:3). Of course, when the Lord speaks, things change. How He physically brought this about is not exactly recorded, though it is a pretty safe bet to say that it has something to do with the flow and quality of light that was initiated on the first day of the re-creation. Increased sin caused a rift with the Lord and in turn He decreased the amount of light needed to sustain the additional years of life. Less light from God means less life in men. (John 1:4.) What is documented is that as the populations of the earth continued to grow others of God's creatures began to take notice.

The Sons of God

That the sons of God saw the daughters of men that they were fair; and they took them wives of all which they chose. There were giants in the earth in those days; and also after that, when the sons of God came in unto the daughters of men, and they bare children to them, the same became mighty men which were of old, men of renown. (Genesis 6:2, 4)

Throughout history and even prior to the creation of the earth, angels (like mankind) are called to follow the will of the Lord. Their current assignment is to be "ministering spirits, sent forth to minister for them who shall be heirs of salvation" (Hebrews 1:14). Upon the original creation, they understood that they were the benefactors of that creation and were elated with anticipation. That jubilation lasted millions of years, but continued to be interrupted and ultimately cut short due to the rebellion of Satan and his companions. The lines between right and wrong were established throughout that time and so were those of the angels that followed after God and those that did not.

Those that stayed with the Lord saw their harmonious society change into a military complex to combat the opposing force. Ultimately that societal attempt was destroyed, but the Lord had another plan and along came mankind. Those angels that remained with the Lord had their priorities changed slightly to accommodate this new creation. They maintained their military structure but also took on added responsibilities by becoming apprentices to mankind, to guide and protect them through times of prosperity and trouble; overseeing their daily lives and providing protection in times of distress. As the population of the earth increased, they were called on to do more and some began to become enamored with the women that they were sent to minister to.

Apparently the enticing lure of human women was too much for some of the angelic hosts to forgo. Certainly, it was some members of the group of angels that the Bible classifies as spiritual wickedness in high places that were unable to restrain themselves from their lusts. (Ephesians 6:12.) They revealed themselves to the women physically and took them for their wives; foregoing the spiritual aspect of heaven and taking on the physical.

Even though they knew the fate of Satan and his colleagues in the physical realm was potentially death, they still decided that it was worth the risk. The outcome from this union between women and angels produced offspring and the Bible says that they were mighty men of renown. Of course this gives unquestionable proof that angels can procreate. They may not join in marriage, but in a physical state they definitely have the ability to procreate. (Matthew 22:30.)

Certainly, Genesis six says that the union of women and angels produced a species of humanoids referred to as giants. To say that a group of angels came and slept with Adam's offspring almost seems ridiculous to write. Such a thought is so far away from the world today that it seems comical. Nevertheless, the Bible extensively documents that these events did indeed transpire.

As previously discussed, in the Old Testament whenever a passage mentions the Sons of God it is always referencing the angelic host. When Satan meets with other angelic management in God's throne room in the first chapter of Job, the other angels are referred to as the Sons of God. (Job 1:6.) Then, in Job 38:7 when the earth was in its beginning stages it says "all the sons of God shouted for joy." Finally, here in Genesis six, the Sons of God is once again referring to angelic beings.

Of a truth, the definition of Sons of God changes following the death and resurrection of Jesus in the New Testament. Now it encompasses all those who choose to call upon the name of the Lord. That is, all angels and humans are called to be the sons of God. "Behold, what manner of love the Father hath bestowed upon us, that we should be called the sons of God" (1 John 3:1). Praise God.

One thing to note is that angels and humans are physically different. When mankind was created, Adam was the first of his kind. He was created in the likeness of God and not made "after his kind" or copied from another similar creature that physically walked the earth. Thus humanity takes on a different physical state than angels, even though angels can be seen and experienced in the physical realm. It is likely that they have some sort of glorified body either similar to or the same type of body that the disciples witnessed when they encountered Jesus after his resurrection. (Matthew

28:9.) He was seen doing things that no other human could do, including spontaneously vanishing and appearing to people. (John 20:19.) Certainly, Jesus' activities gave a foreshadowing of things to come.

Additionally, angels come in various sizes because the Bible says that a person can befriend an angel and not know it. (Hebrews 13:2.) If a person were to meet an angel and not know it then the outward physical characteristics of that angel must be similar to a human's structure. In the Hebrew Old Testament, the word for giant or what is referred to as the offspring of human and angel is *Nephilim*, which is defined as having great size and physical strength. No doubt, this is why the Bible says that the offspring of women and angels produced mighty men of renown. Logic dictates that the angels that came to earth during this period were noticeable because of their large stature.

One indication of angelic size can be seen prior to the re-creation of the earth when angels freely roamed the planet. All things on the earth were of a different enhanced size. This includes much of the earth's vegetation and land animals. Both were generally of a larger stature and size and the Lord designed the environment during those spans to accommodate their increased physical stature. It is likely that they had abilities that normal humans would not have exhibited on account of their increased stature and great strength.

When Abraham met angels along the pathway he knew right away that they were special. Not because they had halos, wings, or any other unique feature, but because of their size. Once he recognized them as angels, he also understood that they had special abilities that humans did not possess. Just like Abraham, Lot was visited by this same pair of angels as he sat by the gate of the city and he too immediately recognized them. (Genesis 19:1.) The only way he would have been able to tell they were angels was due to their stature, because the Bible does not mention any other unique features about them.

Of course, increased stature leads to the obvious conclusion that they were also physically superior. This superiority is well documented throughout the Bible. Many times they are seen dealing swiftly and sharply with men and the elements. Following are a couple of examples of many instances throughout the Scriptures that document angelic prowess.

"And it came to pass that night, that the angel of the LORD went out, and smote in the camp of the Assyrians an hundred fourscore and five thousand: and when they arose early in the morning, behold, they were all dead corpses" (2 Kings 19:35). One angel, in one night, killed 185,000 men! Herod learned of angelic power because "the angel of the Lord smote him, because he gave not God the glory: and he was eaten of worms, and gave up the ghost" (Acts 12:23). Certainly, angelic might is on display throughout Revelation where they are seen killing men and controlling the elements. "And the four angels were loosed, which were prepared for an hour, and a day, and a month, and a year, for to slay the third part of men" (Revelation 9:15). "And after these things I saw four angels standing on the four corners of the earth, holding the four winds of the earth, that the wind should not blow on the earth, nor on the sea, nor on any tree" (Revelation 7:1).

So, angels have power over the environment and when allowed they have the ability to destroy mankind. Thus, in Genesis six where the Bible mentions that angels and women cohabited is another indication of angelic stature, strength, and prowess. It is also a testament to the fact that angels have free will. Although it is likely that Satan had some influence over these particular angels' decisions, they made the choice on their own free will. That choice was to intermingle and produce a subspecies that was both human and angelic.

Undoubtedly, the whole of the event was a debauchery in the eyes of God. The temptation for all things physical is a real part of life even in the spiritual realm. These temptations do not disappear even in the afterlife but are governed by the same laws of God's Kingdom, such as faith, redemption, and deliverance. Certainly, this gives testament to those angels which have remained faithful to the Lord through all the generations of time. They desire to know about the Christ's death and resurrection, because His redemption effects even the angels and their futures in the kingdom. (1 Peter 1:10–12.)

Bodies

The Bible shows that, "All flesh is not the same flesh: but there is one kind of flesh of men, another flesh of beasts, another of fishes, and another of birds. There are also celestial bodies, and bodies terrestrial: but the glory of the celestial is one, and the glory of the terrestrial is another. There is one glory of the sun, and another glory of the moon, and another glory of the stars: for one star differeth from another star in glory" (1 Corinthians 15:39–41). Without recourse the Bible gives specific instruction that different types of flesh are not to be mixed. In this case though, it is not necessarily the flesh that is the problem, for it is apparent that the angelic hosts have a similar physical makeup as humans, due to the fact that they were able to reproduce with women.

The issue is that they reside on a different level of glory. First Corinthians specifically mentions that the glory of the angelic (celestial) body and the glory of the human (terrestrial) body are different. They reside on different sides of eternity, which means that they have differing levels of insight into the Kingdom of God and as such they are looked at differently by God.

One is already eternal and the other was eternal but gave it up for the wages of sin, which introduced the body to mortality, weakness, and death. It is easy to see that on the one side of eternity are the angels, who are also referred to as stars. They are celestial, spiritual, or heavenly in nature and they see the spiritual realm first. Of course, on the other side of eternity are humans, who are first terrestrial, fleshy or earthy in nature; witnessing the physical realm first while being trapped in physical bodies that are waiting to be changed to a spiritual state.

Who then "shall change our vile body, that it may be fashioned like unto his glorious body" (Philippians 3:21)? For a human, only those that choose to believe on the Savior will be removed from a decaying body to a new glorified body. In other words, Adam's original physical body was subject to the decay of sin, but with the coming of Christ the natural can once again be glorified to the spiritual level. First Corinthians proves this out when it says, "So also is the resurrection of the dead. It is sown in corruption; it is raised in incorruption: It is sown in dishonour; it is raised in glory: it is sown in weakness; it is raised in power: It is sown a natural body; it is raised a spiritual body. There is a natural body, and there is a spiritual body" (1 Corinthians 15:42–44).

Paul continues to slam this point home a few verses later, "As is the earthy, such are they also that are earthy: and as is the heavenly, such are they also that are heavenly" (1 Corinthians 15:48). Again, the natural and the spiritual are two different entities. The heavenly is more discerned then the earthly and as such has a higher level of glory

The glory of an angelic eternal body is different than the glory of man's non-glorified weak body. In other words, both men and angels have physical bodies that were obviously comparable in a fashion to be able to produce offspring. "Howbeit that was not first which is spiritual, but that which is natural; and afterward that which is spiritual" (1 Corinthians 15:46). In other words, angels made a choice to forego their primary level of glory for the physical; thereby producing a union between the humans and angels that caused a problem for the Lord.

The Bible goes on to mention the problem with this when it says, "that flesh and blood cannot inherit the kingdom of God; neither doth corruption inherit incorruption" (1 Corinthians 15:50). The seed of angels were already eternal, but the seed of man was death. "For this corruptible must put on incorruption, and this mortal must put on immortality. So when this corruptible shall have put on incorruption, and this mortal shall have put on immortality, then shall be brought to pass the saying that is written, Death is swallowed up in victory" (1 Corinthians 15:53–54). The angels had it backwards. They were already from the incorruptible and they put on corruption, thereby giving into the corruption of the fleshly which eventually led to their death.

So when the seed of angels mixed with the seed of humanity the result was a whole new being. Interestingly, God could not ignore this new species because "God giveth it a body as it hath pleased him, and to every seed his own body" (1 Corinthians 15:38). God's hand was forced to comply with the laws that He established. In other words, He gave this new species a body that was predicated under the circumstances, even though it was not His perfect will.

Corruption cannot inherit incorruption. For these angels that gave up the spiritual for the physical, they were left with an interesting conundrum. They had left their first estate: the spiritual incorruptible and put on physical corruption. In the process they also gave up their rank in the Kingdom of God and they were dealt with accordingly. As for their offspring, they were a product of both the corruptible and incorruptible seed which was short of God's best laid plan. Therefore, their future will likely be determined by whom they believed on while they were on the earth, just like any other human.

Sin

One debauchery that flies in the face of God and still continues today is the elevating of false gods above the Lord. The first two commandments of the Ten Commandments state that, "thou shalt have no other gods before me. Thou shalt not make unto thee any graven image, or any likeness of any thing that is in heaven above, or that is in the earth beneath, or that is in the water under the earth: Thou shalt not bow down thyself to them, nor serve them: for I the LORD thy God am a jealous God" (Exodus 20:3–5). This seeking after false gods and worshipping them are the two commandments that come back again and again to trouble the Israelites.

Upon entering the Promised Land, God gave the Israelites specific instructions to destroy all the inhabitants that occupied the land. On several different occasions they failed to comply with this edict and the result was that they were left with a remnant of people who had a different belief system. On several occasions, the idol worshipping beliefs of partially conquered nations slipped into the Israelites presence and was adopted into their culture. In turn, righteous judges, prophets, and kings, would arise to tear down the statues and poles that were erected and worshipped by the Israelites.

The problem was that once it was unleashed into their midst, the Israelites could not seem to control their overwhelming preoccupation of worshipping something tangible. Even in the short span of 40 days that Moses disappeared in the mountain, by the time he came back the Israelites were already worshiping a golden calf that they had made. (Exodus 32.) Undoubtedly, they were following the techniques of idol worship that they gleaned from their time in Egypt. Nevertheless, the Israelites preoccupation with idol worship caused numerous problems throughout multiple generations.

Idolatry in turn is closely linked with sexual sin in the Old Testament. In Deuteronomy 31:16 it says, "And this people will rise up, and go whoring after the gods of the strangers of the land". Then again in Leviticus 17:7, "And they shall no more offer their sacrifices unto devils, after whom they have gone a whoring." God said that when the Israelites chased after the gods of other lands, that they were whoring them.

One example that is particularly blatant happened in Numbers 22–25. Balak, the king of Moab saw that the nation of Israel was bearing down on his kingdom and he was concerned that they were going to overtake him. The king called upon a man by the name of Balaam whose words were so powerful that a blessing or a curse would respectively cause a whole nation to be prosperous or a failure. Knowing that the Israelites, under the protection of the Lord, were an unstoppable force, he asked Balaam to curse the nation. Unfortunately for the king, Balaam was given specific instructions by God not to curse the nation of Israel. Thus, ignoring Balak's request he was faithful toward God and continued to call down a blessing instead of a curse upon Israel.

The king would not give up, and he continued to increase the prize in order to sway Balaam to curse the nation of Israel. Eventually Balaam was unable to forgo the size of the prize, so instead of calling down a curse upon the nation, he revealed a way to destroy the ranks of the Israelites in a less direct manner than military confrontation. (Numbers 31:16.) His stratagem was to seduce the rank and file of the Israeli men to sin by essentially prostituting the women of Moab. It worked, because the Israeli men were unable to restrain themselves and they entered into sexual sin with the daughters of the Moabites.

This sin led to the introduction of the traditions of the Moabites into the Israeli camp, which opened the door to their idolatry. "And Israel abode in Shittim, and the people began to commit whoredom with the daughters of

Moab. And they called the people unto the sacrifices of their gods: and the people did eat, and bowed down to their gods" (Numbers 25:1–2).

This seduction brought great destruction upon the nation of Israel. The outcome of which angered the Lord and a plague was brought upon the nation killing 24,000 people. (Numbers 25:9.) Of course, it was more than just a sexual act. The Israelites introduced the Moabite culture of Baal-Peor worship into their tents; a sin that brought a death sentence to all who entered into. "Behold, these caused the children of Israel, through the counsel of Balaam, to commit trespass against the LORD in the matter of Peor, and there was a plague among the congregation of the LORD" (Numbers 31:16).

Although the implications above are obvious, Jesus spells it out in Revelation when He says, "But I have a few things against thee, because thou hast there them that hold the doctrine of Balaam, who taught Balac to cast a stumblingblock before the children of Israel, to eat things sacrificed unto idols, and to commit fornication" (Revelation 2:14). Idolatry is fornication and in this light, it can be seen that God does not tolerate idolatry and fornication to other gods. Paul says to, "Mortify therefore your members which are upon the earth; fornication, uncleanness, inordinate affection, evil concupiscence, and covetousness, which is idolatry" (Colossians 3:5).

This is exactly what happened in Genesis as humanity began to spread upon the earth. Jude calls them "the angels which kept not their first estate but left their own habitation," showing that they gave up their spiritual life and took on the physical (Jude 1:6). Hereby, confirming the fact that some of the angelic hosts that initially remained faithful to God during the rebellion of Satan were later swayed by their own lusts and enticed by the seductiveness of God's new creation. This second group of angels was not a part of the original rebellion prior to man because it says that they, "kept not their first estate," which was still heaven.

Those under Satan's rule were already given a type of physical body. Here though, these angels made a choice to take on the temporal because the heavenly was still their first estate. They were still a part of the army of God when they made the choice to forgo God's edicts. They committed a sin by pursuing human women and equally the women entered into sexual relations with the angels.

Undoubtedly, this fornication separated the participants from God and allowed idolatry to enter into their midst. As seen with the Israelites, they likely began to worship the angels and once they took their eyes off of God, they opened the door to all sorts of other idolatry. Both sins are great and have caused cursing instead of blessing on a multitude of nations and generations throughout history. The sin mentioned here is particularly egregious because the angels left their own habitation and went after strange flesh or a flesh that is on a different level of glory than theirs. It is a sin that the Bible warns against on several occasions and Jude compares it to the events of Sodom and Gomorrah:

> And the angels which kept not their first estate, but left their own habitation, he hath reserved in everlasting chains under darkness unto the judgment of the great day. Even as Sodom and Gomorrha, and the cities about them in like manner, giving themselves over to fornication, and going after strange flesh, are set forth for an example, suffering the vengeance of eternal fire. (Jude 1:6–7)

Of course, the events of Sodom and Gomorrah fall right in line with this discourse. In light of this passage and the story itself, it can be seen that God destroyed the cities because of sin that was not necessarily homosexual in nature, but was rather brought about by fornication and lusting after the flesh of angels. Remember that when the angels approached the cities of Sodom and Gomorrah, Lot knew that the visitors were angels. Obviously recognizing them by their stature, Lot called them lords. (Genesis 19:1–2.) Then as they proceeded to walk through the town, the people of the city also recognized them by their stature and began to desire after them.

For certain, their daytime arrival caused a stir among the people and by the time night fell the people of the town were unable to restrain themselves. Obviously, knowing they were angelic hosts, they desired after them. Though the account specifically mentions the men of the town addressing Lot at the front door of his house, it also says that all the townspeople came out. (Genesis 19:4.) It is certainly plausible that the men were there to try and use their strength to physically force the angels to lie with the local women, because they desired a champion amongst them from the offspring.

Here again idolatry and unjustified worship of the angelic hosts caused the people of the town to desire to enter into sexual sin with the angels. So it was not only certain angels that committed sin by entering into relations with women, but it was obvious that it was reciprocated by men and women alike.

In turn, the angels who were specifically sent to the town displayed their power by striking blindness on the people that were pressing in against them, and they ultimately used this power to destroy the city. (Genesis 19:11, 13.) If homosexuality was their only sin, there would have been no reason to quest after the newcomers with such vigor. They were not interested in each other or even Lot's daughters. (Genesis 19:8.) They were only interested in having relations with "strange flesh" or angels. Their determination was very specific in nature. Unfortunately for them, so was the judgment of the Lord.

Satan's Tactics

But why would the angels in Genesis 6:2 make the choice to cohabitate with women knowing the events that transpired on the earth in previous generations? It would seem foolish for a second group of angels to fall into a path of sin having seen the outcome of Satan and the other angels that were in the earth prior to the onset of mankind. Jude goes on to explain, "But these speak evil of those things which they know not: but what they know naturally, as brute beasts, in those things they corrupt themselves. Woe unto them! for they have gone in the way of Cain, and ran greedily after the error of Balaam for reward, and perished in the gainsaying of Core" (Jude 1:10–11).

It is obvious that they sought and desired after the physical realm. Certainly, Satan's continued influence over both the spiritual and physical realm during this age was powerful enough to help coerce them into their bad decision. Also, evil was already in their hearts as they were a contingency of the group the Bible calls spiritual wickedness in high places. (Ephesians 6:12.) It is possible that this group had followed after Satan in the previous era, but never took up physical residence on the earth.

Thus they were easily swayed by listening to the very prince of the power of the air whispering in their ear to tell them what they were missing. In turn, they yielded to the temptation. Overlooking the Lord's previous judgments in the earth, they were easy prey as they fell zealously into all things temporal. They joined with Satan in the belief that this was an opportunity that they did not want to forgo. Satan understood that it was the seed of Adam that would ultimately bring his demise. (Genesis 3:15.) So he must have believed that this would throw an irreversible wrench into God's plan. Therefore, he convinced some of his wicked heavenly colleagues to make the wrong choice.

It must have made Satan happy to see the intermingling of angels and humans, knowing that it would disrupt the pure seed of man and cause a hybrid class of offspring. By controlling that one piece of God's property on the earth, he would again have a foothold on the earth and provide him the opportunity to once again overthrow his Creator. The result would be to catapult him back into power, so that mankind would no longer be a ruling class on the earth. Thus the spirit that now worketh in the children of disobedience, conjured up lustful desire in the hearts of these angels. Convincing them that life on planet earth was better than anything that God offered in heaven. Being free from the constraints of heaven, they would have the ability to do what they wanted, without punishment.

They took the path of things natural and gave up the spiritual, even speaking evil against the spiritual. Greedily corrupting themselves with earthly fleshly gains, they were unable to cease from their sin. (2 Peter 2:14.) Seeking after the things of the world, they are compared to Balaam and Korah who went after the things of the world and not the way of God. Of course Balaam was explained above and Korah was again the gentleman with a small following who rose up against Moses to challenge and overthrow his leadership. Due to their rebellion they were swallowed by the earth and went alive down to the pit. (Numbers 16:33.) Both parties were seeking their own gain and here the angels are compared to them, by being referred to as brute beasts that corrupted themselves with natural things; the incorruptible chased after the corruptible.

This is not all, Jude goes on to use several other analogies of their waywardness. He says that,

These are spots in your feasts of charity, when they feast with you, feeding themselves without fear: clouds they are without water, carried about of winds; trees whose fruit withereth, without fruit, twice dead, plucked up by the roots; Raging waves of the sea, foaming out their own shame; wandering stars, to whom is reserved the blackness of darkness for ever. (Jude 1:12–13)

They are referred to as wandering stars that have lost their way. A prudent picture, because all things are have a specific place and function in God's creation, including the stars. So a star (angel) that is randomly wandering is out of the will of God. They have no shame or fear of God; former trees that were rooted by the river of the Lord are plucked up and now produce no fruit, blown about by the winds of false doctrine and their own wicked ways. They are twice dead; first purged from the vine of the Lord they are dead spiritually, but also they came to earth and took on physical form where they also died in the flesh.

And Enoch also, the seventh from Adam, prophesied of these, saying, Behold, the Lord cometh with ten thousands of his saints, To execute judgment upon all, and to convince all that are ungodly among them of all their ungodly deeds which they have ungodly committed, and of all their hard speeches which ungodly sinners have spoken against him. These are murmurers, complainers, walking after their own lusts; and their mouth speaketh great swelling words, having men's persons in admiration because of advantage. (Jude 1:14–16)

Here it is shown that sex was not their only sin, but apparently they entered into all sorts of ungodly wickedness. Following after their own desires and speaking loud in the things of wickedness, they aroused the interest of humanity that surrounded them and led them astray. Of course their stature and boisterousness caused them to be elevated in their importance, which the Bible calls having men's admiration because of advantage; an exact picture of the activities at Sodom and Gomorrah. So, just like the Israelites who committed sexual sins, then quickly adopted the idolatrous ways of the infiltrators, here too the same sins arose during this age.

Imagine their vanity as they must have thought that they were gods to be worshiped. Believing that there was a loophole in the edicts from the Lord that would have made them exempt from his wrath. Unfortunately for them, this was not the case. The Lord came to execute judgment upon them, and removed them from the earth to a place carved out for them, called the blackness of darkness forever.

The unfolding of these events in Jude is truly a testament to the fact that angels are indeed interested in the things of the earth. (I Peter 1:12.) Many have fallen by the wayside, first in the days of Satan's rule upon the earth and then others that fulfilled their lust toward women in the days of men. No doubt, those angels that have remained faithful to the Lord were excited to see the works of Christ on the cross.

Nowadays, Satan's tactics for the corruption of mankind are more subtle. Since he knows that the blood of Christ was the ultimate sacrifice and it will always reside on the throne, he has gone about attempting to pervert the morality and ideals of the earth's occupants by promoting his crafty rhetoric. He is subtly corrupting the moral fabric of a society by replacing it with a contrary spiel.

It starts with the very creation itself, deceiving people into believing that the creation did not happen, but that it is merely happenstance. In turn, causing people to question the very existence of God and drawing them from the truth of the gospel of the Kingdom of God, toward the lies and deception that are prevalent in the earth today. He is the deceiver and the father of all lies. Using science as a means to show that there is not a need for God in the earth. Instead of using science the way that God intended it to be used: as a method to explore His creation and find out more of who He is through that creation.

Prison

Much like the Lord used the seas to cover a multitude of angelic sins prior to the re-creation; He did it again in Genesis 6–9. Here, He eradicated a wholly different population of angels and sinful men from the earth. That event was the flood of Noah, in which He allowed the whole population on the earth to be destroyed with a flood, except for those whom He spared in the ark.

The fate of those immoral angels was immediate and disparaging. "He hath reserved in everlasting chains under darkness unto the judgment of the great day... suffering the vengeance of eternal fire" (Jude 6–7). He cast them under a judgment that would hold them in chains under the earth forever. On earth the waters receded back to their pre-flood position (that is back to its oceanic state after the re-creation), but for those angels that strayed with women their fate was bleak.

Twice dead, those angels are no longer able to produce fruit and are like shiftless waves of the sea. For them to witness the judgment that the Lord cast upon the original group of angels that walked the earth and yet still choose a path of debauchery was unacceptable to the Lord. During their time on the earth, not only did they cohabit with women, but they chose a path of utter wickedness that angered the Lord.

They had completely turned their back on God, losing even the ability to praise Him. In Hebrew they are referred to as *Rephaim*. "Wilt thou shew wonders to the dead? shall the dead (rephaim) arise and praise thee? Selah" (Psalm 88:10). They had access to the good things of the Lord in heaven and they made their choice to reject their roots, leaving themselves with no fruit and no connection to the Spirit who is fruit. (Galatians 5:22–23.)

They had their days of glory on the earth, wherein they rose up amongst humanity and became kings and men of valor, but their quest for status and accolades left them dead, physically and spiritually. The events of Sodom and Gomorrah, the flood of Noah, and various other Scriptures show that their behavior is unacceptable to the Lord. The dangers of treading into this sin are great and can lead to a penalty of harsh judgment. Lot's wife died for simply looking back at the destruction of the city. (Genesis 19:26.)

The judgment for their sin is clear and has already taken place. "They are dead, they shall not live; they are deceased, they shall not rise: therefore hast thou visited and destroyed them, and made all their memory to perish" (Isaiah 26:14). Their fate is already sealed and they shall remain in the congregation of the dead with no chance of redemption forever. They shall not arise again, which means that they are not entitled to a resurrection and any physical evidence or memory of their activities in the earth has been removed. Once removed they were never to be heard from again, removed to a prison-like place of darkness that reserved exclusively for these disobedient angels.

Peter speaks of the angelic judgment and gives the region a proper name, *Tartarus*:

> For if God spared not the angels that sinned, but cast them down to hell (tartarus), and delivered them into chains of darkness, to be reserved unto judgment; And spared not the old world, but saved Noah the eighth person, a preacher of righteousness, bringing in the flood upon the world of the ungodly. (2 Peter 2:4–5)

These angels are in a division of hell that is prison-like in nature and designed specifically for them due to their unique transgressions. While there they survive in complete darkness until the judgment day. This is the third region under the earth that is a part of the pit. The other two regions, as previously mentioned, are hell and the Garden of Eden (which is now a part of heaven following the resurrection of Christ).

Job points out that although they are strangled in darkness, there is still activity by these individuals. "Dead things (rephaim) are formed from under the waters, and the inhabitants thereof" (Job 26:5). Moses warns against the worship of such things, "Thou shalt not make unto thee any graven image, or any likeness of any thing that is in heaven above, or that is in the earth beneath, or that is in the water under the earth" (Exodus 20:4). Solomon shows that they are congregated together and it is likely that during these meetings they plotted together to take their revenge. (Proverbs 21:16.)

Of course, all of these referenced verses are found in the Old Testament. Even though they were dead, they believed there was still hope there would one day be an uprising amongst Satan and his rebellious ranks that would enable them to reclaim their earthly dominion. It is apparent that their lust for earthly temporal things had utterly consumed them.

During their time on the earth they were great beings of power to be respected, and as such their greedy desire was to once again attain that place of respect they had lost. Therefore, they still had hope that the ongoing rebellion of Satan would win out and restore them to their former glory, freeing them from their chains of darkness. "Hell from beneath is moved for thee to meet thee at thy coming: it stirreth up the dead (rephaim) for thee, even all the chief ones of the earth; it hath raised up from their thrones all the kings of the nations" (Isaiah 14:9). Unfortunately for them, they would find out that Satan's time had also come to an end.

Peter brings this to light in his first book when he says, "By which also he went and preached unto the spirits in prison; Which sometime were disobedient, when once the longsuffering of God waited in the days of Noah, while the ark was a preparing" (1 Peter 3:19–20). Peter reveals one final activity of Christ during his three day stint under the earth. (Matthew 12:40.)

Not only did He obtain the keys of death and hell from the gates of hell and proclaim His victory to the Old Testament saints in the garden, He also went over to Tartarus; preaching to the evil angels that have been locked up in prison since the days of Noah. Or better he proclaimed to the angels that were under the earth, locked in Tartarus that He had conquered the grave. (Colossians 1:23.)

In the blackness of night where they were confined, they would have been unaware of earthly activities and oblivious of their ultimate fate. Therefore, they could not have known the ramifications of Christ's death and what it meant for them until the very Light of Life Himself entered their dungeon and blinded them with the truth of His sacrifice. As far as they knew, they had a chance to be returned to the earth if Satan's continuing rebellion was successful.

Picture their expectation as the doors of their prison cells were opened and the light began to overtake the throes of darkness they had been encased in for millennia. Everything in their being must have been overcome with hope, thinking that the battle was over and they could now return to their former status on the earth, knowing that Satan had won the war.

Imagine their shock and horror as they saw the one standing before them was not Satan, but instead the very Son of God, telling them of His sacrifice for all eternity that ended Satan's chance of victory once and for all. Realizing that death had been conquered, their mood quickly changed as they became cognizant of the fact that their deeds on earth were punishable for all eternity. When Christ left, despair set in and they came to terms with the fact that there was no hope for them, and they realized they would remain in darkness forever! (Jude 1:6.) The battle was indeed won, but the outcome was not what they had anticipated. "Art thou also become weak as we? art thou become like unto us? Thy pomp is brought down to the grave" (Isaiah 14:10–11). Eradicated from the earth they now know that the last nail has been hammered in and their chances of redemption are impossible.

Undoubtedly the angels that still resided in heaven did not want to make a similar mistake. For this reason, outside of a direct edict from the Lord, angels are not seen in the flesh in a fashion that men are aware of. The Lord established a precedent of judgment and seeing the severity of it, those that remain no longer dare cross an edict from the Lord. The only reason they are seen on earth today is by a direct command of the Lord to help mankind.

Furthermore, Christ's resurrection made it clear to both humans and angels that His spiritual and physical sacrifice was for all eternity. "And, having made peace through the blood of his cross, by him to reconcile all things unto himself; by him, I say, whether they be things in earth, or things in heaven" (Colossians 1:20). After He was resurrected, Jesus took His seat at the right hand of God to prove that the lineage of mankind can never again be ruined.

In this one move, He fulfilled a promise to David that his seed would sit on the throne forever while at the same time; He established the pedigree of man throughout all eternity. Additionally, it would also seem that his sacrifice is true for the angels in heaven. Specifically stating that by reconciling all things unto Himself, whether in heaven or on earth, the implication is that they too are no longer under the law but under grace.

The Seed Continues ...

And GOD saw that the wickedness of man was great in the earth, and that every imagination of the thoughts of his heart was only evil continually. And it repented the LORD that he had made man on the earth, and it grieved him at his heart. And the LORD said, I will destroy man whom I have created from the face of the earth; both man, and beast, and the creeping thing, and the fowls of the air; for it repenteth me that I have made them. (Genesis 6: 5–7)

So the Lord destroyed the angels that left heaven and walked the earth. In the same act, He also eradicated their offspring; those that the Bible calls *Nephilim* or giants. His method of destruction was once again a global flood. "But Noah found grace in the eyes of the LORD", so that the seed of mankind could continue in the earth. (Genesis 6:8.) In order for this to happen, Noah was instructed to build an ark. When the rain and waters came, only those in the ark were safe from the perils on the earth. The occupants of the ark were Noah, his wife, his three sons, along with their wives.

Normally this would be the end of the problem, but the Bible informs us that this was not the case. In fact, the Bible makes it clear that the seed of the giants continued after the flood, "There were giants in the earth in those days; and also after that" (Genesis 6:4). While God destroyed the tainted angelic and human seed with the flood of Noah, embedded in the genes of one or more of the Noah's daughters-in-law was still a genetic remnant of these individuals. Even though the Lord erased most of the seed that resulted from the sinful acts of the tainted angels, its genetic markers continued on through the seed of the ark's passengers. Thus more giants were produced with the seed of Noah's children and that seed continued as giants begat more giants, eventually producing whole tribes and races of these beings. Encounters with these giants are found throughout the pages of the Old Testament from Abraham to David.

Many of them were met and defeated by the Israelites shortly after their arrival into the Promised Land. Their first introduction to these giants is a memorable one found in the book of Numbers. Moses understood that the land bordering on the Mediterranean Sea was to be theirs, but the problem was that there were already people occupying it. Many of these people were whole tribes of giants. One of Moses' first tasks upon crossing the Red Sea was to commission twelve spies to do a reconnaissance mission to determine the status of their enemy.

Ten of the spies returned with an evil report saying, "…and all the people that we saw in it are men of a great stature. And there we saw the giants, the sons of Anak, which come of the giants: and we were in our own sight as grasshoppers, and so we were in their sight" (Numbers 13:32–33). The sons of Anak or Anakims were just one of many races of giants that emerged from the offspring of the passengers of the ark. (Deuteronomy 2:11.)

This was a critical point of action for the Israelites and they chose the path of least resistance, which ended up exiling them to the Sinai desert for the next forty years. Their initial faithlessness was so great that God would not even allow them to see how good that they could have lived. The two spies who reported back a good report were the only two people allowed to see the goodness that God had planned for them. (Deuteronomy 1:35–38.) The population of the Israelites at that time was likely over a million people and of that only two men, forty years later, got to see the Promised Land.

It was not until the leadership of Joshua (one of the faithful spies) that this threat to the human population was largely squelched. Once they crossed into the Promised Land, part of their duty was to defeat the giants and others that occupied their land, so that only the seed of mankind would remain and their debauchery would be lost forever.

The fact that these giant nations fought against the Lord's chosen nation shows that they were still wrapped up in the sinful traditions of their forefathers. Under the command of Joshua and a whole new generation of faithful believers, the Israelites were finally up to the task and subsequently removed many of the inhabitants of the Promised Land. The remaining few tribes of giants were conquered by subsequent generations of Israelites, ending in David's generation.

Besides the Anakims there are several other progeny that are mentioned after the flood of Noah. These include, but are not limited to the following tribes: The "Zamzummims; A people great, and many, and tall, as the Anakims" (Deuteronomy 2:20–21). The Emims "Which also were accounted giants, as the Anakims" (Deuteronomy 2:10–11). The Og's were a people in the land of Bashan "which was called the land of giants" (Deuteronomy 3:13). They were smote by the Israelites until none were left. (Deuteronomy 3:3.) In addition to referencing the angels themselves, Rephaim was also a proper noun used to refer to a tribe of giants. (Genesis 15:20.) Their legend continued long into the reign of David due to the fact that a well-known geographic location southwest of Jerusalem was called the valley of the Rephaim. (2 Samuel 5:18.)

Many of these clans made their introduction into the pages of the Bible long before the Israelites encountered them. In fact, giants were prevalent in the days of Abraham. Genesis 14 records the story of Abraham's conquest of several kings who had taken his nephew Lot captive. As the story goes, a group of four kings had formed an alliance together and were invading their surrounding territories. First they smote six different tribes: the Rephaims, Zuzims, Emins, Horites, Amalekites, and Amorites. They then went into Lot's territory and conquered five additional tribes and took Lot as a captive.

When Abraham heard the news, he arose and defeated these invading kings, recapturing Lot. As it has been seen, many of the characters in the story were from the tribes of giants, making it abundantly clear that giants were also prevalent in the days of Abraham. Thus it is no surprise that the people of Sodom and Gomorrah knew the stories of their gigantic angelic ancestors and were quick to recognize that the individuals who entered their city were angels. Obviously the people were aware of their existence and how they came into being.

Though the Bible frequently mentions that the giants congregated together in clans; the story of Goliath points to the fact that this was not always the case. There is no indication in the Bible that the Philistines were a giant people, but rather the Goliath and his siblings were unique. It may have been that the Philistines hired him as a mercenary.

Certainly, it was much less common to witness giants in David's day, as most of them had already been conquered. So in the account of David fighting Goliath, the Bible clearly states that the Israelites were astonished and frightened by the presence of the Philistine champion. (1 Samuel 17:11.) Quite possibly they had never seen an individual so large, but David being a shepherd had travelled through many lands while tending his sheep and in doing so he had most certainly witnessed giants before.

Goliath's height was six cubits and a span or 13 feet 4 inches tall if a cubit is measured as 25 inches and a span is 10 inches. His spear was like a weaver's beam and weighed 600 shekels of iron or almost 23 1/2 pounds. (1 Samuel 17:4–7.) He was truly an enormous individual. Of course the story goes that David being strong in the Lord slew Goliath with a mere stone and removed Goliath's head with his own sword. The remaining contingencies of giants in the earth were subsequently conquered by David and his fellow Israelites. (2 Samuel 21:16–22.) After that there are no other encounters with giants recorded in the Bible.

CHAPTER 19

Noah Built an Ark

Noah

And spared not the old world, but saved Noah the eighth person, a preacher of righteousness, bringing in the flood upon the world of the ungodly... (2 Peter 2:5)

As seen in the previous chapter, God's tolerance level for the sin prevalent in the earth during the days of Noah had been eclipsed. He could no longer stand by and watch the tainted seed of man and angels run rampant on the earth. Even though the angels knew better, they ignored all aspects of God's law and forged on along their wayward path, hoping that the Lord would simply look away. Of course their corruption could not be ignored and those angels are now sitting in prison with no chance of resurrection and it is likely that most of their offspring are in hell awaiting their respective eternal judgment. Without a doubt, God's judgment was correct. The obedience of Noah to protect the human race was the only boon that humanity had left.

Of course, the story of Noah is one of the great stories of the Bible. One single righteous man obediently follows the leading of the Lord and preserves the whole of the human race. Unfortunately, nowadays it is treated as a biblical legend, often portrayed as an ark floating on top of a body of water with a giraffe sticking his head out of the top. The seemingly laughable impossibilities of an event of that magnitude have caused many to pass it off as just another story in the Bible that never could have happened.

337

The truth is the account of the flood of Noah is more than just a story; it was a real event, not only from a scriptural viewpoint, but also from a physical, provable, scientific standpoint. Even Jesus confirmed that the events were real when he said, "For as in the days that were before the flood they were eating and drinking, marrying and giving in marriage, until the day that Noe entered into the ark, And knew not until the flood came, and took them all away" (Matthew 24:38–39).

Still, even though the proof of this historical event was verified by Jesus, there remains a general skepticism about the flood. One of the main issues that arise in people's minds concerning the flood of Noah was its scope. Was the flood a universal, whole earth flood or was it merely a regional, localized flood? Certainly it would be more palatable if it was regional because the amount of water needed to cover a regional area can be much more easily comprehended then the sheer volume needed to cover the whole earth to the depth that the Bible purports.

Unequivocally the Bible is unwavering in its answer, because it specifically says that the waters covered the entire earth. "And the waters prevailed exceedingly upon the earth; and all the high hills, that were under the whole heaven, were covered. Fifteen cubits upward did the waters prevail; and the mountains were covered" (Genesis 7:19–20). Semantics are not an issue, it is clear that the whole earth was covered with water including all the mountains. It does not say that the whole of the world was covered, but rather the whole of the earth and all of the mountains.

If the flood were only regional, not only would it contradict the biblical narrative, but common sense dictates that there would have been other options for the Lord other than having Noah build an ark. If it was only going to be a regional flood, why wouldn't the Lord have just instructed Noah and his family to move to an uninhabited elevated region of the globe while He flooded the rest? Why would He call the animals to the ark, couldn't they too have just gone elsewhere? Does God consistently break His visible covenant promise symbolized in a rainbow that he will never flood the earth again, because regional flooding continues to be a cause of destruction and death across the globe?

No, His visual promise to Noah still stands as a true indication that the flood was universal, which means that it covered the whole earth until even the tallest of mountains were covered with water. Of course, this raises questions concerning the logistical aspects as to how the Lord accomplished this feat.

The Water

During the flood, Genesis says that the waters on the earth were fifteen cubits high and this covered all the high hills and the mountains. Since the sentence is conjoined with an "and," it is a continuation of the thought, which means that both the hills and the mountains were covered. Currently Mount Everest soars above sea level at 29,028 feet, the tallest physical location on the earth and it continues to grow by a few millimeters every year. Presuming that this "uplifting" phenomenon continued since the days of Noah, Mount Everest would be about 43 feet the junior of its current height. Given that Mount Everest was on the earth during the days of Noah, then it would have been the highest point both then and now.

The question then is, would the water that remains under the earth and in the atmosphere been able to produce enough water to cover the earth to that depth, approximately 5 ½ miles deep? The amount would have been three times greater than any amount currently on the surface of the earth.

Scientists say no. Given what is known and taking into account what is believed to exist in the current water table of the earth, there is not enough water to cover the earth to this depth. In the prescribed 40 day time frame, the water table would have needed to rise more than 30 feet (not inches) per hour in order to cover Mt. Everest within the allotted time. Undoubtedly, that is a massive amount of water.

Various theories have been espoused as to how the known water resources of the earth could have covered its entire surface to such a height. Certainly, during the time prior to the re-creation there are several indications within the earth's strata that indicate there were periods of flooding. Without a doubt, the earth's landscape during past epochs shows that there were areas of seas, large lakes, and river beds that are no longer present throughout various parts of the globe.

Whether or not each of these floods were a global phenomenon is difficult to pinpoint, but the general consensus and geological records indicate a strong probability that most of these phenomenon were indeed regional and not global. Therefore, scientifically it is difficult to nail down whether or not there were other instances of global flooding. Nevertheless, regardless of scientific ideas, the fact is that the Bible makes it clear that during the days of Noah that the whole of the earth was covered with water. This is, at least the second time in the earth's history that this had happened, the other instance, of course, occurred in Genesis 1:2. The question still remains then, where did all of this water come from? And did it truly cover the earth to a depth of 5 1/2 miles?

Fortunately, the Genesis account goes on to explain where the water came from, "...the same day were all the fountains of the great deep broken up, and the windows of heaven were opened" (Genesis 7:11). It shows that there were two places that the water came from: the windows of heaven and the deep. Of course, the windows of heaven are a reference to rain falling on the earth and at any given moment it is estimated that there is enough water in the atmosphere to cover the earth to a depth of approximately one inch of water. Certainly, this amount is hardly worth mentioning in the scope of this argument, making it unlikely that the amount of water in the atmosphere would even cause a dent in the overall amount of water necessary to cover the earth.

Realization of this has caused some to purport that there may have been atmospheric differences in those days. One idea is that a canopy of water enveloped the earth in these earlier years. Advocates of this theory have postulated that this is one of the possible reasons for the earliest saints living such long lives. Of course, we previously showed that this was unlikely because it would have caused the surface of the earth to rise to temperatures unsuitable to life, meaning that today's atmosphere remains roughly the same as it was in the days of Noah. So even though it rained on the earth for 40 days, under any reasonable circumstance there simply was not enough rainwater to truly make a huge impact on the amount of water necessary to the cover the earth to any great depth. (Genesis 7:12.)

The other place that the Bible mentions as a possible water source was from under the earth or from the fountains of the great deep. Of course, the word deep has been shown to refer to the vast reservoirs of water on the earth. In the flood of Noah, it is obvious that the water came from under the earth, and the Bible shows that there are still reservoirs of water that remain under the earth. (Exodus 20:4.)

Certainly, it is difficult to ascertain the exact amount of water flowing underground, because we are currently only able to drill through a minuscule portion of the crust to gather core samples. Currently the deepest mining operation in the world works at a depth of a little less than 2.5 miles. In large part, the crust ranges in depth from 3 to 19 miles and makes up only about 2.72% of the earth's volume. One analogy equates the earth's crust to the skin of a peach; unquestionably a minuscule portion of the overall volume of the earth.

Current estimates of the earth's surface water are about 332.5 million cubic miles, or .05% of the earth's total volume. In addition to this, the earth's atmosphere encompasses about 38% of the earth's volume. Obviously, despite these three pieces making up much of the observable universe for mankind, they are still only a small portion of the earth's total volume. The rest of the earth's volume is found underneath its surface and includes the mantle (49.5%) and the earth's core (9.73%). Of course, the massive amount of surface water is minuscule in comparison to the overall volume of the earth's interior.

The obvious insinuation is that some or much of the earth's interior, including the mantle and core are made up of water. Interestingly, scientists speculate that up to ten times the amount of water present on the earth today would be needed in the early stages of the earth's development; but the general theory is that some or most of it would have evaporated away during the earth's formation.

Albeit, from the earth's surface it is difficult to ascertain the makeup of the earth's interior due to the vast distances under the earth that are inaccessible to direct observation. Even massive drilling operations are barely scratching the surface, though there has been talk of a drilling operation that would penetrate the earth's crust at one of its thinnest points. However, this has not happened yet and if it does it will still only be able to sample a miniscule portion of the entire mantle, and will not come even close to the core. Thus, scientists are forced to use other techniques to determine the consistency of the earth's interior.

One of the primary methods of determining the earth's makeup is by monitoring seismic activity around the globe. When an earthquake rattles the surface of the earth, it produces elastic "waves" that travel under its surface. These waves pass through the interior of the earth and can be read by seismic equipment around the globe. These waves have been closely monitored throughout recent years in order to better understand the earth's interior composition. By examining the waves and how they pass through different materials, it is believed that part of the earth's mantle and its entire core are largely made up of liquid metals, most of which are believed to be liquid iron and nickel.

One other method to determine the earth's composition is to analyze objects that have originated from the vast reaches of space and are occasionally seen in the night sky: meteorites. Meteorites are believed to be a glimpse into early planetary development. An analysis of meteorites has indicated that they are composed largely of base elements as well as some water.

By using these various analytical methods, it is believed that the liquid flowing within the earth's core is largely that of nickel and iron, not water. This metallic core has also been attributed to the root source of the magnetic field that protects the earth's atmosphere from the harmful radiation of solar winds. Without this protective shield, much of life on planet earth would be eradicated.

Thus, it has become a generally accepted theory that much of the earth's interior consists mostly of these base metals. It certainly is a plausible explanation of how the earth's magnetic field came into being, but is that the only thing present in the earth's core? Of course, without empirical observation, all of these methods of analysis are still just theory and the interior of the earth is a big place. Could it be that other elements could be found under the earth's surface, like water?

Some propose that there are ample amounts of water under the earth, but it remains trapped in minuscule amounts in the materials that make up the earth's mantle. If one was to add up these minuscule amounts throughout the earth's mantle it would equate to massive quantities of water, which could easily be comparable to the size of seas and oceans. In other words, there are not necessarily whole oceans of water under the surface, but rather individual particles of water mixed in with the surrounding materials in the mantle that equate to significant sea-like amounts. Even if this is the case, it is generally believed that it would not be enough to generate the amounts of water that the flood of Noah's day is apparently suggesting.

Of course, the Bible purports a notion that is contrary to the general scientific community's acknowledgement, and that is that there remain vast reservoirs of water underneath the surface of the earth. In fact, it says that water is the very foundation that the earth is built upon, and that there are huge quantities of water still present under the earth, laid up in storehouses of the deep. (Psalm 104:3, 33:7.) In Proverbs these waters are said to be securely established in their place under the earth, set there from the beginning. (Proverbs 8:28.) Job says that these waters are hid as with a stone, which makes it seem as if they are gathered together in large quantities and withheld from bursting forth to the surface by the crust or mantle. (Job 38:30.)

Certainly, this is exactly the situation that Noah experienced. The waters captured under the earth sprung forth like a fountain and mixed with 40 days of rain to cover the earth. In turn, this eruption of water mixed with the oceans already existing on the earth and caused wide-scale destruction throughout its surface.

The Bible goes on to reveal a little more about the earth's interior workings when it says, "When he prepared the heavens, I (wisdom) was there: when he set a compass upon the face of the depth" (Proverbs 8:27). Of course, compasses are magnets and are driven by the magnetic polarity of the earth. Most definitely, this lends credence to the idea that heavy metals in the earth are a root cause of the magnetic fields encompassing the earth. Notice that the mention of the compass comes before the area that is called the deep. What thickness that layer of "compassing" consists of is unknown. It may be a large area or it may be only a tiny sliver, but it is before the area that the foundation of the earth of the earth rests, which the Bible reports as consisting of water.

Certainly it is plausible that this interior water of the earth may have some unique characteristics that separate it from normal surface water. Indeed it may be some type of elemental rich water designed by the Lord at the creation of the earth. Nevertheless, it is still water and given the volume of the earth compared to the surface water, it is logical that there may be ample amounts of water under the earth's surface. Since the Bible says that the foundation of the earth was established upon a foundation of water it would certainly seem to insinuate that the amount would be similar to what is now referred to as the core of the earth, 9.73% of the earth's total volume. If this was the case then there would be ample amounts of water within the earth's interior to cover its surface during the days of Noah.

Still, the Bible does not specifically state that part of the mantle and the whole of the earth's core is water. True, it was established on a watery foundation, but how much? Is the entire core filled with water, or is it more or less? Obviously, since there is no way to see the earth's mantle or core it may never be known in this dispensation. Therefore, the question still remains, is there enough water in the earth's interior to cover the current surface of the earth to a depth of more than 5 1/2 miles?

For now the answer to the question is possibly. There is certainly enough space under the earth to house enough water to cover it to this depth, but without definitive numbers given by the Bible it can only be theorized. Therefore, it is important to look at other factors that could play a role in the narrative of the flooding account.

The Ark

Make thee an ark of gopher wood; rooms shalt thou make in the ark, and shalt pitch it within and without with pitch. And this is the fashion which thou shalt make it of: The length of the ark shall be three hundred cubits, the breadth of it fifty cubits, and the height of it thirty cubits. A window shalt thou make to the ark, and in a

cubit shalt thou finish it above; and the door of the ark shalt thou set in the side
thereof; with lower, second, and third stories shalt thou make it. (Genesis 6:14–16)

First, it is pertinent to revisit the definition of the size of the ark. When the Lord gives Noah the dimensions of the ark, every measurement in the narrative is defined as a cubit. Cubits throughout the ages have a different length depending on the person doing the measuring. Particularly prior to the birth of Christ and even after, different nations had their own standard of what a cubit was and exactly what a cubit represented.

Without standardized measures to keep track of the length or breadth of objects, items to be measured were generally compared in length to a body part. For example, one society might define a cubit as the distance from the middle finger to the end of the palm. In other cultures it was defined as the length from the middle finger to the waist, which means that depending on the culture the length varied greatly. Obviously, measurements in previous generations were not an exact science, because one person's arm may be substantially different than another person's. Thus not only did different cultures have different definitions of a cubit, even within a culture those definitions changed based on who was doing the measuring. While there are literally dozens of known lengths and volumes of a cubit used by different nations throughout human history, those are only the known measurements.

As a general rule, people have equated a cubit to be 18 inches, which is the average length from a person's elbow to their middle finger. Taking this as the standard and using it as a definition for the ark, it puts the ark at 450 feet long, 75 feet wide and 45 feet high. In fact, a couple of replica arks have been built mirroring these very dimensions. Given these dimensions, it logistically raises the question of whether this size of vessel would be able to fit all of the life forms of the earth, given such a massive creative diversity. Of course, while many would purport it to be unlikely, other experts say that it would be more than ample. Therefore it is necessary to take a closer look to determine if indeed an ark of that size would fit such an enormous creation.

Obviously, since the flood was universal, the ark would have to have been big enough to hold the number of animals that are seen on the earth today. Additionally, due to extinctions in the years following the flood this list would have been even higher, but may have been reduced due to selective breeding of animals by humans. During those days the numbers of domestic animal breeds would have been significantly less, if any. For example, all dog species are believed to have been originally bred from the wolf. In the time since the flood, the breeding and domestication of the dog and its various species would have had enough time to reproduce and grow, given the relatively short breeding spans of the dog. Other domesticated animals and cattle would also fit into this same category. Therefore, it is possible that only one pair of wolves would have entered the ark.

It is also interesting to note that most animal species were welcomed into the ark two by two. Other animals that were considered clean, like cattle and fowls of the air though were taken in seven by seven, which bolstered the amount of space necessary to accommodate them. (Genesis 7:2–3.) The reasoning behind this was two-fold. First, the clean animals could be used as meat for the inhabitants of the ark. Second, a greater population of these species, once they left the ark, would allow their numbers to prevail upon the earth. It is not difficult to see the superior numbers of livestock and migratory birds that reign upon the earth even today. God's plan was to have a greater number of these so that they would be meat for mankind to eat, both during and indefinitely after the flood.

Of course the fish populations in the oceans would not have changed since the re-creation of the earth. Their populations have been flourishing since the re-creation, as the only threat to their survival would have been the food chain itself. Exponentially their numbers would have grown by multitudes more than the land animals due to their continued existence during the flood.

Even after mankind's constant pressure on the ocean by netting, pollution, and habitat destruction, there are still mass quantities of fish in the lakes, seas, and oceans. (Sidebar - Obviously it is unknown if the water in the earth's interior that broke forth was fresh or salt water. Given that it was fresh water, it may help to understand how fresh water fish survived being overtaken by the briny oceans. Certainly, just as there are areas on the earth today where salt and fresh water meet and do not commingle; there must have been pockets of fresh water provided by the Lord that went undisturbed during the flood.)

Undoubtedly, from a logistical standpoint of the ark's space requirements, some animals are small and would occupy a minimal amount of space such as insects, spiders, and amphibians. Others are large and would require ample room to survive; such as mammals, birds, and reptiles. Of course, there are still countless unknown species on the earth, but the current estimated diversity of creation is estimated to be over 31,000 vertebrate animals (mammals, birds, reptiles, amphibians) and another 1,100,000 invertebrate creatures (insects, spiders, etc.)

The Bible does mention that Noah was instructed to bring "every creeping thing of the earth after his kind," which would include the insects also (Genesis 6:19–20). Certainly, they would not have the space requirements that the others animals would have, but could occupy the walls and ceilings on each level. Thus, their impact on the space requirements would be somewhat minimal, but the 31,000 land animals that would have been passengers are a different story. Each one would have its own requirements for food, water, exercise, air, excrement, etc. So the question is, "Would there have been enough room for them all?"

Given the length of a cubit being 18 inches and the ark being three stories high, that would mean that there was approximately 22,500 square feet per level or 67,500 total square feet of living space not including the top deck which had a small one cubit observation room, presumably the area was uninhabitable given the rain. (Genesis 6:16.) By comparison, a "big box store," such as a Target occupy on average 126,000 square feet, with a Super Target sizing in around 175,000 square feet. Frankly, it would seem unlikely that two of each of the land animals on the planet would fit into an area little more than half of the size of a Target store.

Using another common perspective, it may be easier to look at it from the standpoint of boxcars. The average boxcar is approximately 450 square feet, which equates to approximately 150 boxcars as being the living quarters of the ark. Taking all of the animals of the earth and averaging their size, it has been estimated that the average size of all land animals on the earth would be about the size of a sheep or possibly a little smaller.

Approximately 120 sheep could fit into each boxcar if they were packed together like Lego's, which would equate to a minimum requirement of 259 boxcars in order to accommodate one of every animal on the earth; for a total of 518 boxcars for the pair or 233,100 square feet. Of course, this is not taking into account the animals that came in numbers of seven. It is also not accounting for the fact that each of the animals needs room to move and sleep, in addition to storage needs for food and water, etc. All of which Noah and his family were tasked to undertake and provide for them while they were on board. (Genesis 6:19–21.)

Obviously, the math does not equate. Not only that, taking into account the human sanity factor of living in a space a little greater than half the size of a Target store with at least two of every creature on earth, each with their own needs seems unfathomable. Thus it is necessary to revisit a couple of the critical elements of the story.

As has been aforementioned, the length of a cubit can vary from different time periods and cultures. Archaeological finds from the days of Noah concerning standardized measures have come up lacking and may never be unearthed. This was hundreds of years earlier than the first recorded length of a known cubit and arguably the flood would have destroyed any record of Noah's standards of measurement. So without biblical guidance of a cubit's length in those days, it is safe to say that the definition remains unclear. Nevertheless, the Bible does give the dimensions as, "The length of the ark shall be three hundred cubits, the breadth of it fifty cubits, and the height of it thirty cubits" (Genesis 6:15).

One of the most interesting things about the story is that the height of the ark was thirty cubits, but the Bible also states that the tallest mountain was only fifteen cubits. "Fifteen cubits upward did the waters prevail; and the mountains were covered" (Genesis 7:20).

So the entire length that the waters raised was fifteen cubits. This translates to the fact that the height of the ark was twice as tall as the amount that the floodwaters rose, which covered all the mountains of the earth at that time. Furthermore, its length was 20 times as great as the amount of water to cover the highest mountain of the day and its width was over three times the depth of the waters that rose upon the earth. Undoubtedly, a cubit for the Lord and Noah was greater than any one body length.

Certainly, it could be that there were two different measurements for a cubit, one for standard measuring of "household objects" and one for measuring bigger items. Unfortunately, since there is no indication in the narrative that the Lord uses a different length of cubit for a mountain than for the measurement of the ark, it has to be assumed that they were the same length; which means that both the ark and the mountains were measured in cubits and can be compared in size to one another.

Undoubtedly, the believability of the story of Noah centers on the mountains on the earth at the time of the flood. After all, the events of the flood took place only a few thousand years ago. Rational determination of the event says that if a flood of that magnitude during the days of Noah's days did take place, then the earth and most of its landscape would be in approximately the same place. That means the tallest mountain on earth would be approximately the same height as it is now.

Thus, assuming that Mount Everest (20,029 feet) was the tallest point on the earth at the time of the flood and the same analogy was used for a cubit as previously mentioned, then the ark would have been almost 110 miles long! The air is thin at 29,000 feet, but it is really thin and difficult to build at 58,000 feet, the approximate height of the ark given the fact that the Bible was portraying fifteen cubits to be the height of Everest. One hundred years would not have been anywhere near enough time to construct something that large, not to mention the sheer volume of wood and resources that would be needed. Obviously, the absurdity of such a statement points to a discrepancy in the logic. Thus, it is necessary and practical to revisit the size of a mountain in the days of Noah.

Mountains

Who hath measured the waters in the hollow of his hand, and meted out heaven with the span, and comprehended the dust of the earth in a measure, and weighed the mountains in scales, and the hills in a balance? (Isaiah 40:12)

The Bible shows that indeed the earth's landscape has changed since these earlier days. It is an undisputed fact that fossils of sea creatures have been found at the peaks of the highest mountains. Conversely there have been "mountain animal" fossils found in much lower elevations. Of course, scientific projections show that the earth's current mountainous regions are most certainly a result of the earth shifting over a time frame believed to have been millions of years.

The Bible paints a different picture, and hence it is important to decipher what it says about mountains and how they play a role in both the prehistoric and recent landscape of the earth. Mountains are a part of the earth and the whole earth is created, but it is interesting that there is no specific passage that says mountains were created. Whenever they are mentioned in the Bible they are either brought forth or formed, which means that they are temporary fixtures on the landscape of the earth brought about after the re-creation. (Psalm 90:2, Amos 4:13.) As such they are not mentioned in the Genesis account of the re-creation, because they are not a necessity in the earth's landscape.

In other words, mountains are the changing anomaly in the narrative of Noah, because it is certain that there is no way that Noah built a boat that was twice the size of Mount Everest. Therefore the current estimates of millions of years of slowly moving tectonic plates that have caused upward thrust in the earth's crust actually happened within a time frame that was substantially shorter.

Though the Bible is specific that a flat earth is the plan for future generation after the end of this age, there are other passages that reveal the fact that the planet was also non-mountainous in the recent past. (Revelation 16:20) Indeed, biblically there are multiple times in the Scriptures that the Lord is said to have uprooted and overturned prior mountainous outcroppings in the earth before their current configuration. For instance Job says that, "He putteth forth his hand upon the rock; he overturneth the mountains by the roots" (Job 28:9). Here Job was specifically referring to an event that he considered present tense.

Without question, the book of Job is a treasure trove of historical information about creation and the earth's history. It is considered by many to be the oldest book in the Bible. Of course, this has been shown to not be true, given the fact that each of the generations in Genesis wrote about their own existence all the way back to Adam and the re-creation. Nevertheless, the book of Job is believed to take place around the days of Abraham, putting its existence somewhere in the pages of the earliest patriarchs. Job gives a picture of the days prior to the re-creation when he says that it was the Lord, "Which removeth the mountains, and they know not: which overturneth them in his anger. Which shaketh the earth out of her place, and the pillars thereof tremble. Which commandeth the sun, and it riseth not; and sealeth up the stars" (Job 9:5–7).

Of course, the removing of mountains and the shaking of the earth's foundation is contrary to the Lord's original design. The foundations of the earth were established in the beginning of creation never to be removed. (Psalm 104:5.) Yet the Psalmist agrees with Job when he says that during those days, "all the foundations of the earth are out of course" (Psalm 82:5).

Of course, these proceedings were actual events that transpired at a point when the Lord deemed that massive judgment was due. Certainly an event like this is reminiscent of the picture of the earth that the Lord paints in Genesis just prior to the re-creation; for there is no other place in the Scripture that all of these events correlate to.

Thus, when Job mentions that the sun didn't shine and the stars were sealed up, it is likely that the overturning of the mountains in the first part of the verse would have been at least a partial cause of the darkness on the earth. Most definitely an act of that magnitude would have caused a cloud of dust that would have blocked any potential for remaining sunlight, and it may have been partly responsible for the partial destruction of the atmosphere during that age. Undoubtedly, that cloud would have remained on the earth until at least the second day of the re-creation. For without a viable atmosphere or hydrological cycle until the second day, it would not have been able to filter the debris out of the air. Even still, the Bible shows that the dust was not fully settled until the fourth day.

Knowing then that the mountains were removed and the foundations of the earth were out of course during the re-creation helps give additional clarity to the statement that the earth was without form and void. Undoubtedly such an event would have had huge ramifications on the earth. It is certainly possible that the destruction and uprooting of the mountains was the contributing factor for the earth being knocked from its course. The same Psalmist from above goes on to say what the outcome of this mountainous destruction was and will be for those occupying the earth at the time: "But ye shall die like men, and fall like one of the princes. Arise, O God, judge the earth: for thou shalt inherit all nations" (Psalm 82:7–8). Certainly judgment is in their future.

Jeremiah verifies the destruction of the habitation of the angelic hosts and gives one final clue to the puzzle:

> I beheld the earth, and, lo, it was without form, and void; and the heavens, and they had no light. I beheld the mountains, and, lo, they trembled, and all the hills moved lightly. I beheld, and, lo, there was no man, and all the birds of the heavens were fled. I beheld, and, lo, the fruitful place was a wilderness, and all the cities thereof were broken down at the presence of the LORD, and by his fierce anger. For thus hath the LORD said, The whole land shall be desolate; yet will I not make a full end. For this shall the earth mourn, and the heavens above be black: because I have spoken it, I have purposed it, and will not repent, neither will I turn back from it. (Jeremiah 4:23–28)

The order of the events depicted here are just prior to Job 9:5, and it is the very picture of the earth before the re-creation. The earth was without form and void and the heavens had no light; but now a little more of the story is revealed. All the inhabitants were gone, the cities are broken down, and the fruitful place was a wilderness; leaving the whole land desolate because of His great anger. The Lord is wroth and the mountains quaked in His presence.

Combining both passages from Jeremiah and Job helps to paint an exact picture of the earth that is seen in Genesis 1:2. The earth is without form and void. It is dark and the fruitful place (Eden, the garden of God) is now a wilderness, because the reservoirs of the great deep erupted and began to cover the earth. The Lord is so angry that the mountains shake at the very mention of His name.

Ultimately with a blast of His voice, He uproots all of the mountainous landscape. The action is so violent that the earth becomes enveloped in a cloud of dust that casts it into physical darkness, destroying the atmosphere and actually disrupting the planet's orbit. How far out of its orbit is unknown, but it is so dark that the sun does not rise and the stars are absent from the night sky.

Finally, the Lord turns his back on His own creation and the ultimate penalty is invoked: the earth is left in both a physical and spiritual darkness. Hereby, the Bible has painted a complete picture of the events that transpired prior to the re-creation of the earth and what happened during its destruction. After these destructive events transpire, untold generations of time elapse; a gap of time which is witnessed in the geological record of the earth.

Fortunately, the Lord did not remove His presence forever. He develops a plan to rectify these events and begins to execute that plan by bringing back His light to the planet, the very light of the knowledge of the glory of God. On that first day, things began to change. On the second day He restores the damaged atmosphere. Then, on the third day some of the water recedes as the earth reappears, but He leaves a large remnant of the earth still covered with water. Peter describes it as, "the earth standing out of the water and in the water" (2 Peter 3:5). Once the dry land appears, life began to spring forth once again on the planet. And the story continues on through the rest of the Genesis narrative.

Timing

Of course, there is no place in the Bible that specifically exacerbates on the exact time line of the events prior to re-creation, but by combining biblical history with current geological knowledge it is relatively easy to extrapolate a hypothesis.

Given that the height of the mountains during the days of Noah were substantially shorter than they are now, equates to the fact that these events did indeed transpire during the judgment of the angelic hosts. Since the destruction of the mountains happened just prior to the re-creation, when the Lord began to rebuild, the earth would have been largely flat or without form. It does not mention hills, but definitively the mountains had been eradicated from the surface of the earth.

Obviously, by the time Noah sets afloat, there was some topographical deviation because the Bible says that all the mountains of the earth were covered. In other words, there were mountains on the earth by the time Noah came along. The Bible also mentions that when the waters receded after the flood of Noah, the ark came to rest on a range of mountains called Ararat. (Genesis 8:4.) Of course, it has been noted that between the re-creation and Noah there may have been upwards of hundreds of thousands or more years. This would have been more than enough time for the earth to shift and produce upward thrust.

If Adam was truly on the earth for a hundred thousand years or more and the shifting earth pushed certain points upward a few millimeters a year, this would equate to a fairly large mountain. Of course, the Bible does not say what the upward thrust of the mountains was, but there was apparently some upward movement because there were mountains on the earth by the time that Noah went into the ark. While this does not account for the current elevation of the mountains, it does account for some upward movement. (The topography of the earth during this age and the obvious discrepancy compared to modern day topography will be discussed below).

Even by modern definitions, there is no one specific height classification for a rock formation to be called a mountain. For example, Eagle Mountain is the tallest mountain in Minnesota towering in at 2,301 feet. However, in Colorado, Mount Elbert is the tallest mountain and reaches 14,433 feet. Relatively speaking, Eagle Mountain in Minnesota is just a hill compared to Colorado's Mount Elbert. Hence, a more technical definition of a mountain in the United States says that a mountain must have a minimal drop (before one can ascend something higher) of at least 300 feet. This is pretty close to the rest of the world that measures a mountain at 330 feet.

If this definition were carried over to the days of Noah it would help make sense of the fact that all the mountains of the earth were covered by water, if the mountains of the earth were around 300 feet tall. Of course, the exact height of a mountain on the earth during Noah's days may never be known, but it had to have been of a relatively small size, because the ark was twice the height of the tallest one.

For the sake of example, the current international measurement for a mountain of 330 feet will be used to better understand the potential magnitude of the ark. Assuming that the tallest mountain on the earth at the time of the flood was 330 feet above sea level, then that means that 330 feet was equal to 15 cubits. The length of the ark was 300 hundred cubits or 6,600 feet. By definition, one land mile is 5,280 feet, which means that, in this example, the boat was one and quarter miles long! As a comparison, today the largest supertanker that roams the ocean is 1,500 feet long. That's a mere one third of a mile in length. In addition, that would mean that the ark was 1,100 feet wide and 660 feet tall.

Certainly, a vessel of this magnitude would have had ample room to fit the menagerie that showed up as the waters began to overtake the earth. Of course, this is just an example, but knowing that the ark could have been of this significance, points to the fact that the classification of a mountain was substantially less than 330 feet in the days of Noah. Even if it was half this size, it is apparent that the ark was the largest floating vessel ever built and it would need to be to house the vast diversity of the earth's life forms. An ark of that size would be more than seven times today's estimated size of the ark. It seems impossible, but the logic is viable. How else could the Lord fit all the species of the earth into it and how could the ark be twice the size of a mountain and sustain them for so long?

Thus, the fountains of deep were not required to cover the earth to a depth of 5 ½ miles, rather it is apparent that the tallest of mountains on the earth during Noah's time may have been less than a hundred feet tall. Therefore, it is more plausible that all of the high hills and mountains were covered with water within the allotted 40 day time frame. It is also plausible that the fountains of the deep broke forth and significantly covered the mountains of the earth at the time, because an ark that was likely twice as tall as the highest mountain would have displaced an enormous amount of water.

Following are a few facts about the voyage: In Genesis 7:7–9, the floodwaters were beginning to cover the earth and Noah and his family and all the animals entered the ark. These early floodwaters were the start of the actual supernatural event that was to come seven days later. "And it came to pass after seven days, that the waters of the flood were upon the earth… the same day were all the fountains of the great deep broken up, and the windows of heaven were opened" (Genesis 7:10–11).

The amount of time that Noah had to build the ark is unknown, but the Bible points to the fact that it may have been several decades or longer. Noah was 500 years old when he had children. (Genesis 5:32.) Those children were apparently married when he received instruction from the Lord to build the ark. (Genesis 6:18.) He then entered the ark in his 600th year. (Genesis 7:11.) The timeline hinges around when the Lord gave the edict to Noah to build the boat. He may have spoken to Noah shortly after his children were born and predicted their future marriage or they may have already been married. Thus, the timeline is unknown. Nevertheless, the Lord allowed ample time for Noah to complete the task.

Most likely Noah received help from the future occupants of the ark; his wife, sons, and daughter-in-laws, and quite possibly he obtained some help from the neighboring people (some of them possibly giants). It is generally believed that Noah was only in the ark for forty days, but in reality the flood waters covered the earth for exactly one year. (Compare Genesis 7:11, Genesis 8:13–14.) It was the rain and floods that continued upon the earth for forty days. (Genesis 7:12, Genesis 7:17.) Once it was done raining, the waters continued to prevail on the earth for a total of 150 days. (Genesis 7:24.) The rest of the time was spent waiting for the waters to recede and for the ark to come to rest. Of course, all of this took place to dispense great judgment upon a sinful generation of humans and angels and all the inhabitants of the earth were destroyed except for the people on the ark.

One Continent

Thus, it has been seen that the current topography of today has not always been the topography of previous epochs. In fact, it has only been in recent generations that the idea of plate tectonics has become widely accepted as fact. The idea is that the crust is made up of separate plates that "float" above the mantle and have slowly shifted over millions of years into their current location. The merging of these various plates are called fault lines. Where two plates meet can be a volatile place, as they are single-handily blamed as the cause of earthquakes and tsunamis around the globe today.

Prior to their shifting, scientists generally agree that the earth was one landmass and through time it has methodically separated into its current continental configuration. This single landmass has been named *Pangaea* from the Greek meaning entire or all lands. Visually, the idea makes sense; by simply pushing all the continents together it is uncanny to see how well they seem to jigsaw together. To the south would be part of Africa, Antarctica, Australia, and India. To the west would be the rest of Africa, South America, and part of North America. To the North would be the rest of North America, Europe, and Asia and to the east would be the Middle East.

Corroborating evidence for what has been called continental drift can be found in the fossil records of animals that have walked the earth in recent epochs. These records point to the fact that certain animal species can be found on different continents that are now great distances apart. The only explanation for this would be due to a separation in the earth's landscape.

This same phenomenon can be witnessed in the terrestrial architecture; certain rock strata, formations, and deposits are only found in certain areas of the globe that are believed to have been combined at one point. For instance, large deposits of coal can be found in Antarctica, despite it only being "produced" in warmer climates, which proves that Antarctica was not always at the bottom of the earth. Rather it was once located in a climate able to produce the substantial amounts of vegetation necessary to later manufacture large quantities of coal.

Looking again to the topographical layout of the earth when it was one continent, it was noted that the Middle East was once on the eastern side of the map. This entire area is the area that the Bible calls the Garden of Eden in the eastern part of Eden. Of course, as it has been discussed, this region was only a portion of an area that the Bible calls Eden. Prior to the creation of mankind this entire area was called "Eden the garden of God," but it also covered a much larger area (Ezekiel 28:13).

Given the fact that the earth was one continent during this time, it is plausible that much of the exposed landscape of the earth today was previously called Eden. In other words, what emerged from the water on the third day and what mankind currently occupies was formerly Eden, the garden of God. The rest of the earth that was once occupied was destroyed and covered with water during the re-creation. Of course, its exact dimensions are unknown, so this is just a theory based largely on the fact that it was referred to being the garden of God; an area that the Lord had an affinity for and was set apart for Him. Therefore, He resurrected the area during the re-creation for the enjoyment of mankind.

The question that apparently arises then is what time frame is involved for the movement of the earth's landscape? Although it certainly seems plausible that the earth's plates have moved slower in past ages, the Bible depicts a substantially different rate of change in recent times.

Looking back at the events of the re-creation, it can be seen that on the third day the earth came forth as one landmass. "Let the waters under the heaven be gathered together unto one place, and let the dry land appear" (Genesis 1:9). If the waters of the earth were gathered together into one place, then the dry land must have also appeared in one place. In other words, the earth at the time of the re-creation was one landmass (called Eden the garden of God), which would mean that the current configuration and separation of land was brought about at a point sometime after Genesis one and the Bible shows that occurred after the flood of Noah.

Peleg

Approximately one century after the flood dissipated, an individual by the name of Peleg was born. He was the great, great grandson of Shem; the fifth generation from Noah. He was born 101 years after Shem left the ark and he lived for 209 years. At some point during his life the Bible says that the earth changed dramatically. The name Peleg literally means division and it was during his lifespan that the people of the world built a tower in Babel.

> And the whole earth was of one language, and of one speech. And it came to pass, as they journeyed from the east, that they found a plain in the land of Shinar; and they dwelt there. And they said one to another, Go to, let us make brick, and burn them throughly. And they had brick for stone, and slime had they for morter. And they said, Go to, let us build us a city and a tower, whose top may reach unto heaven; and let us make us a name, lest we be scattered abroad upon the face of the whole earth. And the LORD came down to see the city and the tower, which the children of men builded. And the LORD said, Behold, the people is one, and they have all one language; and this they begin to do: and now nothing will be restrained from them, which they have imagined to do. Go to, let us go down, and there confound their language, that they may not understand one another's speech. So the LORD scattered them abroad from thence upon the face of all the earth: and they left off to build the city. Therefore is the name of it called Babel; because the LORD did there confound the language of all the earth: and from thence did the LORD scatter them abroad upon the face of all the earth. (Genesis 11:1–9)

During this age, all the people of the earth were living in one central area and spoke a single language. Unlike Adam's immediate offspring who apparently spread out all over the region, when Noah and his family left the ark their heirs did not journey too far from the nest. For one reason or another they consensually agreed that they should journey away from their current location. They journeyed from the east (the area that was formerly the Garden of Eden), probably looking for a more hospitable place to settle as Eden would have continued to be a harsh desert landscape. Led by a man by the name of Nimrod (the grandson of Ham) they settled on a plain in a land called Shinar and built a town. Obviously, this area had been scouted, named, and determined to be suitable for their needs. They devised a plan to remain unified so they would not be dispersed across the globe. The plan was to establish their name in the earth by building a tower made out of bricks to reach into heaven.

It is apparent that they felt that being a unified force they had no more need for God, and the implication was that they intended to set themselves up as gods upon the earth. Since the mountains of the earth were of little consequence in the landscape, a tower that rose above the tallest points on the earth would have, in their minds, established them as having dominion over all of creation. If extremely tall mountains existed during these days there would have been no need to build a tower, they could have established their superiority by building a city on the side or top of a mountain peak. Since there were none, they built their own; in essence, replacing the mountain or government of God with a man-made mountain.

Their symbolic gesture and attempt to mirror his authority in the earth did not go unnoticed by the Lord. He recognized their heart and realized that their attempt to build a mountain and establish themselves would have been in place of His mountain or leadership. Of course, God is a jealous God. He does not want any other gods or governments to be elevated above Him, which is why there were essentially no mountains on the earth previous to this point.

The Bible is clear that if the people were allowed to become unified together, there was virtually nothing that they would not be able to accomplish. The implication is that debauchery and all sorts of evil would have once again reigned supreme, and God would have been forgotten. It is one of the most defining moments in the history of modern man, for it was here that God changed the course of humanity. Realizing their synergy, the Lord took action before they became too vain and decisive in power.

Aptly named the Tower of Babel, the first thing that the Lord did was to confound their language so that they could not understand each other. God, of course, is the master of all languages, as there are untold countless languages in heaven. (1 Corinthians 14:2.) In turn, He introduced a number of these languages to the earth during the Babel encounter.

It was even harsher than this; because it says that the Lord did there confound the language of all the *earth*. Of course, the word earth is more than just the people and their language. It is apparent that the occupants of the earth at that point were in communion with the landscape surrounding them. Thus, the ability to truly commune with nature had never been lost since the days of Adam, until this point.

Remember that it was the earth that spoke out the first chapter of Genesis and it was likely that Adam transcribed it. Once the Lord confused their language, they lost their ability to understand the language of nature. Thus it is easy to see why the people were joined in one accord, because they were in harmony with the earth and each other; one heart and one mind.

The Lord took it one step further, because He also took the various people who now spoke their respective language and spread them throughout the earth. Since the earth was all one continent, they would have had the ability to easily migrate across the globe unhindered on a relatively flat landscape that consisted of a single continent. The text does not say that they haphazardly meandered to a new location; in fact it says that it was more of a purposeful relocation on behalf of the Lord. "So the LORD scattered them abroad from thence upon the face of all the earth" (Genesis 11:8). It is unknown exactly how the Lord undertook this process or how long the relocation process took, but the people of the earth were displaced all over the globe and congregated together based on their respective new languages.

Although migrations, sea levels, temperature, and several other factors have caused people to move to more habitable locations; there are still tribes of people in the most remote regions of the earth. Speculation is rampant about how they got there, but regardless, it is apparent that it was in fact a fairly recent phenomenon. Although mankind may be tens of thousands of years old, the timeline essentially restarted following the global flood of Noah. The only way for people to reach these remote places was for the earth to have once been one super-continent and even then the passage makes it appear that they were physically relocated by the Lord.

However the Lord ultimately accomplished this feat is undisclosed, but there was one final action that He took during this period of time to solidify the division. He also physically separated the earth. "And unto Eber were born two sons: the name of one was Peleg; for in his days was the earth divided; and his brother's name was Joktan" (Genesis 10:25). Once again, the word earth here shows that it was more than just a division of the population or their language. God also changed the physical layout of the earth, essentially creating the continental separation seen in the earth today.

He did this by taking the descendants of Japheth (Noah's son) as seen in Genesis 10:1–4 and separated them across the globe. "By these were the isles of the Gentiles divided in their lands; every one after his tongue, after their families, in their nations" (Genesis 10:5). The Lord gave the same language to the same tribe and then divided them by these various tribes and families. Once completed, the Lord then broke apart the earth into its current continental configuration, which the text calls islands.

The emphasis here was the division of the land, but it also showed the separation of the people, which was a necessary step to insure the future of mankind upon the earth. He had already dealt with more than one insurgency in the past and realized that the only way to safeguard at least a portion of humanity upon the earth was to divide them. The Lord did not want a repeat in the type of corporate sin and pride that the earth had previously witnessed under Satan's leadership. Dividing the people and the lands across the earth ensured that there would be no continuity and they were left to discover God for themselves.

On account of the division of the earth, the landscape was rearranged into its existing shape, thereby establishing the mountainous regions of the earth today. How He accomplished this is not mentioned, but given the upward thrust of the various mountainous regions it seems apparent that He moved the various continental plates around like a jigsaw puzzle; not picking them up and putting them down like we do, but rather sliding them around like pieces on a board. By doing so He formed the various mountain ranges seen on the earth today. Of course, mountain ranges continue to be a symbol of the separation of mankind across the earth and the establishment of diverse human governments congregated together by speech.

Multiple mountainous outcroppings show that as long as mankind is in the earth there will no longer be complete unity, but instead there is division and instability. Concurring with the establishment of the mountains, the Psalmist says that, "You set the mountains in place by your strength, showing your mighty power" (Psalm 65:6 GNB). The Psalmist did not mince his words. A gradual haphazard random movement in plate tectonics did not bring about their position, but rather they were set in their current place by a mighty God endued with power and strength. Who set the mountains there as a symbol of mankind's current system of governments in the earth. Ultimately, they will all be brought to naught when the Lord returns and once again establishes His holy mountain on the earth; removing all the mountains (governments), and restructuring the earth back to one landmass when he sets up the one true government of God in the earth. (Revelation 16:20.)

Further proof of the division of the earth is found in the seventy fourth Psalm, "For God is my King of old, working salvation in the midst of the earth. Thou didst divide the sea by thy strength: thou brakest the heads of the dragons in the waters. Thou brakest the heads of leviathan in pieces, and gavest him to be meat to the people inhabiting the wilderness. Thou didst cleave the fountain and the flood: thou driedst up mighty rivers" (Psalm 74:12–15).

Many Bible scholars say this passage is a reference to the Israelites crossing the Red Sea. But at no point during the Red Sea crossing did the Lord dry up mighty rivers. He simply held back the waters. Furthermore, at the time of the Red Sea crossing there was no reference to Him needing to change floodwaters or fountains of the deep. Nor does it say in the Exodus account that the Israelites ate the fish of the Red Sea. On the contrary, one of the first things they complained about was the lack of food. (Exodus 16:3.)

Therefore, Psalm 74 is clearly referencing the separation of the earth in the days of Peleg. God is the King of Old that brought salvation by dividing the earth into its modern day continents. Dividing the sea by splitting the earth was His method of salvation for that generation and all of mankind. In addition, it says that the areas that once were wilderness were broken up and one large body of water became the multiple oceans of the earth today. Thus, people of the earth who normally would not have eaten fish were doing so during this tumultuous time as some landlocked areas became coastal villages overnight.

It also states that mighty rivers were dried up, which gives insight into the terrain of the Middle East and what happened to the rivers of the Garden of Eden. It has been shown that the Garden of Eden essentially became a desert after it was swallowed up by the earth, but that does not account for the rivers that were mentioned in the account. Of course, the Bible refers to four rivers that bordered the garden on each side: Pison, Gihon, Hiddekel, and Euphrates. (Genesis 2:10–14.)

As had been discussed, on the modern map there is no geographical location on the planet that meets the criteria of being bordered by four rivers. Even after major events like floods and earthquakes, there would have been some trace remnants of desert rivers in the geological record. This verse explains why there is no trace of them. When the Lord broke the earth apart, some of the rivers that surrounded the Garden of Eden were lost as the earth shifted. Essentially, a new landscape was put in its place and Israel became the connecting point of three continents. Thus it is aptly named the Middle East, because it is the axis point between the continents.

This earthly division brought about in the days of Peleg also helps to explain the location of animal species in various locations around the globe. Once the flood ended it would have been easy for the animals to travel throughout the globe, since the earth was still one continent and relatively flat. Obviously, once they left the ark they would have sought out habitat favorable to their living conditions. As they travelled, they created ranges suitable to their needs. Since the earth was essentially one continent it is easy to see how the various species would be able to navigate to the various remote regions of the earth after the flood.

Today, there are animals that are essentially landlocked great distances from where the ark was believed to have landed. It would have been impossible for these animals to traverse such great distances, travelling through environments that they would have been unequipped to handle. If the earth was split up into the continents of today before they left the ark, then they would have had to travel across large bodies of water and several thousand miles in order to reach their current location. But since the earth was one landmass it explains how some slower moving territorial animals are located in only certain areas of the globe thousands of miles away from the Middle East, while other species are spread out across several continents. This is all due to the fact that when they left the ark, they stepped out onto one continent. Then sometime within the next few hundred years the Lord physically divided them one from another.

In this same respect, it helps to envision how the Lord congregated the animals prior to their entering the ark. Given that the earth was one landmass they would have been unencumbered to freely move across the landscape during the time that Noah was building the ark.

Certainly, it also explains why certain unique geological strata are separated by great distances on different continents. Similar rock formations that were obviously joined at some point in time are now thousands of miles apart. In this same regard, there are some man-made objects on the earth that are hundreds or thousands of miles away from their believed points of origination.

Of course the idea of recent continental restructuring flies in the face of modern scientific theory. The scientific consensus is that it took a couple of million years of minuscule annual movements to have pushed the continents into their current configurations. An obvious disparity between the Bible and science arises in regards to the time frame of the earth's splitting.

Scientifically speaking there is no evidence that the movement of the earth from one single landmass to the divided continents that are known today was a relatively quick event. In fact a "rapid moving earth" has been rejected because it is believed that such forceful actions would have left indelible scarring on the earth's surface. Since these types of striations in various rock formations have never been uncovered or witnessed, the idea of a rapidly moving earth has never been considered.

Genesis never said that it was immediate, but rather that it happened in the days of Peleg, "for in his days (plural) was the earth divided" (Genesis 10:25). Peleg was an individual who lived for 209 years and it is apparent that the word "days" here is once again used colloquially and may be better represented as referring to his generation. That is to say, the Lord did not necessarily cause the separation of the earth's crust in a couple of earth days;

but rather that it may have happened over Peleg's lifetime or a span of time during his life.

Regardless, it still would not match the millions of years prescribed in the scientific method. Recent continental division is not an idea that the scientific community embraces and as such there is no data to back up the argument. Whether there is any scientific evidence or not, the Bible is clear that it was by His hand that the mountains were uprooted, the people were scattered, the land was divided, and the earth's inhabitants were given new tongues.

He is the God of creation and by His power and awesome might He changed the look of the exposed earth to one He deemed conducive to the preservation of man. Therefore, it is not a far stretch of the imagination to say that this happened in a relatively quick fashion. After his humbling experience, Nebuchadnezzar's only statement was one of awe and wonder, "And all the inhabitants of the earth are reputed as nothing: and he doeth according to his will in the army of heaven, and among the inhabitants of the earth: and none can stay his hand, or say unto him, What doest thou" (Daniel 4:35)? He is God, the Creator and Maker of the earth and He has the power to do as He pleases in the earth, as long as it is within the prescribed bounds of His spoken word. That would include His own ability to design and manipulate the earth in a fashion and manner that He sees fit, and it is not relevant whether or not mankind can decipher His methods.

In conclusion, just like the oceans, the mountains were not originally designed to be a part of the earth and at the end of this age, the Lord will once again uproot every trace of these skyscrapers that dot the current landscape, establishing one final time the only true mountain in the earth. Mankind's rule will be gone and the government of God will be established. "For ye are not come unto the mount that might be touched... But ye are come unto mount Sion, and unto the city of the living God, the heavenly Jerusalem" (Hebrews 12:18, 22). When this happens, the covenant of peace and kindness that He has with mankind will never be erased. (Isaiah 54:10.)

The long and short of it is that the earth's landscape has been radically changed based on the actions of the administrators that the Lord placed on its surface. The earth was originally created in a perfect, self-sustaining harmony that was never designed to be a catalyst to sin. Its sole purpose was, and continues to be to glorify God. Once sentient beings were placed on the earth, on account of their sin, its landscape was changed, rearranged, and cursed time and again.

Previously it was angelic sin that caused the earth to sustain untold numbers of cataclysmic events. This period ultimately culminated with the physical destruction of the angelic host and left the earth in ruins. Then, once again, catastrophe struck when man and angels mated; from which He proceeded to save a portion of all life on earth on an ark constructed by one faithful man.

Finally, the Lord intervened at the Tower of Babel to save mankind from itself by physically separating the existing single landmass of the earth into several different continents while simultaneously confusing their speech. Every action that He takes is justified and adequate for the situation at hand. Certainly time will show that during each period of judgment in the earth, the Lord was more than graceful and patient with its inhabitants while He waited for them to get it right. (Psalm 86:15, Matthew 10:26.) "O give thanks unto the LORD; for he is good; for his mercy endureth for ever" (1 Chronicles 16:34).

CHAPTER 20

In Conclusion

In Conclusion

He hath made the earth by his power, he hath established the world by his wisdom, and hath stretched out the heavens by his discretion. (Jeremiah 10:12)

Billions of years ago, God had an idea about a physical universe and a planet that has weathered eons of time and brought life to billions of different species. Part of His plan culminated in the creation of the human race that would one day populate this planet and wonder at His glorious design; instilling in them an inquisitive nature to discover more about its existence.

Admiring the massive diversity of creation, only one thing is for certain; chance is not the creator. Everything is from God, and all that mankind can do is attempt to interpret what God has placed here for humanity to enjoy and utilize. For only God knows the end from the beginning and all points in between. (Isaiah 46:10.)

Unfortunately, human interpretation is often influenced by an enemy that has exerted great power throughout all the ages of the earth. Today, he continues in his wily ways by convincing people that God does not exist and that the creation was really just an accident. Unwittingly, some people get wrapped up in the creation and the interpretation thereof, forgetting about the actual Creator. Duped by the god of this world, they fall prey to his tactics as he subtly injects his ideals into society and turns the truth of God into a lie.

His device, of course, is the exact opposite of what God bestows. "But the wisdom that is from above is first pure, then peaceable, gentle, and easy to be intreated, full of mercy and good fruits, without partiality, and without hypocrisy" (James 3:17). There is no ambiguity in the Word of God, it is always true. What the Bible says about the events of creation is true. Unfortunately, the scientific and Christian communities continue to clash with opposing ideas, questioning everything from logistics to time lines. One side largely heralds an evolutionary process, while the other still generally point to a literal six day creation.

Certainly, there will always be unknowns about the creation, because it seems like the more that is uncovered about the earth and its workings, the more questions arise. The truth is, "He hath made every thing beautiful in his time: also he hath set the world in their heart, so that no man can find out the work that God maketh from the beginning to the end" (Ecclesiastes 3:11). In the end that is the way that it is going to stay.

Though humanity quests to understand all of the mysteries of the universe, we will never know it all. The rest has to be believed through faith, just like belief in the Savior. For many it is easy to believe that He is the Savior, but for some reason it is not as easy to believe that He is also the Creator; despite the two being interchangeable. If He is the Savior, then by necessity He must also be the Creator. "For by him were all things created, that are in heaven, and that are in earth, visible and invisible, whether they be thrones, or dominions, or principalities, or powers: all things were created by him, and for him: And he is before all things, and by him all things consist" (Colossians 1:16–17).

Unfortunately, the ever-expanding scientific knowledge base has led to continuing theories and immense societal influence intended to forgo the fact that God is the Creator, and many are easily deceived. It is this very situation that Paul warned about in Colossians when he said, "Beware lest any man spoil you through philosophy and vain deceit, after the tradition of men, after the rudiments of the world, and not after Christ" (Colossians 2:8). And again when he wrote to the Thessalonians, "Let no man deceive you by any means: for that day shall not come, except there come a falling away first, and that man of sin be revealed, the son of perdition" (2 Thessalonians

2:3). Satan's tricks are very real, but the day will come when his lying and deceptive nature shall be revealed.

Contrarily, God's ways are not difficult; in fact Paul calls it simple. "But I fear, lest by any means, as the serpent beguiled Eve through his subtilty, so your minds should be corrupted from the simplicity that is in Christ" (2 Corinthians 11:3). He has done all He is going to do to convince humanity that He is the Creator. But the basic reality of God is plain enough. "For God is not the author of confusion, but of peace" (1 Corinthians 14:33). "Open your eyes and there it is! By taking a long and thoughtful look at what God has created, people have always been able to see what their eyes as such can't see: eternal power, for instance, and the mystery of his divine being. So nobody has a good excuse" (Romans 1:19–20 Message).

The physical evidence of creation is found in the creation itself. Knowledge and understanding about the creation comes from seeking after the Lord. For "the fear of the LORD is the beginning of knowledge" (Proverbs 1:7) Seeking after the wrong type of knowledge can be costly. Paul warned Timothy about this when he wrote to him to, "Guard that which was committed to your trust, turning away from the profane and empty babblings and opposing views of what is falsely called 'knowledge,' which some, by professing expertise, missed the mark concerning the faith" (1 Timothy 6:20–21 EMTV). He continues in Romans by saying,

> Because that, when they knew God, they glorified him not as God, neither were thankful; but became vain in their imaginations, and their foolish heart was darkened. Professing themselves to be wise, they became fools, And changed the glory of the uncorruptible God into an image made like to corruptible man, and to birds, and fourfooted beasts, and creeping things. (Romans 1:21–23)

Thinking themselves to be something they are not, they forsook the truth and changed it into other things. Forsaking all the brilliance that is God and His creation and clinging to a corruptible lie, they miss the whole of the truth and prescribe to the whims of men. God does not desire that anyone take that path, but rather God desires "all men to be saved, and to come unto the knowledge of the truth" (1 Timothy 2:4). This will ultimately lead to a place where all those who believe will:

> Come in the unity of the faith, and of the knowledge of the Son of God, unto a perfect man, unto the measure of the stature of the fulness of Christ: That we henceforth be no more children, tossed to and fro, and carried about with every wind of doctrine, by the sleight of men, and cunning craftiness, whereby they lie in wait to deceive; But speaking the truth in love, may grow up into him in all things, which is the head, even Christ: (Ephesians 4:13–15)

They are no longer pushed about by every wind of doctrine and ideas of man, where any new scientific idea pushes them into a state of confusion and doubt. Rather they are established in Christ and grown up. They have put on the mind of Christ by faith; and are continually seeking the truth in Him. Of course, that does not mean that they know all the mysteries of the Lord, but that instead they are looking to Him for the answers. (1 Corinthians 2:16.) Because He is the Creator and His Word is full of revelation about creation and the earth's history.

The rest has to be taken by faith, an easy step considering all the measures He has gone through to get His point across: the grandeur of the creation, the guidance from His written Word, and the leading of the Holy Spirit. Any one of these three distinct aspects of His nature, in and of themselves, provides more than enough evidence for a person to believe in Him as the Creator. Yet He freely gives us all three.

Job 38 and 39

In Job chapters 38 and 39, God gives a summary of the events of creation. It is a detailed and largely chronological account of the history of the earth.

Job and three of his friends had been rambling on about the calamity that had befallen Job months earlier, attempting to assess blame and understand his situation. Their conversation had reached a loggerhead, finally allowing a younger man by the name of Elihu who had been respectfully waiting to speak and share his thoughts about Job's situation. He speaks for six chapters and begins to address some of the flaws in the arguments made by his elders, all the while relaying his thoughts. He was doing his best, but ultimately the dialogue amongst Job and his friends had reached the end of the Lord's tolerance, and so the Lord takes over the conversation:

> Then the LORD answered Job out of the whirlwind, and said, Who is this that darkeneth counsel by words without knowledge? Gird up now thy loins like a man; for I will demand of thee, and answer thou me. (Job 38:1–3)

He calls out to Job and says that his ignorance and the words that he has been speaking about his situation are inadequate and meaningless. They have produced a dark cloud in His throne room and now He demands an answer. As the Lord continues on, He demands Job explain the majesty of the creation, for if he can do that, then maybe he is worthy to speak in the presence of the Lord. Of course, Job, like any man, is woefully inadequate to explain the beginning of creation. He continues:

> Where wast thou when I laid the foundations of the earth? declare, if thou hast understanding. Who hath laid the measures thereof, if thou knowest? or who hath stretched the line upon it? Whereupon are the foundations thereof fastened? or who laid the corner stone thereof; When the morning stars sang together, and all the sons of God shouted for joy? (Job 38:4–7)

In the beginning God created the earth. He started by laying the foundation and precisely measured everything down to the smallest details so it functioned to perfection. He established the position of the earth in space and gave it an atmosphere. This passage is speaking of the original creation of the earth that happened in the dateless past. Now, God demands an answer; where were you Job (and all others who profess themselves to be wise), when all of this was going down? Where were you when the cornerstone was laid? The angels were there and witnessed the birth of the earth, but you were not. Can you now determine how it was all set in motion? He continues on with more rhetorical questions.

> Or who shut up the sea with doors, when it brake forth, as if it had issued out of the womb? When I made the cloud the garment thereof, and thick darkness a swaddlingband for it, And brake up for it my decreed place, and set bars and doors, And said, Hitherto shalt thou come, but no further: and here shall thy proud waves be stayed? (Job 38:8–11)

Again, it is the very picture of the earth at the moment of its original creation. The earth is encapsulated in an atmosphere and established upon waters. Waters that are shut up under the earth, held back by what the Bible describes as doors and bars, not allowed upon the face of the earth where His new creation is beginning to take shape.

> Hast thou commanded the morning since thy days; (Job 38:12)

From the beginning, He set the earth in motion by establishing its rotation, distance from the sun, the tilt of its axis, etc. Thereby instituting time and the seasons and establishing it in the heaven. Once it was set up, He left the administration of it to another member of His creation.

> and caused the dayspring to know his place; That it might take hold of the ends of the earth, that the wicked might be shaken out of it? It is turned as clay to the seal; and they stand as a garment. And from the wicked their light is withholden, and the high arm shall be broken. (Job 38:12–15)

The dayspring (Satan) was placed on the earth to care for it and tend to it. He was specifically tasked with its administration and was not to deviate from that task. It was an assignment that was never supposed to end, but the wickedness of His servant brought about judgment. The Lord turned His back on the creation and He removed His Spirit, leaving darkness to cover the earth and shut it up like clay on a seal. Like a garment covering the earth it was cloaked in darkness, withholding light from its occupants, breaking down their strong arm of defenses. The wickedness of Satan and his colleagues was removed and their power was sent to the grave. The oceanic remnants of these events are seen today.

> Hast thou entered into the springs of the sea? or hast thou walked in the search of the depth? Have the gates of death been opened unto thee? or hast thou seen the doors of the shadow of death? Hast thou perceived the breadth of the earth? declare if thou knowest it all. (Job 38:16–18)

The oceans and seas on the earth's surface are a testament to the destructive events that transpired prior to the re-creation. God prepared a place for those that were destroyed; a place under the earth, reserved for Satan and his cohorts and restricted by gates. Death was never meant to be a part of the earth until Satan and his colleagues were sentenced to judgment. Covering up parts of the earth's surface with water, He established physical boundaries that those angels that took up residence in the earth could not cross.

> Where is the way where light dwelleth? and as for darkness, where is the place thereof, That thou shouldest take it to the bound thereof, and that thou shouldest know the paths to the house thereof? Knowest thou it, because thou wast then born? or because the number of thy days is great? (Job 38:19–21)

As the Lord continues to interrogate Job about his knowledge base, He reveals that even through this dark time, He would not abandon His creation, for His light could not be withheld forever. Even though there was destruction and He removed His presence from the earth for a time, things were about to change. His ways are always good and He desired to spread His light upon the earth again.

> Hast thou entered into the treasures of the snow? or hast thou seen the treasures of the hail, Which I have reserved against the time of trouble, against the day of battle and war? (Job 38:22–23)

In the meantime, major earthly function such as snow and hail are stored up while they wait in expectation of returning to the earth. This section also makes mention of the fact that the battle is not over at this point in history. He prophesies about future events in the earth that are reserved for a war that will surely come to pass. For now though, the text continues on with His chronological account of the earth.

> By what way is the light parted, which scattereth the east wind upon the earth? Who hath divided a watercourse for the overflowing of waters, or a way for the lightning of thunder; To cause it to rain on the earth, where no man is; on the wilderness, wherein there is no man; To satisfy the desolate and waste ground; and to cause the bud of the tender herb to spring forth? Hath the rain a father? or who hath begotten the drops of dew? Out of whose womb came the ice? and the hoary frost of heaven, who hath gendered it? (Job 38:24–29)

The damaging proceedings from Genesis 1:2 is over and the events of the re-creation found in the rest of the first chapter of Genesis one are now unfolded, as the earth is being manipulated to bring forth life. Humanity is not yet present on the earth, but the Lord starts to get the earth ready for his arrival. The light begins to dissipate the darkness (day one), the winds begin to blow (day two), and the rain starts to bring forth plant life (day three).

> The waters are hid as with a stone, and the face of the deep is frozen. (Job 38:30)

Still after three days of creation, the earth is out of alignment with the sun. Hence, the oceans of the earth are still frozen. Although plants are growing, they are brought forth on account of the light of the knowledge of the glory of God in Christ Jesus. Therefore, on the fourth day the Lord brings the earth back into orbit and the constellations can now be seen in their rightful place.

> Canst thou bind the sweet influences of Pleiades, or loose the bands of Orion? Canst thou bring forth Mazzaroth in his season? or canst thou guide Arcturus with his sons? Knowest thou the ordinances of heaven? canst thou set the dominion thereof in the earth? (Job 38:31–33)

The earth is no longer shrouded in darkness but rather it is back in its perfect rotational standard. The constellations we recognize today can now be seen and the ordinances of the earth are reinstated. He continues on with more rhetorical questions which are a picture of a functioning earth with one added feature; animals now roam the earth.

> Canst thou lift up thy voice to the clouds, that abundance of waters may cover thee? Canst thou send lightnings, that they may go, and say unto thee, Here we are? Who hath put wisdom in the inward parts? or who hath given understanding to the heart? Who can number the clouds in wisdom? or who can stay the bottles of heaven, When the dust groweth into hardness, and the clods cleave fast together? Wilt thou hunt the prey for the lion? or fill the appetite of the young lions, When they couch in their dens,

and abide in the covert to lie in wait? Who provideth for the raven his food? when his young ones cry unto God, they wander for lack of meat. (Job 38:34–41)

The Lord finishes this section by introducing life to the planet. The earth has now returned to its arranged path; the clouds roll on, the rain and lightning cycle on and off, and the earth is soft and dries up. The lions hunger and hunt and the ravens look for food to feed their young. Sill, God knows all the comings and goings of everything in the earth. Finally, he mentions the uniqueness of the creation of man when He mentions how He gave understanding and put wisdom in his inner parts. In other words, He placed man on the earth and breathed into him the breath of life, distinguishing him from the rest of His creation.

Continuing on in chapter 39, the Lord further expounds on the complexity of His astounding animal creation and implies once again how they were placed here for man's use. Here He speaks of the power and fearlessness of a horse, even while charging into a battle against wielded swords.

Hast thou given the horse strength? hast thou clothed his neck with thunder? Canst thou make him afraid as a grasshopper? the glory of his nostrils is terrible. He paweth in the valley, and rejoiceth in his strength: he goeth on to meet the armed men. He mocketh at fear, and is not affrighted; neither turneth he back from the sword. The quiver rattleth against him, the glittering spear and the shield. He swalloweth the ground with fierceness and rage: neither believeth he that it is the sound of the trumpet. He saith among the trumpets, Ha, ha; and he smelleth the battle afar off, the thunder of the captains, and the shouting. (Job 39:19–25)

Accordingly, these two chapters in Job are an abridged history of the earth from its inception to the time of mankind, as spoken directly by the Lord. He is the Lord: the Creator and Maker of the universe, man, and the angels. He did it all by unfathomable wisdom and only wisdom itself can tell of the power of the Lord.

Final Thoughts

*The LORD possessed me in the beginning of his way, before his works of old.
I was set up from everlasting, from the beginning, or ever the earth was. When
there were no depths, I was brought forth; when there were no fountains abounding
with water. Before the mountains were settled, before the hills was I brought forth:
While as yet he had not made the earth, nor the fields, nor the highest part of
the dust of the world. When he prepared the heavens, I was there: when he set a
compass upon the face of the depth: When he established the clouds above: when
he strengthened the fountains of the deep: When he gave to the sea his decree, that
the waters should not pass his commandment: when he appointed the foundations
of the earth: Then I was by him, as one brought up with him: and I was daily
his delight, rejoicing always before him; Rejoicing in the habitable part of his
earth; and my delights were with the sons of men. (Proverbs 8:22–31)*

He is the God of wisdom and that wisdom is on display throughout the pages of the Bible. It is within its pages that He tells about the creation and all the other attributes of life; but if it is not received by faith then it is all meaningless. "Through faith we understand that the worlds were framed by the word of God, so that things which are seen were not made of things which do appear" (Hebrews 11:3). And it is by faith we understand that of old He laid the foundation of the earth: and the heavens are the work of His hands. (Psalm 102:25.)

His knowledge is insurmountable, His understanding is unfathomable, and His wisdom is unending. There will never be a point throughout all eternity where His wisdom and power will come to an end. He is the architect behind the design and the implementer of all that is seen and known. Thus, it is pertinent to conclude with a few passages about what the Word of God says about the creation.

"The LORD by wisdom hath founded the earth; by understanding hath he established the heavens" (Proverbs 3:19). "And he is before all things, and by him all things consist" (Colossians 1:17). "Which made heaven, and earth, the sea, and all that therein is: which keepeth truth for ever" (Psalm 146:6). "All things were made by him; and without him was not any thing made that was made" (John 1:3). "Ah Lord GOD! behold, thou hast made the heaven and the earth by thy great power and stretched out arm, and there is nothing too hard for thee" (Jeremiah 32:17). "For every house is builded by some man; but he that built all things is God" (Hebrews 3:4). "He is the Rock, his work is perfect" (Deuteronomy 32:4).

"By the word of the LORD were the heavens made; and all the host of them by the breath of his mouth" (Psalm 33:6). "Thou art worthy, O Lord, to receive glory and honour and power: for thou hast created all things, and for thy pleasure they are and were created" (Revelation 4:11). "I know that, whatsoever God doeth, it shall be for ever: nothing can be put to it, nor any thing taken from it: and God doeth it, that men should fear before him" (Ecclesiastes 3:14). "And, Thou, Lord, in the beginning hast laid the foundation of the earth; and the heavens are the works of thine hands: They shall perish; but thou remainest; and they all shall wax old as doth a garment; And as a vesture shalt thou fold them up, and they shall be changed: but thou art the same, and thy years shall not fail" (Hebrews 1:10–12). "O give thanks unto the LORD; for he is good; for his mercy endureth for ever" (1 Chronicles 16:34).

Bibliography

Unless otherwise indicated, all Scripture quotations are taken from the 1769 King James Version of the Holy Bible (Also known as the Authorized Version). Used in the public domain.

Scripture quotations marked (Amplified) are taken from the Amplified® Bible, Copyright © 1954, 1958, 1962, 1964, 1965, 1987 by The Lockman Foundation. Used by permission. (www.Lockman.org)

Scripture quotations marked (CEV) are from the Contemporary English Version Copyright © 1991, 1992, 1995 by American Bible Society, Used by Permission.

Scripture quotations marked (ASV) are taken from the American Standard Version. Used in the public domain.

Scripture quotations marked (ESV) are from the Holy Bible, English Standard Version, copyright © 2001 by Crossway Bibles, a publishing ministry of Good News Publishers. Used by permission. All rights reserved.

Scripture quotations marked (GNB) are from the Good News Bible in Today's English Version- Second Edition Copyright © 1992 by American Bible Society. Used by Permission.

Scripture quotations marked (ISV) are from the Holy Bible: International Standard Version® Release 2.0 Copyright © 1996-2010 by the ISV Foundation. Used by permission of the Davidson Press, LLC. All Rights Reserved Internationally.

Scripture quotations marked (Message) are taken from The Message. Copyright © 1993, 1994, 1995, 1996, 2000, 2001, 2002. Used by permission of NavPress Publishing Group.

About the Author

Andrew Myers is a non-fiction freelance writer. He is an inspired author who is attempting to find truth in the ongoing debate about the origins of the earth and mankind. He currently lives with his family in Minnesota.